ESSAYS AND INTERVIEWS ON CONTEMPORARY AMERICAN POETS, POETRY, AND PEDAGOGY

ESSAYS AND INTERVIEWS ON CONTEMPORARY AMERICAN POETS, POETRY, AND PEDAGOGY

A THIRTY-YEAR CREATIVE READING WORKSHOP

DANIEL MORRIS

Anthem Press
An imprint of Wimbledon Publishing Company
www.anthempress.com

This edition first published in UK and USA 2024
by ANTHEM PRESS
75–76 Blackfriars Road, London SE1 8HA, UK
or PO Box 9779, London SW19 7ZG, UK
and
244 Madison Ave #116, New York, NY 10016, USA

© 2024 Daniel Morris

The author asserts the moral right to be identified as the author of this work.

All rights reserved. Without limiting the rights under copyright reserved above, no part of this publication may be reproduced, stored or introduced into a retrieval system, or transmitted, in any form or by any means (electronic, mechanical, photocopying, recording or otherwise), without the prior written permission of both the copyright owner and the above publisher of this book.

British Library Cataloguing-in-Publication Data
A catalogue record for this book is available from the British Library.

Library of Congress Cataloging-in-Publication Data: 2024936216
A catalog record for this book has been requested.

ISBN-13: 978-1-83999-223-0 (Hbk) / 978-1-83999-224-7 (Pbk)
ISBN-10: 1-83999-223-9 (Hbk) / 1-83999-224-7 (Pbk)

This title is also available as an e-book.

CONTENTS

Acknowledgments vii
Introduction: To Teach Is to Learn Twice (or, Putting the Pieces of My Life's Work Together) ix

SECTION 1: Rereading the Poets, Poetry, and Poetics of My Decade in the Boston Area (1983–1993) 1

CHAPTER 1 Reading Spivack/Reading Myself: A Memoir of Reading a Memoir, Boston 1959–1977; Boston 1983–1993 3

CHAPTER 2 Allen Grossman's Radical Simplicity 21

CHAPTER 3 In Praise of Secular Jewish American Lyric Commentary: Why Bob Dylan and Louise Glück Are Twenty-First-Century Nobel Laureates 31

CHAPTER 4 Preserving William Carlos Williams: Populism, Curation, and Late Avant-Gardism in Kenneth Goldsmith's *Duchamp Is My Lawyer* and Thomas Lux's "Refrigerator, 1957" 49

SECTION 2: Midwestern Avant-Gardism: Essays and Interviews on Experimental Poetics 63

CHAPTER 5 No Sympathy for the Devil of History: On Norman Finkelstein's "Oppen at Altamont" 65

CHAPTER 6 History and/as Language Poetry: Remembering Literary Community through Negation in Barrett Watten's *Questions of Poetics* 77

CHAPTER 7	Tyrone Calling: Torqued Language Poetry and Radical Mimesis in *c.c.*	93
CHAPTER 8	An Interview with Patrick Durgin about Hannah Weiner	123
CHAPTER 9	Tech Support Says "Dead Don Walking": Tradition, the Internet, and Individual Talent in the Poetry of Daniel Y. Harris	133
CHAPTER 10	Interview with Adeena Karasick on *Checking In*	147

SECTION 3: To Teach is to Learn Twice: Poetry, Poetics, and Pedagogy — 165

CHAPTER 11	Convergence Cultures: Modern and Contemporary Poetry and the Graphic Novel	167
CHAPTER 12	Resisting Billy Collins: On Teaching "Introduction to Poetry" in Introduction to Poetry	187
CHAPTER 13	Amiri Baraka's Aesthetic Radicalism: *Dutchman*'s Modernist Roots	199
CHAPTER 14	Two Interviews with Thomas Fink	207

SECTION 4: In My End Is My Beginning: Reviewing Peter Dale Scott and Philip Guston — 229

CHAPTER 15	Reviewing Peter Dale Scott/Reviewing Myself	231
CHAPTER 16	In My End Is My Beginning: Seeing Double at *Philip Guston Now* in the Summer of 2023	241

Conclusion: Goodbye, Heavilon Hall — 255
Index — 263

ACKNOWLEDGMENTS

Many chapters have appeared, often in different forms, and without the author's notes and codas that I have added for this volume, in the following publications. I am grateful to the editors of these publications:

1. "Reading Spivack/Reading Myself: A Memoir of Reading a Memoir, Boston 1959-1977; Boston 1983-1993." The Chapter One Project from Marsh Hawk Press. September 2019.
2. "Allen Grossman's Radical Simplicity." *Evening Will Come: A Monthly Journal of Poetics*. Issue 44, August 2014.
3. "In Praise of Secular Jewish American Lyric Commentary: Why Bob Dylan and Louise Glück are 21st Century Nobel Laureates." *First Of The Month: A Website of the Radical Imagination*. February 1, 2022.
4. "Kenneth Goldsmith's Duchamp is My Lawyer." *William Carlos Williams Review*. 2021, Vol.38 (1), p.80–85.
5. "No Sympathy for the Devil of History: On "Oppen at Altamont." *Where the Wanting Leads Us: Reading the Poetry of Norman Finkelstein*. 2021. Mad Hat Press. Collection edited by J. Peter Moore.
6. "History and/as Language Poetry: Remembering Literary Community through Negation in Barrett Watten's Questions of Poetics." *Talisman*. Issue 46. Winter 2018.
7. "Tyrone Calling: Torqued Language Poetry and Radical Mimesis in *c.c.*" *Talisman*. Issue 47, 2021.
8. "Interview with Patrick Durgin on Hannah Weiner." *Talisman*, 2010.
9. "Tech support says 'Dead Don Walking': Tradition, the Internet, and the Individual Talent in the Poetry of Daniel Y. Harris." *Notre Dame Review*. January 2014.
10. "Interview with Adeena Karasick on *Checking In*." *Talisman*. Issue 48.

11. *Convergence Cultures: Modern and Contemporary Poetry and the Graphic Novel* pp. 526–542 *IN:* Baetens, Jan(ed. and introd.); Frey, Hugo(ed. and introd.); Tabachnick, Stephen E.(ed. and introd.) *The Cambridge History of the Graphic Novel.* Cambridge, England: Cambridge University Press; 2018.
12. "Resisting Poetry and Resistant Poetry: Aesthetics and the Search for Meaning While Teaching Introduction to Poetry." *Something on Paper* (online journal of Naropa Institute). Fall 2014.
13. "Baraka's Aesthetic Radicalism: *Dutchman*'s Modernist Roots." pp. 71–76 *IN:* Calihman, Matthew(ed., preface, and introd.); Early, Gerald(ed., preface, and introd.) *Approaches to Teaching Baraka's* Dutchman. New York, NY: Modern Language Association of America; 2018.
14. Interviews with Tom Fink. 2010 and 2022 in *Dichtung Yammer.*
15. Review of Peter Dale Scott's "Revisiting Jakarta: Internal Turmoil and State Violence in Poetry and Terror" in *Harvard Review.* Number Three. Winter 1993.
16. Review of Peter Dale Scott's *Poetry and Terror. Notre Dame Review.* 2022.
17. "In My End is My Beginning: Seeing Double at "Philip Guston Now." August 1, 2023, *First of the Month.*

I thank my administrative colleagues in the College of Liberal Arts at Purdue University for providing funds to support this book. Special thanks to English department head Al Lopez and to Sorin Adam Matei and Michael Hicks of the Dean's office for administering the grant. I deeply appreciate the thoughtful and timely guidance I received every step of the way from the fine staff at Anthem Press. Special shout-outs go to Jebaslin Hephzibah, Ponni Brinda, and Gomathy Ilammathe. My friend Alec Marsh offered extremely helpful suggestions as I revised the manuscript. Four anonymous readers also provided useful commentaries. As always, shout-out of thanks to my family: Joy, Isaac, Aaron, Hannah, George, and Meyer. I dedicate this book to the memories of my father, Irwin Walter Morris, my brother-in-law Bob Cohen, and my father-in-law George Steele.

INTRODUCTION: TO TEACH IS TO LEARN TWICE (OR, PUTTING THE PIECES OF MY LIFE'S WORK TOGETHER)

To Teach is to Learn Twice, Joseph Joubert (1754–1824, French moralist and essayist)

Writing this introduction at age 61 from my home study in West Lafayette, Indiana, 30 years after I moved to the Midwest from the Boston area to begin my career as a professor of modern and contemporary poetry studies at Purdue, I am drawn to the quotation that serves as my epigraph. "To Teach is to Learn Twice" captures the sentiment behind how and animates why I decided to gather the following pieces into a meaningful pattern in this volume. I first discovered some of the poets I write about in this book when I was in my teens and twenties: William Carlos Williams, T. S. Eliot, Walt Whitman, Allen Grossman, Peter Dale Scott, and Louise Glück. These essays, however, reflect my "learning twice" about how to engage with their poetry as a seasoned teacher and scholar working in a different cultural environment when compared to the social world of my student days. In many chapters, I write in the first-person pronoun. The intimate tone—especially evident in the first two chapters that recall my student years in the Boston area in the late 1980s and early 1990s, my chapter on how I teach a poem by Billy Collins in my "Introduction to Poetry" course at Purdue, and my final piece on Philip Guston—reflect my inability to separate my personal journey from the "thirty-year poetry workshop" as a teacher, literary critic, and poet. This book, then, is as much a study in personal development as it is a work of criticism.

In the early 1980s, I was trained at Northwestern as an undergraduate in New Criticism, a then-dominant, but already waning in influence, formalist approach. Through close reading, we concentrated on distinguishing the intricate design patterns of the poem, which we were trained to regard as a coordinated work of art made out of contradictory elements. Because we were taught to notice how words in poems could have multiple meanings, it was wrong to read poetry for its underlying message. If we tried to explain the significance of a poem in our own words, we were merely demonstrating what New Critical adherents regarded as the "Fallacy of Paraphrase." Perhaps concerned about addressing the controversial political affiliations of Right-wing modernists such as Eza Pound and Left-wing modernists such as George Oppen, instructors who practiced New Critical methods did not encourage students to treat poetry as part of a larger social text that included historical and biographical contexts. They did not emphasize reader reception or interdisciplinary approaches. In creative writing seminars, I crudely practiced the art of the sonnet, the villanelle, the blank verse narrative, and the sestina with distinguished "new formalists" on faculty such as W. S. DiPiero, Mary Kinzie, and Alan Shapiro. As a teacher today, I am grateful for lessons on how to scan a poem to detect the lilt, or rhythmic pulse, of a line composed according to established metrical principles. I also enrolled in a literature course with Paul Breslin, whose landmark approach to contemporary American poetry, *The Psycho-Political Muse: American Poetry Since the Fifties*, appeared with the University of Chicago Press in 1987, three years after I took his class on the topic. As the title of Breslin's book suggests, he was clearly not a New Critic who eschewed attention to biographical ("Psycho") and sociohistorical ("Political") contexts. Instructing a cohort of undergraduates, many of whom were untutored in the fundamentals of the art, however, Breslin preferred close readings of poems by major figures representing the leading schools or movements in American poetry after World War II: Confessionalism (Robert Lowell, Sylvia Plath, Elizabeth Bishop), Deep Image (James Wright), Beat (Allen Ginsberg), New York School (John Ashbery), Second Wave Feminist (Adrienne Rich). We were learning more about poetry than how to distinguish between an iamb and a spondee, but the course syllabus still reflected a limited imagination of the field of contemporary poetry. The only poet of color we read was Derek Walcott, the elegant stylist, and Nobel laureate from Saint Lucia about whom Breslin was working on the book that he eventually published in 2001. Chicago's own Gwendolyn Brooks, a vernacular author influenced by jazz music and performance poetry who chronicled life in Bronzeville, on the city's South Side, the first African American woman to win the Pulitzer Prize for Poetry, and a leading figure in the Black Arts movement, was not mentioned in class. Many poets we studied were queer, but how this dimension of their lives influenced their poetics was not a topic of discussion. Ginsberg's and Rich's ambivalent relationship to their Jewishness was not addressed. Popular poetry and spoken word poets were not on our reading list. When a fellow student, after class, asked Professor Breslin if he could write his final paper on rock poet Jim Morrison's spoken word album, *An American Prayer* (1978), which sold 250,000 copies, Breslin, clearly uncomfortable with the proposal, pondered for a moment, then demurred. "Maybe if you could write something about his music [...]?"

Returning to the East Coast after graduation in 1984, I spent my twenties in the Boston area, first as a creative-writing master's degree student at Boston University (BU). I attended workshops in the same cramped room on the second floor of 236 Bay State Road—a former apartment building near the main campus on Commonwealth Avenue—where in the spring of 1959, Lowell led the most famous poetry seminar ever assembled; the one that included Plath, Anne Sexton, and George Starbuck, who was on the poetry faculty at BU when I attended.[1] An undergraduate in 1959, the young poet Kathleen Spivack was among the other 17 students (besides Plath, Sexton, and Starbuck) who took part in Lowell's seminar. "The experience of being there was nerve-racking," Spivack has stated. I mention Spivack's presence because my response to reading her memoir about Lowell's mentorship constitutes the first chapter of this book.

After BU, I spent six years at Brandeis in nearby Waltham, Massachusetts as a doctoral candidate under the direction of the late Allen Grossman (1932–2014), my major influence, before teaching for two years off the tenure track in the History and Literature department at Harvard, where I reviewed new poetry books for the *Harvard Review*, including a volume by Peter Dale Scott that, for reasons I explain at the end of this introduction, I reproduce in the penultimate chapter of this book. I immersed myself in the Cambridge poetry scene at the Grolier bookstore and at the Blacksmith House, where poetry

---

1 As Gail Crowther reports in "On the Friendship and Rivalry of Sylvia Plath and Anne Sexton": Throughout the spring of 1959, on a Tuesday afternoon between 2:00 and 4:00 p.m., Plath and Sexton shared the same seminar space, room 222 at 236 Bay State Road. This room still exists today: tiny, with creaking wooden floors, a book-lined wall, and three airy windows offering a glimpse of the Charles River. It is a space that seems too small to have housed the personalities of Lowell, Sexton, and Plath. Sexton described it as "a dismal room the shape of a shoe box. It was a bleak spot, as if it had been forgotten for years, like the spinning room in Sleeping Beauty's castle."

The two women spent hours reading their poems, listening to about 18 other students, and taking advice from Lowell about what they were working on. The atmosphere was mostly awkward silences, slight terror at having their poems chosen for discussion, and equal terror at having them ignored. Poet Kathleen Spivack, who attended these classes as an undergraduate student, wrote, "The experience of being there was nerve-racking." https://lithub.com/on-the-friendship-and-rivalry-of-sylvia-plath-and-anne-sexton/ *Literary Hub*. April 28, 2021. Accessed November 7, 2023.

readings were often held, establishing friendships with area poets and writers. Two of them, Joseph Lease and William Corbett, were writing poetry and prose about an intriguing Jewish painter who in his late work that has come to be known as his "Hood" paintings combined abstract expressionism, a complex type of political commentary, and a streetwise sensibility. The painter's name was Philip Guston. He had taught at BU until his death in 1980, but he was unknown to me when I studied at BU in the 1980s. Guston is the subject of Chapter 16.

At Brandeis with Grossman, a bona fide genius (and, in fact, winner of a coveted MacArthur "Genius" grant when I was his student in 1989), and subject of Chapter 2, I absorbed and resisted his unique teachings. An inspirational lecturer and tireless mentor, Grossman combined humanism, formalism, and phenomenology with religious faith in great poetry to, in his terms, protect the image of the person from vanishing. Professor Grossman's graduate seminars at Brandeis were as deep as the ocean, but narrow in scope when compared to what I would now have preferred as preparation for teaching general education courses such as "Introduction to Poetry" at Purdue. His memorable seminars would focus intensively on two, or, at most, three major figures, and each would serve as a foil for the other(s). Whitman and Dickinson; Stevens and Yeats; Rilke, Freud, and Yeats. In office hours, Grossman did encourage me to read contemporaneous poets who were lesser known such as Edwin Arlington Robinson, whose plain-style poems about ordinary citizens such as Richard Cory who endured lives of quiet desperation in the fictional Tilbury Town in Maine influenced Robert Frost. He introduced me to the poetry of Thomas Hardy, best known as a novelist, but whom Grossman taught me to appreciate as a proto-modernist because of his post-Victorian disillusionment, apparent in his focus on cultural disasters such as the wreckage of the Titanic in "Convergence of the Twain" (1912). As I discuss in Chapter 2, Grossman, in undergraduate lecture courses, did help students appreciate the fundamental values of poetry to foster community and develop interpersonal communication skills by referring to nursery rhymes such as "London Bridge is Falling Down" and to popular music lyrics such as "Nothing Compares U." My ears perked up when he did so.

Like Whitman, Grossman was a large and contradictory figure in my eyes. He had the knack for what I refer to in Chapter 2 as "radical simplicity." I recall, for example, Grossman reducing the meaning of lines in all English poetry to three categories: the line of less than 10 positions, the line of 10 positions, and the line longer than 10 positions. The line of less than 10 positions signified spells and incantations. The line of 10—Shakespeare's line in his dramas—represented social discourse. The line longer than 10 conveyed personal transformation. To this day at Purdue, I still tell my students about this approach to help them understand the semantic meaning of line. Grossman's most influential and, for me, readable, publications were Socratic dialogues with former students, most memorably with Mark Halliday in a book-length conversation published in 1992 as *The Sighted Singer: Two Works on Poetry for Readers and Writers*. I participated in a conversation with Grossman on the Native American author Leslie Marmon Silko that was included in *The Long Schoolroom: Lessons on the Bitter Logic of the Poetic Principle* (1997). Grossman could simplify the history of poetry into neat, easy-to-digest, wisdom nuggets, and he could publish conversations with students about poetics. At the same time, Grossman as a writer could be opaque and as a mentor, he could be, like the major modernists he revered, "impersonal." Discussing Wallace Stevens's "World Without Peculiarities" with Halliday in a 1990 "Summer Conversation" that was included in *The Sighted Singer: Two Works on Poetry for Readers and Writers* (1992), for example, Grossman argues that Stevens, in his term, "represses" the personal voice and autobiographical dimensions of his speaker (whose perspective is detached through the use of the third, rather than first, person so typical of lyric address), in order to supply a way out of the speaker's struggles with such issues as the death of parents and an unhappy love relationship in "World Without Peculiarities." According to Grossman, Stevens's impersonal speaker seeks:

> [An] origin of discourse [...] outside of the system constituted by family, by secular instruction and social formations, from the point of view of which "outsideness" it is possible to introduce into the exchange between mortal persons a kind of knowledge which is not vulnerable to the bitter ironies of social construction and vernacular particularity at any given moment in social space and time. The conception of poetry as having its origin precisely in that region which is not determined by the *history* of families and in general the history of acknowledgment, functional and dysfunctional, points in my view to the most powerful benefit that poetry can confer on persons. (148)

Grossman's rhetoric is difficult for me to unpack because he is approaching a specific poem, in this case, "World Without Peculiarities," from the steep and icy peak of abstract discourse about poetry in general. Because I spent years in Grossman's classrooms and in his office learning directly from him, as well as having read much of his criticism (and even edited a collection of essays in his honor in 2004), however, I can take an educated guess on what Grossman is getting at when he refers to as "the point of view of which 'outsideness' it is possible to introduce into the exchange between mortal persons a kind of knowledge which is not vulnerable to the bitter ironies of social construction and vernacular particularity." Unlike my creative writing teachers at Northwestern, Grossman was not a "new formalist" or latter-day New Critic. More so than any other poet or pedagogue on the contemporary scene, however, Grossman maintained a quasi-religious faith in the formal features of poetry—particularly the "line" of the poem—as a graphic manifestation of the difference between natural human speech and the artificial, meaning-bearing dimensions of the poem. If effectively managed, Grossman maintained, the line of the poem could preserve and protect the "visibility" of the "person" across time and space. The problem was that poetry's logic was bitter because the "peculiarities" of individual existence needed to be "repressed" for poetry's "outsideness" to function as a preservative. Reminiscent of Kant's conception of the categorical imperative or the "veil of ignorance" that informs the social justice theory of Harvard philosophy professor John Rawls, the "line" of the poem is the marker of "outsideness" from the "world of peculiarities" that Stevens's poetics seeks to safeguard, but, paradoxically, only through a poetics of "impersonality"—to invoke a famous phrase associated with T. S. Eliot—that chafes against the confessionalist ethos that Grossman's interlocutor, Halliday, represents in his commentary in the "Summer Conversations."

When I set out to write a dissertation under Grossman's direction, I felt, perhaps mistakenly, that the authors I could select and still count on for his expertise were limited to the major modernists—the authors listed above as well as Hart Crane, Frost, Pound, Eliot, and the one I settled on for my thesis, William Carlos Williams. Picking Williams, the doctor poet whose mother hailed from Puerto Rico and who wrote about unheralded people and quotidian topics often set in the industrial cities of Northern New Jersey, such as Paterson, I felt I was rebelling against the High Modernist elitism, opacity, and allusivity that Grossman, the most learned person I have ever met, treated as peers. Williams's "Proletarian Portrait" from the 1930s is typical of the kind of modern poetry I could understand without consulting secondary sources:

> A big young bareheaded woman
> in an apron
>
> Her hair slicked back standing
> on the street

One stockinged foot toeing
the sidewalk

Her shoe in her hand. Looking
intently into it

She pulls out the paper insole
to find the nail

That has been hurting her

As the subject matter and plain wording of "Proletarian Portrait" indicate, I had aligned myself with the "lowest" of the High Modernists. Along with immediacy and accessibility, even a cursory glance at the poem suggests aspects of Williams's aesthetics that I continue to focus on when I teach his work to Purdue undergraduates. Neither a traditional formalist nor a "free" verse lyricist, we notice how carefully he manages the line of the poem through variation in length and the formal device known as enjambment. The speaker's objective tone encourages the reader to empathize with the poor young woman depicted in the poem, rather than, as in traditional lyric poetry, to focus on the speaker's inwardness and vexed emotional condition. The enjambment and disruptive line breaks help readers experience the irritation the young woman is feeling because a nail has lodged under the "paper insole." The poem is something of an updated version of the "Princess and the Pea" fairy tale, but instead of a royal subject from long ago and faraway the main character is a poor working-class woman in the here and now. The line breaks also convey the contemporary, urban tones of jazzy syncopation. As the title suggests, the poem is influenced by visual culture; it is a "portrait," but one animated, like Marcel Duchamp's "Nude Descending a Staircase" (1912). Williams is combining modernist filmic technique with a concern for documenting a little moment of human suffering and the alleviation of pain during the Great Depression. The repetitive use of the gerund ("ing") verb forms—standing, looking, toeing, hurting—suggest the animation of a motion picture. When I teach Williams at Purdue, I emphasize the visual dimensions and multimedia quality of his poetry, as well as how his poetry encourages empathetic identification with the subject matter without overtly emphasizing the thoughts and feelings of the perspectival character or "speaker."

By working on Williams at Brandeis with Grossman, I found myself on the side of what Sly Stone would call "everyday people." The truth was, I was an enthusiastic, but not especially gifted, "everyday" person, not, like Grossman, in Ginsberg's terms, one of the "best minds" of his generation. The fact that I ended up not only writing about Williams, but about his professional relationship with New Directions publisher James Laughlin, and thus about the poet's engagement with the literary marketplace as it intersected with the emerging cultures of advertising, celebrity, and publicity, indicated my resistance to viewing poetry as a replacement for religion in the modern world. Rather, poetry was, as we would now say, a dimension of an intertext, a part of a dynamic cultural web. Poetry, I realized, should be approached in conversation with other arts, including the popular arts, and even advertisements. I was interested in how poetry functioned, however obliquely, as a form of public communication. As Williams himself wrote late in his life in "Asphodel, that Greeny Flower":

> It is difficult
> to get the news from poems
> yet men die miserably every day
> for lack
> of what is found there.

More so than is the case for any of the other modernists whom Grossman venerated, and on a par with Gertrude Stein, whom Grossman did not teach, Williams was, as "Proletarian Portrait" suggests, the most visually oriented poet. Williams was directly in contact with contemporaneous artists, in his case most intimately with Charles Sheeler and Charles Demuth. In the last years of his life, he authored the Pulitzer Prize–winning book of poems, *Pictures of Brueghel* (1962). He cited the abstract expressionist Jackson Pollock in *Paterson* and wrote a poem, "Young Sycamore," based on Alfred Stieglitz's photograph *Spring Showers* (1902). Williams may well have attended the Armory Show of 1913, which introduced Americans to modern European art, and he certainly knew the Dadaists Man Ray and Marcel Duchamp. "The Great Figure" (1921), his poem that inspired Demuth to paint *I Saw the Figure 5 in Gold* (1928) would, in turn, influence the pop artist Robert Indiana to paint *The Figure Five* in 1963. Williams's visual imagination inspires chapters in this book on "Convergence Cultures," which explores how graphic novelists have combined word and image to produce teachable versions of classic poems, and my final piece on Guston, the abstract/pop/political painter about whom I gave my talk for a job in poetry studies at Purdue in 1994. In another chapter, I link Williams to the contemporary conceptualist poet Kenneth Goldsmith through their mutual attraction to Duchamp's "readymades" and the idea of the artist as pointer. By "pointer," I mean an aesthetic guide who does not so much create a new work of art from scratch out of his romantic imagination as reframe already existent elements of material culture. Through repurposing, the artist or author as "pointer" calls attention to the aesthetics of ordinary life.

Eminent teachers such as Breslin and Grossman introduced me to narratives about the history of twentieth-century American poetry. Canonical poets were covered in depth in my classes with them, but, inevitably, much was left out of the story. Oddly, as I reflect on my training, especially at Brandeis with Grossman, who taught for over 30 years at the Jewish-sponsored school after receiving his PhD there in 1960, I realize that the contributions of Jewish Americans to modern and contemporary poetry were barely mentioned by him, if at all. It was only *after* I left Brandeis, and made my way in the Midwest, where I became involved in the Jewish Studies program at Purdue and helped edit *Shofar*, the Midwest Jewish Studies Society's interdisciplinary journal, did I learn of the extraordinarily rich poetry traditions cultivated by Jewish Americans. Jews were leaders in the Objectivist movement, contributed to documentary modes, and, more recently, have made their mark by adapting cutting-edge approaches to poetry such as L=A=N=G=U=A=G=E writing, conceptualism, posthumanism, and multimedia poetics. I mention all this here because, post Brandeis, I recognized that Milton Hindus, a founding member of the Brandeis English department, who still roamed Rabb Hall as an emeritus professor when I was taking classes there, was a notable scholar on the Jewish Objectivist Charles Reznikoff and, before my time, Reznikoff's spouse, Marie Syrkin, a biographer of Golda Meir, was on the English faculty at Brandeis for 16 years. In my presence, Grossman never mentioned Reznikoff, or George Oppen, another leading Jewish Objectivist, and the only memory I have of him commenting on Louis Zukofsky, a third Jewish Objectivist but, unlike the other two I have mentioned, a disciple of Ezra Pound, was to make a general point in a lecture that Zukofsky had written two epics, one called *A* and one called *The*. Displaying the "radical simplicity" that I emphasize in Chapter 2, Grossman addressed the significance of the two articles when thinking about how a poet is imagining the world as either inclusive ("A") or exclusive ("The"). Looking back, it seems like such an odd omission: I was studying in a department that had a direct connection to a prominent movement in Jewish American poetry, but I did not learn about it until I left Brandeis. Gathering knowledge about Reznikoff and Objectivism was part of my discovery of an expanded history of the field as a faculty member in the Midwest. Fellow Jewish Hoosier and Notre Dame English professor Stephen Fredman's book, *A Menorah for Athena* (2001), which I reviewed in *Shofar* in 2003, helped fill gaps in my knowledge of Jewish American modern poetry. In his book, Fredman chronicled Reznikoff's ambivalent relationship as a Jew to the Hellenic realm of the fine arts that gentile imagist poets such as Pound and H. D. embraced with little anxiety. Here is how I concluded my review:

> Unable to view Greek materials with the unselfconsciousness of Pound or H. D., Reznikoff followed Roland Barthes, who argues that "all those outside power are obliged to steal language," by turning the Hellenistic "purity" of imagist style into a hybrid text of ethical criticism and moral insight. Reznikoff's poetry seems to deconstruct the Arnoldian associations of Greek and Jewish writing as mixed legacies for modern Western culture. In blurring the clear line between aestheticism and ethics through his Objectivist work, Reznikoff, according to Fredman, became a pivotal figure in our current revision of the story we tell about modernism, its major players, its tenets, its relationship to modernity. A book such as Fredman's helps us to consolidate the shift in modernist studies from questions of pure form to a wider cultural interpretation of literature that emphasizes the "new historicist" concerns with hybridity, ethnicity, power relations, material culture, politics, and religion.

In chapters on Glück, Kathleen Spivack, Bob Dylan, Kenneth Goldsmith, George Oppen, Thomas Fink, Adeena Karasick, Hannah Weiner, Norman Finkelstein, Daniel Y. Harris, and Guston, I engage in a form of cultural repurposing by "learning twice" about how to attend to other Jewish Americans whose aesthetic contributions were not part of my formal education as a student. As I remarked in my review of Fredman's understanding of Reznikoff's poetry, my study of these culture makers demonstrates my interest in moving beyond "questions of pure form to a wider cultural interpretation of literature that emphasizes the 'new historicist' concerns with hybridity, ethnicity, power relations, material culture, politics, and religion." My essay on Daniel Y. Harris's *Hyperlinks of Anxiety* (2013), for example, specifically addresses from multiple Jewish perspectives—prophetic, diasporic, ethical, Midrashic, gnostic—the vexing problems and sublime potential of disseminating lyrics, the ancient form of transmission and preservation of the singular, private human voice across time and space to an individual reader, in an environment in which e-poetry and digitalized poetics pose a crisis (understood as both opportunity and threat) to traditional page poetry.

Reflecting on how I perceived the cultural landscape of the United States from the perspective of 30 years ago, when I drove my Toyota Tercel from

Introduction xix

Boston to West Lafayette to begin a new chapter in my life as a full-fledged professor—no longer a teacher in training—at Purdue, I must admit that I suffered a version of the East Coast "fly over state" myopia that is imagined nowhere better than in an (in)famous *New Yorker* cover from March 29, 1976 by Saul Steinberg. "View of the World from 9th Avenue" is, according to a commentator on the *Brilliant Maps* website, "a classic map/illustration showing how New Yorkers see the rest of the world":

> The map shows how New Yorkers might see the rest of the world if they faced west on 9th Avenue. Thus, 10th Avenue and the Hudson River are clearly shown, but beyond that it's just a bit of a blur. Canada and Mexico both make it onto the map, sandwiching a very rectangular United States. In total 5 cities beyond New York are included: Washington DC (near Mexico), Los Angeles, Las Vegas, Kansas City and Chicago. Texas, Utah, and Nebraska also make it onto the map.

As noted, I attended college near Chicago at Northwestern, but I brought something of Steinberg's East Coast parochialism with me to Indiana; Steinberg himself made an exception for the Windy City, one of only five metropolitan areas besides New York to appear on his map. In a pleasant way, however, I was quickly disabused of my sense of superior insight into poetics as an East Coast transplant establishing himself in a new community amid the fields of soy and corn in North Central Indiana. During my first week on campus in August 1994, veteran Purdue English professor Neil Myers, a Jew who received his PhD at Harvard and was, like me, a poet and scholar interested in William Carlos Williams, invited me to drive with him the hour South on Interstate 65 to Indianapolis to hear a rising poet he was mentoring, Li-Young Lee, read from his work at the Indianapolis Museum of Art. An extra incentive was that we would also feast on overstuffed Reuben sandwiches on house-made rye, potato pancakes, and Brown's cream soda at the Shapiro's Deli on 38th Street, close to the museum. I was not so far away from origins as I had, foolishly and fearfully, predicted! In my first weeks at Purdue, I would meet other creative ethnic New Yorkers who had set down roots at Purdue or nearby in Indy. Poet Felix Stefanile and his spouse Selma; he was an Italian American, she was a Jew, both born and raised in New York, had lived, and worked in West Lafayette since the early 1960s, where they edited *Sparrow*, a leading poetry magazine that featured formalist verse. In my first weeks on campus, I was befriended by Chuck Wachtel and Jocelyn Lieu, a talented couple who each wrote fiction, taught creative writing at Purdue, and maintained a residence on the Lower East Side, where I would visit with them in the summers. On one memorable summer evening in Manhattan, Chuck, Jocelyn, and I were accompanied by one Hettie Cohen for onion pancakes at a favorite Chinese restaurant in the West Village. After dinner, we walked Hettie back to her loft, which, as I recall, was located near the editorial offices of the *Village Voice*. Did I realize back then that Hettie Cohen was Hettie Jones, the poet and chronicler of the Beat Generation who had once been married to Amiri Baraka? At nearby Butler University in Indianapolis, I attended a Lilly foundation sponsored writing series that each year brought friends from the East Coast (such as Ha Jin, a fellow Grossman student at Brandeis) and Jewish poet heroes such as Gerald Stern, Robert Pinsky, and Charles Bernstein to read. Coincidentally, the poetry scholar and Jewish Studies professor at Butler, Hilene Flanzbaum, had herself been a student of Grossman's as an undergraduate at Brandeis before moving to Philadelphia for her PhD at Penn prior to assuming her academic post in Central Indiana. Small world indeed!

My experience would quickly reveal that I was far from alone in pursuing experimentalism in the arts in the American Midwest. This was especially evident when I attended the annual conference on Twentieth Century Literature and Culture at the University of Louisville, a three-hour drive on I-65 South from Purdue. Directed by the University of Chicago-trained poetry scholar Alan Golding, the "Lurville" conference became a kind of tribal gathering festival in late February for Midwestern avant-gardists to meet, share poetry, talk shop, attend panels on new scholarly work, and, of course, sample the famous bourbon. I pay tribute to Midwestern Experimentalism in six chapters in this book. Essays on Midwestern poets Barrett Watten (a foundational figure affiliated with the Berkeley wing of the L=A=N=G=U=A=G=E movement from the 1970s and now a longtime faculty member at Wayne State in Detroit), Tyrone Williams (a Detroit native, and Wayne State PhD, who taught for decades at Xavier in Cincinnati before accepting a position as a distinguished chair at SUNY Buffalo that he held until his death at age 70 in March 2024), Norman Finkelstein (another longtime Xavier faculty member and frequent participant at the Louisville conference), and my conversation about Hannah Weiner with Patrick Durgin, a University of Iowa PhD and Chicago-based poet and publisher, reflect the degree of my ongoing interest in avant-gardism is now filtered through friendships I have developed with fellow Midwesterners involved in the poetry world. The essays on Watten, Finkelstein, and Tyrone Williams are especially relevant to the overall point of this book, which is that as a teacher of poetry I have continued to educate myself about the complex history of my field. My essay on Watten's historiographical texts *Questions of Poetics: Language*

Writing and Consequences and *The Grand Piano* is explicitly about the process by which the origins of the West Coast Language movement is remembered and how it is situated in relationship to other movements such as Conceptualism. My chapter on Tyrone Williams, a leading African American poet associated with the Language movement, takes Watten's genealogical efforts one step further by emphasizing an aporia within the movement when it comes to highlighting the work of Black avant-gardists. My essay on Norman Finkelstein places the Jewish modernist Objectivist poet George Oppen in relationship to contemporary popular culture through a narrative poem in which Oppen and his spouse, Mary, attend the ill-fated Rolling Stones concert at the Altamont speedway in Northern California. By engaging with Durgin about Weiner, the late experimental New York City-based Jewish American poet who suffered from a psychological disability that literally enabled her to see words affixed to human bodies and whose literary executor, Charles Bernstein, is, arguably, the leading East Coast Jewish American L=A=N=G=U=A=G=E oriented poet, I create direct links between my situation as a Midwestern teacher, practitioner of avant-gardism, and my heritage as a New York Jew primarily trained in the Northeast.

As the first two chapters of this book make clear, I was fortunate to learn from such a distinguished group of poets and pedagogues who informed my formal and informal education from my late teens at NU in the early 1980s until I left Boston for West Lafayette, Indiana to get on the tenure track at Purdue at age 30 in 1994. At the same time, I must admit that when I arrived at Purdue, a public Land Grant school located in a small city in Northwest Indiana, and best known for its programs in agriculture and engineering, I recognized a contrast between my experience as a student who had been trained at cosmopolitan private and "elite" universities and my situation as a teacher of poetry and poetics in general education classes such as "Introduction to Poetry" as an instructor of Boilermakers. In chapters on how I teach Billy Collins's poem called "Introduction to Poetry," "Convergence Cultures," the essay on graphic novel versions of classic poetry, my two interviews with Tom Fink, an Ivy League-educated scholar, accomplished poet, painter, and founding member of the Marsh Hawk Press poetry collective who has spent his career teaching at LaGuardia, a two-year college in the CUNY system, and my commentary on how I situate Amiri Baraka's *Dutchman* (1964) in relationship to the poetry and poetics of T. S. Eliot, I take on the thorny pedagogical issue of how to teach notoriously "difficult" modernist and postmodernist poetry to a wide range of students. My interest, as a scholar and critic, in the relationship of poetry to other arts, a hallmark of my professional expertise, has in part stemmed from my success in introducing students to poetry by placing it in conversation with popular music, graphic novels, painting, social media, and other aspects of everyday life. These topics and approaches animated the poetry of William Carlos Williams, the subject of my dissertation (1992) and first book (1995), as well as the conceptual "found" poetry of the contemporary author Kenneth Goldsmith, about whom I authored a book in 2019. The chapter in this book that includes my commentary on Goldsmith's *Duchamp is My Lawyer*, published a year after my study of Goldsmith had appeared in print, fits well into the theme of this introduction—the idea of learning twice—because, as is evident in my commentary on the curator of the online avant-garde website known as UbuWeb, I link Goldsmith, who was born in New York in 1961, one year before I came into the world in the same city, with the aesthetic tendencies evident in Williams, my dissertation subject who was born in 1883 and died in 1963, a year after I was born.

Before my conclusion, which describes my feelings about cleaning out my office in Heavilon Hall, which has housed the Purdue English department since the 1950s, but which will be torn down later in the summer of 2024, I close the main body of this volume with chapters that exemplify the spirit of the epigram about "learning twice." In the penultimate chapter, I reproduce the review I wrote about *Listening to the Candle* (1992), the second volume in a trilogy of book-length poems by Peter Dale Scott, a former Canadian Diplomat, UC Berkeley professor, and critic of American imperial involvement in Southeast Asia. My review was published first in the *Harvard Review* in 1993, the year before I arrived in West Lafayette to begin teaching at Purdue. I also reproduce a second review of a book by Scott almost 30 years later in the *Notre Dame Review* in 2022. The second review focuses on a prose work Scott coauthored with Freeman Ng, *Revisiting Jakarta: Internal Turmoil and State Violence in Poetry and Terror* (2018). In this late work, Scott, who was in his late eighties when the book was published, tells the story behind the composition of *Coming to Jakarta: A Poem about Terror* (1988), the installment of the trilogy that preceded *Listening to the Candle,* the volume I reviewed before I left Boston for Indiana. Most importantly, Scott in *Revisiting Jakarta* does something courageous and, for me, instructive; whereas *Coming to Jakarta* revealed "the role played by the CIA, banks, and oil companies in the 1965 slaughter of more than half a million Indonesians" (*Coming to Jakarta,* back cover), Scott, on faculty at Berkeley at the time the massacre took place, denied the role his university played in the training of the perpetrators with support from the RAND corporation. Part Mea culpa and part re-memory, I read *Revisiting Jakarta* as Scott's belated forum to address his implicit collaboration with American involvement in

Indonesia, as well as the psychic turmoil that facilitated his erasure of moral responsibility for defending his university at a time when it deserved critique, not succor. What I have taken with me in this collection from Scott's revisiting of his earlier life and work is that willingness to revise one's formative educational experiences in the service of an expanded awareness of its meanings in the light of current understandings and changing conditions. In Chapter 3, for example, I look back at the kind of New Critical approach to teaching poetry that is evident in Billy Collins's pedagogical poem called "Introduction to Poetry." At the same time, I critique Collins's formalism by placing his poem in conversation with poems and song lyrics by Jared Carter, Pete Seeger, and Lucinda Williams that call the reader to think about familial, economic, and political issues that cannot be easily cordoned off from the literary realm.

In chapter 16, I honor my epigrammatic mantra to "learn twice" in a personal reflection on seeing a retrospective of the painter Philip Guston at the National Gallery in Washington, DC, in the summer of 2023. While Guston is a painter, not a poet, I explain the link between my appreciation of his work at age 60 and my journey into the "thirty-year creative reading workshop" as a teacher at Purdue.

A Note on the Organization of This Book

I have separated the following 16 previously uncollected essays and interviews into four sections. Section 1 focuses on the poets, poetry, and poetics that mattered to me the most during my formative years as a graduate student and instructor in the Boston area. The first two chapters offer personal reflections on key mentors—and esteemed poets—Allen Grossman and Frank Bidart. Chapters 3 and 4, which represent recent efforts in cultural criticism, nonetheless return me to William Carlos Williams and Louise Glück, two poets who I read with devotion during my period of graduate training. Williams was the topic of my PhD dissertation (and, eventually, my first scholarly monograph) and Glück (the subject of another early career scholarly book) was among the world-class poets then living, writing, and presenting her work in the Boston area.

On a thematic level, there remain links between Chapters 3 and 4 from Section 1 and what follows in the six chapters of Section 2. My chapter on Glück, for example, emphasizes her Jewishness, and, by placing her in conversation with Bob Dylan, I signal my interest in the relationships between poetry and popular culture. My chapter on William Carlos Williams points forward to Section 2 in its concentration on the conceptualist poet and UbuWeb founder

Kenneth Goldsmith. Section 2, however, differs from Section 1 in that the literary geography shifts from Boston, with its confessionalism and post-confessionalism, to a focus on avant-garde Midwestern poetics. Section 2 also reflects my revised and expanded understanding of the history of twentieth-century poetry in the United States. The essays and interviews that constitute Section 2 are wide-ranging in topic and approach, but what binds them together is that all the poets under discussion except one have lived, studied, wrote, and taught in the American Midwest. The exception, the Winnipeg-born and New York City-based poet Adeena Karasick, became known to me through her performances at the University of Louisville conferences on Literature after 1900, a gathering site for many of the Midwestern poets I discuss in Section 2. In Section 2, I explore contemporary experimental writings that, truth be told, were not emphasized by my teachers in the Boston era when I was a graduate student there.

Section 3 underscores the meaning of this introduction's epigram by emphasizing my writings and interviews on poetry and education. The pedagogical chapters display my ongoing thinking about poetry in relationship to other genres (such as drama and the graphic novel) and, in the chapter on Billy Collins, I continue to challenge New Critical pieties to help my students notice connections between author, speaker, and the situation of poetry in the classroom as a crucial frame of reception. My interviews with Thomas Fink are informed by my efforts to teach experimental poetry in the undergraduate classroom and also express my goal of developing strategies to teach poetry in a way that appeals to contemporary students.

Section 4 concludes this volume with two chapters that convey my experience of the sentiment animating T. S. Eliot's line from "East Coker": "In My End is My Beginning." Eliot's line is the implicit reference point to the portrait of the 1948 Nobel Laureate entitled "East Coker-Tse" (1979) by Philip Guston, that most literary of painters about whom I lectured for my "job talk" at Purdue in the winter of 1994. The other chapter in this concluding section brings together two reviews of writings by Peter Dale Scott, one from the front end and one from the back end of my 30-year creative reading workshop.

SECTION 1

Rereading the Poets, Poetry, and Poetics of My Decade in the Boston Area (1983–1993)

CHAPTER 1

READING SPIVACK/READING MYSELF: A MEMOIR OF READING A MEMOIR, BOSTON 1959–1977; BOSTON 1983–1993

To prepare for teaching a course at Purdue on post–World War II American poets, I'm reading a memoir by a Boston area writer and literary teacher from an earlier generation than my own—Kathleen Spivack. *With Robert Lowell and His Circle* (2012) shows Spivak to have been a confidante of Lowell, Elizabeth Bishop, Anne Sexton, and Stanley Kunitz. All four are now canonical American poets. She arrived in Boston from Cleveland in 1959 at the age of 21 to study poetry. Her first choice of mentor had been Allen Ginsberg, but he was, as might be expected, nowhere to be found in Boston, and so Lowell took her on.

Spivack recounts what turned into an unlikely lifelong friendship of extraordinary intimacy with Lowell. Their connection—a love affair, really, but without the confusions that sex injects in any relationship—only ended with his death, at age 60, in 1977. When she first showed up at his Boston University (BU) office, where he was teaching a writer's workshop, Spivack, by her own account, lacked special qualities. It is unclear why she would have stood out to Lowell as worthy of attention. An alienated young woman hailing from a midwestern college without much experience in poetry writing or literary analysis, she barely knew who Lowell was when they first met. He was entering the magical (if psychically tortured) period that would result in his greatest influence on American letters. He would go on at the end of his life to tell one of his outstanding students and closest friends, the poet Frank Bidart, that he was uncertain of the value of his life's writing, but he was sure he had "changed the game."

When discussing Lowell with Purdue undergraduates—none of whom has even heard of him—it is hard for me to convey just how famous Lowell was when Spivack entered into close terms with him. His last name all by itself garnered respect and fascination. It was an Old Money Boston Brahmin family name with roots dating back to the Mayflower. Ancestors included a Harvard president, and leading poets (James Russell, Amy). Buildings at Harvard were named Lowell, as was the Massachusetts city where Jack Kerouac grew up. At the same time, he appealed to a new generation of young writers because he was something of a bête noir in academic circles. In the late 1950s, he rejected modernist formalism and linguistic opacity. He now favored a subtly well-made, but, on first glance, nakedly revealing, verse style that characterized the addictions, manias, infidelities, and hospitalizations of a speaker that the poet, in a *Paris Review* interview, said he wanted readers to believe was "the real Robert Lowell." In "Skunk Hour" and "For the Union Dead," one sensed how transformational contemporary politics informed and reflected his speaker's unruly nature. One could also imagine other members of his patrician class interpreting his writing as betrayal, an airing of dirty laundry. In "Waking in the Blue," which describes his time at McLean Hospital in Belmont, Massachusetts, Lowell imagined himself with self-effacing humor as a bloated Moby Dick figure weighing 200 pounds after a hearty New England breakfast. He also offered unflattering sketches of other twisted blue bloods who now haunted the madhouse, mere specters of their commanding selves as All-American fullbacks and members of Harvard's elite secret societies. Lowell was of such public stature that when he accepted prison time (later immortalized in his poem "Memories of West Street and Lepke") for his stance as a conscientious objector to World War II (and thus a betrayal of FDR) it landed him on the front page of the *New York Times*.

Lowell was in 1959 teaching what amounted to the most influential creative writing workshop in the country with Sylvia Plath and Anne Sexton among his star students (and co-conspirators in the nascent "confessional" movement) at BU. He was also finishing his game-changing poetry book *Life Studies*. In the late 1940s, Lowell had already gained renown in academic literary culture. By then Old School High Modernists championed his clotted, forbiddingly difficult early poems found in volumes such as *Lord Weary's Castle*, which won the Pulitzer Prize in 1947. His first books were influenced by opaque but sublime modernist authors such as Hart Crane as well as by the weight of his learning in New England transcendentalism and religious Calvinism. (Among his famous early poems was a challenging philosophical meditation on Jonathan Edwards.)

By the late 1950s, however, Lowell had betrayed New Critical pieties about what Wimsatt and Beardsley termed the "intentional fallacy." Contra

Lowell, New Critics separated an author's biographical story from the significance of the work. Lowell, ironically, was thus rejecting the theory inculcated into U.S. academic study of poetry by his Agrarian movement teachers John Crowe Ransom and Allen Tate. By so doing, he'd moved serious poetry off its steep and icy peak and in the direction of a more accessible, overtly political, and personally forthcoming style that became labeled—reductively, by M. L. Rosenthal—as "confessional." His example took root in the work of Sexton and Plath, among others, in what was then, in the era before the proliferation of MFA writing programs, still an insular academic poetry community located in Boston, New York, and with a few emerging outsider figures like Ginsberg hanging out on the West Coast.

Enduring mental illness, Lowell was often during his time with Spivack in a manic phase, which meant on the verge of a nervous breakdown. During such episodes, Lowell would squander class time engaged in an excruciating (and, to those students who had to endure it, painfully embarrassing) private dialogue concerning which poets in his circle were "major" and which "minor." Such classes inevitably preceded the full-blown collapse that led to yet another stay at McLean, a Belmont, Massachusetts hospital for psychically broken (and often artistically famous) patients with financial resources to afford first-rate care on bucolic grounds originally conceptualized by Frederick Law Olmstead in the late 1800s. It was Spivack's misfortune (and, in the end, blessing) to arrive at the great troubled man's office door during a period of disequilibrium; he didn't even remember having accepted the Oberlin fellowship student to attend his seminar at BU. But from the inauspicious first meeting in 1959 at which Lowell offered her half of his sandwich, but no indication that he was willing to sponsor her, Spivack shows how Lowell became her surrogate father and she his unofficial "psychologist," given her penchant for analysis and the steady way about her that he found comforting. Spivack gravitated around Lowell's orbit to the point his Back Bay apartment became her mailing address.

Lowell extended to Spivack access to his private life. Besides studying with him at BU, Spivack attended private tutorials in the attic study of Lowell's Marlborough Street apartment twice a week. One suspected an affair, but that was not the case. Sensing her isolation as a fragile single young woman in Boston, he offered her formal letters of introduction to leading women poets in the area, thus initiating friendships Spivack would enjoy with legendary authors ranging from Sexton to Adrienne Rich to Bishop. A sign of his mania, as well as his inability to maintain proper borders with those near him, Lowell took such a paternal interest in Spivack's personal life that he visited her parents' home in New Jersey to vouch for Spivack's talent. He encouraged her parents to accept poetry writing as her serious life endeavor. He also spoke for Kathleen's choice of a marriage partner, Mayer Spivack, an eccentric inventor with whom she would have children, but eventually divorce. Marital struggle was a common affliction for Spivack and Lowell.

***

On one level, I recognized Spivack's Boston. As in Elizabeth Bishop's "Poem," in which she spots a specific Nova Scotia's farmer's house as drawn in a watercolor "about the size of an Old Style dollar bill" by her Uncle George, I recognized in Spivack's book the streets, buildings, and sharply chill New England light from my own Boston decade (1983–1993). More to the point, as a graduate student at Brandeis, I studied with Frank Bidart, a prominent Lowell student from Spivack's era. More soon on the contours of my relationship with Bidart. On a second level, I read Spivack's initiation into Lowell's inner world with dormant feelings of envy and resentment over my struggle to gain the confidence of students Lowell had championed in the 1960s—many of whom had come into their own as leading writers, critics, and teachers in the 1980s.

Born in 1938, Spivak is 24 years older than I am. Primarily focused on Lowell, Bishop, Plath, and Sexton, Spivak recalls figures who had died before I arrived in Boston. That said, the literary landscape she paints corresponds to the scene as I discovered it after my unemployed single mother, my two brothers, and I moved into the area from South Florida when Harvard accepted my older brother to law school in the summer of 1983. I only met Spivak briefly when I lived, wrote, and studied in the Boston area, but I spent time in her house. Like me, Spivack resided in the blue-collar, but gentrifying, Boston suburb of Watertown. She owned her large old house near Mt. Auburn Street, while my mother, two brothers, and I rented a two-bedroom, one-bathroom apartment. I knew Spivack's place because she rented an attic apartment to Louis Schwartz, a fellow Brandeis PhD student in English, now a Milton scholar at the University of Richmond. I visited Louis to listen to free jazz, discuss metaphysical poetry and its relationship to T. S. Eliot's modernism, or to hang out with an imported beer before heading to the Brattle movie theater in nearby Cambridge for Marx Brothers or Fellini and popcorn with real butter. Further, Spivack mentions her friendships with Bob and Gail Melson, then a young Cambridge couple involved in intellectual endeavors with Spivack and her circle in the 1960s, but who in their mature years have become my professorial colleagues at Purdue—Bob in politics and Jewish Studies; Gail in

Childhood Development—and fellow congregants at West Lafayette's Temple Israel. Those are coincidences, but more significantly, Spivack discusses her comradeship with other poets and scholars of her generation such as Bidart, Lloyd Schwartz, Robert Pinsky, Helen Vendler, and Bill Corbett. Each went on to become an influential literary figure when I was a young poet and scholar pursuing graduate degrees in creative writing at BU and then in modern literature at Brandeis.

Reading Spivack in my fifties I felt an uncanny sense that I could trace my literary family tree to the same legendary roots—Lowell and his circle—from which Spivack blossomed into an award-winning poet, essayist, and teacher on the international stage. I spent significant time with the poets and critics Spivack regards as Lowell's most prominent literary children and interlocutors, Frank Bidart chief among them. Spivack knew the poet and scholar Allen Grossman, who became my PhD dissertation advisor at Brandeis, but did not focus attention on him in the memoir. A Yeats scholar who championed impersonality, Grossman was not a Lowell acolyte, but he had written an important essay on Lowell, and had been an editor of the *Advocate*, Harvard's literary magazine, as an undergraduate there in the late 1950s, before moving on to graduate study and teaching at nearby Brandeis in 1960. (To this day, I hang a poster in my office at Purdue announcing a commemorative reading at Harvard from 1987, a decade after Lowell's death. The event featured Grossman—who read from Lowell's early difficult work, "The Quaker Graveyard at Nantucket"—as well as Bidart, Vendler, Nobel Prize–winning poet Seamus Heaney, and Harvard professor and dramatist William Alfred.) Was I not, in a sense, Lowell's grandchild, given that I studied at Brandeis with Bidart and had frequent contacts with poets (Lloyd Schwartz, Bill Corbett) and critics such as Helen Vendler who took part in Lowell's Harvard office hour workshops and seminars? Did I not spend time lounging on the puffy couch sampling new books at the same shrine of Cambridge poetry—the Grolier—run first by a man named Gordon and then by a woman named Louisa—that Spivack remembers, at first, like me sheepishly, and then more comfortably, entering? Did I not attend the poetry readings at the Blacksmith House or in the Lamont poetry room at Harvard and take part in my own coffee klatches at the Pamplona and Irun cafes? Did I not take classes in the same musty seminar room of a converted brownstone at 236 Bay State Road on the BU campus where Lowell, in the late 1950s, held his workshops with Sexton and Plath before he moved over to Harvard in later years? Did I not myself, after completing my Brandeis PhD in 1992, but before landing a tenure track job at Purdue in 1994, teach literature as a lecturer at Harvard in the same buildings that Lowell had taught his classes on Romantic poetry late in his life? Did I not review poetry for the *Harvard Review* and publish my own poetry in *Agni*, BU's literary journal? Moreover, did not Bidart attend my own poetry reading on campus at Brandeis and at a used bookstore on Moody Street in Waltham? So yes, nostalgic recognition when reading Spivack. But also, an uneasy question. On paper, I seem to have done well. I've published books of criticism and poetry and hold an (increasingly rare) tenured post at a respectable (if provincial) Midwestern state university. Granted that I've built and maintained a solid, if unremarkable, career in the world of letters over the last 25 years, why do I feel regret that, for a time, I was *in* the Boston-Cambridge literary scene Spivack describes in her memoir, but never *of* that world, never embraced?

Lowellian lions for students of my generation—Grossman and Bidart—spent countless hours with me in the classroom and in office hours, but neither offered me anything like the professional (and personal) support that Spivack received for almost twenty years from Lowell. When Spivack received a negative review for her second book of poems in the *New York Times*, she spent the day curled up, like a sick daughter, in bed with Lowell and his wife Carolyn Blackwood. The couple fed Spivack tea and toast, and read her Coleridge, while she self-consciously joked about her Oedipal and Electra complexes until she napped. By contrast, I never saw the inside of Grossman's Lexington house, even as I was his teaching assistant for several years. When I needed Grossman, my PhD advisor, to make a quick call of support to his former Brandeis colleague who now held a chair at another school where I had received a rare campus interview, why had my mentor denied me, falsely claiming he didn't know anybody at the college where I had applied? Why did Bidart, after attending a reading at BU by Language poet Michael Palmer, inform me that he looked forward to being on my PhD thesis committee, but then never mentioned the offer again? Was I such damaged goods?

Perhaps I can't admit to myself that Lowell simply recognized Spivack's gifts in a way my "Lowells" did not recognize mine. Insecure to begin with, however, I have held on to the nagging suspicion that Grossman and Bidart were somehow ashamed of me. However, reading between the lines of her memoir, I offer another theory about why Spivack, so unlike me in this regard, could endure self-doubts about her attractiveness, creativity, intelligence, and social skills to cast aside insecurity and hang in there with Lowell, whose illness could result in split-second shifts from gentle kindness to aggressive critique. Before I put forward my theory, let me express respect for Spivack's sheer spunk and perseverance in the face of Lowell's quixotic moods and overwhelming personality. She endured his hospitalizations at McLean that, at least in the first year, left her marooned in a drab rooming house. Gritty, Spivak absorbed, without being overwhelmed by, Lowell's command of Latin, Roman history, and the English kings, of which Lowell, in his manic phases, believed himself a number.

So, given that Spivack *does not* imagine herself as especially talented, learned, or graceful, and since she *does* describe her doubts about being worthy of attention from Lowell and Bishop, why did she gain admission into the inner sanctum of Boston letters? By contrast, why do I perceive myself, accurately or not, as orphaned by Grossman and Bidart and thus left to fight on my own for a place on the academic margins in a provincial Midwestern town at a university far better known for producing engineers than poets? I think Spivack's accessibility, her receptiveness to new experiences appealed to Lowell and to the others. By contrast, I came across as a brittle guy with a chip on his shoulder. Rather than celebrating my resilience, I was defensive about my modest upbringing. My father had died when I was 11 and I grew up on food stamps in an agricultural town, Homestead, Florida, best known today, if at all, as ground zero for Hurricane Andrew in 1992. It never occurred to me to celebrate an affinity between my obscure background and that of Bidart, who hailed from the farming world of Bakersfield, California. Instead of connecting with other, albeit, older and more accomplished, misfits such as Bidart and Grossman, I was on the lookout for signs of disrespect. When a leading poet such as Mark Strand appeared at Brandeis to give a reading, I chafed at Grossman's request that I find a water bottle for the visiting dignitary. As one who supported himself through graduate school as a custodian at the Waltham Medical Building, I feared the faculty would perceive me as the department lackey. Deep down, I worried I was a water boy (but not heroic like Gunga Din). Unevenly shaven, hair greasy, hands slightly trembling, I feared looking anyone I perceived as my better straight in the eye. I took everyone in the Boston literary world as my superior. Expecting rejection, I rarely asked my mentors for guidance with placing my scholarship and poetry, or for information about securing grants, fellowships, or academic jobs. My slouched bearing and saggy thrift tour tweed announced my lack of self-worth. I recall my trepidation at asking Professor Grossman for a perfunctory recommendation letter *three years into my dissertation project with him*! "My dear boy," he said, stopping to puff his ubiquitous pipe. "If you don't know I will write for you by now, I don't think you have been paying any attention at all these last few years." Reassuring? I guess. Sort of.

Setting aside differences in our levels of talent, gender, and distinct personal dispositions—Spivack (open, warm, willing) and Morris (prickly, resentful, suspicious, self-doubting)—I nonetheless maintain that Spivack's social background helped advance the relationship with Lowell. Spivack enjoyed cultural capital through her father, Peter Drucker, a renowned European Jewish immigrant economic theorist, journalist, and college teacher. My point is not that Lowell accepted Spivack under his wing out of respect for her father. (Perhaps reeling from guilt over the Holocaust, Lowell, who, like Berryman and Plath, imagined himself as an imaginary Jew with obscure Jewish ancestry, may have viewed Spivack favorably in part because she was the child of a diasporic Jewish family.) My main argument, however, has less to do with what Lowell saw in Spivack, than with how Spivack saw Lowell (and, implicitly, how she regarded herself when in the company of famous men and women). I believe Spivack's familial and interpersonal experience with authors and intellectuals when young enabled her to tolerate feelings of inadequacy, ignorance, and not measuring up to Lowell, Bishop, and Sexton.

Spivack recalls years when her father taught at Bennington when now distinguished—but then still relatively unrecognized—poets such as Theodore Roethke and Stanley Kunitz (whose greatest fame came much later, from age 70 to 100!) were teaching there. She describes Roethke as an incoherent depressive who saw himself as a professional failure, toiling in obscurity, passed over by flashier and socially capable younger writers. What is telling for me is that Spivack describes Roethke's insecurities, not as an anomaly faced by one paranoid man, but rather as the typical lot of an author. Roethke dealt with fears of imaginative failure that, she admits, all poets, explorers of the unknown, must endure. Spivack, in other words, did not interpret lack of self-confidence in one's art or social graces as a sign of fundamental, irresolvable personal flaw. I did. For Spivack, insecurity was the common lot of all creative persons, even those as accomplished as Roethke.

Later in the memoir, Spivack recalls discussing the issue of rejection with Lowell and Sexton. Riffing on the language of income investment—a realm I knew nothing about—they settle on a "3 percent rate of return" on accepted submissions to literary journals. It would have been comforting for me to realize that "rejection"—the keyword that I read as defining my Boston decade—was not peculiar to me, and thus was nothing to take personally.

***

Of the generation of poets Spivack identifies as Lowell's primary children, I spent the most time with Bidart. Can anyone claim Lowell and Bishop as symbolic literary parents more so than Bidart? He is literary executor for both Lowell and Bishop and co-editor of Lowell's *Collected Poems*. Spivack writes that

Bishop and Lowell "loved" Bidart like a son. There are accounts that Bidart co-authored (or at least significantly edited and helped shape) Lowell's final poetry books. Bidart's own mature poetry ingeniously synthesizes modernist "impersonality" and postmodern "confessionalism." He evokes the deeply personal explorations of psychic disturbance associated with Lowell, but, at the same time, Bidart distances himself from the speaker through modernist collage techniques and personae (masks)—Herbert White, Ellen West, Vaslav Nijinsky—that recall strategies of authorial detachment associated with High Modernists such as Ezra Pound and T. S. Eliot, authors who Lowell chafed against with his comparatively upfront style.

When I met him, Bidart's main academic job was as a tenured professor at Wellesley College. Because Wellesley had no graduate program, and because of Bidart's respect for Grossman, as well as Brandeis's tradition of supporting outstanding poets—J. V. Cunningham, Adrienne Rich, Mark Halliday, Mary Leader, Alan Shapiro, Timothy Steele, Ha Jin, John Burt, Mary Campbell—who studied or taught there—Bidart offered a course on contemporary poetry on the Waltham campus. Pitched to undergraduates, Bidart, however, encouraged me to audit. After class, he regularly invited me to his office to continue to discuss poetry. These meetings with Bidart resembled the private tutorials with Lowell that Spivack recalls as a cherished part of her education.

What was the texture of the office discussions with Bidart? What, specifically, did we discuss? What was his approach to poetry? Context matters here. Graduate school in literary studies in the 1980s was not the best of times for poets bent on aesthetic appreciation of the literary object, or for those who connected poems to the emotional lives of the people who made them. The 1980s were disorienting for naïve readers. By naïve readers I mean people (like me) who came to poetry and stories because, on a gut level, they (we) felt literature meant something to them (or meant differently in some difficult-to-define but nonetheless self-evident way) than other genres of writing (newspapers, history books).

I recall my first deep connection with literature as a poor, fatherless, alienated Jewish kid from Long Island who found himself at South Dade High School in rural Homestead, Florida in the 1970s. The school's nickname was still The Rebels, a Confederate Flag proudly adorning the gym walls during basketball games against multicultural Miami area schools. The Klan roamed freely down Krome Avenue and U.S. 1. I think of that "shock of recognition" I felt when discovering Kafka, Camus, Mann, T. S. Eliot, and Faulkner. I think of the uncanny feelings of being "at home" and yet never "at home" after finding my way into comparative literature professor Erich Heller's course on

Continental Fiction in the fall of my first year at Northwestern in 1980. I saw on Heller's reading list the authors (and others I had yet to hear of such as Dostoyevsky, Rilke, and Sartre) I had connected with in Homestead, where the other kids assumed I had horns under my hair because I was a Jew. Personal connections to literature (or to use the word "literature"!) seemed beside the point to most graduate students in the PhD program. The post-structuralist climate at Brandeis in the 1980s, ironically, made my meetings with Bidart that much more informative to us both. As Bidart's poetry makes clear, he is a philosophical author with strong interests in metaphysics and religion. His great poem "Ellen West" from *The Book of the Body* (1977) is a meditation on the mind-body problem and on the relationship between presence, absence, and aesthetics through a celebrated set piece on the voice of Operatic Diva Maria Callas as it changed qualities when her body withered in old age. Bidart was by no means anti-intellectual—the dust jacket of his *Collected Poems* offers an etching by Giovanni Valpato of Raphael's *The School of Athens*—and so even if aesthetic appreciation, so-called New Criticism, or biographical approaches to reading poetry were out of favor, Bidart remained curious about trends in Franco-American high theory. He would take what he needed from any influence and leave the rest behind. To the degree I understood what I was reading in classes on Literary Theory, I did what I could to explain to Bidart my notion of "differance," "simulacrum," "contingency of value," "intertext," "subject position," and "death of the author."

Bidart was curious about the theory I was learning from the Yale Mafia's offspring. At the same time, he was working out his own ideas about being, time, language, body, meaning, sexuality, and art. Bidart's poetics were rooted in traditional approaches even as his own poems benefited from avant-garde graphics. He not only focused on how poets made poems (line length, enjambment, pacing, word choice) but also on what poems implied about the emotional and social lives of the authors who made them. An innovator in the use of italics, capitalization, and punctuation to indicate timbre, tone, pitch, timing, and stress, Bidart was especially sensitive to poetry's sound, texture, tone, and graphic appeal. Form following function. He was a bird, not an ornithologist, even as he was not the kind of bird, such as an ostrich, who puts his head in the sand and turns a blind eye to the world as it changes around him. Bidart himself had been a PhD student in English at Harvard in the 1960s, when he first met Lowell. (His thesis was to have been on the poetry of Lowell!). Like T. S. Eliot and Charles Olson, other Harvard graduate students who became famously allusive twentieth-century American poets, Bidart never bothered, officially, to complete his PhD.

Bidart's teaching style was, paradoxically, intensely relaxed. Folding his large pale hands behind the back of his globular balding head as he leaned back in his chair, tipping with his feet the bar that held together the front two legs of the chair, thus lifting the front part of the chair a few inches off the floor, he waited to hear what we thought of the poem at hand. He was performing the quintessential Whitman posture of receptivity to other minds. He didn't need to prepare lecture notes because he taught poems he knew by heart by poets he loved or whom he found perplexingly fascinating. He taught with a microscopic focus on the text. The placement of a period or dash, the choice of colon or semicolon, the cheeky tone of a parenthetical aside (as in the young Elizabeth Bishop's brash remark that she "could read" in "In the Waiting Room"), the esoteric reference, line length, enjambment, or rhythm, these were elements Bidart turned over and turned again with us in class. Bidart used the chalkboard, writing out a line we were debating, and then rewriting it several more times. He would not change a word of the poem in the rewritten versions, but he would break the line in different places. He would try on different punctuation. Watching him tinker at the board, I thought of him, strangely enough, as an expert car mechanic. It was as if he were lifting a line of poetry—instead of an auto chassis—with a hydraulic lift off the pavement (the page) so he could better examine the line. He was, so to speak, checking under the hood, to decide, if anything, what was wrong with the placement of the words, the grammatical markers, the line itself, and what needed repair. Bidart was wary of labels such as "confessional," "beat," "impersonal." Close reading troubled any such categorical definitions.

He was interested in how major (unlike Lowell, Bidart didn't use the term) contemporary poets developed over their careers. He noted that Ginsberg only came into his own in poems such as "Sunflower Sutra" when he incorporated his queer friendship with Kerouac into his narrative poem. Thinking back to his reading list, one could argue that Bidart, a gay man, paid special attention to other gay or queer poets. Ginsberg, Ashbery, Rich, Merrill, Bishop, and Frank O'Hara were among his main subjects, but I do not recall Bidart emphasizing (or concealing) that fact. (He taught Rich's essay on "compulsory heterosexuality".) Bidart discussed poetry as if they were living documents written by full-fledged human beings, many of whom he knew intimately. As with family relationships, the closer one gets to a person the more difficult it becomes to define them by "subject position" or to categorize their motives via an overarching theory or encapsulating phrase. So, it turned out, was the case with poems and poets.

We spent time closely reading poems from Lowell's *Life Studies* (1959). Bidart encouraged us to interpret Lowell's poetry as limited, rather than informed, by the "confessional" label attached to it by critic M. L. Rosenthal. To disprove the "confessionalist" moniker, Bidart paid special attention to the poem "To Speak of Woe that Is in Marriage." As the notes to the poem in the *Collected Poems*, edited by Bidart and David Gewanter, point out, "To Speak of Woe" is itself deeply in conversation with literary and philosophical traditions. The sonnet's title stems from Chaucer's "Wife of Bath"; the epigraph is from Schopenhauer's "The World as Will and Idea"; the poem itself "started as a translation of Catullus's *siqua recordanti benefacta*" (1045). Lowell placed the sonnet in quotation marks because the poem's speaker is not to be confused with a figure for Lowell's autobiographical persona. Rather, Lowell wrote the sonnet from the perspective of the author's wife, the writer Elizabeth Hardwick. In conversation with other poems from Part Four of *Life Studies* such as "Man and Wife," "Home After Three Months Away," "Waking in the Blue," and "Skunk Hour," "To Speak of Woe that Is in Marriage" examines Lowell's well-documented personal maladies, including his mental illness, addictions, manias, marital struggles, and infidelities. One could accuse Lowell of self-absorption because he restricts the lyric domain to the author's quotidian failings, and thus of abandoning poetry's long association with historical, mythic, social, and political themes. However, at Brandeis, Bidart stressed Lowell's extension of his poetic vision beyond the narrow horizon of the monologic self through poems such as "To Speak of Woe" that point to the novelistic qualities of Lowell's autobiographically inflected lyrics.

Bidart was interested in gift-giving and friendship as signs of intimacy and as creative spurs. This is what he especially loved about the poetry of Ashbery's close friend, Frank O'Hara. In "The Day Lady Died" (1964), O'Hara describes with luxurious (even neurotic) detail how he spends his lunch hour (from his day job as a curator at the Museum of Modern Art). He selects unique gifts, as acts of memory and love, for friends he plans to meet at a weekend vacation home (on Long Island, or on Fire Island, where O'Hara died in a tragic accident—or suicide?—when he was struck by a Jeep). In his obsessive, theatrical, even histrionic manner, Bidart clearly relished reciting O'Hara's finicky, exasperated, humorously self-conscious process of indecision about which gifts to buy his friends in "The Day Lady Died." It was not merely about whether to get Patsy some Hesiod, but a specific translation. Bidart emphasized the campy self-mockery about "practically going to sleep with quandariness." He appreciated O'Hara's invocation of taste (the good, the bad, the trashy) as an aesthetic value and interpersonal good. He noted O'Hara's emphasis on specifically branded, often imported, distinctly urban, and idiosyncratic product selections. It was not a carton of cigarettes, but Gauloises, not alcohol, but the Italian herbal liqueur, Strega. The social experience of purchases mattered. O'Hara has not headed to a mall or supermarket, but pops in and out of specialty shops, cash in hand from a bank where he knows the teller's first name. O'Hara is celebrating, in the context of a nascent consumer society, the creation of human significance through the registration of O'Hara's Eliotic "visions and revisions" about what to buy for friends. Part of his gift is the sacrifice (and personal pleasure) of giving up his lunch hour to move through the hot city to buy extravagant stuff for them. A member of the art world who is not made of money—the teller usually checks his balance before handing over the bills—he must draw precious funds to go on his shopping spree. On behalf of friendship, O'Hara has given up time, thought, funds, and endured mental quandary, in anticipation of the desired moment of social exchange. One senses that for O'Hara the payback will be well worth the fuss: the moment of reconnection with the friends and lovers on Fire Island or in the Hamptons. He, too, will enjoy the Strega, Gauloises, and the Verlaine with the Bonnard drawings.

What makes the expectation of presenting gifts to old friends so poignant, and the sense of immediacy and temporal specificity in "The Day Lady Died" so moving, is that it is in the process of buying gifts that O'Hara learns of Holiday's death from the *New York Post*. Knowledge of Holiday's death (as opposed to anticipating his weekend holiday) draws him out of the moment, and away from desirable future images of himself bearing gifts. He turns back toward memories of hearing Lady Day at the Five Spot, a recollection that makes him sweat. The poet of the quotidian, of temporal specificity—"it is 12:40/ of a Thursday" he writes in "A Step Away From Them"—acknowledges the vanishing nature of pleasant experiences and the ephemeral nature of gifts including life.

I rehearse Bidart's celebration of energy, playfulness, as well as pathos, in O'Hara's gift-giving poem for two reasons. First, I recall literal gifts Bidart offered to me and to the other members of his Contemporary Poetry class. On the last class meeting, he brought in an exquisite (and I'm sure quite costly) Black Forest cherry chocolate torte from a special little German bakery that I had walked by with longing many times on Mass Ave just past the Harvard Law School. Getting through graduate school as a janitor and paid-by-the-course composition instructor, I would never have dared step inside to buy dessert there. Bidart, who in "Ellen West" explored anorexia as a metaphysical issue about body, desire, and control, seemed to be signifying with the rich cake the message of LET GO! Moreover, Bidart put in my mailbox in the English Department main office a signed, just off-the-press hardbound copy of his *In The Western Night: Collected Poems 1965–90*. His inscription honors what he refers to as my exemplary care for poetry. What a gift.

Second, I understand Bidart's willingness to take my interest in poetry seriously in our office-hour discussions as a symbolic gift. Thinking of those meetings today, I feel pride, gratitude, and I am even a little humbled. Here I was discussing poetry, not merely with a scholar or teacher in the field, but, as Spivack's memoir makes clear, with the most trusted and revered heir apparent to the two most influential and canonized American poets since World War II—Lowell and Bishop.

I think of how overcome I was in reading Spivack. Envy, resentment, anger, and regret took over when I remembered how I felt that Bidart and Grossman didn't lift me into their circle in the way Lowell and Bishop and Sexton lifted Spivack. Yet as my account of my relationship with Bidart at Brandeis makes clear (even to thickheaded me!), Bidart did honor me. It would require another long essay to describe, but Grossman, too, provided me with incalculable attention and unforgettable knowledge that I bring with me into the classroom, study, and writer's desk each day. I regret that I have waited so long to recognize my Boston years as a gift that has only grown in value over the decades.

Coda

After reading my chapter, a friend and fellow modernist scholar, Alec Marsh, noted that I did not emphasize my own accomplishments as a poet. He also pointed out that I did not offer an evaluation of Spivack's poetry. I address both of these omissions below.

On my own poetry

I first published this chapter in 2019 as my contribution to Marsh Hawk Press's "Chapter One" series about writerly beginnings. As the press's official website reports, Marsh Hawk, a non-profit juried collective founded in 2001, publishes titles that "often highlight the affinity of poetry, memoir and the visual arts." I have been an active member of the Marsh Hawk collective since 2004, when the press published my first book of poems, *Bryce Passage*. Over 20 years, I have published three more volumes of my poetry with the press, guest-edited the *Marsh Hawk Poetry Review*, edited manuscripts of other members, and served as a reader for the press's annual poetry prize competition.

While I am a proud member of the Marsh Hawk collective, I view my day job as being a professional literature teacher, scholar, critic, and editor. At night, on my own time, I write poetry and do what I can to support Marsh Hawk, a small independent press that has managed, through the hard work of its members, to survive for so long. In terms of my poetics, my association with Marsh Hawk is telling because it is very much a New York City-centered collective. Many of the press's founding poets studied with and/or were influenced by New York School and Jewish objectivist poets such as David Ignatow, George Oppen, John Ashbery, Kenneth Koch, David Shapiro, Barbara Guest, and Frank O'Hara. Like Marsh Hawk colleagues such as Stephen Paul Miller and Jon Curley, my poetry has the raw, comical, talky edge one finds in some New York School poets (as well as in Allen Ginsberg and David Antin). Tracking my own scholarly interests, however, I have incorporated into my New York School style the defamiliarizing elements of Language poetry and conceptualism. As with other Marsh Hawkers such as Thomas Fink and Burt Kimmelman, my work exhibits a graphic, even visual, dimension. I'd like to think of myself as a poet for the eye (the page) as well as for the ear (the voice.)

On the poetry of Kathleen Spivack

By contrast to my relationship to poetry writing as an avocation that is adjacent to my job as a literature professor, Kathleen Spivack is an established, if not canonical, professional poet and teacher of creative writing in Boston and Paris. Born in 1938 to Jewish refugees from Hitlerism, and still publishing her poetry and fiction well into her eighties, Spivack combines meditative, lyric, and narrative modes in the more than four hundred poems she has published in journals, anthologies, chapbooks, and full-length volumes. Only six years older than fellow Lowell student Plath, and a decade younger than Sexton, the other legendary confessional female poet who studied with Lowell at BU in the late 1950s, Spivack's poetry, so careful in its wording and restrained in its emotional tenor, resembles neither Plath nor Sexton in sound or sense. Nor does Spivack's writing display a pronounced interest in the political activism or social documentarian dimensions of Adrienne Rich (born 1929) or Muriel Rukeyser (born 1913). Spivack has, at times, veered in the direction of political commentary in her poetry, but the results have been subpar. In "Jane Witnesses the Destruction of the World," for example, her speaker, walking through Harvard Square during the Vietnam War period, "averts her eyes" to where "Asian bodies lie." As Peter Klappert remarked in a 1974 issue of *Parnassus: Poetry in Review*, "the childlike rhymes, are embarrassing rather than universalizing; it is a shame to have 'Asian bodies' used in this all-too-poetic way." A survivor of the confessional generation of writers, so many of whom died prematurely, sometimes by suicide or substance abuse, Spivack's sensibility reminds me more of Elizabeth Bishop's in its reticence than of Lowell's with his penchant for unrestrained self-disclosure.

Comparable to her contemporary, Mary Oliver (born 1935), Spivack is a careful observer of nature, the weather, and wildlife. The final lines of "Flying Inland," the title poem to her 1973 collection, illustrate her deft touch, skill at managing rhyme, diction, and line, and careful eye when observing nature and the animal world: "Five seagulls, circumflex accents, drift by—/nothing to speak of in the heaving sky." Like Louise Glück (born 1943), one could describe Spivack as a post-confessional Jewish female lyric poet with a strong narrative bent. Like Glück, Spivack is not especially interested in exploring her Jewishness in her poetry, however, and she does not offer strongly worded critiques of patriarchy. That said, Spivack does represent unfulfilled desires in marriage through a detached, third-person perspective in "He Doesn't Move" (1981): "He doesn't move in bed/is not alive/she keeps breathing, as if giving a sign/she knows she is wanting/but to tell/him is somehow worse." In "He Doesn't Move" and other poems from the 1970s and 1980s, Spivack offers insightful commentary on the quiet desperation of the domestic experience of a sensitive middle-class New England woman. She is married, but one senses her isolation and psychic pain. In "Private Pain in Time of Trouble," a frank, first-person lyric, Spivack's speaker, seemingly in mourning for a failed pregnancy, imagines her heart as an eggplant: "How can I sustain/this troubled swelling:/my heart like an eggplant,//blackened, bulbous, grows too greedy:/ bruised and sorrowful,it will not let its great loss go,//wanting to be pendulous with child."

Writing in mournful, often witty, sometimes comical, but always clear-eyed tones about sexuality, depression, and interpersonal struggles, Spivack occasionally seeks the protective lens of personae (Helen of Troy in the poem "Mythmaking" and in the "Jane Poems," which allude to Yeats's Crazy Jane, for example). More often, she distances herself from the psychic pain of her subject matter by selecting a limited third-person perspective and narrative mode that is closely aligned, and yet differs from, the first-person vocalizations that confessionalists of a prior generation encouraged readers to associate with the unmediated experience of the authorial self. A winning example of Spivack's ability to approach serious issues of loneliness and unfulfilled desire in the bedroom with a comic flair—the deliberately all-too-obvious symbolism is funny—occurs in "Outboard Engine": "At night/he turns to her in bed/

after a long absence/and talks intensely about motors./How he is buying this one and that one and that/one, prying open their insides and lubricating."

"The Young Woman Who Went Deaf," which, like "Outboard Engine," appeared in *Poetry* magazine, is another good example of how Spivack negotiates lyricism with narrative to produce a post-confessional poetics that balances self-disclosure with self-restraint. Here are the first five couplets: "All spring the snow fell/she knew she was losing her hearing.// Her husband spoke to her / and backed away, leaving.// She could not hear what he was saying:/'goodbye,' he mouthed.// Her children signalled her:/they were like goldfish in a bowl,// swimming away, and thick glass grew/In front of her eyes." Set at the edge between sound and silence, "The Young Woman Who Went Deaf" self-consciously meditates on the limits of the confessionalist ethos in which a voicing of the isolated self will somehow lead to the solace of acknowledgment and, in the end, affectionate understanding.

CHAPTER 2

ALLEN GROSSMAN'S RADICAL SIMPLICITY

As a graduate student in English at Brandeis in the late 1980s and early 1990s, I was not only drawn to Allen Grossman's theatricality and charisma, but also to his pragmatism and what I will be calling his radical simplicity. As *Publisher's Weekly* has noted, Grossman's lyrics highlight his "interest—or better, faith—in poetry's capacity to perform distinctly human acts of preservation." His example was not of the romantic poet chasing an elusive blue flower in the English Lake District. Instead, Grossman argued, poetry, traditionally, was how cultures disseminate history and myth, promote values such as honor, courage, and compassion, and confront loss and change. Grossman spoke of Hesiod, the ancient Greek lyricist whose poetry in *Works and Days* offered instruction on practical matters for an agricultural community comparable to a Farmer's Almanac. Poetry was how people "across time" (another Grossman formulation) expressed hope, like a message in a bottle tossed into an ocean, that someone on the other shore (read symbolically, as in Dickinson's poem "I cannot live with you," as the gulf of "despair" between self and other) would care enough to listen and respond.

In the 1980s, I had been a typical autobiographical storyteller in college at Northwestern and in the fiction-writing master's program at Boston University in the year before starting graduate studies at Brandeis. In stories, I was "acting out," or, more generously, "working through," private traumas including the death of my father, Ernie, when I was 11 and he 45, and an emotional breakdown I suffered in my sophomore year at Northwestern. I hadn't realized until Grossman offered a wide-angle perspective that my stories were of a piece with innumerable calls into the wilderness uttered by lost souls in hopes of being heard, understood, and loved. But Grossman's message was more complex in its focus on intersubjectivity. The lyric concern, counterintuitively, was not on preserving the authorial image, but rather on protecting the image of the beloved, the "you" addressed by the speaker. This emphasis on the figure of apostrophic address was so, even as, ironically, we remember the name and face of Shakespeare, and not the "dark lady" whom the Bard considered comparing to a summer's day (and decided not to), and even as he promised the beloved at the end of Sonnet 18:

> But thy eternal summer shall not fade,/ Nor lose possession of that fair thou ow'st;/ Nor shall Death brag thou wander'st in his shade,/ When in eternal lines to time thou grow'st:/ So long as men can breathe or eyes can see,/ So long lives this, and this gives life to thee.

However unexpected, an apparently narcissistic lyric such as "When I have Fears" by John Keats was, Grossman stated, motivated less by Keats's anxieties about mortality—he died at 25—and more by his concern that upon his death he will no longer be able to cast eyes upon, and put pen to paper to represent, Fanny Brawne, the "fair creature of an hour, That I shall never look upon thee more, Never have relish in the fairy power, Of unreflecting love."

Grossman's theory was that poetry at its best was interpersonal and outer-directed, but also poignant because it expressed the reality that life is beautiful because fragile and inevitably involves (again, another Grossman term) vanishing. All that is human perishes and rots, wrote Yeats, in a comment Grossman, who authored a study in 1970 on Yeats's early poetry, liked to repeat. Salt and ice make for the best packing. Symbolically, "salt and ice" referred to poetic form. In "Sunday Morning," "death," wrote Wallace Stevens, an American modernist touchstone for Grossman, "was the mother of beauty." Grossman thus invoked a straightforward, but provocative, idea. Poetry was not, as I had thought, in the business of "self-expression"—as in the hackneyed creative-writing teacher's encouragement to find one's "voice"—but rather in the business of constructing an *image* of self in a valued form he termed "personhood." Grossman, as Micah Towery reports:

> [S]ees persons as "value-bearing," and he differentiates persons from "selves" along this line of value. The self is something that can be discovered or found. The self is what Freud parsed: a hurricane of secret desires, phobias, and complexes. Persons, however, are what poets write about; they are "artifacts." Now, to say it is a construction of sorts, does not mean it has no "presence." I don't think of this construction as a mask, a falseness, something that obscures, but rather the actuality of what we perceive when we encounter others. In other words, I experience "Micah Towery" as a

self—*my*self. You, however, encounter me as an object (in the Thomistic sense), but more: a person. You encounter my presence through my writing.

Towery emphasizes two key points about Grossman's poetics. The first is that poetry is not narcissistic, but rather, as noted above in remarks about Keats, driven by a wish to imagine the beloved, as well as to elicit a response from another. The lyric yearning was not for knowledge of self so much as it was for how to project an image of self that could be "encountered" by another. The second point is that poetry functioned through what Grossman called a "bitter logic." By "bitter logic," he referred to a fundamental, and unbridgeable, difference, between my ordinary sense of self—flesh and blood Danny—and the representational image of "Danny" that might bestow upon me rights of appearance as a "person." Because of the difference between self and personhood, lyric appearance entailed experiential loss.

Among suspicious Brandeis graduate students with a populist bent who'd never heard him teach, Grossman's reputation was as a hermetic elitist. They may have passed by an open auditorium door while he lectured in bardic tones. In the hallways of Rabb, which housed the English department, they may have noticed his gray suit and tie (even on non-teaching days), smelled his pipe, and overheard him utter terms such as "crepuscule" and "liminal" in an elevated tone and with the long "a" sounds of someone trained in a New England Prep School even though he was a Jew from Minneapolis whose father had been a Chevy salesman. It was, from the outside, easy to caricature him as a Boston Brahmin wannabe. (I am reminded of the fact that T. S. Eliot was born in St. Louis but in recordings sounds as if he were raised in an English manor.) Those who didn't study with him may have assumed Grossman scorned popular culture, a prevalent area of scholarly inquiry among younger faculty and graduate students in the 1980s and 1990s. But part of Grossman's genius was that he paid respectful attention to all sorts of cultural expressions, high and low. He regarded a line such as "Nothing compares to U" from a Sinead O'Connor (by way of Prince) song, not only as a meditation on what it feels like to have your heart broken, but also as declaring the inadequacy of lyric—of figurative language—to reduce suffering through the detection of common elements of feeling in apparently unlike objects. Nothing compares to you. No logic of substitution, no way to use language or imagery to displace loss. Loss is total, unavailable to redemption through imagination. When John Lennon was murdered in Manhattan in 1980, Grossman spoke of a headline he read in the newspaper: "The Day the Music Died." It was, I knew, the line from Don McLean's elegy to Buddy Holly, "American Pie" (1971). Grossman saw depth in the saccharine remark. He noted the phrase concerned the death of "Music," not the "musician." When I fumbled with my pronunciation of Ludwig Wittgenstein, he reminded me of the Mel Brooks movie: "Frankensteeeen."

Given his reputation as what one fellow graduate student who loved him called "The Grand Poohbah," Grossman's appeal to me was, surprisingly, his ability to simplify poetic knowledge, boiling it down to fundamental truths. (The Grossman course the Teaching Company selected to tape for their Superstar Teacher series was called "Poetry: A *Basic* Course.") In a definitional sense, he was a radical thinker if we remember the word "radical" means "root," not "way out." He was, by contrast to "way out," "way in" because of his interest in discovering the foundational sources and traditional functions of poetry. One influential essay, which first appeared in *TriQuarterly,* focused on the masculine (Orphic) and feminine (Philomel) myths of poetic origination. His telling of the Philomel story was enthralling and disturbing. It showed the relationship between sexual violence—the rape of Philomel—that included the cutting off her tongue by a mad king so she could not announce the perpetrator—and the displacement of voice to a form of writing as Philomel knits information about her assailant and is transformed into a singing bird. The story fit Grossman's thesis that poetry was a "last resort" precipitated by literal or figurative "blockage" and vocal disability. We recall Dickinson's comment, "Because I could not say it, I wrote it out in verse." Grossman's ability to manage the incidents of poetry into archetypal formulas came out of structuralism as well as what Wallace Stevens in "The Idea of Order at Key West" called the "rage for order" so typical of the High Modernist sensibility.

To illustrate his point about the link between poetry and loss, Grossman, again displaying a simplifying bent, divided poems about love into three temporal categories. Love poems could focus on anticipation (before), consummation (during), or conclusion (after). Why could one find in any garden-variety anthology countless poems or turn on the radio and listen to pop song after song (and he would include song lyrics as poems) about anticipating, as the Beatles sang in a euphemistic metonym, "to hold your hand"? And, Grossman asked, why so many poems and lyrics about the actuality, as Neil Sedaka wrote, "that breaking up is hard to do"? Grossman pointed out that few poems existed about the actual *being in the moment* of passionate love. (He cited Shakespeare's "Phoenix and the Turtle" as an exception.) Why so few? Because, Grossman, following Saussure, answered—when did he not have a brilliant response?— of the absent-based character of language. Poetry was a bitter art because it solved isolation, but was also the intractable source of alienation from experience. Ironically, even tragically, words, brought forth to draw us together through communication, take the lover, even for that split second in which mind shapes feelings into words, away from fervor, now cooled into what Eliot called a "formulated phrase." The language of love also was the language of loss. When I think of what a love poem expressing ardor might sound like, I imagine disco songs with ecstatic but incomprehensible and yet erotic utterances such as "Love to Love Ya Baby" and "I feel love" by Donna Summer or the deep moans of Barry White on "Can't Get Enough of Your Love, Babe." The moment of insatiable desire, disco hits announce, is no time for analytic reflection, but intense devotion to physical stimulation and emotional sensations that, the songs seem to say, defy language.

Given the "bitter" logic of poetry as based in absence, and specializing in anticipation and aftermath, but not equipped to satisfy our desire for representation as the equivalent of experience, I wondered what was the utilitarian purpose of poetry? Here Grossman noticed the intuitive way children played games involving poetic language. Such games, he argued, implicitly expressed the understanding that patterned wordings might create, at least temporarily, order and harmony in the face of an uncertain reality in which, as Yeats wrote, things fall apart.

Grossman asked us to consider the singing game, dating from the late Middle Ages, "London Bridge is Falling Down My Fair Lady." Far from what Frost in "Mending Wall" would call "merely another outdoor game" that "comes to little more," Grossman read "London Bridge" as an essential example of his pragmatic theory. In poetry lectures, he made the children's ballad seem as crucial an expression of human fragility as lyric masterpieces by Shakespeare, Milton, and Wordsworth. (In fact, Grossman, again with radical simplicity, divided poetry into two main formal subgenres: lyric and ballad. The lyric, he explained, was the high cult version of the verbal art because of its focus on individuation and interiority. We associate a specific author with "voice," and the 10-position line approximates the length of a typical conversational statement. The ballad, by contrast, was the poetic expression of the "folk" because of its communal features—its four-beat/three-beat alternating measure is associated with low church hymnal—and lack of certain authorship.)

His close reading of "London Bridge" was a classic instance of radical simplicity. Who pays attention to the words and situation of a nursery rhyme? It is about a symbol of culture, beauty, and the ability of ordinary people to move from one place to another despite the natural impediment of a river by way of a majestic human construct—The London Bridge over the Thames. At the same time, there is a crisis of catastrophic dimensions—London Bridge is Falling Down! We don't know why it is collapsing, but the children sense that the crumbling bridge illustrates a larger truth about the conflict between nature and culture. They notice—as the aristocratic "Fair Lady" does not, and so needs to be alerted to the fact—that a brilliant material construct designed to assist citizens as they travel through the environment was itself vulnerable. Grossman went on to note the rhyme was not (at least not only) an expression of a speaker's fears about personal upset. It attended to troubles faced by another vulnerable person: "my fair lady." Continuing to "close read" the nursery song, he showed its art doubled as a motivational speech act—metrics and choreographic movements by performers—illustrate the message: "Build it up with brick and clay [...]"

Looking back at my academic history, I notice my search involved finding an older Jewish male mentor to fill the void I felt after my father's early death. Jewish men such as Jeff Lipkis at Northwestern, Leslie Epstein at Boston University, Grossman at Brandeis, and Daniel R. Schwarz at Cornell have all served as surrogate father-figures for me. Grossman's personal history, however, made it unlikely that he could deal with my early traumas because he was still overcoming his own. As I learned about Grossman's personal history, I realized his theory that poetry was a "last resort" for people in trouble who felt unable to communicate in a face-to-face encounter was not merely disinterested intellectual inquiry. As an undergraduate in the 1950s, he'd left Harvard because he lost the ability to speak. The legend, circulated among adoring and at times bewildered students, went that he ended up in Chicago, semi-homeless. The story continued that he spent the bitter Chicago winter wandering downtown streets. His only contact was a psychiatrist whom he saw irregularly. One of Grossman's most accomplished mature poems is "The Woman on the Bridge Over the Chicago River," the title poem from a 1979 volume, his first with New Directions Press. The poem inaugurates the first section of the book, entitled "The Fame of Tears." I mention the section title because, like a surreal version of Genesis in which the substance of God's creativity is composed of tears, each of the poem's eight stanzas involves a different part of the cosmos that is defined by weeping. In stanza one, the moon, stars, wind, and sea are composed of tears. In stanza two, insects and reptiles' weep. As the stanzas continue the division of the world into weeping elements takes on an abstract, even philosophical, cast as concepts such as "Eternity" and "Time" and "Nothing" and "Ideas" cry. From the cosmic perspective of a world made of tears in the first four stanzas (the first half of the poem), Grossman in the second half hones in on what I believe—based on rumors of his vocal disability when he left Harvard to undergo psychological treatment in Chicago in the 1950s—to be the poem's autobiographical dimension. Moving from celestial, to earthly, to metaphysical dimensions of a world made out of tears, Grossman in stanza five imagines, with the detachment of third-person perspective, anecdotes of human weeping in urban, suburban, and modern industrial contexts that include "steam engines" and a "sad family/in the next house over" who cry so much that they are "staining the dim blind." There is a "small boy in a coat" who sobs in a tent in stanza five, and the same boy appears in stanza six as he hears the "grieving sound of his own begetting" suggesting a psychosexual dimension to his bathetic audio-visual reception of a mourning world. In the penultimate, seventh stanza, Grossman, writing in the present tense about an event that he will, in the final stanza, reveal to have been a memory, suggesting trauma as past and present indelibly blur, alludes to his mute wanderings in Chicago during his college years:

> It is cold and snowing
> And the snow is falling into the river.
> On the bridge, lit by the white shadow of
> The Wrigley building
> A small woman wrapped in an old blue coat
> Staggers to the rail weeping.
>
> As I remember,
> The same boy passes, announcing the fame
> Of tears, calling out the terms
> In a clear way, translating to the long
> Dim human avenue.

Even huge fans, such as his student, the poet Mark Halliday, have lamented the abstraction in Grossman's poems. I think of the critique of his abstractionist bent—one indebted to his tonal similarities with Wallace Stevens—because I notice how drawn I am to the ending of "The Woman on the Bridge." I am relieved when Grossman mentions the "Wrigley Building." The Chicago landmark locates the tender and yet still cerebral (the self-conscious division of the cosmos into realms of tear-filled beings and units reminding us of Genesis) remarks in a "confessional" anecdote. The moment is especially moving because the emphasis is not on Grossman's suffering, but rather on his witnessing the disoriented woman in the "old blue coat" who staggers to the bridge railing over the Chicago River. Even here Grossman—whose lone scholarly book concerned symbolism in Yeats—is working with archetypes rather than merely recalling quotidian private memories. One senses the "Wrigley Building" signifies the alienating "shadow" of urban capitalism and the unsatisfying realm of consumerism in which chewing Wrigley's Spearmint Gum offers false promises of beauty, health, and pleasure. The "small woman" is less an individual from Chicago reacting to a specific (in the poem unspecified) history of pain than an allegorical figure who stands for the concept of Suffering. Those reservations aside, I am drawn to the image of college-aged Grossman, wandering in the snow in downtown Chicago, and coming across another sufferer. (I drifted down Chicago streets, disoriented, as a Northwestern student in the early 1980s). One weirdly senses that the woman somehow represents the poet's mother. Grossman would often comment that the poet's task was to "translate" (a word he uses at the end of the poem) the "mother tongue" into literary language that produces that value-bearing conception of significant appearance that Grossman regards as "personhood." One realizes the final stanza suggests the symbolic moment of initiation into poetic election. His task will be to "translate" the "mother tongue" of "tears"—the natural language of embodied lamentation over the human condition of separation and dissolution (even the snowflakes are melting into the river)—into a public expression. The poet invokes the Homeric term "fame" for distinguished recognition. As in Homer, fame entails a loss of natural being, but also dignity, if not redemption, to what had previously been an emotionally rich, but not distinguished (everyone and everything is weeping) condition:

> announcing the fame
> Of tears, calling out the terms
> In a clear way, translating to the long
> Dim human avenue.

In the poem, an isolated young man observes the woman in the frigid and alienating urban setting. Somehow, Grossman recovered from his inability to speak. Big time! In fact, his voice in lecture halls was so authoritatively booming that auditors believed he'd accessed the sources of inspiration that compelled ancient bards to recite tribal histories. Grossman's voice represented supreme power and unquestioned authority over subject matter and stunned the audience. Words poured out of his mouth in lecture halls, but he needed an official forum and well-built auditorium as well as for the roles of lecturer and auditor to be defined before he could begin his utterances. Grossman spoke a lot of words in lecture halls and office hours, but rarely, at least in my experience, in relaxed forms such as a friendly conversation over coffee. In fact, Grossman, mysteriously, once told me, "poets cannot have friends." Another time, at a rare departmental picnic to celebrate a nice spring afternoon following a poetry reading, Grossman ambled over to the party in his ubiquitous suit and tie, however hot the day. He stood yards away from the rest of the group, smoking his pipe and looking off into the distance. I came up to him. "Why are you standing so far away from everyone else? Why don't you join the party?" "I gave that up a long time ago." I was his student as well as a teaching assistant for a good four years; he never asked me to his house in Lexington or out to have dinner with him at a restaurant in Cambridge. (This may say as much about my social awkwardness and inferiority complex as about Grossman's impersonality.)

He wasn't the type of beloved teacher known for inviting students over to his home for tea or port and chat or for holding seminars in a funky café. But like an evangelical preacher, he announced the good news of poetry as THE form to, in Grossman's words, protect us "against our vanishing" by placing the ephemeral human voice into the sturdy time capsule of well-made lines and memorable rhythms of verse. And it *did* feel like preaching, to the converted (as in my case) or the unconverted (the great unwashed masses of Brandeis undergraduates who needed to take his introduction to humanities courses). Now a long-time professor of poetry at Purdue, it only becomes more astonishing when I think of his dedication to students. By contrast to my minimalist attitude toward Office Hours, my mentor, Professor Grossman, each week posted a sign-up sheet on the door of his cave-like corner office in Rabb Hall. The sheet, and I am not exaggerating, consisted of rows of black lines assigned to 15-minute time slots, that, taken together, added up to a minimum of 15 *hours* a week of "office hours." Each Monday morning, students, undergraduate, graduate, and even junior professors, would wait by the door, pen in hand, ready, like Christmas shoppers waiting for Black Friday deals, to ink their name to prime times, often taking three or four 15-minute slots to guarantee an especially detailed private session. Often, after the official slots were filled, you would notice extra slots penciled in underneath the official, black-lined time slots. And, inevitably, one would arrive early outside Grossman's office for the coveted meeting only to hear his deep voice, heavy laugh, and the odor of pipe smoke amid a current meeting that, inevitably, would be somewhere in the middle of a session. It was like an airport on a harsh weather day, little planes like me waiting for the green light to jump off into the transcendent skies of Grossman's healing vision of poetry.

Works Cited

Allen Grossman. *The Woman on the Bridge Over the Chicago River.* New York: New Directions Press, 1979.

"Allen Grossman." *The Poetry Foundation Website.*

John Keats. "When I Have Fears." In *Poems, Poets, Poetry: An Introduction and Anthology,* edited by Helen Vendler. Boston: Bedford, 1997, p. 17.

Review of *How to Do Things with Tears. Publishers Weekly.* March 26, 2001, p. 85.

William Shakespeare. "Shall I Compare Thee to a Summer's Day?" (Sonnet 18). In *Poems, Poets, Poetry: An Introduction and Anthology*, edited by Helen Vendler. Boston: Bedford, 1997, p. 521.

Micah Towery. "Blogging through Allen Grossman, Part 1: The Role of Poetry." *The The.* February 9, 2010.

William Butler Yeats. "Easter 1916." In *Poems, Poets, Poetry: An Introduction and Anthology*, edited by Helen Vendler. Boston: Bedford, 1997, p. 26.

CHAPTER 3

IN PRAISE OF SECULAR JEWISH AMERICAN LYRIC COMMENTARY: WHY BOB DYLAN AND LOUISE GLÜCK ARE TWENTY-FIRST-CENTURY NOBEL LAUREATES

Seven decades after what Benjamin Schreier calls, "the dominant event of Jewish American literary history," which is the "'breakthrough'—the irruption in the 1950s of Jewish American writers like Bernard Malamud, Philip Roth, Saul Bellow, and Grace Paley into the heart of American cultural scene," two Jewish American lyricists have received the Nobel Prize for Literature in a span of four years: Bob Dylan (born Robert Allen Zimmerman in Duluth, Minnesota in 1941) in 2016 and Louise Glück (born in New York City in 1943 and raised on Long Island) in 2020 (Schreier, 2). Superficially, Glück's Nobel complicates the meanings of the Dylan Nobel, a rebalancing to achieve equilibrium with a kind of an "equal and opposite" reaction to Dylan: Male/Female; popular musician/academically sanctioned page poet; folk-rocker whose anthems inspired the civil rights movements of the early 1960s/apolitical lyric poet of the private sphere. In fact, like Dylan, Glück practices a recognizably contemporary secular Jewish American strategy of revisionary poetics. She draws together disparate cultures—Jewish, European, American—and makes them her own. By considering Jewish identity as a consensual relationship to the recollection of a prophetic strain of sociopolitical history (Dylan) and personal history (Glück) through revisionary relations to literature, myth, and religious texts, we may consider the two Nobel laureates' creative readings of classical texts as a type of commentary expressing their secular Jewish sensibilities. For Dylan and Glück, Jewishness is a way of thinking about revisioning texts. The literary inheritance is not considered sacred and so becomes available to variation through the author's willingness to talk back to it.

In *Bob Dylan: Prophet, Mystic, Poet*, Seth Rogovoy argues that one way to approach Dylan's lyrics "is to read them as the work of a poet mind apparently immersed in Jewish texts and engaged in the age-old process of midrash: a kind of formal or informal riffing on the texts to elucidate or elaborate upon their hidden meanings" (Rogovoy, 6). He continues:

> Perhaps the most famous of these riffs takes place in one of Dylan's best-known songs, 1965's "Highway 61 Revisited," his whimsical retelling of the Akedah, the story in which G-d commands Abraham to bind Isaac as if for a sacrificial offering, which Dylan posits as a conversation between two jaded, "cynical hipsters," U.S. Route 61, incidentally, is the main highway leading from New Orleans to Dylan's birthplace in Duluth, Minnesota. (6)

In *Chronicles*, Dylan himself interprets "Highway 61" as the literal and figurative pathway that, like the Mississippi River, links the Minnesota native to the roots of country blues in Louisiana and the Mississippi Delta:

> I always felt like I'd started on it, always had been on it and could go anywhere from it, even into the deep Delta country. It was the same road, full of the same contradictions, the same one-horse river towns, the same spiritual ancestors. The Mississippi River, the bloodstream of the blues, also starts up from my neck of the woods. I was never too far away from any of it. It was my place in the universe, always felt like it was in my blood. (Dylan, 240–241)

In "Highway 61 Revisited" (1965), Dylan affiliates himself with the origin story of the Delta Blues. It was, after all, at the crossroads of Highway 61 and Route 61 in Clarksdale, Mississippi that Robert Johnson was said to have sold his soul to the devil in a Faustian bargain for creative inspiration. In "Highway 61 Revisited," Dylan crafts a secular Jewish commentary work by self-consciously refashioning the Delta Blues tradition of Johnson and Mississippi Fred McDowell to serve personal, political, and creative purposes. Dylan's ingenuity emerges through his combining the sonic features of traditional acoustic blues—Philippe Margotin and Jean-Michel Guesdon note that it was a "blues song in B flat, giving tribute to Robert Johnson and Blind Willie McTell"—with the "energetic blues-rock song [sound] carried by the electric guitar of Mike Bloomfield, who confirmed his virtuosity on the bottleneck" (Margotin and Guesdon, 199). As David Dalton points out, the lyrics specifically reference Fred McDowell's "61 Highway Blues," the penchant in blues songs to engage in magical numerology, and the blues tradition of including an "outlandish cast of characters" in the lyric (Dalton, 127–128). Dylan's lyricism is also influenced by the French surrealist Arthur Rimbaud, the streetwise sensibility of the peripatetic Beat icon Jack Kerouac, and the biblical resonances to Genesis 26, which, as Margotin and Guesdon argue, enabled Dylan, whose father's name was in fact Abraham, to associate his rebellion against his father's middle-class, Midwestern values with his "decision to become a musician" (Margotin and Guesdon, 198). Displaying, in Dalton's terms, a talent for "projecting his personal situation into a mythic dimension," Dylan's contemporary secular Jewish revisionary sensibility enables him to put local and international creative resources into play to produce "a toxic cartoon denouncing American culture that somehow involves him and his dad, Abe (with whom he had an estranged relationship), in a diorama from Genesis" (Dalton, 128). Dylan's midrashic mashup of sources and influences becomes what Dalton calls a fusion of "the political, historical, and personal into a hornet's nest" that critiques American culture's "slick surface and commercial jive promising impossible things" (Dalton, 129). As in "Highway 61 Revisited," Dylan's "Blowin' in the Wind," combines African American sonic features with biblical resonances to explore contemporary themes. Margotin and Guesdon note that "Blowin' in the Wind" not only borrows language from Ezekiel and Isaiah, but also the "melody, as Dylan admitted, was musically based on 'No More Auction Block,' a spiritual that he heard Delores Dixon sing every night with the New World Singers at Gerde's Folk City" (Margotin and Guesdon, 51). As with "Highway 61 Revisited," Dylan's creativity emerges in "Blowin' in the Wind" through his revisionary strategies. He reframes biblical prophetic language and a melody associated with African American spiritual traditions to speak to what Margotin and Guesdon describe as "universal themes that resonated in 1962 amid the Cold War and the struggle for recognition of civil rights" (51).

Seth Rogovoy ties Dylan's protest songs to how biblical prophets "pointed out the hypocrisies and errors of their subjects' ways, warning of punishments that could befall them and suggesting paths toward collective redemption" (Rogovoy, 9). By contrast, Richard F. Thomas, a Harvard Classics professor, links Dylan to Horace, Catullus, Ovid, and Virgil in *Why Dylan Matters*. Focusing on "Lonesome Day Blues," from *Love and Theft*, for example, Thomas hears lines from Virgil's *Aeneid* "loud and clear" to Dylan's "I'm goin' to teach peace to the conquered/I'm gonna tame the proud" Dylan's lyric closely resembles how Anchises' "instructs his son from the Underworld on just how

Rome is to rule the world: "to teach the ways of peace to those you conquer,/to spare defeated peoples, tame the proud" (Thomas, 7). As Thomas writes, the "idiom, rhymes, and music of these lines belonged to Dylan, but the thought and diction, rearranged by Dylan, came from Rome's greatest poet, Virgil" (Thomas, 7). To cite one more example of Dylan's intertextual bent, in "Who Killed Davey Moore?," a 1963 topical song about the death of a prize fighter, Amit Chaudhuri writes that "the material comprises the American folksong, the children's rhyme, the public tragedy and the narrative taken directly from the newspapers" and subjected to the sort of estranging synthesis in which [as Dylan notes] "nothing's been changed [...] except for the words."[1]

Glück's *Triumph of Achilles (1985)*, *Ararat* (1990), *Meadowlands* (1997), and *Vita Nova* (2001), illustrate her long habit of amplifying the weight and scope of her personal style of poetry by connecting individual poems into collections that frame the experience of contemporary speakers against the template of international literature ranging from Homer to Virgil to Ovid to the Brothers Grimm to the Bible to European modernists such as Yeats and Auden. Glück often invokes Jewish sources in her poetry, but she limits their meanings to make room for the value, or emotional impact, of adversarial materials such as those found in Greek myth. "Mount Ararat" from *Ararat* discusses the family plot at the Jewish graveyard (named Mount Ararat), where her father and one of her sisters are buried. As with Dylan's "Highway 61 Revisited" in which "God said to Abraham, 'Kill me a son,'" Glück in "Mount Ararat" imagines the Jewish God as a ruthless deity. She describes Mount Ararat as a place "dedicated to the Jewish god/who doesn't hesitate to take/a son from a mother" (Glück, *Poems: 1962–2012*, 213). By contrast to the Jewish God who destroys families in "Mount Ararat," Glück represents the God-man Achilles in "The Triumph of Achilles" as a classical figure who embraces life, suffering, and the inevitability of death with a kind of Nietzschean intensity. In "A Parable," from *The Triumph of Achilles*, she describes the pattern of King David's biography as following the "trace" of "a mountain." The mountain's "arc" illustrates the shape of David's narrative from obscurity to the incline of power, to a social decline brought about by the excesses of his sexual appetite and political ambition. Glück connects King David to Sisyphus, the legendary first murderer, by preceding "Parable" with a poem about the Greek mythic character

---

1 See Amit Chaudhuri. "Bob Dylan is not the first songwriter to win the Nobel prize for literature." *The Guardian*. October 21, 2016. https://www.theguardian.com/books/2016/oct/21/dylan-is-not-the-first-songwriter-to-win-the-nobel-prize-for-literature

entitled "The Mountain." In "Mount Ararat" and "A Parable," as well as "Day Without Night" and "Saints," Glück interprets Hebrew Bible stories by juxtaposing them with classical myths and then by connecting the ancient sources to her own experience, sometimes, as in the work of other contemporary Jewish feminist midrash poets such as Alicia Ostriker and Jacqueline Osherow, from a gendered perspective. She maintains a balance between the lyric, with its emphasis on a first-person retelling of subjective experience, and what Maerra Y. Shreiber refers to as a "cross-cultural exchange" (Shreiber, 164). By commenting on Jewish as well as non-Jewish texts, Glück imagines a more "heterogeneous, inclusive version of Jewishness," as well as honors "individuated emotive experience" alongside "collective diversity" (Shreiber, 165–166).

Whereas Dylan, at least in his brief but signature phase of engaged folk singing from around 1962 to 1964, wrote and performed songs that commented on racial injustice, nuclearism, and the growing involvement of the United States in military activity in Southeast Asia, Glück has made a difference within literary culture itself. Most prominently, she has attempted to fuse modernist impersonality with postmodern confessional modes by working in a mode reminiscent of late nineteenth-century British authors such as Robert Browning and Alfred Lord Tennyson, the dramatic monologue or persona poem, but also, à la James Joyce in *Ulysses*, by affiliating the contemporary quotidian experience of middle-class American culture with mythic and narrative templates drawn from ancient and modern world literature. Besides the title poem, other poems from *The Triumph of Achilles* that emphasize classical material include "The Reproach," an apostrophe to Eros; "Night Song," which Glück has herself read as a reflection upon the figures of Eros and Psyche; "The Mountain," which discusses the myth of Sisyphus; and "Mythic Fragment," which recalls Ovid's story of Apollo and Daphne, who, to avoid the "captivity/in praise" from the "stern god" who is also her suitor, turns for help to her father, the river god Perseus, who transforms her into a "tree forever" (Glück, *Poems: 1962–2012*, 156). As Helen Vendler points out, since a myth such as that of Daphne and Apollo is already known to most readers, "interest consequently has to center almost entirely on interpretation and manner" (Vendler, 438). In "Mythic Fragment," Vendler continues, Glück's retells the myth as a "Freudian story, the tale of a girl too much in love with her father to accept a lover," and as a "modern story of virginity, revealing its roots of incestuous desire" (Vendler, 438–439). As Vendler's commentary indicates, *The Triumph of Achilles* turns to the mythic mode for the detachment that allows Glück to explore components that would have likely been subjects for the analytic process she had undertaken years earlier. Ever evolving,

Dylan and Glück, regularly engage with a lyric practice that has been identified by the late German-Jewish Yale literary theorist Geoffrey Hartman as a "struggle for the text." By so doing, Dylan and Glück participate in a recognizably Jewish tradition of creative commentary on canonical proof texts that include, but are not limited to, the Old and New Testaments to Homer and Virgil, and to Romanticism and Modernism. I claim the revisionary tendency in their lyricism to be the thread that binds Dylan to Glück and links them both to a significant aspect of a contemporary secular Jewish kind of creativity. Both are diasporic Jews who do not reject their Jewish identity, but do not make it central. They are weaving and constructing identities out of multiple strands, in Dylan's case American folk art—besides Guthrie, Dylan early on revised songs associated with African American blues composers and performers such as Jesse Fuller, Bukka White, Memphis Minnie, and the Reverend Gary Davis—being the strongest and in Glück's case European high culture.

Born two years apart, Dylan and Glück are only the 11th and 12th U.S. citizens to win the Nobel for Literature. Three other Jewish Americans had previously won the prize; all were immigrants: Saul Bellow, born in Quebec, in 1976, Isaac Singer, born in a village near Warsaw, in 1978, and Joseph Brodsky, born in Leningrad, in 1987. Other than T.S. Eliot and Brodsky, who emigrated in 1972 at the age of 32, Dylan and Glück are the only U.S. lyricists/poets—and, with the exception of Eliot, a British citizen, the only U.S. born lyricists—to win the Nobel. (Glück is the 16th female laureate). Given, as Schreier argues, the immigration narrative has been the only "real theory" that has "been able to carry any currency" to explain the "breakthrough" of Jewish American culture in the United States, we can understand Bellow, Singer, and Brodsky. What theory of Jewish American literature explains Glück and Dylan? Assimilation? A celebration of Jews as a model ethnic group that now, in Schreier's terms, represents "confidence, security, and success" (Schreier, 2)? The Jew, again following Schreier, "as the representative modern figure," or, perhaps, as a nod to the values of ethnicity, difference, and multiculturalism in a global period marked by reactionary white nationalist movements (Schreier, 3)? None of these explanations fits for Dylan or for Glück, mercurial figures attracted to masks that destabilize authorial identity. Bestowed in the wake of the Black Lives Matter Movement, immigration conflicts on the Southern border of the United States, and Trumpism, Glück's Nobel came as a shock even to herself. Rather than defining herself in an interview with Alexandra Alter in the *New York Times* as a Jewish American (from a Jewish Hungarian background on her father's side), she describes herself as "Completely flabbergasted that they would choose a white American lyric poet. It doesn't make sense."[2] Dylan famously changed his family name from Zimmerman, but it is inaccurate to suggest he did so to erase his personal history as a Bar Mitzvah in 1954, a member of a close-knit community of Jews in Hibbing and Duluth, Minnesota, a summer participant at Camp Herzl "about a hundred miles south of Duluth," and a third-generation immigrant whose "grandfather had come over from Russia in the 1920s. He was a peddler and made shoes" (Heylin, 28; 22). An ongoing project that spans six decades, Dylan's mythologization has made room for multiple revisions of self. His self-fashionings range from Oklahoma native Woody Guthrie's orphaned son, to electrified urban neo-Beat hipster in dark jeans, shades, and puffed-up hairdo, to smiling Nashville country boy, to Born Again Christian, to Hasidic Jew, to entertainer on an endless tour, to Sinatra-like crooner of pop standards on *Shadows in the Night* (2015).[3] Seth Rogovoy comments on how Dylan—like Glück—imagined his identity as a performance subject to constant change. Following Woody Allen's *Zelig* (1983), a "fictional documentary about the life of

---

2 In the *Guardian*, Alison Flood reports:

> At Glück's UK publisher Carcanet, which has published the poet for more than two decades, Michael Schmidt said staff were 'completely surprised' at the news but also 'astonished at the justice of the win': 'What the Academy seems to have done is they've gone for a poet who is, in a sense, aesthetically, imaginatively, at odds with the age,' Schmidt said. 'She's not a cheerleader. She's in no way a voice for any cause—she is a human being engaged in the language and in the world. And I think there's this wonderful sense that she is not polemical, and maybe this is what's being celebrated. She's not a person trying to persuade us of anything, but helping us to explore the world we're living in. She's a clarifying poet. There doesn't seem to be much political engagement in her poems. They're really about the individual human being alive in the world, and in the language.'

See "Louise Glück wins the Nobel prize in literature." *The Guardian* https://www.theguardian.com/books/2020/oct/08/louise-gluck-wins-the-2020-nobel-prize-in-literature?ref=upstract.com&curator=upstract.com

3 In *Bob Dylan Behind The Shades: A Biography,* Clinton Heylin writes that while many biographers read Dylan's "desire for a new identity" through a mythologization of his origins that erased his Jewishness as a sign of Jewish self-hatred, the early self-fashionings may have stemmed less from "a rejection of his Jewish identity" and more from "a rebuttal of the limits placed on imagination on the bulk of the citizens of Hibbing" (22) and "an attempt to disavow his small-town background" as well as the "undercurrent of anti-Semitism" faced by the small, close-knit Jewish community of Hibbing, which was dominated by "an essentially Catholic infrastructure" (22).

human chameleon Leonard Zelig, a man who becomes a celebrity in the 1920s due to his ability to look and act like whoever is around him," one could argue that Dylan's identities—portrayed for example, in Todd Haynes's 2007 film *I'm Not There* by itself reflects the uncertain relationships to identity—to whiteness—that characterize one dimension of contemporary secular American Jewishness (IMDb).[4] At the same time, Rogovoy notes in "Bob Dylan's Ten Most Jewish Songs" that while Dylan has rarely foregrounded his Jewishness, as when he engaged with Lubavitch Hasidism, he has rarely concealed his Jewish heritage:[5]

> This son of a middle-class appliance salesman from the Upper Midwest, who grew up with a Yiddish-speaking grandmother down the hallway in an extended Jewish family that was at the nexus of Jewish life in Hibbing, Minn.—mom was president of the local Hadassah, and dad was president of B'nai B'rith—wound up making several trips to Israel in the late-1960s and '70s (during one visit, he even began the application process for moving his family to a kibbutz). He sent his children to the same Jewish summer camp in Wisconsin that he attended for four or five summers as a teenager.
>
> By the time he arrived in New York City's Greenwich Village, he intended to make a name for himself on the folk scene—and that name was Dylan, not Zimmerman (the name is German and not Jewish, anyway, although his forebears were from Russia), and Bob fashioned himself a latter-day Woody Guthrie (as it turns out, Guthrie himself had a whole secret Jewish

---

4 *Zelig* information from https://www.imdb.com/title/tt0086637/
5 As David Cloud reports,

> Dylan has dabbled in Lubavitch Hasidism, an ultra-orthodox form of Judaism, suggesting that he was exploring his Jewish roots. "Bob Dylan, the Midwestern Jew who drifted away from Judaism while pursuing his career as singer and songwriter, appeared at synagogue prayers on the Yom Kippur Day of Atonement and was honored with a call to the reading of the Torah, according to Shmais .com. He attended the Chabad synagogue of Beth Tfiloh in Atlanta, Georgia. The crowd of 900 other worshippers quickly identified the 66-year-old Dylan, whose original name is Robert Zimmerman. He was called to the sixth of seven parts of the Torah reading and remained for the sermon and the memorial service of Yizkor." ("Day of Atonement Draws Dylan to the Torah," *Arutz Sheva*, Israel National News, Sept. 24, 2007)

See "Bob Dylan." *Way of Life Literature*. Updated March 16, 2015 (first published May 29, 2001) https://www.wayoflife.org/reports/bob_dylan.html

side to his work, born of his close relationship with his mother-in-law, Yiddish poet Aliza Greenblatt). [Rogovoy, "Bob Dylan's Ten Most Jewish Songs."]

Like Dylan, Glück eschews an ethnic identification with Jewishness in most of her poetry. An exception would be "Legend" from *Triumph of Achilles* (1985), in which she recollects the family "legend" told of her paternal grandfather—and by so, extension to the "legend" of the early twentieth-century Jewish American immigration narrative associated with the Ellis Island experience. Glück may wish to resist an ethnic identification of the self because of her fear that it would limit her scope, but "Legend" reveals an escape from one's familial background—and the Ellis Island immigrant narrative—is not possible. Like Dylan, Glück does not choose a single mythic template or intertextual echo to address current events or personal issues. Neither fully assimilated figures nor representatives of multiculturalism, I regard Glück and Dylan as, if not exactly "non-Jewish" Jews, then ambivalently Jewish, or only sometimes overtly Jewish Jews. To varying degrees, both participated in an upbringing that included Jewish cultural practices and education, Dylan more so than Glück, who has written to the author that she "had a rudimentary Jewish upbringing," that she grew up in a "Jewish suburb, but Jewish practice was, as I remember, casual," and that she "rebelled early against a religious education, partly because it was an education in addition to music lessons, dance lessons, and so on." Dylan and Glück occupy different relations to mainstream versions of literary culture, but both engage in a recognizable pattern of Jewish revisionary strategies to compose and decompose their lyric personae. Like Dylan, Glück's primary engagement with Jewishness involves how she positions her personae in literary, mythic, and folkloric environments. Both frequently create commentary lyrics on biblical and other non-Jewish classical texts ranging from Homer to fairy tales, to modernists such as Yeats in Auden in Dylan's case to create a surreal/prophetic atmosphere in iconic songs such as "Blowin' in the Wind," "All Along the Watchtower," and "A Hard Rain's a-Gonna Fall."[6]

For Dylan and Glück to win the prize only four years apart is unusual, but also, in both cases, the subject of debate about what the Nobel Committee was

---

6 Margotin and Guesdon point out, for example, that Dylan's "Gates of Eden" (1964) was influenced by William Blake's *The Gates of Paradise* (1793) and Dylan's "As I Went Out One Morning" (1967) was inspired by W. H. Auden's "As I Walked Out One Evening" (170;284).

trying to say by awarding each the coveted literary award.⁷ Dylan's award was contentious because many observers regard him as a producer and performer of cultural productions that are undeniably significant and influential, but in a genre—the popular recorded song—that exits *outside* the traditional "literary" genres (page poetry, narrative fiction, drama), and so not worthy of the Literature Prize.⁸ The Nobel committee picked Dylan for "having created new poetic expressions within the great American song tradition." They

---

7 Unlike Dylan and the Austrian novelist Peter Handke, who won in 2019, Glück's selection is neither surprising nor scandalous. As Daniel Trotta and Anna Ringstrom reported in Yahoo News (October 8, 2020), however, commentators have interpreted Glück's selection as a way for the Nobel committee to make amends for the controversial choices of Handke in 2019 and Dylan in 2020:

> Glück's Nobel prize followed years of controversy surrounding the literature award, but [Academy Permanent Secretary Mats] Malm sidestepped questions about whether Glück was chosen to address any related concerns.
>
> Alluding to past disputes, he told reporters: "I'd say that in our Nobel (prize) work the crisis hasn't been decisive."
>
> In 2019, the Academy exceptionally named two winners after postponing the 2018 prize in the wake of a sexual assault scandal involving the husband of one of its members.
>
> The secretive, 234-year-old Academy later announced changes it billed as improving the transparency of the awards process.
>
> But one of the literature laureates announced last year, Austria's Peter Handke, had drawn international criticism over his portrayal of Serbia as a victim during the 1990s Balkan wars and for attending the funeral of its nationalist strongman leader Slobodan Milosevic.
>
> The 2016 literature prize granted to American singer-songwriter Bob Dylan polarized opinion over whether a popular musician should be given an award that had been largely the domain of novelists and playwrights.

See: Bianca Britton, CNN report, "Peter Handke's Nobel literature prize win sparks outrage." Updated 3:59 PM EDT, Fri October 11, 2019 https://www.cnn.com/2019/10/11/europe/peter-handke-nobel-prize-criticism-intl-scli/index.html).

8 Dylan was not the first Nobel Laureate in Literature to have excelled in music; that honor would belong to Bengali author and musician Rabindranath Tagore (1861–1941) who in 1913 "became the first non-European to receive the Nobel Prize for Literature." https://www.britannica.com/biography/Rabindranath-Tagore; Britannica.com; author is W. Andrew Robinson; "Rabindranath Tagore Bengali poet."

also honored his "profoundly sensitive, fresh and beautiful verse, by which, with consummate skill, he has made his poetic thought, expressed in his own English words, a part of the literature of the west." Already a household name with 11 Grammy Awards, an Academy and a Golden Globe award to his credit, as well as induction into the Rock and Roll Hall of Fame in 1988, some asked if Dylan needed a Nobel, a form of global recognition sometimes awarded to relatively obscure authors from less powerful countries than the United States.[9] Anna North, for example, acknowledges that Dylan is a "brilliant lyricist," but she feels awarding the Nobel to a popular songwriter amounted to a lost opportunity for the Nobel committee to recognize an underappreciated author in a traditional literary genre: "Yes, it is possible to analyze his lyrics as poetry. But Mr. Dylan's writing is inseparable from his music. He is great because he is a great musician, and when the Nobel committee gives the literature prize to a musician, it misses the opportunity to honor a writer."[10] Stephen Metcalfe acknowledges Dylan's "almost unparalleled influence": "It was Dylan, more than anyone, who took Truth from out of the Victorian attic and put it into rock 'n' roll; put it on the AM radio."[11] At the same time, in this sense like North, Metcalf remains opposed to Dylan's Nobel on the ground that Dylan is more of a cultural phenomenon than a poet whose skills with language match up to mainstream academic page poets such as, in Metcalf's example, Richard Wilbur.[12] Following my main argument about Dylan and

---

[9] Supporters have emphasized Dylan's impact on popular music. Stephen King, for example, says that "without Dylan, Paul Simon maybe ends up in the Brill Building, writing songs like 'Hey Schoolgirl' like he did in the beginning."
[10] Anna North. "Why Bob Dylan Shouldn't Have Gotten a Nobel." *The New York Times.* October 13, 2016.
[11] Stephen Metcalfe. "Bob Dylan Is a Genius of Almost Unparalleled Influence, but He Shouldn't Have Gotten the Nobel." *Slate.* October 13, 2016. https://slate.com/culture/2016/10/why-bob-dylan-shouldnt-have-gotten-the-nobel-prize-for-literature.html
[12] Comparing a passage from a Wilbur poem to a Dylan lyric, Metcalfe writes:

> Wilbur has spent a lifetime refining an ancient practice, of making a hard, seemingly intractable thought dance to the rhythm of his chosen words—and in so doing, in working through the difficult thought, for a moment, the cosmos is placed at our fingertips. In the second, which is from my favorite Bob Dylan song by far, the words are colloquial, spare, painterly, and without the accompanying music, inert. The first is poetry, the second are lyrics. You don't go to the hardware store for oranges, as they say, and if you want poetry, you don't go to Bob Dylan.

Glück as contemporary secular Jewish Americans whose creativity stems from their revision of prior texts, I regard Dylan as a revisionary artist who is taking inspiration from different traditions. Discussing the contemporary secular Jewish revisionary project that binds together Dylan and Glück, Ethan Goffman writes that such a project asks the contemporary secular Jewish artist to be "cosmopolitan and multicultural, to be diasporic but also integral to the new culture and an innovator within that culture as a way of fitting in while not jettisoning one's Jewish identity entirely."[13] Following Goffman, we may say that critics of Dylan's Nobel do not fully appreciate that he, like Glück, appealed to the selection committee because he, like Glück, is a wide-ranging, revisionary figure, a cosmopolitan internationalist who also sympathizes with local cultures.

The Nobel Prize in Literature is, of course, awarded to an author of literary distinction, but because it is well known that the selection committee's decision is also a form of social and political commentary, it is unsurprising that observers try to interpret what the selection committee was trying to say when a new laureate is announced. If Dylan signifies the Jewish artist as an unruly figure who, as it were, draws outside the lines, disturbing the boundaries between insider and outsider, as simultaneously a countercultural figure and iconic voice of the social protest movements of the 1960s and a media mogul who recently sold the rights to his song catalog to Universal Music Publishing Group for a reported $300 million dollars, Glück's selection represents the Nobel's appreciation of a poet who, as it were, thinks inside the box, thus stabilizing the meanings of genre terms such as "poetry," and "lyric," and "literature." [14] Given the traumas the world—and America—endured in 2020—it struck many observers—including Glück—as peculiar that the Nobel

---

13 Ethan Goffman. "On Contemporary Jewish American Secular Creativity." Unpublished manuscript.

14 Anastasia Tsioulcas writes, "Nearly 60 years after writing such counterculture classics as 'Blowin' in the Wind' and 'Like a Rolling Stone,'" Bob Dylan has sold his entire songwriting catalog—more than 600 songs—to Universal Music Publishing Group in a deal announced Monday morning by Universal.

The agreement was first reported by the *New York Times*, which said it is worth more than $300 million. The deal with Dylan may be the highest price ever paid for a musician or group's songwriting rights. (Universal has not disclosed the purchase price.) "Bob Dylan Sells Songwriting Catalog in 9-Figure Deal."

(NPR: https://www.npr.org/2020/12/07/943818966/bob-dylan-sells-songwriting-catalog-in-nine-figure-deal) December 7, 2020 11:28 AM ET

Committee would turn to an apolitical bona fide lyric page poet whose work seems to fit squarely inside traditional, canonical, and academically sanctioned interpretations of literary merit. Is it odd that a Jewish American woman would come to represent the safety and comfort of the status quo in 2020? If you are thinking that in some symbolic way Glück represents a postmodern version of Emma Lazarus's open-armed Lady Liberty, or the stereotypical Jewish mother or Yiddishe Mama, you would be off course. The Nobel Committee's citation does appreciate Glück's penchant for treating "radical change" with "clarity" and "biting humor." Representing personal and familial trauma ranging from a sibling's death to a battle with anorexia nervosa, to divorce, to psychological disability, to ambivalent expressions of desire and repulsion in sexual relations, one may contextualize Glück's selection during a worldwide pandemic and an American president who engaged in documented cases of sexual violence toward women. By and large, however, Glück's poetry steers clear of identity politics and multiculturalism. Eschewing the role of poet as activist, she mocks social-oriented authors as "stadium poets" in her Nobel lecture. Glück attacks "stadium poets" such as Dylan, but, unwittingly, she has in common with Dylan her situation as a diaspora Jew, clinging to some aspect of her identity but largely revisioning other identities to create a new identity as an American but also, for Glück, an inheritor of European culture. Like Dylan's, Glück's contemporary American version of Jewishness is characterized by a protean sensibility that imagines the self as an elusive trace of allusions through masked performance. As with Dylan's metamorphic self-fashionings, Glück appears to some readers as a feminist, to others a Jew, a postmodernist, a confessionalist, a modernist, a religious author, a mystic, an elegant stylist, a blunt poet, a bitter poet, an ecofeminist nature poet, a pagan poet, a cultivated poet, an elegist, a lyric poet, a narrative poet, and, as Lynn Keller argues, an antifeminist poet who "raises crucial, disturbing issues about women's complicity in their own oppression" (Keller, 123). As with Dylan, Glück's various masked identifications are symptomatic of her enactment of a dialogue between identity as biological essence and identity as a usable social construction in which the subject is in a state of constant flux of verbal recasting of self in different disguise. My argument is that Glück and Dylan are contemporary secular American Jewish cultural figures because they reflect the situation of contemporary secular American Jews whose subject positions function as figurative spaces, enabling the author (Glück; Dylan) to operate within the frame of literary or musical conventions that convey established values from the past through texts, even as these conventions are recast to remain relevant to the author's experience in the present tense. Glück's poetry and, for that matter, her relationship to such patriarchal constructs as the Western literary canon and to the Jewish God, Yahweh, are traditional in that she employs the voices of characters from ancient narratives and sacred texts to amplify her experience beyond personal circumstance. Following Hartman's understanding of Jewish ways of reading as a Midrashic "struggle for the text" through creative commentary on canonical proof texts, however, Glück and Dylan can interrogate the source material and make it conform to their life and times without having to "confess" to the reader or listener the details of their autobiographical existence, the disclosure of which defines the speaker's vulnerability in most recent lyric poetry.

If we regard Glück's selection as a realignment of the Literature prize to a narrower understanding of how to define the literary than was the case with the Dylan selection, I also consider both selections, in different ways, as implicit critiques of Donald Trump, another prominent American born in the early 1940s. Like Dylan, who was named a Nobel laureate by the Swedish Academy on October 13, 2016, less than a month before the American presidential election took place, Trump is a cultural and political figure associated with New York City. Representing one road not taken by Trump, Dylan's version of anti-establishmentarianism and populism understands institutions of political power as obstacles to real change. We think of songs such as "Masters of War" and "Only a Pawn in their Game," as well as lines from other iconic songs such as "It's Alright, Ma (I'm Only Bleeding)," in which even the president of the United States must stand naked, and "The Times They Are A Changin'," in which senators and congressman are urged to stop blocking the halls to inhibit political transformation. Trump used the presidency as a bully pulpit to announce a nativist form of populism that raged against urban elites and multiculturalists. Contra Dylan, Trump's message empowered racial and ethnic resentment among working-class rural whites, the very audience that Dylan saw as "pawns" in the game of elites who wished to divide races and classes to maintain social, economic, and political power. We may think of the Dylan Nobel as less about rewarding an individual and more about honoring a person who stands as a symbol, a voice that spoke for a generation in the early 1960s on behalf of civil rights and against war and the culture of nuclearism.

What about Glück as a response to Trumpism? The Nobel Committee noted that one reason they rewarded Glück was that she deployed international mythic templates that counteracted the committee's disappointment with America's isolationism, anti-immigrant policies, provincialism, and withdrawal under Trump from international treaties. Glück's poetics represent an implicit rebuke to Trumpian isolationism, bombast, and American provincialism.[15] In *The Triumph of Achilles*, Glück implicitly expresses an appreciation for universal values through an international perspective. She deals with typical lyric themes such as taking the risk to love what one knows must be lost, but, as Helen Vendler has commented, Glück gives "experience the permanent form of myth," without, as in the "confessional" poetry of Robert Lowell and Sylvia Plath, attempting to make the author's autobiographical experience itself mythic. Discussing the universalizing role of myth in "The Triumph of Achilles," Caroline Malone writes, "myth allows Glück the distance to approach what is most intimate and vulnerable—to love another human being. The godlike Achilles finds himself grief stricken over the loss of his beloved Patroclus. This loss forces Achilles to confront his own mortality. With these new boundaries of self, Achilles is able to achieve his greatest triumph: Becoming truly human." In "The Triumph of Achilles," Glück sets the relationship between Achilles and Patroclus at the intersection between friendship—defined by the principle of democratic sameness (they wear the same armor)—and the hierarchical principle of difference that characterizes both the feudal model of master-slave relations and the aristocratic attitude toward warfare that produces the significance of few individual warriors at the cost of the destruction of the anonymous many whose stories are left untold. "Always in these friendships/one serves the other, one is less than the other: the hierarchy/is always apparent" (Glück, *Poems: 1962–2012*, 159). In Glück's complex presentation of friendship, competition for mastery and empathetic identification with the partner coexist. Glück's treatment of friendship as well as how she imagines characters in "The Triumph of Achilles" who renounce their desire for affection as a strategy to achieve their goals of making themselves known to the beloved also connects to the poetics of commentary, which I am

---

15 The Australian critic Ian Warden has read Glück's decision to focus on Emily Dickinson's "I'm nobody—who are you" in her Nobel lecture as an implicit rebuke to Trump's excessive Tweeting and publicity seeking: "In her acceptance lecture, Glück testifies that her favourite poets and poems are the antithesis of the Trumpian 'Look at me! Listen to me! Mate with me! I'm Somebody!' way of doing things. She, Glück, loves Dickinson's poem in praise of 'nobodyness' because it is a poem not brayed to a whole bog but just spoken, quietly, intimately to one reader at a time."

Reading it as a teenager, Glück remembers, she knew that "she [Dickinson] had chosen me, or recognised me."

"We were an elite, companions in invisibility, a fact known only to us [...] I believe that in awarding me this prize, the Swedish Academy is choosing to honour the intimate, private voice [...]"

identifying as a Jewish dimension of her work. As the Bible scholar Michael Fishbane has observed, the Midrashist sublimates the desire for recognition of his or her originality by performing the apparently subservient role of commentator.[16] At the same time, the self-effacing acts of analysis and explanation become a veiled statement of freedom, creativity, aggression, and originality, which emerge in relationship to reading the Torah. The Midrashist intends to reassess the Bible's meaning by filling in gaps and hollow places, thereby reconstructing scripture as a polysemous text, while appearing to submit to its influence through appraisal of its timeless values.

Dylan's midrash on the Akedah in "Highway 61 Revisited," noted earlier in this chapter, illustrates Fishbane's observations. Contra Abraham's submission without question to God's commandment to bind Isaac in Genesis 22, "Abe" in the song, at first, says, "'Man, you must be puttin' me on.'"

> Oh God said to Abraham, "Kill me a son"
> Abe says, "Man, you must be puttin' me on"
> God say, "No." Abe say, "What?"
> God say, "You can do what you want Abe, but
> The next time you see me comin', you better run"
> Well Abe says, "Where you want this killin' done?"
> God says. "Out on Highway 61"

As if he were negotiating with another human being, Hipster Abe's initial response—"Man, you must be puttin' me on"—suggests the patriarch's willingness to challenge God's threatening command. In this way, Dylan's Abe's differs from the silently acquiescent Abraham of Genesis 22. Dylan emphasizes Abe's agency, and thus his humanity, but we must still face his unsettling willingness to ignore God's recommendation to "run" away from God (and, presumably, to ignore God's command to kill innocent children) and instead to encourage God to command him to kill: "Where you want this killin' done?" In the end, Dylan has turned the Akedah into a black humor type of anti-war commentary, one in which the elders relish the opportunity to send the young into harm's way. In his book on the patriarch, Alan Dershowitz regards the Abraham of the Akedah story as "the world's first Jewish fundamentalist—a man who elevates faith over morality, fundamentalism over reason" (36). To a degree, Dylan rejects the biblical version of

---

16 See Michael Fishbane. "Inner Biblical Exegesis: Types and Strategies of Interpretation in Ancient Israel." In Hartman and Budick, *Midrash and Literature*, 19–40.

Abraham as faithful to God in "Highway 61 Revisited" and replaces it, not with the moralist Abraham of the Sodom story, but with an interrogative version of the patriarch who pivots between resistance and vehemence. A disturbing aspect of Dylan's song is, in fact, how quickly Abe's initial resistance to killing a son in the name of the lord shifts to a willful agreement to do so. In the Sodom story, as Dershowitz points out, Abraham, like a pugnacious defense lawyer, negotiates a principled agreement—a contract—with God in which "the presence of a certain number of innocents [ten] among the numerous sinners of Sodom will result in the 'whole place' being spared" (20). As with Glück in "The Triumph of Achilles," Dylan in "Highway 61 Revisited" reflects in emotionally ambivalent ways on a human relationship—Abraham and Isaac—in the context of a hierarchical relationship involving a human and a God. Both of our newest Jewish American Nobel laureates put their Midrashic imaginations to work to explore the fragility of human relationships in the face of inhuman terrors.

Works Cited

Alexandra Alter. "'I Was Unprepared': Louise Glück on Poetry, Aging and a Surprise Nobel Prize." *The New York Times*. October 8, 2020. https://www.nytimes.com/2020/10/08/books/louise-gluck-nobel-prize-literature.html

Bianca Britton. "Peter Handke's Nobel Literature Prize Win Sparks Outrage." Updated 3:59 PM EDT, Fri October 11, 2019. https://www.cnn.com/2019/10/11/europe/peter-handke-nobel-prize-criticism-intl-scli/index.html

Amit Chaudhuri. "Bob Dylan is Not the First Songwriter to Win the Nobel Prize for Literature." *The Guardian*. October 21, 2016. https://www.theguardian.com/books/2016/oct/21/dylan-is-not-the-first-songwriter-to-win-the-nobel-prize-for-literature

David Cloud. "Bob Dylan." *Way of Life Literature*. Updated March 16, 2015 (first published May 29, 2001). https://www.wayoflife.org/reports/bob_dylan.html

David Dalton. *Who is that Man? In Search of the Real Bob Dylan*. New York: Hyperion, 2012.

Alan M. Dershowitz. *Abraham: The World's First (But Certainly Not Last) Jewish Lawyer*. New York: Schocken Books, 2015.

Bob Dylan. *Chronicles: Volume One*. New York: Simon & Schuster, 2005.

Michael Fishbane. "Inner Biblical Exegesis: Types and Strategies of Interpretation in Ancient Israel." In *Midrash and Literature*, edited by Hartman and Budick, 19–40.

Allison Flood. "Louise Glück Wins the 2020 Nobel Prize in Literature." *The Guardian*. https://www.theguardian.com/books/2020/oct/08/louise-gluck-wins-the-2020-nobel-prize-in-literature?ref=upstract.com&curator=upstract.com

Louise Glück. "Nobel Prize Lecture." December 8, 2020. https://english.yale.edu/news/department-news/louise-glucks-nobel-prize-lecture

———. *Poems: 1962–2012*. New York: FSG, 2013.

Ethan Goffman. "On Contemporary Jewish American Secular Creativity." Unpublished.

Geoffrey Hartman. "The Struggle for the Text." In *Midrash and Literature*, edited by Hartman and Sanford Budick. New Haven: Yale UP, 1986.

Clinton Heylin. *Bob Dylan Behind The Shades: A Biography*. London: Faber and Faber, 2011.

Ian Jack. "Rabindranath Tagore was a Global Phenomenon, So Why is He Neglected?." *The Guardian*. May 7, 2011.

Lynn Keller. "'Free/of Blossom and Subterfuge': Louise Glück and the Language of Renunciation." In *Word, Self, Poem: Essays on Contemporary Poetry from the 'Jubilation of Poets'*, edited by Leonard M. Trawick. Kent: Kent State University Press, 2003.

Stephen King. "Why Bob Dylan Deserves the Nobel Prize." *Rolling Stone*. December 7, 2016. https://www.rollingstone.com/music/music-features/stephen-king-why-bob-dylan-deserves-the-nobel-prize-105313/

Caroline Malone. "The Ambivalence of Being in Glück's 'The Triumph of Achilles.'" October 8, 2020. https://blog.bestamericanpoetry.com/the_best_american_poetry/2020/10/the-ambivalence-of-being-in-glucks-the-triumph-of-achilles-by-caroline-malone.html

Philippe Margotin and Jean-Michel Guesdon. *Bob Dylan: All the Songs (The Story Behind Every Track)*. New York: Black Dog and Levanthal Publishers, 2015.

Stephen Metcalfe. "Bob Dylan Is a Genius of Almost Unparalleled Influence, but He Shouldn't Have Gotten the Nobel." *Slate*. October 13, 2016. https://slate.com/culture/2016/10/why-bob-dylan-shouldnt-have-gotten-the-nobel-prize-for-literature.html

Daniel Morris. *The Poetry of Louise Glück: A Thematic Introduction*. Columbia, MO: University of Missouri Press, 2006; reissue 2021.

Anna North. "Why Bob Dylan Shouldn't Have Gotten a Nobel." *The New York Times*. October 13, 2016. https://www.nytimes.com/2016/10/13/opinion/why-bob-dylan-shouldnt-have-gotten-a-nobel.html

Seth Rogovoy. *Bob Dylan: Prophet, Mystic, Poet*. New York: Scribner, 2009.

———. "Bob Dylan's Ten Most Jewish Songs." *The Forward*. May 24, 2020. https://forward.com/culture/447127/bob-dylans-10-most-jewish-songs/

Benjamin Schreier. *The Rise and Fall of Jewish American Literature: Ethnic Studies and the Challenge of Identity*. Philadelphia: University of Pennsylvania Press, 2021.

Maerra Shreiber. "Jewish American Poetry." In *The Cambridge Companion to Jewish American Literature*, edited by Michael P. Kramer and Hana Wirth-Nesher. Cambridge: Cambridge University Press, 2003.

Richard F. Thomas. *Why Dylan Matters*. New York: HarperCollins, 2017.

Daniel Trotta and Anna Ringstrom. "American Louise Glück wins Nobel Prize for Literature." *Yahoo News*. October 8, 2020.

Anastasia Tsioulcas. "Bob Dylan Sells Songwriting Catalog in 9-Figure Deal." *NPR*. December 7, 2020 11:28 AM ET. https://www.npr.org/2020/12/07/943818966/bob-dylan-sells-songwriting-catalog-in-nine-figure-deal

Helen Vendler. *The Music of What Happens: Poems, Poets, Critics*. Cambridge, MA: Harvard UP, 1988.

Ian Warden. "Donald Trump's on the Way Out, but will his Croaking Ever End?" *Canberra Times. Com*. December 19, 2020. https://www.canberratimes.com.au/story/7054495/mating-call-of-the-45th-president/

CHAPTER 4

PRESERVING WILLIAM CARLOS WILLIAMS: POPULISM, CURATION, AND LATE AVANT-GARDISM IN KENNETH GOLDSMITH'S *DUCHAMP IS MY LAWYER* AND THOMAS LUX'S "REFRIGERATOR, 1957"

Populism, Curation, and Late Avant-Gardism in Kenneth Goldsmith's *Duchamp Is My Lawyer*

In justly celebrated poems such as "Between Walls," "Proletarian Portrait," "To a Poor Old Woman," "Poem (As the cat [...])", and "This Is Just Say," William Carlos Williams encourages readers to focus on parts of the world that they might otherwise ignore. In "Between Walls," for instance, the poet locates "broken // pieces of a green / bottle" in the "back wings" of a "hospital where / nothing // will grow" (CP1 453). Unlike the organic sublimity found in romanticism, the inert "green" glass can "shine" because Williams, the urban modernist, applies form and language to curate a place where Depression era hoboes sought warmth from a homemade fire and wine. I thought of the curatorial function of "Between Walls" when reading *Duchamp Is My Lawyer: The Polemics, Pragmatics, and Poetics of UbuWeb* (2020) because the leading contemporary conceptual poet and critic Kenneth Goldsmith (born 1961) inaugurates his history of UbuWeb, the website he created in 1996 to curate avant-gardism, with a comparable example of how to encounter artifacts behind another sort of respected institution: "Invisible to the bustling crowds at the main entrance on Fifty-Third Street, there's a back door to the Museum of Modern Art (MoMA) in New York City that few know about," writes Goldsmith (1). MoMA's former Poet Laureate then explains why the usually "desolate" back door that commands "only a lonely intern sitting at a desk" is, in fact, the portal outsider artists use to enter their work into the museum with no questions asked. It turns out that in the 1970s, a MoMA librarian named Clive Philpot "decreed that anybody could mail anything to the MoMa Library, and it would be accepted and become part of the official collection" (1). Through the literal and figurative "back door," MoMA has added "anywhere from 100,000 to 200,000 artists to the collection" (1). As Williams understood in "Between Walls" and as Goldsmith demonstrates in spades throughout *Duchamp Is My Lawyer*, "the back door is a powerful tool. While all eyes are elsewhere, magical things can happen in the margins. Andy Warhol once said that if you want to collect something in New York, you have to find out what it is that nobody else wants and collect that. Before long, everyone will want it" (2). Curating the culture of outsideness and making its artifacts widely available through a form of piracy that doubles as an act of preservation, Goldsmith's UbuWeb follows Williams in bridging the gap between populism and avant-gardism. In "This Is Just to Say," which I focus on in the second section of this chapter through a reading of Thomas Lux's revision of the Depression era "found" poem in "Refrigerator, 1957," Williams channels Duchamp by repurposing a "forgive-me" note as iconic modernist artifact. Through an incredibly old technology—the poetic line—Williams transports to a wide audience of readers the note he placed on his kitchen table at Nine Ridge Road, and which he originally intended for one reader, his spouse Flossie. The line signifies the movement of the note's language of forgiveness into an art world realm that encourages diverse types of inquiry and appreciation. As with Williams in "This Is Just to Say," Goldsmith, through the new media intervention of UbuWeb, imagines copying as a transformational aesthetic procedure. "More than a century ago, Marcel Duchamp legitimized recontextualization by taking a urinal and putting it on a pedestal. The act of moving something from one context to another was an act of transformative use," writes Goldsmith (74). A late avant-gardist, Goldsmith manages digital resources to frame and conserve strange media from the past. His fundamental concern with copying as a radical gesture of cultural transformation resonates with the reproductive aesthetics I associate with modernist avant-gardists such as Williams and Duchamp.

Following Warhol's compulsive strategy in *Time Capsules* (1974–1987), where "the distinctions among collecting, curating, archiving, and hoarding collapsed into an artistic practice," Goldsmith assembles, documents, and distributes peculiar sonic, visual, and textual artifacts via UbuWeb (12). Combining reframing techniques Marcel Duchamp developed in "Fountain" (1917) with the ludic impulses that animated Duchamp's *L.H.O.O.Q* (Mona Lisa With Moustache; 1919), Goldsmith doubles down on Dada. We may, however, distinguish Goldsmith's practice from Duchamp's. Duchamp tweaks the admittedly postcard version of Da Vinci's masterpiece, so familiar that when it was stolen from the Louvre on August 21, 1911—possibly as a prank by Picasso and Apollinaire—it was not until August 22 that anyone noticed La Gioconda had gone missing. Goldsmith, by contrast, exhibits rarely seen artifacts belonging to the avant-garde itself. Preserving unusual music, film, art, and poetry in the spirit of fandom, not professional curation, he preserves the rebellious ethos of avant-gardism while removing its baggage of elitism, imperialism, masculinism, and militarism (the term avant-garde, of course, refers to soldiers on the vanguard of a battle zone). As Goldsmith freely admits, UbuWeb is an amateurish endeavor. "The site is filled with the detritus and ephemera of great artists better known for other things," Goldsmith writes (4). Indeed, silly curios proliferate on UbuWeb: Pop entertainer Marie Osmond reciting Hugo Ball's Dada Poem "Karawane," William Burroughs singing with The Doors and REM, the electronic music (not the painting) of Jean Dubuffet, the videos by Richard Serra, not the metal sculptures, the country music of sculptor Julian Schnabel. UbuWeb also features outsider artists such as David Daniels. A once-promising painter who was rejected by leading abstract expressionists in the 1950s, Daniels remade himself in the 1980s as a Bay Area digital artist/poet. Using an early version of a personal computer and Microsoft Word, he composed visual poems "entirely of alphanumeric text and printers' characters" (217). By proposing "a different sort of revisionist art history based on the peripheries of artistic production rather than on the perceived, hyped, or market-based center," Goldsmith remixes avant-garde historiography (4–5).

UbuWeb occupies an ambiguous position in Goldsmith's career as cultural provocateur of the digital age. In *Duchamp Is My Lawyer*, he emphasizes his role as a free information activist, but we may regard UbuWeb as a gigantic example of a time-consuming procedural "uncreative" art project that involves reframing information technology. We must also remember that UbuWeb is a process and practice, not a finished product. Borrowing a term coined by Dan Graham, a conceptual artist who edited a number of *Aspen: The Multimedia Magazine in a Box*, a precursor to UbuWeb published between 1965 and 1971, Goldsmith thinks of UbuWeb as a piece of "in-formation": "Graham called this form of art not 'information' but 'in-formation,' claiming that the form and distribution of information and ideas are restless and ever changing. What appears in a magazine at one moment can reemerge as a museum exhibition" (208). He applies principles that animated *Aspen* for the digital environment: "When Word documents can become PDFs with a click, which can then be spammed to a listserv, which can then be printed out, the materiality of that artifact is constantly and restlessly 'in-formation' while at the same time remaining 'information'" (208).

The title of Goldsmith's book illustrates his advocacy for, to put it politely, sharing language without fretting about who "owns" a phrase. It was Virgil Abloh, not Goldsmith, who uttered the "Duchamp is my lawyer" comment in an interview. An Illinois-born fashion designer of Ghanaian descent, Abloh paints over clothing and footwear branded with famous names to increase the value of the readymade without, as Goldsmith notes, "acknowledging sources" (74). "Following Abloh's lead, UbuWeb can be considered one enormous appropriative artwork, a giant collage, which appropriates not a single object but rather the entire history of the avant-garde" (74). Recasting poesis as a transgressive activity involving ripping and sharing hard-to-find artifacts produced by other hands, Goldsmith boldly flaunts the fact that UbuWeb runs afoul of copyright rules. Is Goldsmith a cultural Robin Hood or an Al Capone?

> By the letter of the law, the site is illegal; we openly violate copyright norms and almost never ask for permission. Most everything on the site is pilfered, ripped, and swiped from other places, then reposted. We've never been sued—never even come close. UbuWeb functions on no money—we don't take it, we don't pay it, we don't touch it; you'll never find an advertisement, a logo, or a donation box. (4)

Part Diaghilev, part Benjamin of the *Arcades Project*, part Warholian collector, part Duchamp, part Bill Graham, part P.T. Barnum, Goldsmith accrues symbolic capital by enabling everyone access to Stan Brakhage videos, Allison Knowles Fluxus performances, and Yugoslav Black Wave Cinema. Rather than questioning community values and contesting legal perspectives on obscenity, as did modernists such as James Joyce, D.H. Lawrence, and Radclyffe Hall, Goldsmith's radical gesture involves challenging legal norms about who (if anyone) owns creative productions. Anti-capitalist and anti-copyright, we may interpret Goldsmith's idiosyncratic selections for UbuWeb as subjective acts by an avant-garde auteur.

Goldsmith's oeuvre displays a kind of monomania. Collector and celebrant of celebrity, Warhol is foremost among Goldsmith's experts. To compose *Fidget* (1998), for example, Goldsmith

> used a dictaphone to note as much of as many of his body's movements as he could, keeping a verbal record of what happened when he walked

across his bedroom, shook his head or performed more intimate functions. This volume charts the results in 11 sections, corresponding to Goldsmith's eleven hours awake that day, in clear homage to the hour-by-hour chapters of Joyce's *Ulysses*—that most bodily of modernist masterpieces. (*Publisher's Weekly*).

Monomania indeed! And yet a pleasure of reading *Duchamp Is My Lawyer* is to find Goldsmith honoring champions of the free information movement other than himself. Through interviews and straightforward reporting about unsung digital curators such as Dušan Barok, who founded Monoskop in Slovakia in 2004, Goldsmith dons the persona of an empathetic magazine journalist. He chronicles efforts by a ragtag band of eccentric collectors as well as recounts efforts by legal scholars who develop arguments for why pirated sites should fall into the category of "fair use." Given Goldsmith's observation in *Uncreative Writing* that, "[t]he act of choosing and reframing tells us as much about ourselves as our story about our mother's cancer operation," we are startled by his use of terms of interpersonal affection and individual integrity such as "care," "sincerity," "trust," and "devotion" when celebrating pirates such as Barok (9). Goldsmith cherishes fellow underground renegades because they, like he, are those who "love[s] and cherish[es] obscure artifacts" by treating "[p]iracy [as] preservation" (39). Tones of tenderness, kindness, and responsibility abound in *Duchamp Is My Lawyer*. "It's funny what a little human discourse can do," Goldsmith states, recalling his successful quest to convince the lawyer for the public television station WNET to rescind its cease-and-desist order for *An American Family* (1973) because of UbuWeb's honorable intentions (61). Punning on the pre-capitalist concept of folklore, Goldsmith, sounding like a Blakean Lamb, not a Blakean Tyger, states that "[f]olk law works best through reason, politeness, and common sense" (62). Such a passage demonstrates the astonishing transformation in Goldsmith's sensibility, especially when compared to how he revels in "forcibly suppressing a student's 'creativity' by making them plagiarize and transcribe" in the description of his University of Pennsylvania seminar in 2011's *Uncreative Writing* (9).

It is difficult for me not to read his "Why Can't We Be Friends?" self-fashioning in *Duchamp Is My Lawyer* as Goldsmith's riposte to critics who excommunicated him from the poetry world after he performed "The Body of Michael Brown," a conceptual poem based on the autopsy report for the African American man slain by a white police officer on the streets of Ferguson, Missouri in 2014. Illya Szilar's withering response to his performance of the poem at a conference at Brown University is characteristic: "Goldsmith could have let the singular being that was Michael Brown, be heard, but, in the end, he did not have the compassion, the empathy, or the humility to do it. And because of this, he failed his art, he failed his audience and, he failed Michael Brown." Contra Szilar's condemnation of him for lacking compassion, empathy, and humility, *Duchamp Is My Lawyer* displays Goldsmith fulfilling an ethics of caring about others who care about conserving odd things. Caring is at the heart of this tender homage to eccentric collectors who have put themselves at legal risk to share their obsessions. A mea culpa, as well as a paradoxical self-celebration in the democratic tradition of Whitman, Stein, Williams, and Warhol, Goldsmith acknowledges that he was "too slow in diversifying [a] site" that, at first, relied too heavily on "a legacy of dead, white, straight, European, male artists" (46). Since around 2010, UbuWeb, he notes, has done more to highlight the contributions to the avant-garde by people of color. He also laments his obnoxious inclusion on the site of a "Wall of Shame," which pilloried culture makers who encouraged cease-and-desist orders that have sometimes forced Goldsmith to remove work from UbuWeb.

Writing *Duchamp Is My Lawyer* in the wake of "The Body of Michael Brown" fiasco, Goldsmith makes absolutely no mention of his prior efforts as a conceptual poet, nor does he discuss his vexed relationship to the poetry world. If the poetry world has shut its door on Goldsmith, *Duchamp Is My Lawyer* reveals that he remains welcomed in the pirate librarian underground. Goldsmith notes that Duchamp "once made a door hinged between two frames that was always open and always shut. The door closed one entrance when it opened the other" (3). He analogizes Duchamp's "pendulous door" to UbuWeb as a conservatory that is "[o]pen and closed, pirate and legitimate, serious and playful" (3). I regard Duchamp's door as a metaphor for how Goldsmith situates UbuWeb as a pivotal threshold in his evolving career as a poet, pedagogue, and provocateur. As much as his book signifies his farewell to the poetry world, it chronicles his essential work as a free information activist. And yet, because we can understand UbuWeb as Goldsmith's crowning achievement as poet laureate of the digital era's information technology, I suspect he is leaving the door open to be welcomed back into the poetry fold.

"Born of the spirit and born again": Reading Thomas Lux's "Refrigerator, 1957" as Refurbished Williams Ice Box

Remarking on Williams's "Between Walls" and Goldsmith's UbuWeb, I noted that each enacts the Duchampian project of pointing out the value of unacknowledged parts of the social text through acts of cultural conservation. In

"Poem (As the cat [...])," Williams opens the imagist Depression era poem by using enjambed lines to literalize the ongoing movement of the cat, which, amusingly, will end up sticking a hind leg into a flowerpot:

> as the cat
> climbed over
> the top of
>
> the jamcloset

In the context of a chapter that is, in part, titled "Preserving William Carlos Williams," and that explores poetry as a form of cultural preservation, I draw attention to line four, "the jamcloset." According to the "Definition.net" website, a jamcloset is "a coldroom that is meant to be used to store things such as canned foods." Written in an economy of scarcity, the "jamcloset" suggests an environment in which food storage is a central problem of domestic life for the people who share their limited space with the climbing cat. At the same time, Williams is calling attention to the preservative (jam as fruit and vegetable preserve) function of poetry itself as a "jamcloset." This is especially the case when examining a self-reflective work such as "Poem." Punning on enjambment (the word jam is inside enjambment), Williams recasts the poem as a jamcloset to preserve a filmic representation of the cat's syncopation. Williams's manipulation of line breaks—enjambment—contributes to how the poem curates a quotidian moment that the author has noticed and found worthy of documentation in an art world context.

Like Duchamp, Williams and Goldsmith help us to revise, or, to use the epigrammatic term from my introduction, "learn twice," how to come to terms with banal aspects of the quotidian world we struggle to appreciate as fresh because we thought they were already too well known to even notice, much less value for aesthetic significance. By reframing the material culture of everyday life, Duchamp's "Fountain," Goldsmith's transcription of the entire September 1, 2000 issue of the *New York Times* in *Day* (2003), and Williams's forgive-me note in "This is Just to Say" help us to see the world in new ways through a poetics of defamiliarization that emphasizes audience reaction. As art historian John Russell has written of Duchampian readymades: "Objects of everyday use are combined in an irrational or nonutilitarian way to produce something that we recognize as having a strange power and a presence all its own" (178). In the second section of this chapter in which I reflect on how two contemporary authors preserve Williams's poetics, I will be working meta-textually—that is to say, applying the principles of conceptual art to poetry's relation to itself. In "Refrigerator, 1957" (1997), the late Massachusetts-born and Boston-area educated poet Thomas Lux (b. 1946–2017) absorbs (regurgitates?) into his own poem the previously digested images and tropes from "This Is Just to Say" (1934), the depression era icebox found in Williams's imagistic lyric. Like UbuWeb, Lux's poem serves the late avant-gardist function of providing a conservational space of archival memory, not only for "This Is Just to Say," but for a theory of imagining poetry as a technology to meditate on the relation of imagistic and symbolic readings of common literary tropes. Like "This Is Just to Say," Lux's poem involves refrigeration, fruit, desire—to eat or not to eat—and thus the theme of interpersonal ethics. The poem also serves as an opportunity for Lux to consider the pre-history of the object—a three-quarter full jar of Maraschino cherries he finds as he remembers, as an 11-year-old child, noticing in the otherwise spartan refrigerator of his Cold War era ancestors.

In contrast to Harold Bloom's notorious theory of influence anxiety, I argue that Lux's refrigerator—a typical figure for poetry as conservatory of human, and thus perishable, value; Yeats famously stated that all that is perishable rots and that salt and ice made for the best packing—should not be read as a postmodern appliance the contemporary poet invokes to push out of memory Williams's outdated modernist ice box. Rather, I metaphorize the refrigerator in Lux's own terms from the first line of his poem—as a "vault," that is, an enclosure designed to protect things of value. Williams's "This Is Just to Say" describes the speaker's unrestrained desire. Lux thus explores the interpersonal problem of consumption in an economy of scarce resources. The "I" in Williams transgresses upon a promise—an implied social contract—to resist taking away from the beloved other—the "you" with which he has agreed to share what is deemed good—what he strongly assumes not only belongs to her, but what has accrued special worth by virtue of her willingness to abstain from immediate pleasure. In "This Is Just to Say," the "you" delays gratification so that anticipation itself becomes a form of excruciating pleasure. One may think of Lux's persona as a belated version of that "you." In the end, he is Williams's ideal reader and his poem is a form that allows us to think of Williams's note as having been, in Hegelian terms, "born of the spirit and born again." If so, we may then consider the jar of "beautiful" Maraschino cherries Lux finds in the "Refrigerator, 1957" as a metonym for "This Is Just to Say," one container within another container. Understanding his own image container ("Refrigerator, 1957" as a vault-like archive of aesthetic value), Lux's speaker concludes that he "never ate" a cherry from the jar because "I knew it might be missed/and because I knew it would not be replaced/and because you do not eat/that which rips your heart with joy" (lines 35–40).

Lux reanimates Williams's lyric in an act of writing that is also a creative revisioning of what has come before. He regards his speaker's recollection of pulling open the vault-like handle arm of the refrigerator's quintessentially late 1950s massive, slick white, and excessively heavy metal door (with the balloon-like rounded contours so prevalent in 1950s U.S. industrial design) as a literal act of opening himself up to a cold, interior space. Pulling open the handle also figuratively inaugurates Lux's imaginative re-entering into the cold interior space of personal and historical memory via his imaginative response to the spartan, but idiosyncratically perplexing contents—pedestrian potatoes *and* the sexy, "on fire" cherries he finds in there. "So much depends upon" one thinks when reading Lux's entry into a familial history inscribed in three homely objects he remembers noticing in the relatives' refrigerator when he endured "an entire/childhood of dull dinner" (lines 22–23): a single boiled potato honored with preservational significance through its encasement in a bag, a chicken carcass encrypted in a piece of precious tin foil, and, the anomaly that becomes the navel through which he enters the poem as a contemplative space of complex personal meaning, a three-quarter full jar of Maraschino cherries embalmed in thick sweet artificial-tasting syrup.

At first behaving toward his ancestors like Bloom's anxious ephebe toward the strong literary predecessor, Lux's verbally gifted middle-aged persona comes to terms with the three items—potato, carcass, cherries—via a condescending tone. His verbal manner speaks to his wish to deflect attention from his position of isolation from a community of interpretation that would have regarded a potato, carcass, and syrupy cherries as worthy of conservation. Occupying the position of rhetorical abundance as he gazes upon a frigid scenario characterized by absence and lack, he interprets the little there is to see as a manifestation of a condition of fear of the indulgence his fanciful rhetoric calls to mind. Lux's speaker is not shy about showing off his figurative chops. In the first half of the 40-line contemplative poem, he displays his imaginative skills with discursive flourishes to demonstrate how the belated author's image-making exceeds the paltry occasion.

I mentioned how Lux's speaker compares the fridge to a vault, but he will go on to associate the cherries in the set of the moribund utilitarian spud and bones to "strippers/ at a church social" (lines 15 and 16). Besides comparing the bottled-up (sexually repressed) "foreign" cherries as quite literal forbidden fruit to strippers, he personifies the cherries as "exotic,/aloof, slumming" in "such company" (lines 11–13) as potatoes and soup carcass.

Is it a stretch for me to consider the speaker here as comparable to that of a stripper at the church social? He is engaged in a burlesque performance in a pious space involving the creative shedding of his performative inhibitions to provide libidinal satisfaction for an audience of voyeurs who may look but dare never touch the desirable merchandise. He imagines himself quite haughtily in the first half of the poem as the ultra-hip, gender-crossing, and liberated figure of imaginative excess, the one in the rhetorical position of having, not wanting. By contrast, he ridicules the sexually pent-up conservatism of the frigid owners of the fridge, whom he regards as excessive hoarders of bland, pedestrian foodstuffs. Channeling the unruly speaker in "This Is Just to Say," who helps himself to the plate of cold sweet plums even though he indulges during a period of economic scarcity and he knows his wife is counting on them to break her fast, he is asking who saves one potato and a chicken carcass and refrains from opening the lid of those "heart red, sexual red, wet neon red,/shining red in their liquid" Maraschinos? Who saves such stuff, Lux wonders, in the high-flying U.S. economy of the 1990s, or during the post–World War II heated-up economy in the 1950s when stagnant Depression era factories, at first repurposed to manufacture planes, tanks, and supplies for GIs, were repurposed once more to supply new veterans and their families with refrigerators and tail-finned cars to reach their suburban homes where baby-making was booming? Implicitly, Lux's speaker, at least in the first half of the poem, displaces the consumerist "I" from "This Is Just to Say." He relegates the relatives to whom belongs the vault-like refrigerator, potatoes, carcass, and uneaten cherries, to the position of the retentive "you" from "This Is Just to Say." The relatives, at least at first, are the ones into "saving," not consuming.

The first 20-lines of "Refrigerator, 1957" deal caustically with the problem of economic scarcity, but Lux addresses an issue quite different from the crisis of unrestrained consumption that animates "This Is Just to Say." Initially, Lux critiques his relatives' retentiveness. He mocks their fear of dipping deeply into the jar of cherries, like plums a symbol of that which brings momentary satisfaction from a state of perpetual want. His tone implies that the relatives who own the refrigerator should be less like Williams's "you" who "saves for breakfast" and more like the "I" who takes now, worries later. They should give in to desire, let go. But precisely in the middle of the poem—at line 20—the speaker's relation to the anal ancestors shifts from condescension to admiration. To his surprise, Lux realizes it is *his* speaker—the consumer age, linguistically dexterous, assimilated American who has never known material want—who occupies the position of wanting, not having. (We as readers would have expected immigrants from Bohemia who, the speaker will go on to surmise, endured the Ellis Island experience of coming "over from the old country"—line 26—and the poverty and danger of "a sweatshop," to be in need, not the speaker.) The turn from bathos to pathos occurs when Lux rolls what he calls "the only foreign word I knew" (line 17)—the word *Maraschino* in his mouth. Rehearsing the proper noun on his tongue a second time, he feels its strangeness—in his term—foreignness:

> Maraschino cherries, maraschino, the only foreign word I knew. Not once
> did I see these cherries employed: not in a drink, nor on top
> of a glob of ice cream,
> or just pop one in your mouth. Not once. (16–21)

In the first lines of the poem, Lux connects phrases of negation signifying lack and absence—"and on the shelves: not a lot" (line 2) and "This is not/a place to go in hope or hunger" (lines 6 and 7)—with his skepticism that conjuring up common objects associated with stingy relatives who provided only "an entire/ childhood of dull dinners" could provide for him juicy imaginative fare. It is as if he projects his pent-up frustration of his inhibited youth onto relatives who had next to nothing in their (from his point of view) "vault" refrigerator to offer him as fodder for a middle-ager's childhood revery. But his tune changes when he tastes the word *Maraschino* (a word, after all, with "no" as its final syllable). He realizes the provincial limits to his own linguistic capacities and exposures, limits corresponding to his own prior incapacity to imagine his way into the refrigerator with an empathetic imagination that would, if activated, bear creative fruit. The lyric's final movement enacts that empathetic imagination, indirectly acknowledging that underwriting Lux's pyrotechnic performance remains, unconsumed, unconsumable, Williams's spare imagistic message in a bottle. The "I" of "This Is Just to Say" reports, after consumption, to his beloved that the plums were "so sweet" and "so cold." By contrast, Lux ruminates, admittedly in a bathetic, tongue-in-cheek fashion, on the potentially symbolic weight of the cherries for his poor relations and on the value of his preserving the cherries as a sign of respect for his relatives. He calls them "family heirlooms" and "status symbols/bought with a piece of the first paycheck/from a sweatshop" (lines 24–26), and after considering the three-fourths uneaten cherry jar (remember "This Is Just to Say" was a poem of three stanzas, four lines each), he regards the jarred cherries as his inheritance (someday mine,/then my child's [lines 33–34]). Unconsumed, but preserved, he comes to see the uneaten cherries in their artificial liquid as containing special merit once he perceives them with what art critic Arthur Danto refers to as an "aesthetic attitude":

> They were beautiful
> and, if I never ate one,
> it was because I knew it might be missed
> or because I knew it would not be replaced
> and because you do not eat
> that which rips your heart with joy. (lines 35-40)

In the last 20 lines, Lux has leaped into an imaginative historical reflection on his Bohemian (not so much Bohemian as Greenwich Village antiestablishment art crowd as Central European pig farmers) relatives. He wonders what kind of backstory is contained in the cherry jar. (Appropriately, Wikipedia informs that Maraschino cherries were in fact originated in nearby Croatia.) Alas, rather than a sign of his relatives' hangups, the uneaten cherries signify Williams's imagistic gambit: well-managed language can offer preservational value to what is precious, vanished, and vanishing.

Coda

Thomas Lux died in 2017 of lung cancer at age 70 in Atlanta, where he had been teaching at Georgia Tech since 2001. A graduate of Boston's Emerson College in the 1970s and a native of Northampton, Massachusetts, from a working-class background, he was a notable figure on the Boston-Cambridge poetry scene in the 1980s when I was a graduate student in the area. I encountered "Refrigerator, 1957," however, in an anthology of contemporary poetry I was using for an "Introduction to Poetry" class at Purdue. I decided to teach the poem because I recognized Lux's name from my Boston years and was curious what this poet, whose name and face I knew but whose poetry I had never read, was about. As I taught the poem, I projected my own interest in Williams's poetry onto Lux's poem. This was in 2014. I drafted a version of the reading of "Refrigerator, 1957" that became the second section of this chapter, found Lux's email address on the Georgia Tech website, attached my reading of his poem, and pressed send. In my email to him, I asked him a question about interpretation and intention. Was my reading legit even if the poet did not consciously intend "Refrigerator, 1957" as a revision of "This Is Just to Say"? Here is his email response to me:

I've only read a few other scholarly essays on my work. I found yours fascinating and, of course, you discovered things about the poem I didn't know. I never consciously was aware of the WCW plum poem connection. And, of course you're right: fruit, refrigerator, desire. Someone called it "delirious" in a review and I THINK it was meant in a good way. It's hard to argue with any other connection you make between the poems. You see the refrigerator EXACTLY. I loved the detail of the origins of the maraschino—I would have figured more Mediterranean. To be mentioned in the same essay with Dr. Williams is an honor. I'm glad the poem engaged you enough to write about it. You got it and you taught me something about it. You got the family and the historical context. I've read Herb Leibowitz's WCW bio and like it very much. Ditto Mariani's. And I judged this year the WCW Award for the Poetry Society of America. So, again, it's an honor. Re intention and interpretation: perfectly legit if you or another scholar reading something I (or any poet) wrote comes up with readings the poet didn't consciously intend; if they're not a million miles off mark, that's fine. We do that all of the time. It might be a problem if the poet is obscure or "difficult" and the critic becomes the person who stands between the poor dumb fuck of a reader who is just not smart enough to understand the poem. Your essay certainly didn't do that or have that tone. Cheers, Tom

In line with my readings of Lux's "Refrigerator, 1957" and Goldsmith's UbuWeb, I now see my acts of reading poetry, teaching poetry, writing about poetry, and, through the magic of the internet, reaching out to poets who I admire, as contributions to how poetry can serve as a form of cultural conservation and interpretive conversation. When one reads, teaches, and writes about a poem, one is calling it to mind and so breathing new life into it, preserving its memory for a new audience. At the same time, the act of reception is itself a creative refashioning that simultaneously preserves and alters the poem under discussion. My act of reading Lux's poem, and including his response to my reading of it as part of this chapter, enhances the dialogic quality of reading as a form of conversation and co-creation. Lux has passed on in the decade between my first encounter with his poem and my composition of this chapter. Lux's poem, itself about refrigeration as a postwar version of Yeats's idea of "salt and ice" making the best packing for what is perishable, helped me to "learn twice" about Williams, my dissertation subject from three decades earlier. In helping me remember my own past, I help us remember Thomas Lux.

Works Cited

Arthur C. Danto. "The Artworld." *Journal of Philosophy* 61, no. 19 (October 15, 1964): 571–584.

Kenneth Goldsmith. *Uncreative Writing: Managing Language in the Digital Age.* New York: Columbia UP, 2011.

Thomas Lux. "Refrigerator, 1957" (1997). In *Contemporary American Poetry: A Pocket Anthology*, edited by R. S. Gwynn and April Lindner. New York: Pearson Longman, 2005.

Publisher's Weekly. "Fidget". (January 19, 1998). www.publishersweekly.com/978-1-55245-076-5

John Russell. *The Meanings of Modern Art.* New York: Harper and Row, 1981.

Illya Szilar. "The Body of Michael Brown: A Response to Kenneth Goldsmith." *HuffPost.* March 18, 2015. Updated December 6, 2017. https://www.huffpost.com/entry/the-body-of-michael-brown_b_6891114

Helen Vendler. *Poems, Poets, Poetry: An Introduction and Anthology.* Boston: Bedford, 1997.

William Carlos Williams. *Collected Poems: 1909–1939, Volume One.* New York: New Directions Press.

SECTION 2
Midwestern Avant-Gardism: Essays and Interviews on Experimental Poetics

CHAPTER 5

NO SYMPATHY FOR THE DEVIL OF HISTORY: ON NORMAN FINKELSTEIN'S "OPPEN AT ALTAMONT"

In "Making The Ghost Walk About Again and Again: History as Séance in the Work of Susan Howe," an essay in *On Mount Vision: Forms of the Sacred in Contemporary American Poetry* (2010), Norman Finkelstein writes, "Functioning as a medium, Howe in effect channels the controversies and debates, the accusations and denials, the spilled blood and spilled ink, and finally, the centuries of chronicles and scholarly research. The poem restages an already highly theatrical chain of events." Finkelstein's comments on Howe as a "medium" resonate with his role in "restag[ing] an already highly theatrical chain of events" connected to the titular subject of "Oppen at Altamont" (2009), among his most visible, and, in my view, most compelling, recent poems. Extending over 39 stanzas, divided into two parts, and running vertically along three distinct columns, the poem first appeared in April 2009 in *Smartish Pace*, and then in *The Ratio of Reason to Magic: New & Selected Poems,* (Dos Madres Press, 2016). Jerome Rothenberg also featured "Oppen at Altamont" on his blog in *Jacket 2* (August 6, 2016). Recalling his reading of Howe, Finkelstein oscillates between subjective, Gnostic, and archival modes in his re-presentation of the audio-visual array of materials that constitute the source texts for "Oppen at Altamont."

Especially in the middle of the three vertical columns, Finkelstein (b. 1954) imagines himself as a speaker with a personal stake in the story he is telling (and to be more precise, *to the story of how he has accessed the story* he is telling). As the poem's title predicts, *the story of the story* concerns the peculiar fact that the objectivist poet George Oppen, born in 1908 and so around age 60 at the time, and one of Finkelstein's most enduring influences, joined his wife, Mary, also born in 1908, at the notorious free outdoor rock festival at an obscure

Northern California raceway on December 6, 1969.[1] Toiling in a period he describes as characterized by "endless simulacrum," Finkelstein struggles to channel Altamont as historical event while honoring an aesthetic commitment to what Louis Zukofsky, in his introduction to the 1931 "Objectivist" issue of *Poetry,* described as "thinking with the things as they exist."[2] In a literary séance that invokes Oppen as the poet's guiding spirit, Finkelstein nonetheless questions the possibility of recovering the value of his precursor's combination of a Heideggerian epistemology and a poetics devoted to clarity, materiality, limit, ethics, sincerity, and direct witness.

In "Oppen at Altamont," Finkelstein enacts an archival poetics comparable to Howe's, which, as he remarks, combines Gnosticism, lyricism, and historicism. "Oppen at Altamont" also recalls, in form, theme, and sensibility, Oppen's *Of Being Numerous,* which won the 1969 Pulitzer Prize for Poetry. In *Of Being Numerous,* Oppen, prophetically, expresses curiosity about "a new generation" (28, Section 26) while exploring themes he and Mary would witness at Altamont to assess their place in a changing world: "There are things/We live among 'and to see them/Is to know ourselves'" (*Of Being Numerous* Section 1, page 9).[3] In a raucous environment, Oppen

---

[1] Regarded as the zenith of the triumphant return to the garden movement, The Woodstock Music and Arts Festival occurred on August 15–18 at Max Yasgur's farm in Bethel, New York. As Dave White has written, "heat, rain and mud didn't do much to break the spirit of the 450,000" for whom "peace, love and flower power reigned." Occurring just four months later, Altamont signified the nefarious end to Woodstock's, and, by implication, the decade's, more hopeful aspects.

[2] Zukofsky quoted in Peter O'Leary, "The Energies of Words." Poetry Foundation website. https://www.poetryfoundation.org/articles/69068/the-energies-of-words Originally published June 12, 2008.

[3] In the opening stanza of part 2 of the left-hand column of "Oppen at Altamont," which Finkelstein devotes to the perspective of "the poet," he rehearses the Heideggerian concepts of "Dasein" from *Being and Time* that influenced Oppen:

> The space of possibility
> is always limited:
> the past *is*
> because it *has been*
> insofar as we
> *have been thrown*
> insofar as we
> *are fallen*
> insofar as we
> may project ourselves
> *forward*

writes, speech fails to ground the self in the world while negotiating differences between persons: "It is not easy to speak//A ferocious mumbling, in public/Of rootless speech" (*OBN* Section 17, p. 21). "Of Being Numerous" and "Oppen at Altamont" are assemblages of discrete and yet interrelated pieces of text. In this sense, we may compare both texts in their inchoate affinities to what Finkelstein in his poem refers to as "freeze frames" from *Gimme Shelter*, Albert and David Maysles and Charlotte Zwerin's 1970 film documentation of The Rolling Stones's 1969 U.S. tour. Recalling a Howe-type séance, which necessitates the poet to "channel" and to "restage" already theatricalized historical material, Finkelstein devotes the right-hand column of "Oppen at Altamont" to generating verbal equivalents—word pictures—to archive, and, implicitly, to enable critical commentary upon, *Gimme Shelter*. Finkelstein reads *Gimme Shelter* as an indelible part of Altamont's situation as a historical event. He coordinates quotations from an Oppen interview about his Altamont experience first published in *Ironwood* and Jagger quotations from *Gimme Shelter* in which the singer engages in futile declarations of communitarianism designed to quell the increasingly violent crowds. He incorporates other quotations from *Gimme Shelter*, including a metafictional scene in which Jagger appears in the filmmaker's editing studio as the Maysles cut their documentary film. Finkelstein also incorporates Oppen's comments about a reading tour he canceled for *Of Being Numerous*, and a bit of conversation between Finkelstein and fellow English professor Alan Golding as they ponder the meaning of Oppen's appearance at the ill-fated concert. As in a Howe literary séance, Finkelstein pulls these fragmentary materials together into a historical recuperation. On a formal level, he evokes the Maysles brothers' cinema verité approach to composition as a type of found art. In *Gimme Shelter* and in "Oppen at Altamont," the auteur/poet has based the artifact on the historical record while subjectively rendering the presentness of the past by selectively recomposing disparate audio-visual materials that are "then put together in the cutting room."[4] As Finkelstein stated to me in an email: 'I wrote the poem from 2/28/06 to 3/3/06, though I had been planning it and gathering documentary materials for some time before." In cinema verité, the director treats frames of film and pieces of sound as distinct material entities that he or she "put[s]

---

4 "Rather than following the usual technique of shooting sound and pictures together, the film maker first tapes actual conversations, interviews, and opinions. After selecting the best material, he films the visual material to fit the sound, often using a hand-held camera. The film is then put together in the cutting room." ("Cinema verité"; online *Encyclopedia Brittanica*).

together in the cutting room." Just so, Finkelstein's process involved "gathering materials for some time before" he assembled the textual "freeze frames" into a mosaic of three vertical strips.

Critics such as Henry Gould have placed Finkelstein alongside peers such as Peter O'Leary, Joe Donahue, and Ed Foster as key members of a New Gnostic movement in poetry. Finkelstein and the other loose band of authors may chafe against the group designation, but we should recall that Mount Vision is part of the title Finkelstein selected for his 2010 study of the place of the spiritual in contemporary poetry. I mention the title of Finkelstein's critical book here because the term Mount Vision resembles Altamont. Both place names suggest an elevated space of access to transcendence. In "Oppen at Altamont," however, Oppen's strong suits—materialist objectivism, a concern with the limits to human speech, and the relation of history to representation—chafe against the New Gnostic yearning for sublimity. In "Oppen at Altamont," Finkelstein's mash-up of sensibilities ranging from Oppen's to the Maysles Brothers' to Howe's to Allen Ginsberg's to Mick Jagger's traces a chaotic narrative in a form that pivots between rational organization and cacophonous disorientation. Revealing authorial subjectivity, "Oppen at Altamont" criticizes the irresponsibility of an unlimited version of the ecstatic poetics associated with Jagger's dangerously ambitious performativity. He also questions Oppen's ethical culpability as a laconic bystander to the Altamont disaster. For Oppen, Altamont signifies the most distressing implications to his concerns about speech as a meaningful form of public communication in an unruly environment, but Finkelstein contemplates the adequacy of Oppen's reserved posture during the distressing concert. "Oppen at Altamont" describes concertgoers as involved in erotic self-satisfaction and yet Finkelstein describes the music as unassigned to any individual voice. At the same time, Finkelstein quotes Oppen as perceiving the "long hair" audience as seeming "to be mourning." One surmises the long hairs are mourning, proactively, a reading such as Finkelstein's own. Interpreting Altamont as a profane version of what René Girard would refer to as ritualized sacred violence, Finkelstein laments how Jagger reigned over a communal Death Drive at the Speedway. Presiding over a mass event that came to "identify death/with a kind of ecstasy/so that the crowd/takes over in a darkness/closely akin to joy," Jagger fancied himself a bardic conjurer in possession of dark knowledge, but "Oppen at Altamont" represents him as a venal fraud. Jagger is most certainly helpless to control the crowd he has whipped into a frenzy once the crush of fans near the small, makeshift stage at the speedway—only a thin cord separated the stage from the fans—forced audience members forward, where some accidentally bumped into the Hells

Angels' bikes.[5] Described in the poem as "this medieval prince,/troubadour of darkness/self-appointed but/delegated," Jagger tried to pass himself off as a populist by concluding the Stones's U.S. tour with a free west coast concert. Finkelstein, by contrast, perceives Jagger as a greedy aristocrat. On his American tour in 1969, as Joel Selvin has noted, Jagger wanted to establish his street cred at a point in rock history when the genre was tilting away from the English Invasion and in the direction of bands developing in the Bay Area (Santana, The Grateful Dead, the Jefferson Airplane, and Janis Joplin among them). Cynically, Jagger sought to benefit from the free outdoor event at Altamont by profiting from *Gimme Shelter's* ticket receipts. Jagger confused the corporate Death Drive with a desire for the erasure of self and the extinction of the discerning sensibility responsible for the consequences of language. Such discernment characterizes the reticent sensibility of Finkelstein's speaker as he channels Oppen's legacy. Jagger never took responsibility for the bloody aftermath of his oracular pretense. *Gimme Shelter* and "Oppen at Altamont" also document how festival staff escorted Jagger off the stage and to safety in San Francisco via helicopter. By contrast, Meredith Hunter, a fan in the first row repeatedly stabbed by Hells Angels member Al Passaro, bled to death because no helicopters were available to shuttle him to a Bay Area trauma center. A communal instance of the repetition compulsion of traumatic events at Vietnam and at Altamont, Finkelstein interprets the helicopter in his poem as at once reminding us of and shielding us from the terror of "the fall of Saigon/reenacted endlessly/in a musical."

In the essay on Howe from *Mount Vision*—the phrase Mount Vision appears in Howe's poem "Thorow" (1990)—Finkelstein offers a salutary, if still paradoxical, way to understand a visionary poetics as in the service of recuperating historical understanding:

---

5 Selvin writes that Jagger "seemed lost" as he was unable to control the crowd (207):

> The full enormity of the situation was crashing down on the Stones finally. The rushed preparations for the show, the absence of a police presence or any sort of practical security for that matter, the low stage, the scorched earth from the campfires of burnt garbage, the bad drugs and strong wine, the physical harm to the members of other bands who'd played that day, and the very real danger that the Angels posed—all of it seemed to converge in this moment of the Angel grabbing the microphone. The audience and everyone around the stage had known for hours that Sam Cutler was not in charge of this show; now it was clear that the Rolling Stones were not in charge either. (208)

In Howe's work, the visual and aural elements are equally important, which is why "You're hearing something you see." Indeed, the strangely "unreadable" print collages found in most of her poems could be viewed as materializations of dead voices, both from old books and historical personages, which partially reveal themselves through the "medium" of the text. Her reference to her "hand receiving orders from somewhere" also points to the poem as séance: spirit writing, taking written dictation from spirits guiding one's pen, was a specialty of many mediums and a favored mode of communication with the dead. [6]

In his Howe essay, and, by extension, in "Oppen at Altamont," Finkelstein explores the contradictory mixture of violence, representation, history, and memory that he associates with René Girard's theory of violence and the sacred: "Indeed, the sacred may be understood as containing within itself the notion of blasphemy or transgression. At such moments—and they are ubiquitous in Howe's work—the poet approaches what Girard calls 'the two faces of the sacred—the interplay of order and disorder, of difference lost and retrieved'" (Violence, 257). An archival pastiche as well as a coherent spatial display with the three vertical columns divided into two sections, "Oppen at Altamont" most certainly exhibits Girard's "interplay of order and disorder, of difference lost and retrieved." In the left-hand column of the poem, Finkelstein focuses on themes of "mourning," prophecy, and the contested relationships among generations in a crowd that is "always at risk/as power is unleashed." This last theme seems inevitable. Mary and George were 40 years older than most who attended Altamont. On a historical level, the left-hand column's description of a "spike" that, the poet says, can lead to a knife, refers to Pesaro's weapon. On the level of visionary poetry, Finkelstein is referencing Genesis 22, the Akedah, or the binding of Isaac. Translating Altamont as the High Mount, we may link the concert location to the biblical situation at Mount Moriah. However obliquely, Finkelstein has joined historical and visionary modes in a fashion reminiscent of his critical treatment of Susan Howe. He reads Hunter's murder at Altamont as a perverse Midrash on Genesis 22. In opposition to Genesis 22, however, in which the Angel's voice calls Abraham to halt his murderous intent, it is the Hells Angel, Passaro, who murders Hunter, an innocent member of the younger generation.

In his representation of Oppen in the left-hand column, Finkelstein casts the objectivist poet as a "meditative man." Oppen, the poem declares, was able to "honorably keep/His distance" from Altamont's mayhem. Oppen certainly avoided Jagger's irresponsible solipsism, and yet one senses Finkelstein considers Oppen's circumspection and detachment as themselves signs of impotence in the face of a public crisis.

> But to what degree
> does one withdraw from the stage?
> Oppen cancels his reading tour—
> "woke up one night in the absolute certainty
> that I could not do it…
> cannot, cannot, perhaps particularly
> with the expansion of voice in Numerous
> I cannot make a Chautauqua of it,
> cannot put myself so thoroughly INTO it,
> like a Ginsberg."

Finkelstein implicates Oppen in Altamont's catastrophe if only because the objectivist poet's diffidence about overstepping his bounds as a speaker on behalf of other minds discouraged the beloved precursor from participating in "a Chautauqua," Oppen's surprisingly derogatory term for an outdoor cultural event that features audience engagement in a carnivalesque atmosphere. In an email to me, Finkelstein described the middle column as reflecting the view of "the poet." There are, however, quotations that appear in the left-hand column—that is, the column Finkelstein devoted to The Rolling Stones—that reference Oppen's published views. Oppen and Jagger primarily appear in opposite columns in Finkelstein's poem, but "Oppen at Altamont" is concerned with generational affiliation as much as it is with generational conflict and so the lines between Oppen and Jagger blur into one another from time to time. The poem's middle column, which Finkelstein refers to as "the poet" column, refers to Finkelstein, but also to Oppen and to Ginsberg. Contra Oppen, Ginsberg represents an embrace of the "Chautauqua" style of interaction between singer and audience that Finkelstein reads as foreshadowing Jagger's tragic misinterpretation of the Hells Angels as benign participants in a collective celebration of music, youthful experimentation, and freedom from the restraints of conventional behavior:

> Who once invited
> the Angels to
> a Dylan concert, calling
> them "our outlaw
> brothers of the
> counterculture"

In the middle column, the poet repudiates Ginsberg's legacy by casting the Beat icon's impulsive poetics as predicting the naïve, deluded, and hubristic behavior of a Jagger. Jagger and Ginsberg, however, are not the only singers that

Finkelstein associates with "unleashing/energies" through expansive song. The phrase "unleashing/energies" resonates with Oppen's concern that the "expansion of voice in ["On Being] Numerous" replicates the unauthorized voice of the "people" or "crowd" that Finkelstein, in the middle column of "Oppen at Altamont," associates with unregulated violence. In an email to me, Finkelstein said he is "responding most centrally" to section 10 of *Of Being Numerous:*

> Or, in that light, New arts! Dithyrambic, audience-as-artists! But I will listen to a man, I will listen to a man, and when I speak I will speak, tho he will fail and I will fail. But I will listen to him speak. The shuffling of a crowd is nothing—well, nothing but the many that we are, but nothing.
>
> Urban art, art of the cities, art of the young in the cities—The isolated man is dead, his world around him exhausted
>
> And he fails! He fails, that meditative man! And indeed they can not "bear" it. (section 10, p. 15)

Alluding to a passage in "Of Being Numerous" that follows Oppen's powerful line about "the bright light of shipwreck," and that appears in a section associating "that light" with the "Dithyrambic," we realize that Finkelstein is correlating Oppen's poetics and Jagger's theatrics at Altamont with rhythmic performance in ancient Greek Dionysian ritual festivals. Finkelstein himself rehearses Ginsberg's oracular, anaphoric, and dithyrambic type of rhetoric in his poem, but this festive style describes Jagger's inability to distinguish persons representing real and present dangers from a dandified, androgynous, and theatrical fantasy of Satanic Dionysian revelry: "Who once invited the Angels to a Dylan concert, calling them 'our outlaw brothers of the counterculture.'" Focusing on Whitman's penchant for self-celebration rather than on Whitman's coincidental interest in representing the crowd with a formal approach to managing lines and strophes that distinguish between part and whole, Finkelstein casts Jagger's performance at Altamont as creating a paradoxically "masturbatory atmosphere" that doubles as an impersonal love fest in which "the songs [...] are no one's own."[6] Jagger can, unconvincingly, and

---

6 And indeed "everyone
    turned very sharply
    into himself or herself.
    Kind of a masturbatory
    atmosphere."

with a tragic lack of success, urge the unruly crowd to "show/we're all one," but that only leads to the problem that "The Crowd" is "always at risk" as "power is unleashed." As Burt Hatlen has written, Oppen, too, was concerned with "the ontology of the human collectivity" and the "ongoing life of the people 'en masse'."[7] Oppen writes in "On Being Numerous": "We want to say//'common sense'/And cannot" (part 26) and, in part 9, Oppen writes, "Whether, as intensity of seeing increases, one's distance from Them, the people, does not also increase." Oppen is attracted to and repelled by "The absolute singular," which is "the bright light of shipwreck." He and Mary attended Altamont, but "Oppen at Altamont" describes them as seeming "odd" "to any of the festive youth/unstoned and thoughtful." Like Oppen before him, Finkelstein seeks accuracy in representation through documentary methods while acknowledging the inevitable role mediation plays in distorting our recollection of the past. "Oppen at Altamont" suggests the limits of representation in that "neither the Maysles nor mine/can present this passage," this "sickening acceleration/that no poem may stop."

Like Oppen before him, Finkelstein occupies a circumspect posture. He approaches writing with a pronounced concern for the ethics of speaking on behalf of others when the outcomes of his utterance may conceal truth, blur distinctions between discrete entities, or encourage violence. Like Ginsberg before him, Jagger, by contrast to Oppen, signifies in Finkelstein's poem the cultic singer. At Altamont, Jagger seems woefully unprepared to deal with the aftermath of his Bacchanalian performance. He failed to assess the outcomes of his speech acts or to take responsibility for performing in a manner that contributed to an atmosphere that encouraged irrational behavior. Self-scrutiny was not Jagger's strong suit. The middle column of "Oppen at Altamont," by contrast, is devoted to Oppen's ambivalence about the efficacy, outcomes, and questionable legitimacy of the poet who elects, on his own authority, to speak on behalf of a group. Oppen's poetry conveys to readers the sense that silence may well be preferable to speech in certain situations. As with the physicians' Hippocratic Oath, Finkelstein recommends that at least the poet do no harm. When describing his and Mary's experience at Altamont, Oppen's focus is on describing with fidelity the physical scene itself: "*the irrigation canals*" and "*walking under the high-tension wires over the brown hills.*" "Unstoned" and "thoughtful," Oppen uses language to establish a material world outside the self. The goal

---

7 Hatlen quoted in Marjorie Perloff, "The Shipwreck of the Singular: George Oppen's 'Of Being Numerous'" http://bigbridge.org/BB14/PerloffShipwreck.pdf

is to dispute nihilism. Oppen's limited poetics contradicts Jagger's use of language to promote a romanticized assessment of simulacrum.

The middle column of "Oppen at Altamont" emphasizes the poet's ambivalent, even contradictory, and, at times, bitter, relation to speech. Speech acts, the poet states in the middle column, range from "corrupted" to essential components of a functioning polis: "we are able to live/only because some things have been said." Speech contributes to the "corruption" Finkelstein refers to as "endless simulacrum," which he associates with *Gimme Shelter*, a representation indelibly intertwined with our memory of the murderous incidents at Altamont. Oppen and Finkelstein seek to distinguish corrupt speech from speech that promotes communication between persons, but in part 2 of the middle column, Finkelstein abandons hope that he can recover Oppen's Heideggerian claims that speech can push through falsehood to enable us "to live." Each of the three short stanzas in part 2 casts a Platonic pall over Finkelstein's recovery of Dasein. Instead of being, Finkelstein seeks stillness. In part 2 of the middle column, one could say the poet, paradoxically, prefers the stasis of photography to the temporal conditions of writing, or film for that matter. This is so even as the poet wishes to situate representation and reality in a proximate relationship that provides a counterweight to "endless simulacrum." In "Oppen at Altamont," Finkelstein associates "endless simulacrum" with the oscillation between Altamont the concert as actual event and Altamont as it appears in *Gimme Shelter*, as well as with the specific image of the helicopter, which played a key role in Altamont, the contemporaneous Vietnam War, and, more recently, the Broadway musical *Miss Saigon*.[8] To my surprise, the elegiac tone of part 2 of the middle column reminded me of Wallace Stevens's very late poems. In

---

8 The image from *Gimme Shelter* of the Stones whisked by helicopter in and out of the clogged mayhem symbolized the disconnection between the self-proclaimed populist rock stars and the audience (including the Oppens, who parked their car a mile from the site and walked from there to the concert). Hunter may have died because helicopter service to San Francisco hospitals was unavailable to him because it was occupied by the entertainers. Helicopters, of course, also served as a key symbol of the Vietnam conflict, then raging and tearing the nation apart. Helicopters serve as a kind of historical marker of America circa 1969. Helicopters serve not only as a privileged form of transport from a violent scenario at Altamont but also as an iconic reminder of the archetypal mode of transporting "grunts" into Vietnam war zones and often injured soldiers out of harm's way to MASH units. As Finkelstein told me in an email, the image of the helicopter also showed up, to his dismay, on the set of the Broadway musical *Miss Saigon*, a reminder of a culture of "endless simulacrum" that has transformed a bloody and divisive war in

"This Solitude of Cataracts" (1954), for example, Stevens's speaker admits, "He never felt twice the same about the flecked river,/Which kept flowing and never the same way twice." At the risk of courting death as a form of stasis, "He wanted to feel the same way over and over" and to "walk beside" a river "flowing the same way" and "beneath a moon nailed fast" in "a permanent realization" (*Collected Poems*, 449). At the end of the middle section of "Oppen at Altamont," the poet stands helpless, like Walter Benjamin's Janus-faced Angel of History, as he surveys his contribution to an endlessly repetitive loop of tragedy and defeat. At the same time, he acknowledges that no poem, no representation, may stop time or alter what happened at Altamont. Drafting "Oppen at Altamont" at age 60—comparable to Oppen's age in 1969—Finkelstein must have experienced the chill of time's swift passage. And yet the two stanzas preceding the concluding one represent an "endless simulacra." In the third to last stanza, history becomes frozen, as in a broken film loop, now The Stones escape the deadly havoc at Altamont via helicopter.

Finkelstein has described the right-hand column of the poem as devoted to Jagger and The Rolling Stones. He does name Jagger and Charlie Watts, the band's drummer, in the right-hand column, but I would describe this column as repeating in words what Finkelstein twice in the same column refers to as "freeze frame" images of Altamont from *Gimme Shelter*. The verbal equivalents of film stills range from depicting Jagger "helpless onstage" as he shouts platitudes of unity to the unruly crowd, to Charlie Watts, the Stones's drummer, staring "in reverie" at a mosaic scene reminiscent of a "biblical painting" in which the Hells Angels clear a "path to the stage" for the performers "as the bikes roar through." In a disillusioned metacommentary on the outcome of his ekphrasis, Finkelstein, in part 2 of the right-hand column, admits his repetition of prior representations about Altamont has failed to provide the reader with a relation to the event that might promote a cathartic working through of trauma. The poet acknowledges his representation to be one more sounding in an echo chamber that veils, rather than reveals, history, but such an analysis cannot alter a baseline fact: a discredited maker, Jagger, "stares at us forever." It is not Oppen's ethical poetics that remains visible at the end of the poem, but the face of the thoroughly commercialized singer who failed to read his audience while "No arbitrary freeze-frame/neither the Maysles nor mine/can prevent this passage."

Vietnam into a prop on a Broadway stage. The poster for *Miss Saigon* features an Asian-looking ideographic brush stroke that in part resembles a helicopter.

In "Reticence and Rhetorics: The Poetry of George Oppen," Michael André Bernstein emphasizes Oppen's treatment of his writing as "a storehouse of gathering from different domains of experience," but also as revealing, "an equally strong sense of the limitations in any one man's mind or language, limitations that severely restrict how much of that larger world he can honestly (again, the unavoidable word) grasp" (234–235). In "Of Being Numerous," Oppen expresses uncertainty about the outcomes of his speech acts. He is especially concerned with the difficult, if not impossible, goal of writing a type of meditative poetry that succeeds as few poems have done in negotiating the relationship between speaker and audience without falling into nihilism or unauthorized speech on behalf of other persons who can do simply fine speaking for themselves. Finkelstein's "Oppen at Altamont" honors his precursor's willingness to document a reality beyond the self while acknowledging the limitations of speech to stop violence, to uncover the thoughts of other minds, to alleviate trauma, or to enable readers to achieve a sense, after Heidegger, of ever Being There.

Works Cited

Michael André Bernstein. "Reticence and Rhetorics: The Poetry of George Oppen." In *George Oppen: Man and Poet*, edited by Burton Hatlen. Orono: The National Poetry Foundation, 1981, pp. 231–238.

Norman Finkelstein. "Making The Ghost Walk About Again and Again: History as Séance in the Work of Susan Howe." In *On Mount Vision: Forms of the Sacred in Contemporary American Poetry*. Iowa City: University of Iowa Press, 2010.

———. *The Ratio of Reason to Magic: New & Selected Poems*. Loveland, OH: Madres Press, 2016.

Henry Gould. "'I Gather the Limbs of Osiris': Notes on the New Gnosticism." *Coldfront*. May 9, 2014. http://COLDFRONTMAG.COM/I-GATHER-THE-LIMBS-OF-OSIRIS-NOTED-ON-THE-NEW-GNOSTICISM/

Peter O'Leary. "The Energies of Words." Poetry Foundation website. https://www.poetryfoundation.org/articles/69068/the-energies-of-words. Originally published June 12, 2008.

George Oppen. *Of Being Numerous*. New York: New Directions Press, 1967.

Marjorie Perloff. *The Shipwreck of the Singular: George Oppen's "Of Being Numerous."* http://bigbridge.org/BB14/PerloffShipwreck.pdf

Joel Selvin. *Altamont: The Rolling Stones, The Hell Angels, and the Inside Story of Rock's Darkest Day*. New York: Harper Collings, 2016.

Wallace Stevens. "The Solitude of Cataracts." In *The Collected Poems of Wallace Stevens*. New York: Vintage, 2015, p. 449.

Dave White. "Woodstock 101: Four Days that Changed the World." *ThoughtCo*. March 17, 2017. https://www.thoughtco.com/history-of-woodstock-748354

CHAPTER 6

HISTORY AND/AS LANGUAGE POETRY: REMEMBERING LITERARY COMMUNITY THROUGH NEGATION IN BARRETT WATTEN'S *QUESTIONS OF POETICS*

In *American Literature*, J. Peter Moore reads silence as a dimension of the vernacular discourse in Amiri Baraka's *The Dead Lecturer* (1964).[1] Moore understands Baraka's privileging of silence as a "fugitive effort" that signifies resistance to hegemony, but that also initiates community through "opacity" (791). Baraka's subject position, generational situation (he was born Everett Leroi Jones in Newark in 1934), and poetic affiliations—he wrote *The Dead Lecturer* on the cusp of his participation with the Black Arts Movement in Harlem after abandoning the Beats following Malcolm X's assassination in 1965—differ markedly from the subject of this chapter, Barrett Watten. Born in Long Beach, California in 1948, Watten, a founding member and historiographer of the Bay Area Language Poetry movement, majored in biochemistry at Berkeley when *The Dead Lecturer* appeared in print. At the same time, Watten in *Questions of Poetics: Language Poetry and Consequence* (2016) argues that Language Poetry, which occurred as a belated rhetorical response in the mid-1970s to the limits of the Free Speech Movement at Berkeley, abides by a poetics that foregrounds obduracy as a form of vernacular expression. As with silence and silencing as notable components of dissident group formation in Baraka, Watten does not only imagine negation as a key feature in Language Poetry's resistance to hegemony, but also frames negation as a means of signifying a community of

---

[1] J. Peter Moore. "A silence that only they understand": Amiri Baraka and the Silent Vernacular of *The Dead Lecturer*. *American Literature* 1 December 2017; 89 (4): 791–820. doi: https://doi.org/10.1215/00029831-4257859

outsiders who may "remain conscious within a language of systematic denial" through "techniques of subtraction and refusal of closure that lead beyond formal composition (tonal or atonal) to nonintentionality and sound in postwar and contemporary avant-gardes" (179).

Language Poetry is a type of opaque writing that negates ease of reader receptivity.[2] This negation occurs even as Language poets self-consciously design texts that maximize the range of responses to the materiality of language itself understood as a meaning-bearing construct subject to an endless deferral of conclusive receptivity through the withdrawal of difference between poesis and textual critique. At least in theory, Language poetry's ludic qualities upend the Neo-Liberal fetishization of the consumable object as a transparent form of private property available for monetization through a market economy. Appropriating Moore's understanding of the fugitive purposes of silence and the vernacular in Baraka's watershed book of poems from 1964, I am reading Watten's account of Language Poetry in *Questions of Poetics* as, in Moore's terms, a "willful failure to comply to standards" of normative discourse. As with the vernacular, Language Poetry in Watten's recuperative historiographic treatment of the avant-garde movement in *Questions of Poetics* and in *The Grand Piano* collective autobiography project (2006–2010), featured the communal value of resistance as a non-normative social formation. Ironically, the poetry community's *failure* to stick together over the ensuing decades merely underscores the unruly role negation has played in the development of a movement bent on resisting containment via periodization. In a study that as a rule averts emotional expressivity as a residue of lyric subjectivity, Watten's acknowledgment, even embrace, of fissure, abandonment, and incompleteness as characteristics of his attempt in *The Grand Piano* to historicize Language Poetry as a canonical movement signals a poignant aspect of *Questions of Poetics*. Language Poetry conveys a communitarian ethos and yet tolerates, even courts, dissolution as a constituent feature of a poetics that resists distinctions between primary

---

2 In *A Critical Dictionary of Psychoanalysis*, Charles Rycroft defines "Negation":

> Process by which a perception or thought is admitted to consciousness in negative form, e.g., the onset of a headache is registered by the thought, "How lucky I am to have been free from headaches for so long"; the fact that a figure in a dream stands for the mother is admitted by the statement, "It wasn't my mother anyhow.; (The point here is that none the less the idea that it might be the mother must have occurred for it to be denied.) Not to be confused with denial; negativism. (108)

A Critical Dictionary of Psychoanalysis, New York: Penguin, 1995. Second Edition.

textualization and secondary contextualization. In his reception of *The Grand Piano* in *Questions of Poetics*, Watten regards the 10-part collective autobiography he designed and published from his current home base in Detroit as creating a space of "multiauthorship at a crossroads where friendship, community, and writing meet" (125). At the same time, he acknowledges that "differences and conflicts" among the 10 authors involved in the group project led to "the fault lines of negativity" and "dissent from collective forms" (128) that, in turn, led Bob Perelman to abandon his role in *The Grand Piano* prior to the completion of the series. According to Watten:

> Bob worries that the turn to language cancels the presence and immediacy he finds to be a central concern of writing (and of the contingency of community, as present rather than an artifact of the past), throwing out the baby (presence) with the bathwater (tradition) leads him to preserve the fault lines of negativity among us as a fact of literary value and friendship. (128)

Fragmentation becomes a characteristic of the consequential afterlife of Language poetry, which Watten treats as holding an insecure but identifiable relationship to more recent movements such as Conceptual Writing and Flarf. We think of Language poetics as materialist. Watten's oddly dislocational historicism, however, interprets his movement as an ineffable conceptualism that simultaneously moors and dislodges the text from a specific time and place. What does success for Language poetry look like, I wondered, given Watten's consideration of the movement's obscurity, dissensus, and defiance of closure as privileged versions of terms that, as Moore argues with Baraka, are usually viewed as disappointing indications of malfunction.[3]

In "On the Advantages of Negativity," Chapter 5 of *Questions of Poetics*, Watten shows partiality toward negativity in a nuanced appreciation and sensitive close reading of fellow Language Poet and longtime Fordham University Political Science professor Bruce Andrews's appearance on Fox News's *The O'Reilly Factor* (November 2, 2006). In the segment of the right-wing program entitled "Outrage of the Week," O'Reilly challenges Andrews's decision to include Robert Sheer's *The Five Biggest Lies Bush Told Us about Iraq* (2003) on a reading list for a course on "Analysis of International Politics." Watten especially

---

3 I understand closure in psychoanalytic terms as a breach in the fictive bracket persons may impose upon immediate events as dissociated from subsequent linguistic remediation.

admires Andrews's refusal to accept O'Reilly's premises or, conversely, to vigorously defend his decision to teach Sheer, which Watten describes as "a signal instance of negativity" (172). In Bartleby fashion, Andrews neither affirms nor denies O'Reilly's HUAC-like Red Baiting characterization of Andrews as in agreement with Sheer's positions in *The Five Biggest Lies Bush Told Us about Iraq* (2003). Watten concentrates on how Andrews questions the questioner, challenges O'Reilly's premises, and refuses to succumb to O'Reilly's "assumptions" about the relationship between the professor's views and his inclusion of Sheer on a reading list (174). By so doing, Watten connects Andrews's negativity (his obduracy) to the political valence of Language Poetry, which signifies a noncompliance with "the dominant discourse network" (Moore, 791).

Watten implicitly links Andrews's negativity to other examples of the poetics of obfuscation that occurred prior to the birth of Language Poetry, but which in retrospect has motivated his reading of the relationship between difficult poetry, disruptive politics, and critical obduracy. A case in point is Watten's analysis of Allen Ginsberg's response—documented in the film *Berkeley in the Sixties* (1991)—to a reporter's questions about his role in a 1965 Vietnam Day Committee march from Berkeley to the Oakland Army Base:

> Reporter to Ginsberg: Go ahead, just react.
>
> *Ginsberg:* Well, what do you want? A reaction to what?
>
> *Reporter:* React to the greatness of the march, of the day, as a victory or what? Are you happy with it?
>
> Ginsberg, *into camera, singing:* Hari om namo shiva, hari om namo shiva, hari om namo shiva. *[Looks at reporter and nods] (29)*

For Watten, the Beat icon illustrates, *avant la lettre,* how a Language poet may use silence, absurdism, indirection, and the privileging of an otherness that is left untranslated, if not fully untranslatable, to disrupt normative politics in ways that could not be accomplished through resorting to a coherent enactment of Free Speech. Since the release of University of Chicago president Robert Zimmer's "Chicago Statement" (2015), I would argue that social conservatives have appropriated the meaning of the Berkeley Free Speech movement from 1964. Following the Chicago statement's insistence upon "free, robust, and uninhibited debate and deliberation among all members of the University's community," conservative commentators, legislators, and university administrators have mandated the protection of "diverse" voices (that is, Christian conversative, pro-military, and pro-business advocates) against silencing in an atmosphere they characterize as a hotbed of Leftist groupthink dominated by intolerant "tenured radicals."[4] The subversion since 2015 of the Berkeley Free Speech movement, in which "students protested the university's restrictions on political activities on campus" and "sit-ins and demonstrations escalated into a series of large-scale rallies and protests demanding full constitutional rights on campus," lends credence to Watten's argument that Free Speech is an incoherent ideological construct. From Watten's point of view, defamiliarizing cultural activities such as Ginsberg's incantations and Language writing's defamiliarization techniques may serve as linguistic critiques of political discourse.[5] According to Watten: "Ginsberg's answer to the reporter's awkward question is a perfect non-explanation of his perspective on the march, as well as of his politics: the mantra *hari om namo shiva*" (30). As with his reading of Andrews on *The O'Reilly Show*, and his understanding of Language Poetry's inscrutability, Watten is claiming Ginsberg aims for what Watten defines as a use of language that expresses a desire for "opaque emancipation" that expresses aims that "cannot be communicated transparently" (32).

In *Questions of Poetics*, Watten frames Language Poetry from Berkeley in the 1970s as a belated linguistic response to the poet's own, at times traumatic, involvement with the limits of the Free Speech movement. His study also confronts the fiction of liberalism's tolerance for dissent, and the state-sponsored violence that enforced these limits in the mid to late 1960s. As noted in *Questions of Poetics*, Watten was in fact a student at Cal in the late 1960s, graduating with an AB in biochemistry in 1969, the time and place he defines as one layer of the foundation for the subsequent development in the 1970s of Language Poetry as a nonstandard discursive performance.[6] Retroactively, Watten interprets Language Poetry as a response to the limits of Free Speech at Cal during the protest movement as documented in the film *Berkeley in the Sixties*, which Watten comments upon in detail in *Questions of Poetics*. Watten was among those who attended California's flagship public university at a time when modest tuition enabled young people of modest means to matriculate there. He represents his

---

4 "What is the Chicago Statement?" FIRE website. https://www.thefire.org/research-learn/adopting-chicago-statement
5 "Free Speech." University of California at Berkeley website. https://www.berkeley.edu/free-speech/
6 Watten had attended MIT before transferring to Cal, where he would return in the 1980s for a PhD after taking an MFA at Iowa.

movement's esoteric relationship to mimesis as a rejection of the academic, civic, and political environment that denied Free Speech to Cal students.[7] In a reading that lends bathos, not pathos, to his historiography, Watten associates the distribution of tear gas via military helicopters to disperse a Free Speech rally in the Bay Area with gas bombings in Southeast Asia. In this reading, the children of California's middle class morph into displaced victims of U.S. imperial rage. Negating lyric convention as a symbolic reflection of a discredited liberalism, Language Poetry becomes an allegorical instantiation of and disruptive commentary upon the limits to Free Speech imposed upon outspoken, but silenced, UC activists.[8] By invoking *Berkeley in the Sixties*, director Mark Kitchell's 1991 documentary about Cal in 1964, Watten troubles our ability to locate the origins of Language Poetry in time and space because the "event" of the Berkeley Free Speech movement cannot be separated out from the subsequent layers of its historiographical imagining in films such as Kitchell's and in Watten's own remarks in *Questions of Poetics*. He also connects Language Poetry's pre-history at Cal with actions by the Black Panthers, who sell (but initially do not read) Mao's *Little Red Book* to progressive students outside the gates of the Berkeley campus to earn funds to buy weapons. He links Language Poetry with the subsequent postcolonial theories of Gayatri Spivak, whose figure of the subaltern, "the voiceless other outside the total system of Western reason and its self-confirming construction of alterity, who has no voice and cannot speak" is read as anticipated by Kerr's silencing of Cal protestors (412). Not merely an art world intervention, Language Poetry, Watten argues, is rooted in the embodied experience of engaged, activist, populist, vernacular, historical, communitarian, and resistant student protestors on the front lines of a global conflict that stretches from Berkeley to Southeast Asia.

Primarily white, mostly male, mostly straight, and attending elite universities, Language poets are in this study remembered as locking arms and

---

7 In 1964, Cal president Clark Kerr barred Mario Savio, Jack Weinberg, and Michael Rossman from placing tables to distribute anti-war literature at Sproul Place on the Berkeley campus. Kerr was a leading proponent of defining the public research university as a component of the knowledge industry. Kerr viewed Cal in terms of its use value. Cal, Kerr argued, could grow the nation's GDP in postmodern times in ways comparable to how the railroads and the automobile industry enhanced the nation's economic progress in modernism.

8 Watten notes: "I was among the crowd of students underneath the helicopter attack. My next 'turn' was to poetry, specifically the Iowa Writers' Workshop, where I was referred by Josephine Miles and Robert Grenier, arriving in January 1970." (Note, p.231)

standing shoulder to shoulder with brothers and sisters in a political movement that was far more queer, multicultural, embodied, engaged, pop cultural-oriented, friendly to difference, and communitarian than the literary movement is often remembered to have been. As opposed to his repudiation of Conceptual Writing as excessively reliant upon formalist concerns to promote its situation as a break from Language writing, Watten remembers Language Poetry's origins in the context of what Moore, writing on Baraka, calls a "cultural tradition of vernacular aesthetics" that eschews "avant-garde insularity" (793).

Contesting the critique of Language Poetry as a formal movement in opposition to and exclusive of poets of color, women, poor persons, and queer poets, Watten in *Questions of Poetics* recalls an initiatory scene for Language Poetry that occurred at a coffee shop in Berkeley in which he and Ron Silliman meet Lyn Hejinian. The initiatory scene is complex in terms of the politics of gender relations and the formation of Language poetry. On the one hand, Watten represents Hejinian as part of the foundational trio, and so critiques of the movement as male-centric would be overstated. On the other hand, the foundational moment has the whiff of what Eve Sedgwick would have described as a homosocial event "between men." As Watten acknowledges in his recollection of the movement's primal scene, Hejinian's appearance seems to bring out a belated adolescent rivalry between Watten and Silliman as they wonder between themselves whether Hejinian has ever read Milton:

> Beyond the admission of belatedness (often associated with narratives of beginning) in this passage [from the *Grand Piano* in which Hejinian recalls meeting Watten and Silliman at a Berkeley café in 1977], the homosocial moment of interpellation or hailing is important. The two men's anxiety over Milton's influence on a woman poet, an association with Lyn's imagined class background and real Harvard education, was a challenge to patrilineage and homosociality in the early stages of group formation. Lyn likely remembers this moment of challenge because that is what it was: in asking for her literary credentials, the two males playfully (or offensively) resist (or agree to) modification of their 'original' compact, which will be deepened as collectivity develops and expands. (124)

Milton, as William Blake understood, is a politically radical figure. Notably, he wrote a treatise on divorce, educational reform, regicide, and republicanism. His *Aeropagitica* (1644) argued in favor of free speech and a free press. According to Blake, Milton in *Paradise Lost* represented the combative romantic artist who chafed against the restraints of hierarchy by being of Satan's party without knowing it, but Milton also represents, more so than any other English poet besides Shakespeare, a fixture in the high English canon. Uncomfortable with representing the history of Language Poetry as fixed, and, therefore, as a movement that is now still, rather than actively ongoing, Watten is challenging traditional ideas of linear narrative historiography. In this sense, we may regard *Questions of Poetics* as sharing the historiographical mindset that informed *Bad History* (1998), Watten's book of prose poems in which the "event" of the Persian Gulf War (1991) and its historicity cannot be separated from the layers of its mediation, including the poet's own. As Philip Metres notes: "Bad History's jacket blurb suggests that the poem both invokes the Poundian epic (it is a poem 'including history') and counters it ('In [...] Bad History, history includes the poem') by questioning the notion that the text can somehow exist outside of history while attempting to record history."[9] Turning his attention from war history to literary history, Watten continues to trouble the concept of "event" in *Questions of Poetics*. He represents Language Poetry as forged a decade before he met with other Bay Area figures at coffee shops to organize cultural endeavors that he would, in retrospect, regard as formational activities to a movement whose significance was unpredictable. The meanings of Language Poetry have unfurled via an array of historicist interventions of which *Questions of Poetics* and *The Grand Piano* are major instances.[10] As in William Faulkner's quip from *Requiem for a Nun* (1951), "The past is never dead. It's not even past," Watten displaces the foundation of Language Poetry into moments prior to its inscription and anterior to what is commonly regarded as its periodic heyday in the late 1970s and 1980s. Destabilizing the concept of history as a settled agreement about the meaning of events that exist outside of our linguistic constructs, Watten understands Language Poetry as a response to the "falseness of public language" and to the "inadequacy of language to history" (66), as well as to the encounter with "the limits of the system" of American liberalism that occurred during the clampdown on the Free Speech movement in Berkeley, a decade prior to the formation of Language Poetry.

In Chapter 4, "Periodizing the Present," Watten links the Japanese-born (but, from 1965, New York-based) conceptual artist On Kawara's date

---

9 See Philip Metres. "Barrett Watten's Bad History: A Counter-Epic of the Gulf War." Postmodern Culture. 2003. https://pmc.iath.virginia.edu/issue.503/13.3metres.html.
10 The Grand Piano was in fact the name of "a coffeehouse at 1607 Haight Street, where from 1976–1979 the authors [of *The Grand Piano* collective autobiography] took part in a reading and performance series" [*The Grand Piano* book flap].

paintings, "which bring together form and history" (156) to *The Grand Piano* (2006–2010), "in which the defamiliarizing New is read in relation to historical frames" (156). Watten's historicist reading of Language Poetry as steeped in a 1960s radicalism also, paradoxically, critiques the Free Speech movement. At the same time, his placement of Language Poetry exceeds a fixed periodization. Language Poetry is protected from the danger of supersession by "the proliferation of post-avant strategies" (154). By contrast, he treats Conceptual Writing as, ironically, not conceptual because the emphasis is on the material dimensions of what he regards as a sterile formalism. "Conceptual writing is concerned with repurposing existing forms of language, as does Language writing, rather than dematerializing existing conventions of art, as does conceptual art" (155). Far from an unmediated expression of a "pure present" (158), Conceptual Writing is in fact a hypermediated (and thus, like Language Poetry, materialist-oriented) practice. Rather than inaugurating a new period in literary history, Conceptual Writing is merely a rehashing of twentieth-century projects "from Dada cut-ups to John Cage's and Jackson Mac Low's chance procedures to the New Sentence and OuLiPo" that, pre-dating Language Poetry, used "repurposing" and "citational methods" for defamiliarizing projects. By contrast to Conceptual Poetry, which Watten regards as neither an unmediated "pure present" nor a significant advance over past practices of appropriation, Language Poetry is aligned to the temporally disjunctive and spatially uncontainable processes found in On Kawara's date paintings, known collectively as *Today* (1966–2013). Kawara's art defies periodization because his "oeuvre as a whole is organized as an archaeology of representations of time that reflexively engages the temporal frameworks—or periodized/ing history—that it was produced in" (149). Through his reading of Kawara's date paintings, Watten, by analogy, can frame Language Poetry as a practice that one may date as a movement that Watten helped found in the Bay Area in the mid-1970s, but the Language movement may not be reduced to that single historical frame. As *The Grand Piano* and *Questions of Poetics* indicate, the ongoing reinscription of the significance of the movement has extended into its reception as a reauthorization that, Watten contends, he and other early proponents of the movement neither could have predicted nor have produced at the time of the movement's origination. *Questions of Poetics* historicizes, and in this sense periodizes, Language Poetry. Watten narrates Language Poetry's pre-history in the Free Speech struggles of the 1960s. He also conceives *The Grand Piano* and *Questions of Poetics* as part of the ongoing "*social formation* of the avant-garde" through the construction of "interpretive frames" (14). Moving away from an understanding of the Language poem as a distinct materialist work, he deliberately blurs the lines between reading and writing, production and consumption, historiography and poetics, poetic practice, literary history, embodied protest, and cultural theory. A paradoxical history, *Questions of Poetics* negates traditional conceptions of the genre as consisting of divvying up events, understood as value-bearing outside of their representation, into a neatly demarcated past, present, and future. "Like artistic production, the reception of the work of art is also a construction of value. Works of literature and art are valued not only in terms of their individual merits but also as representative of their periods, genres, and schools—each a material construction above the level of the author or work" (16).[11]

Just as Watten designs his critical/historical/autobiographical prose to cast Language Poetry as currently resonant, he also wants to receive the movement most likely to supersede Language Poetry, Conceptual Poetry, as one that "still depends on past art production to give it meaning and value" (17). Watten, for example, reads fellow Language poet Ron Silliman's *The Alphabet*'s use of proceduralism and attention to typography as at once anticipating and superseding in quality later conceptual projects such as those put forward by Kenneth Goldsmith:

> *The Alphabet* often anticipates—and does advance work for—later conceptualist strategies that provoke uncertainty over whether a given work needs to be read, once its procedures are noted. Silliman's procedural forms may be read as early (and more complex) examples of conceptual writing, long before the movement was announced as an alternative to Language writing. (93)

Watten is overstating the case because of his investments in promoting the work of a fellow member of a movement each helped to found. He distinguishes

---

11 Watten adds:

> Writing in the present about writing in the past creates a double register of temporality and historicity: the past becomes a shifter, as the present continually changes meaning and value. Similarly, the date paintings of On Kawara, as an exemplary meditation on presentism and periodization in conceptual art, create a dynamic in which the present in which the work is made (identical to the date depicted on the paining) shifts into the past immediately on completion. The date as a referential shifter (between present and past) keeps the periodization of On Kawara's serial work open, until it ends (or until one of the conceptual strategies he uses terminates). [17]

Silliman from Goldsmith by claiming that while Goldsmith places value in a "pure present," *The Alphabet* (2008) is simultaneously a conceptualist project of linguistic dissociation from referent *and* "a historical reference or an event itself" (93) that provides information about the Vietnam War, the Manson murders, the Gulf War, and the Los Angeles riots of 1992. Like Silliman, Goldsmith has used processes of arbitrary proceduralism such as the alphabet to construct frames for his appropriative uncreative writing in books such as *Capital* (2015). It is, however, inaccurate to suggest Goldsmith is exclusively offering, as Watten claims, "a defamiliarizing, inauthentic presence in its chosen forms of writing, an open-ended allegory for the 'homogenous empty time' of the reified lifeworld as an opaque reinscription of preexisting language" (156). A major Goldsmith work such as *Capital* does work with "preexisting language," and does touch on the themes of reification and defamiliarization, but at the same time, as with Watten's version of Silliman, *Capital: New York, Capital of the 20th Century* (Verso: 2015) is brimming with historical information and is itself a significant historical event.

To conclude (and to return this chapter to remarks I made at the outset) I am aware that my decision to begin this chapter on *Questions of Poetics* by connecting the role of negativity in Baraka and Watten is perverse. Unlike Baraka, Watten in *Questions of Poetics* wrestles with the conundrum of representing what Moore calls "fugitive resistance" from a position of whiteness and class privilege. Further, Watten and Baraka opposed each other in a well-publicized, contentious, and feisty debate about the history of Language Poetry at a conference held at the University of Maine at Orono in 2000. That said, if verbal conflicts with other contemporary culture workers at public forums—Robert Duncan, Donald Pease, Juliana Spahr—barred me from making analogies between Watten's poetics and that of others, I would be limited in doing what Watten himself wants readers to do, which is to offer a revisionary history (and pre-history) of Language Poetry in relation to movements often viewed as antithetical to his own. Verbal sparring at literary events has been par for the course for Watten at least since the 1970s. This is so even as I would characterize his written work as detached, objective-sounding, and impersonal in tone and even as he comes across in person (in the few times I have met him in non-confrontational situations) as a mild-mannered, Clark Kent-looking, bespeckled, late middle-aged academician in khaki pants and button down. Lore of Watten's heated conflicts, however, have become legendary within certain circles interested in how new poetics does or does not interact with politics, the academicization of alternative cultures, and especially how race, class, and gender are represented (or not) in new poetry movements. As Robert

Archambeau has suggested in a blog post on Watten's critique of panel presentations on the Robert Duncan-inspired New Gnosticism movement at the Louisville Conference on Language and Literature since 1900, such conflicts remain for Watten traumatic memories at once recalling and stunting his responses to emotionally stunning verbal ripostes with revered elders. Trauma may be one reason the tone of *Questions of Poetics* is so remote, at times impenetrable. This is so even as the history Watten recalls is intimate, and even as, in his own view, a good deal of his critical study could be dismissed as a potentially illegitimate "biographical indulgence" (207) offering "the genealogy of the poet/critic" (217). In the book's concluding chapter, Watten goes so far in the direction of self-analysis that he offers a close reading of his own poem "Radio." He also recalls a reading, first published in *The Constructivist Moment* (2003), of a drawing he did at age five of a "head of a king's son" (207). He must have composed the drawing during an experience of real-life trauma involving a father and a son: the juvenile's artwork was made "about the time my father was stationed on a destroyer and in Japan during the Korean War" (207).

We have learned from theorists such as Cathy Caruth in *Unclaimed Experience* (1996) and Dominick LaCapra in *Writing History, Writing Trauma* (2001) that silence, negation, amnesiac forgetting, resistance to closure, temporal displacement, and a lack of access to feeling are characteristic (non) responses to trauma. Emphasizing how forms of obduracy, anamorphosis, and negation motivated difficult writing as a site for dissent and community formation among Language-oriented poets in the late 1970s in the Bay Area, Watten in *Questions of Poetics* recalls (again, by vacating an emotive register) traumatic experiences. Trauma range from being a victim of a state-sponsored helicopter-distributed chemical attack on Bay Area protesters in the late 1960s, to the run-ins with Baraka and Duncan, to his recollection of the drawing he made when he was five years old and his father was on a destroyer ship near Japan during the Korean War. The austere language and chill tone through which he recalls these experiences deprives (negates and silences) the reader from experiencing pathos. Watten's historiography lacks vivid representations that would re-create the emotionalism, lyricism, and linguistic intensity that one expects to find in a more traditional memoir. Without knowing Watten's backstory, I suspect a reader would be surprised to realize Watten's investment in recalling the history of a movement he has devoted his adult life to developing and to keeping relevant in the face of threats by upstart movements such as Flarf, conceptual writing, The New Gnosticism, and the New Narrative. In *Questions of Poetics*, Watten treats the high-profile conflicts with Baraka and Duncan in flatly stated and objective-sounding footnotes. He displaces these conflicts away from the main body of the work in the spatial sense that he relegates the discussion of the Baraka and Duncan events to endnotes. Watten enacts negation through silence. He suppresses the emotional significance of face-to-face performances in a study that regards what happened in the past, as in his reading of Carla Harryman's *Adorno's Noise* (2008), as an "archive [...] motivated by a negativity at its core—of trauma, unrepresentability, nonidentity—and each unfolds at the boundary between narrative and nonnarrative, the visible and the opaque" (102–103). A freezing of feeling (it was Dickinson who wrote that such a "formal feeling" tends to follow "great pain") is part of how Watten treats with asbestos gloves moments of explosive fissure and generational (with Duncan) and racial and generational (with Baraka) conflicts. Such incidents, I trust Watten would maintain, are always already fictive constructs. It is not that the footnotes on the Duncan and Baraka conflicts are uninformative. They are. Watten's point is that we should interpret face-to-face events within the context of an unfolding historiography of a poetics movement whose significance remains undetermined outside of an ever-expanding horizon of critical interventions at conferences, in journals, blogs, and reappraisals such as *Questions of Poetics* and even this essay for that matter. For Watten, the dustups with Baraka and Duncan are themselves textual events available to reinscription, commentary, historiography, performance, language, and theory. The endnotes devoted to them are primarily a spur to promote further reading, reflection, and commentary as the footnotes include a bibliography of published commentaries, interviews, and theoretical underpinnings that suggest the ongoing significance of the debates in terms of the ongoing unfolding of the historiography of the poetics project.[12] It is as if what must have been stressful and even disheartening conflicts did not happen to Watten, and I believe he would in some sense claim the events did not happen to him, or, better, that the "him" of the representations of these events is a separate entity from the feeling person who experienced the conflicts. In similarly uninflected rhetoric, Watten uses a passive sentence structure to foreground the agency of language

---

12 Watten writes:

> The conflict over the poetics of presence and translation erupted as a moment of dissensus between me and Robert Duncan during an evening, sponsored by the San Francisco Poetry Center, devoted to the work of Louis Zukofsky shortly after his death in 1978. Many references to the event appear throughout *The Grand Piano*; see also Jarnot, "San Francisco is Burning," chap. 61 of *Robert Duncan*. (244). (On the politics of empty signifiers, see Laclau, Emanicipations(s), chap. 3. (231)

over and above the agency of the embodied participants in his (non)memory of the especially consequential conflict between himself and Robert Duncan at an event in honor of Louis Zukofsky in the late 1970s. In retrospect, Watten has viewed the conflict with Duncan as setting Language Poetry back a decade and observers have told me the Zukofsky event was an experience of upset to Watten.[13]

A study of the contested roots and undetermined consequences of an influential, if often disparaged, literary movement, Watten in *Questions of Poetics* claims distinctions earlier generations of critics have made between the production and reception of poetry are moot when it comes to understanding the kinds of writing he values the most. Watten disputes W. K. Wimsatt's interpretation of the poem as an object of desire that is distinct from the critical response to it. Watten, by contrast, aligns his poetics with the unstable interaction between poet (and/as) critic and/or critic (and/as) poet found in William Carlos Williams's genre-busting *Spring and All* (1923), the hybridic lyric/essayistic writings of Charles Olson, and the poetics fostered in Donald Allen's 1960 *The New American Poetry*. Donald Allen, of course, included work by Baraka, as well as figures such as Ginsberg, Robert Creeley, and Denise Levertov, all of whom take their place as precursors to the version of Language Poetry that Watten develops in *Questions of Poetics*. As in the texts put together by Williams, Olson, and Allen, Watten blurs the lines between poetry and theory, primary and secondary texts, poet and theorist, writing and reading, work and commentary, text and context, unsettling language, and disruptive politics. History and poetry are one. Watten privileges the idea of the "poem as an expanded

---

13 Recalling Watten part in a discussion of the New Gnosticism at a conference in Louisville, Robert Achembou writes:

> Here's what I think was at stake: the return of the repressed, or the revisiting of trauma. The best way to get at this may be to come back to a moment, now legendary in certain poetry circles, when a young Watten had a very public run-in with Robert Duncan, a kind of godfather of the New Gnosticism (and the primary subject of Peter O'Leary's study *Gnostic Contagion*). The late David Bromige told the story well, maintaining, in an interview, that Watten was "the arch villain" of poetry in Duncan's eyes, because Watten and the Language poets were, for him, "the New Criticism come again. It was everything he, Robert, and his gang, had defeated [...] and now it was going to come back again." For Duncan, Watten represented "poetry written by critics, and a very buttoned down kind of poetry too [...]" Matters came to a head, says Bromige, at a conference in 1979, when Watten and Duncan were going to speak about Louis Zukofsky.

object" (201). Calling "for wider horizons of interpretation and meaning," he explores "the formal construction of the work in relation to external, cultural logics" (210) beyond New Critical assessments of the poem as a distinguished object removed from the web of critical scrutiny that invests libidinal significances upon a linguistic formation of elevated significance (201).

Advancing a provisional claim for Language Poetry's place in literary history, Watten remains mindful, however, that periodization at once affirms the movement's epochal significance, but also threatens to contain its ongoing relevance to the development (and critique) of upstart movements such as Conceptual Writing and Flarf whose proponents have claimed to have superseded Language Poetry. Unlike Marjorie Perloff's interpretation of Language Poetry as a primarily formalist/aesthetic period in a "series of avant-gardes" (7), Watten argues that the progressive political resonances evident in Language Poetry's pre-history reveal an aporia in subsequent movements such as Flarf and Conceptual Writing that, allegedly, have displaced it in the 2000s. During the civil wars of the 1980s and the pluralist movements of the 1990s, Language Poetry has been critiqued as, variously, narcissistic, elitist, "hostile to identity politics" (6), and as promoting a "contextless formalism divorced from any specific political, cultural, or expressive aims" (5). More recently Language Poetry has been criticized as authoritarian in its claims to have been the first and last true avant-garde movement in poetics. Watten's goal is to restore the "historical crises that gave Language writing its necessity" (5).

Works Cited

Robert Archambeau. "'Where's It Coming From?': Barrett Watten, Robert Duncan, and the New Gnosticism in Poetry." *Samizdat Blog*. February 24, 2013.

Cathy Caruth. *Unclaimed Experience: Trauma, Narrative, and History*. Twentieth Anniversary Edition. Baltimore: Johns Hopkins University Press, 2016.

William Faulkner. *Requiem for a Nun* (1951). New York: Vintage International Reprint Edition, 2012.

LeRoi Jones (Amiri Baraka). *The Dead Lecturer*. New York: Grove Press, 1964.

Dominick LaCapra. *Writing History, Writing Trauma*. Baltimore: Johns Hopkins University Press, 2001.

Philip Metres. "Barrett Watten's Bad History: A Counter-Epic of the Gulf War." *Postmodern Culture*. 2003. (https://pmc.iath.virginia.edu/issue.503/13.3metres.html.)

J. Peter Moore. "'A Silence That Only They Understand': Amiri Baraka and the Silent Vernacular of *The Dead Lecturer*." *American Literature* 89, no. 4 (December 1, 2017): 791–820. https://doi.org/10.1215/00029831-4257859

Charles Rycroft. *A Critical Dictionary of Psychoanalysis*. Second Edition. New York: Penguin, 1995.

Eve Kosofsky Sedgwick. *Between Men: English Literature and Male Homosocial Desire*. New York: Columbia University Press, 1985.

Barrett Watten. *Bad History*. Atelos Press. 1998.

———. *Questions of Poetics: Language Writing and Consequences*. Iowa City: University of Iowa Press, 2016.

———, Editor. *The Grand Piano: An Experiment in Collective Autobiography*. Detroit: Mode A., 2006–2007.

CHAPTER 7

TYRONE CALLING: TORQUED LANGUAGE POETRY AND RADICAL MIMESIS IN *c.c.*

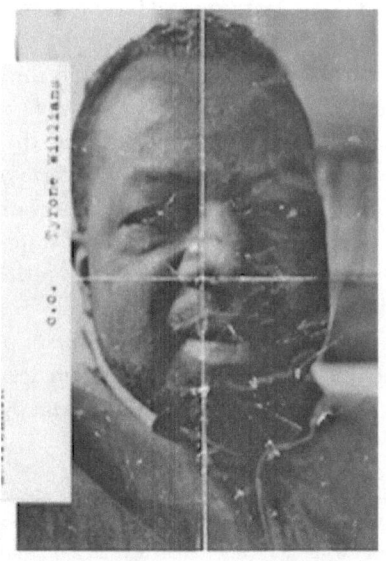

Tyrone Williams (1954–2024) chose *c.c.* as the provocative title for his debut full-length poetry book in 2002. In a cover photograph featuring the author's face, Williams's mouth is closed, but he stares back at the reader, as if returning a summons into subjectivity: Hey you! Who are you? (The title to Section Five of *c.c.* is, in fact, "Who Is It").[1] As section titles "Calling Cards," "Called

---

1 As with closed captioning, another meaning of the "c.c." abbreviation, Williams's title suggests a relationship between a written text and the spoken word in a visual field. The

Card," and "Cold Calls" indicate, Williams's volume concerns being called and calling back, but *c.c.* is not an invocation of immediate orality. Imagining the lyric voice as a trace of graphic textuality, Williams in *c.c.* calls back to a critical apparatus for contemporary Black poetics that Aldon Nielsen refers to as the "nearly hegemonic assumptions about the nature of the relationship between African-American oral traditions and writing, with a clear privilege given to the prevailing ideal of the oral" (24).[2] At the same time, by publishing *c.c.* with Krupskaya, a leading Bay Area independent press associated with the Language movement, Williams is calling back to a group of formalistically progressive (open form) poets who, following Cathy Park Hong's critique, did not emphasize racial justice in its inaugural period. By calling back to both "African-American oral traditions and writing" and to Bay Area Language poets, Williams self-consciously engages with theorists such as Derrida and Benjamin, who regard belated writing as a form of translation. Literature, for Williams, as for Derrida and Benjamin, is full of potential. It is always a form of translation of prior texts and thus always exhibits the connections between writing and the "afterlife."[3]

Williams's title challenges the reader to translate the repetition of a letter and a dot into metonymic signs for communication forms that are implied, but, for the most part, hidden. We cannot avoid the observation that although the poet is interested in reception as a form of call and response, he is also aware that his desire for recognition by an audience as a "voice" worth hearing—or as a "voice" even able to be heard by others—will not be a straightforward transaction between writer and reader. Rather, the response to his intensely mediated call will require special efforts by readers to decipher the significance of his call.[4] An African American poet who focuses on the material fact of the

---

need for "closed captioning," however, implies a disability on the part of the reader or viewer to hear the speaker without an additional textual apparatus.

2 *See* Nielsen's *Black Chant: Languages of African-American Postmodernism*. Cambridge University Press, 1997.

3 For more on the "text-in-afterlife," a thesis that understands texts as inextricable from the texts they translate and the texts that translate them, see *Afterlives: Benjamin, Derrida and Literature in Translation*, a thesis submitted to the University of Manchester for the degree of Doctor of Philosophy in the Faculty of Humanities 2016 by Edmund Chapman.

4 I appreciate Williams's concerns about reception of his calls. In *c.c.*, Williams's poetics features what Nielsen, writing on the concrete work of Julia Fields, refers to as a "poem that graphically remasters history, using oral and graphic tradition, orature and historical document, but using them in a fashion that must be seen to be heard" (Nielsen, 30). Adding

open form text, rather than imagining his text as a transparent transcription of orality, we can appreciate why Williams would be concerned with reception. Whereas Lorenzo Thomas has argued that "visibility [for a Black poet] depends upon the emergence of an aesthetic or political program that provides a convenient rubric or perhaps a fortunate commercial interest" (Thomas, 222), Williams's poetics defies affiliation with a "convenient rubric." Writing poetry that refuses, in the words of Allison Cummings, to choose between two "artistic imperatives—to write the revolution or to write the process of linguistic revolution" that, she adds, "have often been felt as competing, contradictory demands," Williams, however obliquely, documents persons, events, movements, and experiences associated with twentieth-century African American political, economic, athletic, legal, religious, gustatory, musical, and literary activity (Cummings, 4). At the same time, his poetry courts personal invisibility by engaging with a formalistically progressive literary movement—the Bay Area Language movement—that, following Park Hong, did not emphasize racial justice.

c.c. displays far more white space per page than printed text, but I read erasures, absences, and the unsaid as bearing meaning. The long section called "Cold Call," for example, consists of 15 pages of footnotes appearing on the bottom of pages that are, otherwise, blank. Do we read whiteness as blankness, or as that which need not be stated, because assumed to be the case in the first place? *c.c.* verges on weightlessness. It is spectral, ghostlike. A heavy text that weighs in at 95 pages, *c.c.* is, nonetheless, "difficult" in Charles Bernstein's sense of Language-type poetry that resists consumption.[5] What language there is in *c.c.* is splayed all over the page as if language were a visual manifestation of historiographical rupture. (The concluding section of the book, called "tag," suggests graffiti, a children's game in which someone is "it," and a slip of paper on which to list the price of an item for sale.) If *c.c.*'s front cover image frames the poetry to come as uttered by an African American male

---

to Williams's reception troubles is the fact that he is writing in the wake of a moment in which, as Nielsen argues in *Black Chant: Languages of African-American Postmodernism*, made work such as his own difficult to see and to appreciate. "Too much current theorizing about black poetics secures its success with a critical readership by eliminating from consideration those poetic practices that might disrupt totalizing theories of what constitutes black vernacular" (18).

5 *c.c.* is playful, punning, filled with the vernacular, but it is a "difficult" book in the sense of the term Charles Bernstein puts forward in his parody medical condition advertisement essay, "The Attack of the Difficult Poem."

author in early middle age, the back cover frames the poetry that has come before as a contribution to the "afterlife" of Bay Area Language-oriented poetics circa 1975. Framed between covers that send out contradictory messages to the reader, how closely are we to align the poetry with the author's subject position? Following Harryette Mullen's critique of the assumption that "'avant-garde' poetry is not 'black' and that 'black' poetry is not formally innovative," *c.c.* is simultaneously a work of African American historiography *and* a Language-oriented exploration in writing beyond, after, before, or other than an expression of a speaker's unmediated "voice."[6] "Double consciousness gets swept aside/by polyentendres, duck-rabbits, wavicles. /Neither waving nor drowning, we tread water/like a page turning in a book," writes Williams in "I Am Not Proud To Be Black" from a section called "Who Is It." The passage invokes the legendary concept from *The Souls of Black Folk* (1903) in which Du Bois argues that the selves of "Black Folk" are split through white interpellation: "the sense of looking at one's self through the eyes of others." At the same time, Williams replaces Du Bois's reading of African American alienation as a calcified interpretation of race relations while signaling affiliation with a principle of avant-garde representation: the undecidable relationship between sign and signification. As Williams stated in an interview with Joshua Marie Wilkinson, the poet's work is "a critique of calcification in all its modes—the

---

6 Williams's "impure" Language poetry stands in contrast to what John Yau refers to as "pure" avant-gardist art that erases identity from the equation. In "'Purity' and the 'Avant-Garde,'" Yau writes:

> As the white cultural gatekeepers frame it, experimental writers of color either don't exist in the "colorless" (read "white") world of the "avant-garde," or they are late arrivers, like hyenas feeding off the carcasses left behind by white writers.

I am uncomfortable with the association of the work by an African American poet with the concept of "impurity," because such a formulation may veer towards repugnant ideas of an African American poet somehow "polluting" or "sullying" a "pure" good thing. But I am choosing to hold on to the Yau reference here because it puts in play a challenge to conceptions of poetry as "pure" in the sense of autonomous, of poetry as having no relation to a rhetorical aspect or speech act dimension that connects poetry to action through language as a form of doing. Here I am referencing the complex discussion of the relationships between poetry, rhetoric, and (often unintended) consequences in David Bromwich's *How Words Make Things Happen* (Oxford UP, 2019). I add that Harryette Mullen wrote in 1996, "the assumption remains, however unexamined, that 'avant-garde' poetry is not 'black' and that 'black' poetry, however singular its 'voice,' is not 'formally innovative.'"

http://bostonreview.net/poetry/john-yau-purity-avant-garde

objective/subjective divide, class/coterie scales, the construction of race and ethnicity according to a biologism dependent on an absolute nature/nurture distinction." "I Am Not Proud To Be Black" differs through negation from James Brown's Black Power hit "Say It Loud ~ I'm Black & I'm Proud" (1968). In Williams's poem, there is no immediate lyric "I" to announce racial pride à la James Brown. In fact, there is no "speaker" to say anything, much less to say it "loud." A dazzling array of repurposed écriture, "I Am Not Proud To Be Black" is an exceedingly allusive and exceedingly elusive, 15-part sonnet-like sequence. The form refers, ironically, to the quintessential European poetic structure for lyric expression: the sonnet. In a style that Henry Louis Gates might describe as signifying, the poem refers to "white" canonical authors such as Shakespeare ("suffer the slings/and arrows of *et tu* transfiguration" [67]), T. S. Eliot ("narcotic nonsense, never to wake us" [64]), Milton ("Yet we cannot simply stand and wait/for deliverance [63]) and the previously quoted Stevie Smith, whose contribution refers back to Stephen Crane's "The Open Boat." "I Am Not Proud to Be Black" is, self-consciously, composed of "variegated vectors, these conflicting and overlapping methods" (61).

Discussing Erica Hunt, Harryette Mullen, and Gwendolyn Brooks as African American women poets who write poetry that emphasizes graphic texture, Allison Cummings notes that

> where the Black Arts movement and much poetry influenced by it called for audiences to recognize a new racial pride and a coherent group identity, poststructuralist writing, language writing, and poetry in their wake called for readers to question the literary and linguistic formulations of identity, to distrust the "I," and to interrogate fictions of autobiographical progression, coherence, or consistency within subjectivity. (Cummings, 5)

Incorporating elements of the Black Arts movement into his poststructuralist writing, Williams's sonnet sequence reads like a zigzag, even inchoate, repetition of tag-like nods to twentieth-century African American cultures that signify Cummings's "new racial pride and a coherent group identity." Section Fourteen, for example, by itself lists the "Nation of Islam, Republic of New Africa, NAACP,/Congressional Black Caucus, talented tenths," as well as "Moore v. Dempsey, Plessy v./Ferguson, Brown v. Board of Education, Shaw v. Reno" (72). The author does not tip his hand toward political preferences, distinctions of value, or his views on the relative merit of social, legal, intellectual, and political movements. On the one hand, the list includes 1969s' "Republic of New Africa," which promoted separatism as its leaders "made plans for armed resistance and a prolonged guerrilla war."⁷ On the other hand, the reference to "Brown v. Board of Education" connotes mid-1950s' integration and non-violent systemic revision of American race relations through legal means and legislative methods. The list portends a mood of what Williams, elsewhere in the poem, refers to as "sublime despair" (73). I say, "sublime despair" because his poem recites a litany of twentieth-century headlines of hope for African American emancipation from oppression, but also a collage of contradictory gestures that leave the "we" in a treading water situation—"neither waving nor drowning." In an essay consisting of a nuanced historical analysis of ambivalence toward communism among African American intellectuals such as Richard Wright and Ralph Ellison, Williams highlights Harold Cruse's challenges to Civil Rights Movement integration including Cruse's argument that integration destroyed Black Power and undermined the black underclass. Williams dismisses Du Bois because of what the poet elsewhere calls a calcified mode of seeing the world through a series of misleading binaries. In the interview with Wilkinson, however, Williams acknowledges the "paradox that political efficacy depends on blocs, groups, social formations [...] must put up a common front of solidarity." Disengaged from political efforts of a separatist or integrationist variety, the "we" deal with linguistic defamiliarization and remediation, rather than direct forms of political action: "we turn/the page. We begin outside the book/but the text is everywhere we turn,/a finishing fable" (60).

In the passage quoted above, and at other places in *c.c.* that reference everything from Pullman Porters to Black Panthers, "I Am Not Proud To Be Black"

---

7 The online site *Black Past* reports:

> The Republic of New Africa (RNA) is a black nationalist organization that was created in 1969 on the premise that an independent black republic should be created out of the southern United States of South Carolina, Georgia, Alabama, Mississippi, and Louisiana, which were considered "subjugated lands." The group's manifesto demanded the United States government pay $400 billion in reparations for the injustices of slavery and segregation. It also argued that African-Americans should be allowed to vote on self-determination, as that opportunity was not provided at the end of slavery when the 14th Amendment to the U.S. Constitution incorporated African-Americans into the United States. The economy of the RNA was to be organized based on *ujamaa*, Tanzania's model of cooperative economics and community self-sufficiency. Citizens of the proposed RNA would have limited political rights, unions would be discouraged, freedom of the press would be curtailed, men would be forced to serve in the military, and polygamy would be allowed.

https://www.blackpast.org/african-american-history/republic-new-africa-1968/

reads like a Black History Month highlight reel. In terms of African American literary aesthetics, the poem, similarly, pivots from the poetry of Ishmael Reed and Amiri Baraka to work by Anne Spencer and Robert Hayden. Williams cites "Those Winter Sundays" in *c.c.*, a race-neutral memory poem about a son who never thanked his father for keeping the house warm and his son's shoes polished before churchgoing. In "I Am Not Proud To Be Black" there are nods to non-violent civil rights activist Rosa Parks as well as Jamaican-born Colin Ferguson, who murdered six on the Long Island Railroad in 1993. There is the story of the "glamorous," but "broke" "showgirl" dancer Harriet Browne as well as a reference to O. J. Simpson as *The Labors of Othello Simpson* (66). All of it exists in a procedural web that we may read, as they are internal to the poem, as expressions of "disfigured hope" (60), or, else, as at another point, as cynical simulations of clichéd Black stylings: "But in what does this preservation/ of African American culture consist? It can/hardly consist in anything more than eating/black-style food, listening to black-style music [...]" (71). Asserting "the text is everywhere we turn" in part two of the poem, Williams contributes to a revisionary historiography of Language poetics in its "afterlife."

Born in Detroit, Michigan, where he would go on to earn three degrees in English at Wayne State, including the PhD in 1990 for a dissertation on "Open and Closed forms in 20th Century American Poetics," and, beginning in 1987, a literature professor at Xavier in Cincinnati before accepting a distinguished chair position at SUNY Buffalo after decades of service at the Ohio Jesuit institution, Williams, as noted, has published his first poetry book with the distinguished Bay Area independent press Krupskaya in 2002. By publishing with Krupskaya, Williams is connecting his experience as an urban male African American Midwestern author and teacher with a Bay Area cultural movement from the 1970s that critics have taken to task for racial insensitivity. Cathy Park Hong, for example, regards Language writing as part of an avant-garde that has been antithetical to identity politics to the point of insensitivity to the roles race, class, gender, and ethnicity play in the composition of a cultural imaginary that Language writers wished to upend through linguistic defamiliarization.[8] A translational rereading of Bay Area Language writing

---

8 In the *Denver Quarterly* interview with Joshua Marie Wilkinson, Williams reflects on his working-class roots and penchant for experimental writing in Detroit:

> I grew up in a working-class family—my dad worked in all three of the plants (Chrysler, Ford, GM) before driving a truck for a distilled water company; my mother was, for a while, a housecleaner in a home for retired women (all white) before she began working in the public schools–and I had a number of service jobs

history, *c.c.* shares affinities with recent writing by Lyn Hejinian, who in "En Face" (2015) recalls the lacunae of race "back in the era of the long becoming of the Language writing movement" from about 1975 to 1990. Acknowledging the importance of writers of color including Lorenzo Thomas, Erica Hunt, and Harryette Mullen, Hejinian admits, "we [white Bay Area Language poets] thought and talked well about power structures, gender, capitalism, imperialism, and we spoke very little, if at all, about race." One could say Williams's volume serves as an announcement—his "calling card"—of his arrival Out West as a bona fide "difficult" poet. He is identifying, after all, with a publisher known for releasing books by (paradoxically) well-established language-oriented white authors such as Judith Goldman, Kevin Killian, Rob Halpern, and Laura Moriarity.[9] Williams's writing calls back to a racialized past in poems such as "Study of a Negro Head," but also to a prior historicizing that imagined Language-oriented writing as race-blind. His poetics recover the fact that Language writing is, and has always been, inflected by an African American aesthetics that preceded it. As Hejinian now acknowledges, Black Arts Movement poets influenced her work, as did authors such as Zora Neale Hurston, who, Hejinian notes, understood signifying in "Some Characteristics of Negro Expression" (1934), "as a fundamental strategy for innovative and subversive language practices and first brought some of its usages to the attention of white readers."[10] In her belated recovery of African American contri-

---

(shoe salesman, grocery store clerk, etc.). My Detroit is labor intensive in every sense of the phrase. So it's safe to say that my poetry, though it has changed over the years, has perhaps become more complex (though I was writing "experimental" poems under the influence of the Cass Corridor radical/post-hippie scene around Wayne State long before I'd heard of avant-garde movements like the Language Poets), is informed by a working-class/labor ethos.

9 As his first book of poems, *c.c.* represents Williams's entrance into the situation of the publicized self as a posthumous authorial trace. We may think of the authorial self in *c.c.* as wearing a death mask or as the subject of a defacement, to use Paul de Man's term from his essay "Autobiography as Defacement."

10 In an interview with Joshua Marie Wilkinson, Williams notes that he was, from an early age, attracted to the Black Arts Movement and to becoming a "grammarian" of the "English Language." Williams states:

I've always been fascinated—since the age of 13—with the Black Arts Movement and some of its practitioners who insist/remind us that we always speak the language of those who kidnapped and enslaved us. At the same time, this "we" is crucial to my sense of our historicity, the obvious fact that "I" and everyone I

butions to Bay Area Language poetry, Hejinian, in 2015, attempts an act of ideological desublimation. Writing four decades after her initial contributions to the movement, her goal is to make apparent that which was always already there, but hidden from view: "it wasn't because it [that is, 'Black American linguistic innovation'] wasn't there." Like Hejinian, Williams revisions the Language movement by publishing with a Bay Area press in 2002. He is involved with the African and African American traditions defined by Hurston in 1934 and Henry Louis Gates in 1988 as "signifying"—"formal revision that is at all points double-voiced" (Gates 26).[11] Williams's poetics are doubles in the dizzying array of multiple senses that includes an indeterminate relationship between voicing and texting (Gates's "Talking Book" as "the fundamental repeated trope of the black tradition" [45]).

Given that Williams challenges associations of Bay Area experimentalism with whiteness via the photograph of the African American male figure on the front cover of *c.c.*, what to make of the fact that two white avant-gardists, Susan Howe and Nathaniel Tarn, endorse the book on the back cover? Howe's blurb mentions that Williams "explores the boundaries between poetry, politics, and history." She leaves out the fact that Williams is a Black man or that race is an overt issue in *c.c.* Howe never mentions that *c.c.* deals with South

---

know have only known "this" language. But the gap between what happened to our predecessors/ancestors and the experience of those born in the Western hemisphere is the space of play, of irreverence—I don't "revere" the English language but I use it and, on occasion, abuse it. Having written that, I am a grammarian—I was taught by pre-integration "Negro" teachers who taught what we today call "linguistics" in ordinary English classes in elementary and junior high school. And what I learned from Mrs. Ewing—for example—of the world is that every grammatical marker is purposeful, that every torque of the language renders "meaning" problematic—which seems to me the precise "condition" of African-American existence in particular and "American" life in general.

11 In *The Signifying Monkey*, Gates quotes Bakhtin scholar Gary Saul Morson on the concept of double-voicedness:

The audience of a double-voiced word is therefore meant to hear both a version of the original utterance as the embodiment of its speaker's point of view (or "semantic position") *and* the second speaker's evaluation of that utterance from a different point of view. I find it helpful to picture a double-voiced word as a special sort of palimpsest in which the uppermost inscription is a commentary on the one beneath it, which the reader (or audience) can know only by reading through the commentary that obscures in the very process of evaluating. (Gates, 56)

African Apartheid, quotes a Dunbar poem in which the speaker cannot get his voice across in the poem, and collates "found" passages regarding a "Blonde Negress" at a museum with the first line of "The Dark Brother," a sonnet by Lewis Alexander, which begins, "'Lo, I am black but I am comely too.'" (43). Howe doesn't mention that *c.c.* pays "homage to Ola Mae Quarterman, a black civil right fighter" (95) ("Bottom Left Corner Folded 'In'" (12), "Hayes Williams, one of the first prisoners whose conviction was overturned due to DNA technology" ("Upper Right Corner Folded 'In'" (15), and to Arthur Bell, the first African American dancer with New York City ballet who, at age 71, was found by a social worker, homeless and disoriented in Brooklyn. ("Upper Left Corner Folded 'In'" [13–14], 95). Nor does she note a poem from the graffiti-type "Tag" section that ends the book, which alludes to "Strange Fruit" lynching. Tarn's longer endorsement focuses on Williams's tonal complexity, "formal invention," invocation of "character," and, in a nod to the language of race, claims Williams bridges a gap "above all between African American concerns and those of the plain vanilla majority." Back cover endorsements are not book reviews, much less essays. Nonetheless, Howe's omission of "African American concerns" and Tarn's reading of Williams's work, not as an expression of "African American concerns," but rather as a halfway house—a mediatory "bridge"—between two racially encoded groups, are telling aporias on the book's back cover that suggest the reception troubles Williams's title has anticipated on the front cover. Howe and Tarn regard the relations between "caller" and "called" in *c.c.* as post-race or as an intervention in what Williams refers to as a "calcified" social world in which a "Black" author expresses "concerns" to a "white" audience.

In its absence, Howe's endorsement speaks to the avant-garde erasure of markers of subject position that Williams himself critiques in a *boundary 2* essay from 1995. For Williams, formal inventiveness among African American poets has tended to be "invisible in American Literary History" because the focus has been on "thematic Blackness" (128). Among the exceptions, Williams states, would be Ed Roberson, whose poems such as "Bird's Blake," which references Charlie Parker and William Blake, exist on the "margins" of a Black Arts movement "aesthetic criteria for authenticity" (128). Like Roberson in "First Person," Williams throughout *c.c.* foregrounds what critic Tristram Wolff calls "the feeling of being watched by an outside eye" (553). Beyond "being watched," Williams's thoroughly mediated lyric "I" reflects the poet's reframing of prior texts authored by other hands. Paradoxically, Williams's "authenticity" is the product of his creative refashioning of prior texts. As Wolff notes in his essay on Blake and Roberson, the residue of Romanticism appears in Roberson in what he, Wolff, calls a "coeval" sensibility. By "coeval," Wolff refers to multiple time frames that inhabit the same space. In Williams's case, "coeval" poetics takes the form of hyper-referentiality. "Cold Calls," for example, includes two pages of "End Notes" with 15 citations. References range from poems by Dunbar and Claude McKay to poems by William Wordsworth and Miller Williams to critical texts including Du Bois's *The Souls of Black Folk* and Elaine Scarry's *The Body in Pain* to citations from the *New York Times* science section about how stars form from "surrounding gas clouds" (40). Williams's "coeval" poetics challenges "authenticity," a conception of the relationship between lived experience and representation that Williams complicates, if not rejects. Williams connects Roberson's poetry with language experimentalists and ethnopoets such as Robert Duncan, Jerome Rothenberg, Nathaniel Tarn, Nathaniel Mackey—queer, Jewish, Black authors—who represent "several lines on inquiry" of which the quality of "ethnic/racial authenticity is only one part" (129). Roberson is an important model for Williams in *c.c.* because the poet born in Pittsburgh in 1948 draws on the "limitless possibility in the sign systems, languages and art of any number of Western and non-Western cultures" (129). For Roberson, according to Williams, "Blackness is not a fixed standard (biologically or culturally)" (132–133). As in his reading of Roberson and Erica Hunt, Williams is exploring concepts such as the marginal, the intersectional, the in-between, and a zone of uncertainty in his poetry (133).

Comparable to poetry by Roberson and Hunt, *c.c.* is an avant-gardist project that emphasizes the inextricably intertwined relationships between race and representation. In the section entitled "Called Card," for example, Williams foregrounds the problematic issue of how white Europeans represented and displayed African bodies in poems such as "Study of a Negro Head" and "El Negro." In "Additional Notes," Williams notes that "El Negro," more familiarly "El Negro of Banyoles," is the name given to the stuffed body of an African man displayed in Europe 1916–1917. In 1995 his remains were returned to Gaborone, Botswana. "'Study of a Negro Head' is the title of an Albrecht Durer drawing" (95). The identity of the sitter for "Negro Head" is unknown, but because Durer drew the image in 1508 during the period of the Transatlantic Slave Trade, commentators speculate that Durer may have met his subject when he visited Bellini in Venice, a port city. The Slave Trade tended to benefit Europeans through the importation of raw materials from the Americas, so it remains a mystery where Durer, the German, met his subject.[12]

---

12 http://cghs.dadeschools.net/african-american/europe/durer.htm.

"Study of A Negro Head" is difficult to unpack because it begins with an abstract, self-reflexive, and paradoxical reflection on the relationships between verb forms, language, image, reality, time, and history: "This recalls a future" (33). Refraining from offering a typical ekphrastic translation of images into words, Williams's elaborate attention to how grammar, and especially verb forms and tenses, shape the meaning of Durer's drawing in words, indicates the poet's understanding of writing as a creative response to representations in their "afterlife." The first word in the poem, the pointer, "This," for example, is a slippery term that can function as a pronoun, an adjective, or an adverb. It is especially difficult to decide the referent to "This" in the case of a self-reflexive poem that references a "study" drawn by a German artist around 500 years ago. The "study" itself represents an unknown individual who served Durer as the model for a "type," a racialized categorization of personhood. Is Williams saying "This" poem recalls Durer's drawing as projecting "a future" in which the image of the facial features of a "Negro Head" will be, from the prospective temporal perspective of 1508 used—misused—in subsequent centuries to authorize pseudo-scientific claims to white supremacy?[13] We must remember that Williams's facial portrait adorns the cover of *c.c.* He identifies the Durer image as a precursor to his own: "hand-made, maiden/drawing of my face in 1528" (33). Rendering time as multilayered and multidirectional, "Study of a Negro Head" traffics in retrospection and prophecy. The poem imagines Durer's perspective on the "Negro Head" as a projection of a future work of art (a study toward a finished painting, a version of "The Adoration of the Magi"). We may think of the visual study of a racialized head circa 1500 as a problematic contribution to the cultural imaginary that inaugurated European exploration into the "new world" and increased the Transatlantic Slave Trade that eventually brought Williams's ancestors to the "New World."[14] "This" poem

---

13 One article on the drawing suggests the image may have served as a model for Durer when he drew studies of the Magi for his 1504 oil painting *The Adoration of the Magi*. Since that painting was completed four years before the drawing, I am skeptical about this theory.
14 In *Stony the Road: Reconstruction, White Supremacy, and the Rise of Jim Crow*, Henry Louis Gates notes that in the nineteenth-century era of "racial science" in the United States, pseudo-scientific studies, including those by the then renowned Harvard natural science professor Louis Agassiz, "argued that people of different races were actually of different species" (Gates, 59). Gates notes that Philadelphia doctor Samuel George Morton, in his 1839 book, *Crania Americana; A Comparative Views of the Skulls of Various Aboriginal Nations of North and South America*," used "the shapes and sizes of their skulls" to assign a "ranking of races" with the "Caucasian race at the top" and "Ethiopians, or black people, at the bottom" (Gates, 60).

is, of course, itself a "Study of a Negro Head." The student doing the studying is not Durer 500 years ago, but Williams, calling back to the image from around the year 2000. Williams is a "Negro Head" in the sense that he is an African American contemporary intellectual. He is a reader/viewer who identifies with the "Negro Head" as subject and object. He is reflecting on a reflection of another person ("a Negro Head") by another artist (Durer). Williams devotes the fourth line of his poem to one word: "Indefinite." The word is an adverb for unclear or of "without clear limits," but in a grammatical sense an "indefinite article" is a noun, "the grammatical name for the words 'a' and 'an' in English or words in other languages that have a similar use" (*Cambridge Dictionary* online).

Like other parts of *c.c.*, "Study of a Negro Head" defies straightforward interpretative readings. Nonetheless, when I return Williams's call as an active respondent who pieces together significance from the bricolage of textuality, as well as ponder the implications of the abundant white space that surrounds the wording, a reading (or series of readings) emerges. For example, I wonder about the relation of the word "Indefinite" to Williams's decision to indent the term toward the right margin, leaving about a one-inch space instead of text to the left of the word. The space feels meaningful, even as the meaning is uncertain, "indefinite." The white space can signify as an erasure of language or as the language of erasure. We can read the space as a blanket of white (supremacist) coverage that violates through concealment African American inscriptions that might otherwise contest a racist imaginary. Despite the abundance of negative space, pieces of the archive have found their way into "Study of a Negro Head." Writing exists as mangled trace of prior racialized inscriptions. On a formalist level, Williams's admission of so much negative space may be his nod to affiliation with schools of alternative U.S. modernist and postmodernist poetics such as Olsonian "Open" field as well as an African American poetics in which space may indicate a syncopated jazz beat. The line following "Indefinite" is justified on the left margin, but is cast as a parenthetical aside and in the form of an interrogative: "(forced march? Ticker tape? Brownian?)." Without resorting to Google, I decipher the first two phrases without trouble. Not specifically historicized in the poem, a "forced march" calls to mind the "trail of tears" marches that befell Eastern Woodlands Indians in the Jacksonian era (1830s) as well as the Bataan Death March. What about Brownian? One meaning of Brownian as an adjective for movement would be "Brownian Motion," which, as *Encyclopedia Britannica* reports, refers to "any of various physical phenomena in which some quantity is constantly undergoing small, random fluctuations." The phrase fits Williams's practice of copying "found" material in which "fluctuations" occur through the movement of something from one place to another.¹⁵

c.c. is a titular abbreviation, a metonym for something, but for what? I am not sure, but I am confident there is more than one "what" to unpack. Carbon copy? Pre-email "literal" carbon copy? Email era use of a now defunct, technologically transcended, and yet linguistically preserved term for transmitting the same message to multiple receivers? "Black" author as a "Carbon" (coal-colored) "copy" (mockingbird mimic) of a "white" discourse? "Black" author as a "Carbon" (coal-colored) "copy" of a "black" discourse such as the Black Arts Movement in which Amiri Baraka (then LeRoi Jones) wrote in "Black Art," "We want a black poem. And / a Black World. / Let the world be a Black Poem"?¹⁶ An originary, non-racially marked author of universalist import because, as Wikipedia notes, "Carbon compounds form the basis of all known life on Earth, and the carbon–nitrogen cycle provides some of the energy produced by the Sun and other stars [...] Carbon occurs in all known organic life and is the basis of organic chemistry." A copy of carbon transformed through time from the soft common substance into the hard bright light substance of immense value, the proverbial diamond in the rough? Carbon copy as a sec-

---

15 Brownian Motion "was named for the Scottish botanist Robert Brown, the first to study such fluctuations (1827). If a number of particles subject to Brownian motion are present in a given medium and there is no preferred direction for the random oscillations, then over a period of time the particles will tend to be spread evenly throughout the medium." https://www.britannica.com/science/Brownian-motion

16 According to Dorothy Wang,

> Poems by minority poets are almost always judged on the basis of their thematic (sociological, ethnographic) content in the "traditional" or "mainstream" poetry world and rarely on their formal or aesthetic structures, properties, modes—in other words, what makes poetry poetry and not a memoir or treatise. But the flipside of the same coin is true in the world of "innovative" poetry and poetics, where the "absence" of obvious racial identity is to be applauded—for not exhibiting the hallmarks of "bad" poetry (read: "identity poetry" [read: "minority poetry"])— and this criterion, too, is content-based, albeit in negative form. A poem without any overt ethnic or racial markers is assumed to be racially "unmarked." Little or no attention is paid to how poetic subjectivity, which overlaps with but is not limited to racial subjectivity, might inhere in a poem's language and formal structures—in what is unsaid or unspoken at the level of "content" but manifested through aesthetic (poetic) means. (Wang, *Boston Review* 2015)

http://bostonreview.net/poetry/dorothy-wang-jim-crow-color-blind-poetics

ondary audience? As something overheard? We could keep playing, creating correspondent interactions with the signs in a kind of call-and-response gesture. What comes to our minds? CC Mitch Ryder and the Detroit Wheels? A doubling on Stevens's "Comedian as the Letter C," the serio-comic long meditative lyric invoking Crispin's failed journey South to a tropical landscape to rejuvenate his language and thus transcend his drab New England quotidian life that ends *his* first book, *Harmonium*? The graded marks given by the teacher on the average student's report card? Christopher Columbus?

A term used to define the placement of text in a formal letter after the closing salutation, CC is related to another abbreviation, PS (Post Scriptum; "written after"). The connection between the formulaic procedures followed by letter writers, and Williams's proceduralism in *c.c.* is apparent in his imitation of what he calls, in an interview, "the formal 19th c. greeting card format of four of the poems in c.c." ("Bottom Left Corner Folded 'In'"; "Upper Left Corner Folded 'In'"; "Upper Right Corner Folded 'In'"; "Lower Right Corner Folded 'In'"). Given what I noted earlier about Williams's poetics as a translational form of literary afterlife, it is useful to think about *c.c.* as a complex rendering of a text "written after." Williams suggests this reading of *c.c.* through his decision to assign his volume's epigraph to Emily Dickinson's concluding epistolary remarks (and tombstone engraving): "Called back.//Emily//--May 1886".[17] As Craig Dworkin remarks, *c.c.* is, on a formal level, at points a carbon copy without an original, or a copy with an erased original. A 15-page section of *c.c.*, "Cold Calls," as Dworkin notes, features "appropriated, collaged, and recontextualized language *as* a citational system of footnotes hugging the bottom of the page and referencing endnotes" (11–12). As with much else in *c.c.*, it is a fool's errand to summarize, paraphrase, or read "Cold Calls" as if it were a mimetic poem with transparent meaning. That said, we notice patterns in

---

17 On Emily Dickinson's tombstone, rather than *died* or *returned to the Lord* or *left this world*, it reads: CALLED BACK.

Emily Dickinson
Born
December 10, 1830
Called Back
May 15, 1886

As those two words were the last she wrote, in a letter to her cousins, but also the title of a novella she loved by Hugh Conway. See Casey N Cep's "Called Back." https://www.theparisreview.org/blog/2013/10/30/called-back/

the citational materials. For example, the first "footnote" poem—at the bottom of the otherwise empty page 39—quotes from a passage about the topic of "spatial/temporal lacuna" as related to "temporary disruption" or "permanent abortion—of service," and then shifts to "an example of such disruption, failure, and breakdown" in Dunbar's "Ships That Pass in the Night." Dunbar, at times, wrote in a vernacular style and, at times, in a style reminiscent of traditional European lyricism complete with iambic pentameter metrics. "Ships That Pass in the Night" is of the latter sort. Dunbar's poem thus "mimics" a white-encoded poetics, but the content of "Ships" comments on the spectral quality of a voice that does not maintain vitality and connection to an authorial embodiment. "Voice" is transferred through a "vessel" that we may compare to the poetic artifice itself: "My voice falls dead a foot from mine old lips/ and but its ghost doth reach that vessel/passing, passing." Taken together, the "footnote" emphasizes the relation between images and words, as well as pre-established structures of representation and the failure of the form to enact the speaker's desire for self-expression.

The first "footnote" poem in "Cold Calls" recalls Williams's focus on the disrupted relationship between image (the cover photograph of the poet) and reader expectations for a style of writing that will serve as a narrative caption to authorial experience as "voice." The third "footnote" poem, about racial violence and South African apartheid, includes bits of a news report involving a "foreign respondent," a description recalling Williams's interest in calling and returning calls through correspondence. Chopped up into a rush of headline passages gleaned from the *New York Times* and separated, à la Dickinson, by dashes, the poem alludes to the 1993 gang murder of Amy Biehl, a white Stanford-educated Fulbright recipient who served in Cape Town as an anti-Apartheid activist. In a terrible irony, "a crowd of [black] youths" shot Biehl to death as an act of revolutionary violence. The footnote to the poem states the murder contributed to the end of apartheid: "South Africa is free today because of the bloodshed," according to a quotation linked in the "End Notes" section to the *New York Times*. The footnote is indeed a "cold call." It offers a "cold"—in the sense of extreme emotional restraint to the point of heartlessness—recollection of a brutal murder that may, from the perspective of Realpolitik, have helped dismantle South African apartheid. Williams's rendering is also "cold" in the sense that the writing seems uninflected, objective, a recording of facts about one incident that contributed to the history of a racist system and, potentially, its undoing. How does this "cold call" about the murder of a Bay Area-educated white female activist, mistaken by young African males to be supporting apartheid, relate to Williams's investigation of interracial politics in avant-garde poetics? We noted that in the Dunbar poem, a Black poet experiences the loss of voice through mimicry of a white style. Here I turn to Harryette Mullen's invocation of the term "aesthetic apartheid" in her response to Ron Silliman's "Poetry and the Politics of the Subject" (*Socialist Review*, 1988). As Randall Couch reports, Silliman argues that "women, people of color, sexual minorities, the entire spectrum of the 'marginal'—have a manifest political need to have their stories told" in a more conventional form than those progressive poets who identify as members of groups that have been "the subject of history" (65). Mullen regarded such a cordoned-off version of avant-gardism as "aesthetic apartheid": "Ron Silliman did us all a favor," she has said, "when he articulated what I consider a productive tension between content and form, between identity and innovation."[18]

The two "footnote" poems from "Cold Calls" I have described so far deal with racial conflict and disfigurement. Other "footnote" poems are not so obviously about race, and are not about race or racism at all. One "footnote" poem, for example, refers to the September 11, 2001 attacks on the World Trade Center. The poem offers the perspective of terrorists, who view the passengers on the jet that crashed into the towers as "sinful" (51). The poem also offers the viewpoint of Christians who read the tragedy as a religious apotheosis: "Crashing into a skyscraper, a Boeing jet 'disgorged its sinful passengers'" and "from which their spirits 'floated upwards towards a glowing image of Jesus high in the clouds'" (51). "Footnote" poem four, again not focused on African American experience, collates imagery from Wallace Stevens, John Keats, Homer, Beckett, and the tales of Scheherazade's "thousand-plus deferents" with references to the economics of credit lines and "bulk mailings." The "intent" of this poem, I argue, is to imagine the roles of hope, longing, and patience as venerable aspects of how culture and economics function, grow, and sustain themselves in the face of cessation. We think of the image of Penelope weaving and unweaving Odysseus's shroud to ward off the suitors in Ithaca. We recall the constant jabbering of the bums Vladimir and Estragon

---

18 As Randall Couch reports, Mullen "is committed to working, in Duke Ellington's phrase, 'beyond category;' to continually 'rewriting and revising' identity; and to 'overcoming 'aesthetic apartheid' and cultural difference' (Kane)." See Randall Couch: "A Eurydice beyond my maestro: Triangular desire in Harryette Mullen's "Dim Lady" https://www.asu.edu/pipercwcenter/how2journal/archive/online_archive/v2_4_2006 /current/in_conference/couch.html and Daniel Kane. "Poets on Poetry: Daniel Kane Interviews the Poet Harryette Mullen." *Teachers & Writers – Poets Chat* June-July 2002

as they wait for Godot. As in *Godot*, Williams has sent out his calling cards, has made his cold calls, in writing *c.c.* He has thus expressed a desire for communication, for connection with an audience of readers. In an entrepreneurial sense, he has invested in the possibility of a return on his bulk mailings.[19]

If we regard c.c. as an abbreviation for carbon copy, we are inclined to ask about the relationship of an original work to a copy of that same work? We must historicize the topic. Neoclassical poets in the English tradition such as Alexander Pope understood the art of copying a masterwork as a test of skill and a healthy nod to traditional masters. In the twentieth-century era of copyright law and the cult of artistic originality, by contrast, copying is an area of aesthetics interrogated by experimental visual artists ranging from Marcel Duchamp to Sherrie Levine. Their goal is to challenge legal definitions of authorship and ownership of representations, as well as to interrogate the commodification of creative expression in an art world in which symbolic capital translates into serious green in late capitalism. A key point that Gates makes about signifying in his classic study, and that Williams demonstrates in his essay on conceptualism and radical mimesis, is that, in a Derridean sense, there is a difference in the same when a writer or artist copies an "original." In an interview, Williams remembers Mrs. Ewing. She was a linguistics-oriented "pre-integration 'Negro'" teacher from whom he learned "every grammatical marker is purposeful" and that "every torque of the language renders 'meaning' problematic." He notes that her teaching is related to the "'condition' of African American existence in particular" and "American life in general." *c.c.* indicates that Williams paid deep and abiding attention to the lessons Mrs. Ewing taught at Durfee Junior High School.[20] In the essay on "Radical Mimesis," Williams uses the term—"torque"—that he learned from Mrs. Ewing to describe how Phyllis Wheatley, the first African American and among the first women to publish a book of poems in North America,

---

19 According to Wikipedia: "Amy Elizabeth Biehl (April 26, 1967 – August 25, 1993) was an American graduate of Stanford University and an Anti-Apartheid activist in South Africa who was murdered by Cape Town residents while a black mob shouted anti-white slurs. The four men convicted of her murder were pardoned by the Truth and Reconciliation Commission." en.wikipedia.org/wiki/Amy_Biehl

20 According to the *Detroit Free Press,* Durfree was slated for closure in 2017 because of poor performance: "More than 120 schools were on the state's 2015 list of Michigan's bottom 5% of schools, including 47 schools in the Detroit district. Durfee has been on the list since 2014. "*Detroit's Durfee school to shut as district, state debate closure list.*" Ann Zaniewski, *Detroit Free Press.* Jan. 5, 2017

expressed difference through emulation in *Poems on Various Subjects, Religious and Moral* (1773). Describing Wheatley as a precursor to the "Mockingbird" school of African American female poets such as Georgia Douglas Johnson, Williams writes of Wheatley's "On Being Brought from Africa to America":

> I believe that it is possible to argue that mimesis, as deployed by certain artists, at certain moments, did serve to critique hegemonic cultural values. [...] Wheatley relies on her ability to manipulate grammar and syntax to turn the tables on her Christian enslavers. She torques the language and grammar of her benefactors to create a space for an African subjectivity presumed to have been fully suppressed by her enslavement and subsequent exposure to "good" values.

In his essay on radical mimicry, Williams argues that we cannot separate the meaning of copying from the evolving literary-historical contexts in which the writer or artist makes the copy.[21] Writing in the wake of Duchampian concep-

---

21 In the following passages from "Radical Mimicry," Williams locates Wheatley's poetry at a transitional moment in the history of literary emulation:

> Thus Africans capable of reading and writing in European languages had to concern themselves with questions of the optical and linguistic vis-a-vis the readymade, that is, vis-à-vis the African body. To wit: despite her visual appearance as an African, a readymade presumed inured to nurture, to learning (as opposed to mimicry), Wheatley proved herself able to overcome the handicap of the optical, and thus her "nature," by emulating in writing the English poetics of the 18th c. So baffling was her achievement, the shock of the new to 18th c. Bostonians, Wheatley had to undergo an oral defense of her work before eighteen esteemed gentlemen of the city. In what sense, however, can I claim that her poems, however novel, registered protest? In what sense can some of her poems be understood as enacting torqued mimicry or radical mimesis?
>
> Mimicry of the European in form, mode and apparent "message" was believed to be the best proof that the interior life of the African was not an effect of the exterior, debased sign of the skin. But mimicry, as imitation, was already on the wane as a positive aesthetic value in the 18th c. as the doctrine of originality, intimately connected with the social, cultural, and political revolutions in Europe and its various colonies, began to seize hold of the European imagination. It is this value that Jefferson deploys to

tualism and in the midst of Goldsmithian uncreative writing, which troubles legal definitions of intellectual property rights, Williams is playing with the idea of carbon copying as a form of ludic subversive activity. Williams, however, is claiming a special meaning for the art of the copy in the context of African American signifying practices.

In *c.c.*, Williams's "carbon copy" poetry negotiates unstable relations between repetition and alteration in a process that simultaneously preserves the "original" (the historical "foundational" text) and erases its prior meanings through the replacement copy. In "The Work of Art in the Age of Mechanical Reproduction" (1935), Benjamin famously suggested the art copy lost the "aura" of the original. He viewed the loss of "aura" in positive terms. In the age of the aura, the viewer received art independently, as a form of distanced contemplation of a ritualized work. Without the aura, art reception becomes a form of communitarian immersion that occurs, for example, when we go to the movie theater to catch a flick. One needs, as does Williams, to recognize, as Benjamin did not, that works by a replicator such as Sherrie Levine, in "carbon copy" works such as "After Walker Evans" (1981), themselves take on the "aura" of originality through the historical context of art world theory. Repetitions become valuable, ironically "original," conceptual projects. Williams has engaged with conceptualism in an article on "radical mimesis," a term coined by Judith Goldman, an author associated with Krupskaya Press. Whereas Duchamp and Levine put forward "readymades" or copies of prior artworks to expose the relation of the art market to commodity capitalism, Williams engages with the art of the copy to interrogate how African Americans have been misrepresented in prior art and writing:

> While the debate within these conceptual fields turns on the relationships among the optical, the readymade and language, I want to widen the scope of Goldman's argument by demonstrating how the concerns of conceptualism in general, that is, in the plastic, visual and verbal arts, are analogous to the concerns of some Negro, colored, and even black writers from the 18th to the mid-20th century in the United States, not as conceptual

---

disparage Wheatley. As applied to the writing of Africans, free or enslaved, originality was tantamount to another revolution, as destabilizing to the European world view as the Copernican one, since it implied that African and European subjectivity might be indistinguishable from one another.

aesthetic issues per se but as flawed and inadequate "representations" of the African human.

In his essay on radical mimesis, Williams notes the racist attitudes towards Phyllis Wheatley held by "Enlightenment" thinkers such as Thomas Jefferson. Jefferson claimed that Wheatley's poetic "mimicry" of "white" styles was the exception that proved the rule that African Americans in general were inferior beings who lacked creative imagination and mental powers.

From the point of view of European descendants unable to fathom the possibility of subjectivity on the part of Africans, the African who spoke English "well" may have been a novelty, capable of mimicry, but the African capable of writing English well was, by definition, a protest novelty. Whereas the ability to speak English could be, and often was, attributed to the propensity for "imitation" among Africans (connected to their "innate" talent for music and dance), the ability to write English suggested the ability to reason and think, that is, to forge original thoughts. The demonstration of these skills thus offered a counterargument to, a protest against, the general belief that Africans were incapable of the reasoning attributed to Mongoloids and Caucasians.

"Happy Fault," the first poem in the sequence entitled "Carded," Williams tells us in "Additional Notes," is "dedicated to Phyllis Wheatley." (95).

Like other sections of *c.c.*, "Happy Fault" resists paraphrase or easy interpretation.[22] Nonetheless, the poem suggests how ideological control of the subject takes place when one is "called" by another who possesses a greater degree of state power, such as when a police officer shouts, "hey you!" The speaker of "Happy Fault" is responding to a call, a knock at the door, or a telephone call. (Published in 2002, Williams wrote "Happy Fault" when people still used landlines, not cell phones). "Happy Fault" begins: "Who was it/Was it for me,/you, or some/misnomer,/wrongly called" (21). In the next movement of the poem, however, it is difficult to know exactly who is speaking and to whom.

---

22 According to Brian Kelly in Catholicism.Org: "Happy Fault" refers to the "Church's prayer "O Felix Culpa" (O Happy Fault) which is sung within the *Exultet* (otherwise called the Paschal Proclamation) during the Easter Vigil service. "O Happy Fault that merited such and so great a Redeemer!" What I had passed over thoughtlessly, however, was the previous verse of the hymn: "O truly necessary sin of Adam, which the death of Christ has blotted out!" *"O happy fault that earned for us so great, so glorious a Redeemer."* – St. Augustine.

Williams does not link the general pronouns such as "who," "you," and "me" to any specific names or characters. Instead, he recalls a scene of violence against a speaker, disabling speech: "tongue torn out,/favoring a hand?" I think of the story of the Rape of Philomel by Thracian King Tereus as told in Ovid's *Metamorphosis* and retold in Eliot's "The Waste Land." In the Philomel narrative, a politically empowered male cuts off the tongue of the female rape victim to deny her speech, and thus testimony. Unable to announce the rape through speaking, however, she weaves the story into a tapestry. A story associated with the origins of female creativity as related to the aftermath of physical trauma and the blockage of speech, we may link the Philomel story to Wheatley's poetics. Like Philomel in the sense that she did not feel she could speak directly about her oppression, even in her poetry, Wheatley needed to express protest indirectly, through "mockingbird mimicry."

As in "Study of A Negro Head," in which future and past merge as the speaker reflects on a Durer drawing that, he notes, may resemble his own appearance, "Happy Fault" begins as a response to a prior call. As "Happy Fault" progresses, however, the one "who beckons" is aligned with a potential version of the speaker of the poem as a "future 'I'" (21). Williams selects the future-perfect form (indicating completed action) to describe the paradoxical sense that the precursor has already arrived, and, paradoxically, is still on his way to arrival—"Who will have/arrived"—but the self that arrives is in imperfect form—limping, "belated, 'off-line'" (21). The last part of "Happy Fault" returns to the opening query about the identity of the caller. The focus shifts, however, from an interpretation of "called" as referring to the person who has beckoned the speaker to a reading of "called" as meaning "referring to" someone or something as if that someone or something were something else. In this case, the speaker is wondering about who "called" into being ("referred to") a chain of referents: "'Christians, Negroes,' 'Negroes, black as Cain,' but Cain,/ nothing but Cain/with impunity?" (22). The speaker is asking tough questions about the relationships between African Americans to aspects of Judeo-Christianity. He is asking how the chain of associations between "Christians" and "Negroes" has devolved into an association of "Negroes" with "nothing but Cain," the Old Testament biblical figure associated with banishment, marking, and fratricide.

Williams himself deciphers "c.c." as the abbreviation for titles to three of the five sections in the volume: "Calling Cards," "Called Card," and "Cold Calls." These phrases are themselves common, if outdated, vernacular expressions associated with business or social communication, but they also remind us of Althusser's theory of how the state produces subjects through authoritative beckoning. As in signifying practices defined by Hurston and Gates, the three section titles suggest how both readers and writers respond to the call of language as a form of the afterlife by expressing a willingness to call back in creative response to prior representations. Poetry is a meeting place between reader and writer, but the location for this meeting in *c.c.* is uncertain. The relation between material text and semantic meaning is unstable, but Williams deciphers *c.c.* through a section title that refers to a telephone salesperson engaging in a commercial transaction with a stranger ("Cold Call"). Another section— "calling card"—may suggest a material sign to express the prior appearance of a visitor who, now absent, has left a trace of an attempt to meet another person, then absent. The card serves as a trace of a desire for a future meeting between two absented persons. The titular abbreviation c.c. suggests an analogy between the publication of the first book of poems and/as an author's Calling Card. If Williams is likening an old-fashioned "calling card" to a twenty-first-century publication of a physical book of poems put out by a small independent press (in this case, Krupskaya), then he is, by analogy, suggesting the physical object he has produced is already a trace of an atavistic mediation of intersubjectivity. No doubt, calling cards (as a method to prepay long-distance telephone calls) and print volumes of poetry still exist, but they recall, nostalgically, critically, an earlier moment in the communication arts.[23] In *c.c.*,

---

[23] I associate Calling Cards in the United States with a segregated genteel society, as described in this commentary on the history of the form from the American Stationery website:

> A society woman's calling card "follows her everywhere she goes, remains when she is gone, and is the recognized representative in the payment of social debts when personal attention is impossible." Gentlemen and children also dropped visiting cards along with these "ladies of fashion," primarily in the 18th through the early 20th centuries.
>
> Calling or visiting cards first employed in 15th century China and later used by the aristocracy of 17th century became popular with England's nobility and rich in the 1800s. The cards served a number of social purposes, such as a means of introduction, to further acquaintanceship, to express congratulations or condolences, and to provide notices of arrival or departure. Card etiquette had strict rules.
>
> Generally, the bearer waited in a carriage, enlisting a servant to deliver the calling card. The bearer folded a corner if delivering the card in person.

Williams sends out a kind of calling card, but he also explores the idea of being "Carded," the title of the second section of the book. We regard the act of being "carded" as a threatening activity if read, for example, in the context of the "Black Lives Matter" movement, or the current situation of immigrants from Central America and Mexico at the Southern border of the United States. In both cases, being "Carded," or a "routine" identification check performed by a government official, could endanger the safety, freedom, and welfare of a person who "looks like" the person photographed on the cover of "c.c." Brook Tankle's sepia-toned black-and-white cover photograph depicts Williams staring at the camera. What is notable to me is that the copy of the author photograph selected for the cover looks like it has been mistreated. Crumpled, scratched, and marred, someone deliberately folded the copy of Williams's image into four identification card-sized quadrants. The white crease marks create a cross shape in which the vertical and diagonal quadrants meet at the poet's left nostril. The meaning of the white cross crease is uncertain, but it appears to me as if Tyrone is in the crosshairs of a rifle's scope. Alternatively, the cross suggests a religious symbol. Given the history of Ku Klux Klan cross burnings, however, the cross as a religious symbol connects back to the sense that Williams notes the danger in racialized representation. Tankle has lit the photograph so that the left side of Williams's face is much lighter in tone than the right half, which is very dark and shadowy. Because Williams foregrounds the relationship between image and identity in poetic sequences such as "Calling Card," I surmise he is noting how hue—and especially dark versus light—impacts how viewers interpret the person—the face—within a racialized environment. In

---

This first call rarely resulted in a face-to-face meeting as the conveyor generally expected to deliver the item to a servant and leave. Stringent rules prevented awkward situations. Socialites desiring a relationship with a particular person or family dropped off a card and returned home. The receiver replied with their own card in a few days, inviting the initiator back for an in-person visit. If the aspiring socialite received the answering card sealed in an envelope or did not receive a return card, it meant to maintain social distance.

https://www.americanstationery.com/blog/the-history-of-the-calling-card/
For Williams, "calling cards" are no longer a material part of a feminized parlor game played in the United States by white aristocrats, and often performed by their Black servants, who were following strict protocols of behavior in delivering, receiving, and responding (or delaying a response) to the card exchange.

"Face *Qua* Flash Card," a conceptual "found" poem in the "Carded" sequence, Williams investigates how persons are marked according to stereotypical categories of language use and appearance. Splayed out on the page with ample amounts of white space separating the segments of the poem from one another, "Face *Qua* Flash Card" represents a defamiliarized array of racialized, class-based, and, in general, prejudicial observational phrases. A bottom note links the phrases to a "State Department/Customs/INS Key" for evaluating (and rejecting based on appearance) potential immigrants at a border or airport: "slimy looking," "wears jacket on shoulders w/earring," "no way [...] poor, poor, poor," "avoids eye contact," "smells" (24). Spread out in a jagged manner around the middle and right part of the page are names associated with Asian, Middle Eastern, Hispanic, and Indian groups: "Mohammed/Wong/Miguel/Swami/Chang." There are also five uppercase abbreviations that, a note at the bottom of the page tells us, relate to INS code for "rich kid," "looks poor," "talks poor," "looks rough," and "take care." "Face *Qua* Flash Card" appears in the "Carded" section of a book titled "c.c.," which may stand for "calling card." The book cover, as noted, includes an author photograph. When taken together, all these aspects of the poem's context suggest that Williams is exploring relationships between image, identity, and coded interpretations (including racist, classist, and xenophobic) of "types." His poetry engages, often in ludic, punning, parodic ways that signify, in Gates's sense, and unsettle, the "looks" and speech practices that are, in "Face *Qua* Flash Card" stereotypically pejorative elements of a racist imaginary.

In the essay on "The Authenticity of Difference" in African American poetics, Williams examines the uneasy relationship between author photographs and poetry texts that, he claims, may serve as "captions" for the visual depiction of the poet. In his essay, Williams pays special attention to the relationships (or lack of relationships) between author photographs, endorsement "blurbs," and the poems within the volume. Williams advocates for "de-captioning textuality," by which he means he does not want the poem, and especially the traditional autobiographical narrative poem, to serve the "normative function" of a "caption" in relation to the author photo (134). He favors a poetry such as Hunt's that exists "within and outside constituted identities" (135).

> Still, one could ask if the narrative/lyrical traditions in which [Elizabeth] Alexander, [Natasha] Trethewey, and Rita Dove work do not reduce their texts to captions, a nonpejorative utility if one writes in order to make oneself visible. For the consequence of writing in a way that

de-captions textuality, that separates it from its normative functions as caption or blurb, is precisely invisibility. (134)

In his 2015 essay, Williams focuses on the problematic relationships between author image, narrative visibility, and poetry texts as "captions." His commentary indicates his concern with a text's availability to be "automatically assimilated to ethnic, racial, or even gender-based politics" (134). *c.c.*, ironically, foregrounds Williams's photographic image, not in a small square the size of a driver's license picture on the back flap, but rather on the front cover and of the size that occupies the cover's space. This photograph is in your face.

Taken together, *c.c.*, the book title, and the front cover image of Williams represents provocative, even contradictory, gateways into the difficult text that follows. I use the adjective "difficult" to describe Williams's poetry in the way Bernstein does in *Attack of the Difficult Poems (*2011), as the site of potential reader anxiety that, Bernstein advises, tongue in cheek, may be overcome with due diligence on the reader's part: "Don't let the poem intimidate you! Often the difficult poem will provoke you, but this may be its way of getting your attention" (5). Bernstein's kidding aside, I have treated my difficulties in reading *c.c.* as a crucial element of my response to Williams's poetics. Rather than withdrawing from attending closely to the text because of its challenges to immediate intelligibility, I regard difficulty as itself a meaningful aspect of my experience of *c.c.* I also find myself thinking about Bernstein's comments on the "difficult poem" as "an unusual problem" in a racialized context even as Williams's poetry, like that of Erica Hunt, functions "within and outside constituted identities."

For Bernstein, "difficult" poems are problems. For Du Bois, an existential crisis for Black Folks was not *having* problems, but *being* a problem. We recall Du Bois's comments from *The Souls of Black Folks*: "Herein lie buried many things which if read with patience may show the strange meaning of being black here in the dawning of the Twentieth Century. This meaning is not without interest to you, Gentle Reader; for the problem of the Twentieth Century is the problem of the color-line." Parodying an infomercial discourse on how to treat a disease or affliction with a salve, pill, cream, or medical procedure, Bernstein treats difficult poems as a source of reader anxiety and a way for the author to get "your attention." "So the first step in dealing with the difficult poem is to recognize that this is a common problem that many other readers confront on a daily basis. You are not alone!" (4). Symptoms of difficulty include "elevated linguistic intensity; textual irregularities; initial withdrawal (poem not immediately available); poor adaptability (poem unsuitable for use in love letters, memorial commemoration, etc.); sensory overload; or negative mood" (4). How does a reading of a difficult poem as source of reader "intimidation" and as an attention-getting device function in the context of "difficult" poetry by Tyrone Williams, a "Black male author from Detroit," who courts and resists association of his writing with his subject position?

On his website *Heretofore*, Williams displays a small-c catholicity in his enumeration of musical tastes and influences. Prominent "COMPOSERS and ARRANGERS" include African American jazz and soul stylists ranging from Ellington and Strayhorn to Miles and Sonny to Stevie and Smokey Robinson. Williams varies his selections in terms of genre, but his choices are mainstream when compared to free jazz experimentalists such as Anthony Braxton, Sun Ra, Ornette Coleman, and Roland Kirk, none of whom make the list. When it comes to the contemporary avant-garde, we find British electronica figure Brian Eno and punk rocker Joe Strummer from The Clash. Alternative white female folkies such as Maggie Roche and Katie McGarrigle make the list. Most striking to me is Williams's emphasis on white male composers associated with the Great American Songbook and Broadway: Leonard Bernstein, Hoagy Carmichael, Harold Arlen, Cole Porter, and Burt Bacharach and Hal David. These composers produced numbers for the stage that African American jazz legends such as John Coltrane, Sarah Vaughan, Louis Armstrong, Ella Fitzgerald, and Carmen McRae reimagined as syncopated standards. As with Coltrane, Vaughan, and the others I have mentioned, signifying on traditional texts is most certainly a part of Williams's modus operandi. Williams's list of musical influences helps me think about how to read the "difficult" poetry in *c.c.* In the end, I read his poetry as a form of resistance to stereotypical identifications of his writing with a reductive understanding of his subject position. *c.c.* is and is not connected to the cover image.

Works Cited

Walter Benjamin. "The Work of Art in the Age of Mechanical Reproduction." In *Illuminations: Essays and Reflections,* edited by Hannah Arendt, translated by Harry Zohn. New York: Mariner Books, 2019.
Charles Bernstein. "The Attack of the Difficult Poem." In *Attack of the Difficult Poem.* Chicago: University of Chicago Press, 2011.
David Bromwich. *How Words Make Things Happen.* Oxford University Press, 2019.
Casey N. Cep. "Called Back." *Paris Review.* October 30, 2013. https://www.theparisreview.org/blog/2013/10/30/called-back/
Edmund Chapman. *Afterlives: Benjamin, Derrida, and Literature in Translation.* A thesis submitted to the University of Manchester for the degree of Doctor of Philosophy in the Faculty of Humanities, 2016.

Randall Couch. "A Eurydice beyond my Maestro: Triangular Desire in Harryette Mullen's 'Dim Lady.'" https://www.asu.edu/pipercwcenter/how2journal/archive/online_archive/v2_4_2006/current/in_conference/couch.html

Allison Cummings. "Race and the Critical Reception of Gwendolyn Brooks, Erica Hunt, and Harryette Mullen." *Frontiers: A Journal of Women Studies* 26, no. 2 (2005): 3–36.

Paul de Man. "Autobiography as Defacement." In *The Rhetoric of Romanticism*. New York: Columbia University Press, 1984.

W.E.B. Du Bois. *The Souls of Black Folks*. 1903. New York: Bantam Classics; Bantam Classics edition, 1988.

Craig Dworkin. "Textual Prostheses." *Contemporary Literature* 57, no. 1 (Winter 2005).

Henry Louis Gates. *The Signifying Monkey: A Theory of African American Literary Criticism*. New York: Oxford University Press, 1988 [Reissued 2014].

———. *Stony the Road: Reconstruction, White Supremacy, and the Rise of Jim Crow*. New York: Penguin, 2019.

Lyn Hejinian. "En Face." *The Boston Review*. 2015.

Grant Jenkins. "Feeding the Gods: An Interview with Harryette Mullen." *Rain Taxi* 10, no. 3 (Fall 2005).

Daniel Kane. "Poets on Poetry: Daniel Kane Interviews the Poet Harryette Mullen." *Teachers & Writers – Poets Chat*. June–July 2002. http://www.writenet.org/poetschat/poetschat_h_mullen.html

Harryette Mullen. "Poetry and Identity." In *Telling It Slant: Avant-Garde Poetics of the 1990s*, edited by Mark Wallace and Steven Marks. University of Alabama Press, 2002, pp. 27–31. 446 (book article).

Aldon Lynn Nielsen. *Black Chant: Languages of African-American Postmodernism*. Cambridge University Press, 1997.

———. "Black Deconstruction: Russell Atkins and the Reconstruction of African-American Criticism." *Diacritics: A Review of Contemporary Criticism* 26, no. 3–4 (1996): 86–103.

Cathy Park Hong. "Delusions of Whiteness in the Avant-garde." *Lana Turner*. No. 7 November 3, 2014.

Kathy Lou Schultz. "Rock and a Hard Place: Erica Hunt and the Poetics of African-American Postmodernity." *How2*. Vol 1. No. 5 March 2001. https://www.asu.edu/pipercwcenter/how2journal/archive/online_archive/v1_5_2001/current/index.html

Ron Silliman. "Poetry and the Politics of the Subject." *Socialist Review*. July–September 1988.

"The History of the Calling Card." https://www.americanstationery.com/blog/the-history-of-the-calling-card/

Lorenzo Thomas. *Extraordinary Measures: Afrocentric Modernism and Twentieth-Century American Poetry*. University of Alabama Press, 2000.

Dorothy Wang. "From Jim-Crow to 'Color-Blind' Poetics." *Boston Review*. 2015. http://bostonreview.net/poetry/dorothy-wang-jim-crow-color-blind-poetics

Joshua Marie Wilkinson. "Interview with Tyrone Williams." *The Denver Quarterly*. Accessed via *Omnidawn* April 12, 2009.

Tyrone Williams. *c.c.* San Fran.: Krupskaya, 2002.

———. "The Authenticity of Difference as 'Curious Thing[s]': Carl Phillips, Ed Roberson, and Erica Hunt." *boundary 2* 42, no. 4 (2015).

———. "The Radical and Bourgeois Leftism of Harold Cruse." In *Black Writers and the Left*, edited by Kristin Moriah. Cambridge Scholars Publishing, 2013.

———. "Radical Mimesis: Conceptual Dialectics and the African Diaspora." *Omniverse*. http://omniverse.us/tyrone-williams-radical-mimesis/ This paper was given at the Celebrating African American Literature conference at Penn State, October 26, 2013.

Tristram Wolff. "Being Several: Reading Blake with Ed Roberson." *New Literary History* 49 #4 (Autumn 2018): 553–578.

John Yau. "'Purity' and the Avant-Garde." *The Boston Review*. 2015.

CHAPTER 8

AN INTERVIEW WITH PATRICK DURGIN ABOUT HANNAH WEINER

Author's note: I first met the Chicago-based poet, scholar, teacher, publisher, editor, and community activist Patrick Durgin at a panel devoted to William Carlos Williams at a Modern Language Association meeting. Years later, I became especially interested in two of his projects, *The Route*, co-authored with Jen Hofer (2008) and *Hannah Weiner's Open House* (2007), a collection of works by Weiner that Durgin edited and published with his imprint, Kenning Editions. *The Route* and Weiner's *Weeks* (1990) involved the authors' use of electronic media to create poetry intended for the printed book. An experiment in digital citizenship, Durgin and Hofer's *The Route* consists of 13 lengthy emails to each other drafted between 2001 and 2006 followed by 13 conventional mailings in which they collaborate on "Open Letters" addressed to other experimental cultural works. They question the premise of interlocution by interrupting how we typically define markers of identity such as self, other, subjectivity, witness, difference, authorship, and readership. In *Weeks*, Weiner anchors her 50-week diary based on her experience of sitting in front of the TV set in her Manhattan apartment in 1986 while transcribing a cacophony of pithy, if disturbing tidbits gleaned from local and national news programs. I included chapters on *The Route* and *Weeks* in *Not Born Digital* (2016), my study of texts that exist on the edge of traditional page poetry and postmodern electronica. It was in the context of my research into Weiner's poetics, so influential to areas ranging from Language Poetry to the poetry of disability, along with new media studies, that I initiated the following conversation with Patrick Durgin, which originally appeared in *Talisman*.

Morris: Can you begin by telling me how you were introduced to Hannah's work? What was it about her work that led to your extraordinary devotion to it? Did you, like me, have the chance to hear Hannah's voice through recordings of her legendary performances? When did you realize Hannah would become a major scholarly interest of yours? Were you concerned (or liberated) about the "risks" of working on an obscure figure associated with "Language" poetry, a movement that is not accepted in all parts of the academy?

Durgin: I would have first encountered her work in Douglas Messerli's anthology *From the Other Side of the Century: A New American Poetry 1960-1990,* a book that was my introduction to a good many poets whose work I would later read, enjoy, and study intensely. But it might have equally been the other important anthologies of this ilk, that I somehow missed at the time (the early-mid-nineties). I was soon engrossed in a large-scale study of the work of Jackson Mac Low and was quickly made aware of the affinities between them; for instance, according to *In The American Tree* and "Language" Poetries, Mac Low and Weiner are the prescient elders of Language Writing. I don't think it's wrong to say so, but I was always aware that they were a part of earlier movements, and those investments compelled them as much if not more than those of the early Language writers. I had not read an entire book of Weiner's work, though, until I received a copy of *Spoke* from my friend and mentor Adalaide Morris. This was important because Weiner's work is best taken in whole, and many of her books are single series, and some of her series were even too large for a single book (e.g., *Clairvoyant Journal*). At the time, Buffalo's Electronic Poetry Center was a treasured source for work by and about contemporary and modernist poets of interest, and their Weiner page filled in a few of the gaps. When she died, I had just begun to read her work, and the tributes that were turning up on the EPC were moving and provocative. So, I gradually accumulated as many of her books as I could find, including the cassette (pre-mp3!) of the Clairvoyant Journal. I was hoping to study with Bernstein and eventually did—also with Robert Creeley, Susan Howe, and others during the late heyday of UB's Poetics Program—and so, although the values that marginalized Weiner's work seemed to me askance, I was introduced to her work and encouraged to explore it in depth within an academic context. To me, the real risk had more to do with adjudicating those values and not with securing marketability as a scholar.

By the time I came to Buffalo in early 2000, I recognized that her work would play an important role in my dissertation, as it had begun to play in my own poetry. As Bernstein is executor of her literary estate, I gained full access to her archives and procured copies of out-of-print material. I was also tapped to typeset Page and uncovered some more recordings of Weiner in performance, all of which was transformative; the extreme care with which she combined the written and the verbal was unlike anything I'd encountered outside of perhaps someone like Amiri Baraka. In the last year of writing the dissertation, I also put together the online edition of *The Early and Clairvoyant Journals* at the Archive for New Poetry in San Diego. That was when I gathered most of the unpublished material that would appear in *Hannah Weiner's Open House*, too. A year later, in 2005, I became interested in the burgeoning field of Disability Studies. And emboldened by personal interests in the field, began looking at ways that Weiner's work could benefit certain inquiries key to theorizing disability. The last three years have been an extension of that, for me, though with the publication of *Hannah Weiner's Open House*, I've seen her work receive a lot of attention from other quarters, not all of them academic by any means. I'm pleased that interest in her work continues to broaden, beyond the designation of Language Writing. From what I can tell, Language Writing is largely accepted within academia, but very often only as a foil. But it could be said that Weiner's work exemplifies the variety or singularity of particular practices so branded. Perhaps her work will play some small part in doing justice to the greater swathe of late twentieth-century American experimentalism. Because her work so vividly demonstrates that by experimentalism, we also mean something like experiential, a core value of writers and critics otherwise openly hostile to poetry in the radical modernist tradition.

Morris: I was interested in your mention of disability to focus on the materiality of language. Disability Studies has become a prominent aspect of cultural studies, but my sense has been that the focus has been on the disabled body more so than on disabilities or differences of minds. How does your story, and Hannah's, contradict or in other ways relate to the common image of the relation between mental disability and creativity, the image of a Van Gogh, "suffering for his sanity" as in that corny song by Don McLean? My sense is that creative work, especially group performances at her legendary living room gatherings, really did have an influence in allowing Hannah to endure the voices she heard and saw all over the place. Was it her ability to transform these material manifestations of language into performance art that helped her deal with what might otherwise have been a terrifying phenomenon?

Durgin: I should stress that Weiner and I probably only share the fact of having been diagnosed—it's an odd thing to endure and to process, of course. Whatever suffering we endured, mine has surely been comparatively mild. I doubt there's much of a fit, and so I don't try to massage the history. But more importantly, I am on principle reluctant to make analogies with my experience and that represented in Weiner's work, or to seek out similarities under the sign of disability. Disability theory has sometimes brilliantly posed questions of difference, and that's where its value resides, in my opinion: reopening the problem of the subject as subject to social models of biological elasticity. You're right that the focus has been on bodies, and caution is due since disabilities associated with the psyche have been overwhelmed by the recent turn to psychopharmaceutical explanations. My sense was that Weiner's work could tell us something about attribution, radical modernist poetic form and process as an alternative means of attribution, but not as a form of overcoming, cure, or healing as defined by psychiatric discourse. This is why, in one sense, her diagnoses are immaterial. But in another, they can be the focus. In an article I recently published in *Contemporary Women's Writing*, I discuss her work in a Deleuzian ("literary clinic") framework in order to avoid the mad genius cliché; for Deleuze, literature is a means of diagnosis, and of generating percepts that do confer power where it was withheld by certain regimes of power. This obviously, to me at least, resonates with how Weiner pitched her later writing projects, really from 1974 onward. Hence, she demonstrates something that disability theory might otherwise only discuss. All of this falls under the rubric of what I call "psycho-social" disability, which I develop in a separate but related article.

By her "legendary living room gatherings," do you mean the rehearsals for the *Clairvoyant Journal* tapes? Or are you referring to the pre-clairvoyant "open house" event? Maybe it can be useful to conflate the two. Her early work in performance, but also her early, New York School inflected poetry indicate that she was interested in the sort of semiotic questions that the later clairvoyant phenomena would amplify. The onset of seen words signals a new direction for the form and content of the work, which then revolves around self-care and political agency, harnessing the feminist reflections from previous years and putting them to new and somewhat more interesting work. She was deeply community-minded at all times, of course, and my research has given me reason to believe that she came to see her role as a sort of poet-seer (something Jerome Rothenberg insists upon). But then she sometimes seems to believe that the contemporary poet-seer has a legitimate sacrifice to make. So that between periods of lucidity and always with an abundance of humor, she might have stoked the fire. But it's difficult to lose sight of the fact that she understood the rhetorical value of madness as a trope, one that could be implemented in the search for something far from solipsism or prophecy. In any case, she outpaces the seemingly ubiquitous trope of the mad genius. And this is something that allows her to achieve sincerity and to sharpen her critical acumen in one and the same gesture.

The relation between psycho-social disability, diagnosis, subjectivity, and creativity dovetails with the question of marginalization and stigmatization. My initial forays into the field of disability studies represented a collaborative exploration of the way classism and ableism conspire to render the academy an often unaccommodating and potentially hypocritical site for institutional critique as well as creative expression. Together with three other scholars, and based on mutual contributions to threads in the "Disability Studies in the Humanities Listserve" (or "DSHUM"), I conceived and eventually took part in a panel at the 2007 Society for Disability Studies conference. This was my first public airing of the work on psycho-social disability. In editing and publishing *Hannah Weiner's Open House*, I did hope to facilitate disability theory's access to Weiner's work, and certainly these things coincide in my own work. But other scholars have found different foci. Judith Goldman has done impressive work on the semiotics of power in her work, Juliana Spahr very recently on class and place in "Radcliffe and Guatemalan Women," and Maria Damon on clairvoyance, Jewishness, and trauma. I have also seen Weiner's influence on younger poets and artists grow.

Morris: In your introduction to *Hannah Weiner's Open House*, you describe her participation with "an unprecedented confluence of poets, performance and visual artists including Philip Glass, Andy Warhol, Carolee Schneemann, John Perrault, David Antin, and Bernadette Mayer." Given your background in music and arts communities, I wondered if Hannah's linkages with these fascinating people working in various but interconnected media was part of what so appealed to you about her? Do you feel you have ever been part of such a multimedia world as Hannah played a part in the 60s and 70s? Has creative culture in the U.S. changed so much in the last 30 years that such a merging of various talents is less likely, especially given the academization and commercialization of underground cultures that we have already discussed? Can you give us more details about Hannah's Open Houses and her Happenings that sometimes took place at her job at A.H. Scheiber?

Durgin: If anything, it seems like media, linguistic, and generic crossovers of the past 30–50 years have culminated in an environment less likely to uphold high- and low-art distinctions. John Lennon's abdication into Fluxus and Yoko Ono's sphere of influence is an important precursor. If you look at Warhol's association with the Velvet Underground, you see that it seems more and more arbitrary, for all its initial commercial importance. The original New York punk scene coalesced around the Mercer Arts Center, before landing back in the bars. Patti Smith, Tom Verlaine, and Richard Hell incessantly cited the French Symbolist poets, Blake, the abstract expressionists; see also Greil Marcus' now canonical ancestry where the Sex Pistols were concerned, once the mid-seventies were reached and, back in New York, the Talking Heads began their successful foray into both museums and the suburban cinemaplex. See also Richard Prince and Gerhard Richter gracing Sonic Youth album covers. There's a band that has become an exhibit; Sensational Fix unfortunately isn't slated to visit the American continents, however. (Their curatorial work and songwriting have involved Dodie Bellamy, Nate Mackey, and Eileen Myles; Thurston Moore wrote an excellent review of Jesse Seldess' *Who Opens.*) Currently touring the U.S. is an exhibit by the brilliant visual and kinetic artist Olafur Eliasson, who has also worked as lighting designer for his Icelandic compatriots, Sigur Ros. As for poets, ongoing experiments in poets theater, neo-Benshi programs and new media outlets have made multidisciplinary work seem like something one ought to try. Sadly, I know of no further documentation of pieces like Weiner's "Hannah Weiner at Her Job," the piece wherein she invited an audience to witness her workplace routine in a high-art context. One of her "Street Works" had her sweeping the sidewalk in the guise of an "unknown collaborator." But, again, there is no documentation beyond what I included in *Open House.* In January, at a Links Hall event here in Chicago devoted to Weiner's legacy, Lee Ann Brown staged a rendition of the collaborative "Fashion Show Poetry Event" that represented one of the most striking examples of the "confluence" I mention in the introduction. By featuring the early happenings (a term I'll use loosely here) she devised so prominently, the book deliberately begs the question. One reason for the sparse documentation of these sorts of happenings then and now is the challenge conceptual work presents to the museum/gallery system. Such venues sometimes still struggle to accommodate intermedia work, but especially the ephemerality of performance.

Less well known is the way that art, music, and poetry are now committing to less rarefied contexts. For instance, one could draw a line between Weiner inviting an audience to "her life" and contemporary poet and labor activist Mark Nowak's "poetry dialogues" with Ford autoworkers in the United States and South Africa, striking clerical workers, and Muslim nurses. It'd be a squiggly line. But that's the reward of pursuing the appeal of multidisciplinarity and collaboration. I'm afraid my own work has been less uniformly invested in intermedia, translation, and all of these forms of implication, though I have collaborated with visual artists and a bit with poets theater and electronic music. I'm currently working on an anthology of poets theater with editors Kevin Killian and David Brazil, and it has emboldened me to complete a play that's been faltering in various stages for years. I don't and haven't felt that "creative culture" per se has discouraged this sort of thing, though work like Weiner's has clearly encouraged it (as well as certain sampling techniques the "flarf" and "conceptual" poets employ). I'm not sure anything beyond certain forms of new media poetics can make quite as radical an impact as the happenings of the sixties, though. In a lot of cases (e.g., Sonic Youth's *Goodbye 20th Century*), the results can feel redundant, though thankfully less so, for me at least, than another Audenesque sonnet. I ducked into the AWP conference when it was here this winter, and I didn't really see any attention given to this sort of crossover. Creative writing culture is still manifestly page-bound, for better or worse.

Morris: I remember my advisor Allen Grossman—an expert on Yeats—saying that contemporary poets had "lost their nerve" in their general unwillingness to extend their reach beyond social discourse and to follow Yeats into the realm of the mystical, esoteric, visionary. Grossman mentioned James Merrill as an example of a contemporary poet who DID consult with Ouija boards to make his poems, but here Grossman noted that Merrill hailed from a super-rich family (I believe connected with Merrill Lynch) and so stood outside the commercial nexus for contemporary poetry. I mention all this because if nothing else Hannah Weiner is quite literally a visionary author. She herself wrote that she "got fired" from a publishing house for "associating with aliens," discussed "astrals," and noted that "in 1970" she became "extremely psychic." She famously responded to a "hidden teacher" called "Paw"—who keeps her "under control"—and another called "chawho." Do you read Hannah in the line of visionary/shamanic authors—Blake, Yeats, Ginsberg, Merrill? Do you see a place for the visionary in contemporary poetry? Is this visionary element one of the aspects in which Hannah differs from other New York School and Language poets? Does her visionary aspect relate to her felt connection with Native American and Indigenous cultures, including her extraordinary interest in the case of Leonard Peltier? Is she in line with Biblical Jewish visionary figures? She told Charles Bernstein in a radio interview that she was descended from the Levis—landless, hidden teachers.

Durgin: As Mac Low once said to me, "Too much hocus pocus for my tastes." Or at any rate, I find it takes all my nerve to confront and appropriate the material world. Grossman would be right, if there weren't so much in the immediately preceding history to persuade one that bravely confronting the otherworldly source of all beauty and truth weren't really just solipsistic recourse (e.g., Andre Breton's paranoid narcissism, which, nonetheless, generated great work). I'm a post-humanist in that I deny religion when its core tenets are hegemonic; most often the supernatural or spiritual realms allow and even force us to dodge and defile humanity or basic ethical requirements of survival, yet I have no faith that all will be put to right in the assertion of my humanity. The very openness of religious metaphor is what has made it a generative resource, whether it's the "white Buddhism" (Jonathan Stalling's term) of Leslie Scalapino or the Yogic and antiparacolonial mimicry of Weiner's "silent teaching." The literariness derives not from metaphoricity but from its literalness. Weiner's "disability" would be pertinent there, far more than in any reading of her later work as an edifying tale of overcoming. But Weiner is not a post-humanist in this sense, and there's a real fascination with her extra-sensory sources that allows her to illuminate problems of gnosis and direct action—ultimately, of course, political problems. Is the seer seeing a valid model for this problem, or is it another form of compensation, an ideological subterfuge? Perhaps a bit of both. One thing that happens in her work is that, through the potentially problematic claims of access to Indigenous spiritual and cultural forces and sources, she shifts the balance, such that what is esoteric is her peculiar narratives, her neo-primitivism. It becomes a sign. I think the best of the visionary/shamanic authors manage this, and then take those signs to task. Blake certainly does.

Morris: You mentioned in an earlier response that you were interested in narrative, and in Hannah as a narrative poet. One of the things I love about her work is the way she deepens our sense of the multiple psychic textures of moments. She instructs readers about how to read the multi-texture of her lines by suggesting the conventional line simply can't reflect all that is going on at the moment of composition. So, she tells us that "the CAPITALS gave me orders, and the underlines or italics made comments." There is a sense things are going on psychically above the line, below the line, but also simultaneously. It is truly a multi-voiced text and the act of composition is one of the events she is narrating, although by no means the only event. I also love her ideas about interruption: "The sentence is always interrupted." To some degree this captures the busy, interpersonal quality of Hannah's life with a phone ringing, maybe friends stopping by, as well as the frenetic quality of a mind that might shift from remembering she needs to pick up something at a grocery store for a party to observations about the colors of words she sees on her body to a dream she had to something regarding her "professional" career as a poet and performance artist to her concern for American Indians.

Can you talk about your sense of Hannah as a "narrative" writer? You mention I think that she is one that is better read in larger units than in small pieces, that her work needs to be thought of as, if not a whole, than large movements. Can you talk about her sense of the line and the way it does and does not reflect narrative and compositional time?

Durgin: That's a great question. And your account is a lucid summation of where I learned to begin rereading her work. In "Mostly about the Sentence," she emphasizes that her clairvoyant work initially comprised a sort of "novel," by which she meant, I take it, a fundamentally prose and narrative mode of working. This is elaborated on in her interview with Bernstein for *The Line in Postmodern Poetry,* where she refers to her work as "large-sheet poetry." She begins with a prose template, bound to the margins (of her typewriter or notebook page). The interruption comes from the verse elements that emerge from the disharmonious and/or choral effusions of the "voices." So, she is always responsible to and for her prosody and with a meticulousness that matches that of Mac Low, no small feat. When I apply the term "avant-garde journalism" in my introduction to *The Early and Clairvoyant Journals*, I am trying to capture this amalgam generically. When you see the manuscripts, I think you see the hybridity of the form so vividly, I felt it needed a name. Another implication of this term is the pursuit of instantaneous reportage, of simultaneity. It's something more than Mac Low's simultaneities, though obviously informed by them and earlier performative and intermedia practices that achieve their effects only in the momentary occurrence of their realization, literally in concert. This affects our expectations as readers of narratives even beyond the graphic "interruptions" of her unorthodox, quasi-concrete surfaces; the "orders" reach out to us. It's really lyric apostrophe, but it is also silent teaching. The needle's constantly in the red, as the struggle to transcribe the moment of composition is itself, in part, composed of our own struggle. You root for her, but you know there's nothing more to root for than yourself, what is present to you.

CHAPTER 9

TECH SUPPORT SAYS "DEAD DON WALKING": TRADITION, THE INTERNET, AND INDIVIDUAL TALENT IN THE POETRY OF DANIEL Y. HARRIS

Author of *Hyperlinks of Anxiety* (2013), Daniel Y. Harris (b. 1962) is a Paris-born, University of Chicago-trained experimental poet, artist, and divinity scholar with a special interest in Jewish mysticism and hermeneutics. At a lecture called "Post-Digital American Jewish Poetry" at the University of California, Irvine, Harris describes his task as reassembling Web detritus into a Golem, "Technology and hyperreality meet Judaic midrash and Biblical exegesis in stanzas which seek to create a human being from the refuse of bandwidth." In *Hyperlinks of Anxiety,* Harris positions himself as an ambivalent ventriloquist of the human voice. He is an old-school page poet—"an analog/ in an age of digits" (32)—announcing his situation as an author writing on the cusp of the Brave New Web environment. He suggests "an age of digits" simultaneously amplifies and extinguishes the value of his current practice through the dissemination powers of an intelligent machine. In "Emoticon" he writes: "Unhip to need/to be here, but the way back is splayed:/he can sit and click, exchange/ links, but the state of bandwidth/is skin, the widget in the corner of the screen/ exudes the bot of bodies. Digitally,/he clones and is multiple again." He continues: "He logs on./The domain is as big/as a yotta" (6). Given that a "yotta" is the largest unit prefix in the international system of units (Wikipedia), we note Harris's ambivalence toward entering literary voice on the web as a sublime event. In "Emoticon," the Brave New Web expands personal visibility on such a monumental scale that traditional notions of identity and romantic ideas about creative self-expression are put in question.

In "Confessions of a Blogger," Harris addresses with typical ambivalence his motivations for and concerns about the outcome of achieving the common philosophical desire to (literally and figuratively) go "in search of myself" by entering his name and texts on the web: "digits/for countless others probing/ the Net for my name—/me numbered, me squared/to a thousand and one/ nights of the Boolean me:/tapered/linkrot of vanity/shaping me as helicoid/ in search of myself" (3). His title winks back to the groundbreaking "confessional" movement of the 1950s (think Lowell, Plath, Berryman). Fifties "confessionalism" was self-consciously rejecting Eliotic "impersonalism" and returning American lyric to a Wordsworthian self-expressionism with a touch of Catholicism through reference to the expiation of guilt via confession, as in St. Augustine. The irony, of course, is that Harris's crisis in large part concerns the deconstruction of the relationship of "voice" to "author" to "authenticity" to "word on page" that Fifties "confessionalists" such as Lowell privileged in phrases such as "Yet why not say what happened?" from "Epilogue" (1977). The idea of "confessing"—in either a religious or a lyric autobiographical— manner via the digital environment of blogworld seems absurd. And Harris echoes Pound's Mea culpa keyword in the *Pisan Cantos*—"vanity"—by associating authorial presence with a web world animated by Boolean logic—composed of algebraic combinations of "and," "or," and "not"—in a form Harris likens to a minimalist term related to the geometry of space. (A Helicoid concerns the minimal surface having a circular helix as its boundary. It is the only ruled minimal surface other than the plane.) Harris suggests the paradoxical nature of Web existence in the passage above. As in the Arabian Nights folk tales, the dissemination of the poet's name and story becomes a textual form of survival that defers execution.[1]

Poetry may be a form of textual survival, but Harris acknowledges that whatever sense of identity is transmitted via the Web is not merely publicized

---

[1] "The main frame story concerns a Persian king and his new bride. He is shocked to discover that his brother's wife is unfaithful; discovering his own wife's infidelity has been even more flagrant, he has her executed: but in his bitterness and grief decides that all women are the same. The king, Shahryar, begins to marry a succession of virgins only to execute each one the next morning, before she has a chance to dishonor him. Eventually the vizier, whose duty it is to provide them, cannot find any more virgins. Scheherazade, the vizier's daughter, offers herself as the next bride and her father reluctantly agrees. On the night of their marriage, Scheherazade begins to tell the king a tale, but does not end it. The king, curious about how the story ends, is thus forced to postpone her execution in order to hear the conclusion. The next night, as soon as she finishes the tale, she begins (and *only* begins) a new one, and the king, eager to hear the conclusion, postpones her execution once again. So it goes on for 1,001 nights." (Wikipedia)

through narrative, but rather identity is dispersed into rhizomatic combinations of storylines, themselves the product of algebraic set theory logics and spatial designs that take the "confessionalist" far away from, as in Lowell, a "life study" in which the speaker simply says what happened. In "Confessions of a Blogger," Harris continues, the translation of "self" into the virtual realm distorts or even destroys authorial intent, but, ever the knotty self-ironist, Harris also suggests that his "original" voice was nothing to write home about in the first place because "his" language was always already uncivilized (too early) and commodified (too late) for significance. The blog realm seems of a malicious intent, with its own cruel wish to "break/me, pulp my savage accent,/my hack-herd packing words/in viruses with a thin/mdash" (3).

A page poet, Harris nonetheless approximates the bewildering explosion of personhood in a web realm by giving voice to the displaced Other through a virtually untranslatable opaque verse style: "Diaspora the body in all places/ at once," he writes in "The Agon Poems" (29). His book specifically addresses from multiple Jewish perspectives—prophetic, diasporic, ethical, midrashic, gnostic—the vexing problems and sublime potential of disseminating lyrics, the ancient form of transmission and preservation of the singular, private human voice across time and space to an individual reader, in an environment in which e-poetry and digitalized poetics pose a crisis (understood as both opportunity and threat) to traditional page poetry.

A University of Chicago Divinity School graduate with a thesis guided by the hermeneutist Paul Ricoeur on the role of Kabbalah in the works of Moses de Leon, Gershom Scholem, and Harold Bloom, Harris's website lists a genealogical ancestry that includes a composer, members of the French Resistance during World War II, archeologists, the chief Ashkenazi Rabbi of Paris, and an eighteenth-century paternal ancestor who was a prominent Lithuanian Rabbi, Talmudic scholar, and Kabbalist. Given Harris's fascination with deep genealogical personal history and its relationship to Jewish hermeneutics, mysticism, and political resistance to overwhelming state terror during the Shoah, it is fitting that although he remains a traditional—if brutally obscure—page-oriented author with a modernist disposition, his lyrics reflect on how the mediation of voice in a digital format will impact poetry's primordial function of preserving the human image across time and space. Harris regards the realm of hyperlinks as the ultimate vehicle to conserve and disseminate words and images. At the same time, he worries that the new media environment for poems resembles the Kabbalist's broken vessel, shattering text, rather than shards of glass. At other times, he fears, the hypertextual environment seems like a decidedly non-kosher Octopus. Its dangerous tentacles are bent on choking out the personal voice and exhausting the human body with a vengeance reminiscent of the Shoah that his grandparents actively resisted. Harris records his sense of appearing as a trace in the aftermath of a catastrophic alteration to personal presence in "I": "I, barcode and libido of might am here/ after rapture, extermination and fetish."

Designed for the page, his poetry is by necessity hyperlinked. I say this because one is pretty much forced to read Harris's book while remaining online to Google for definitions of unusual concepts and esoteric terms associated with Greek philosophy and Jewish hermeneutics, aesthetics, and religion. Examples include "Theomorph," "pantomorph," "Opuscule," "Khidr," "Yotta," "Methexis," "Henosis," "Shevirah," "Shekinah," "helicoid," "amygadale," and "Notarikon." One thus reads Harris in the interstitial space between page and web, where his esoterica becomes heteroglossed in ways that take the reader on lines of flight that defy authorial intention. Consider my web-assisted experience of deciphering the following passage from "The Ballad of Don Notarikon":

> With spiritus, golemic hurl of speckled air,/my brain spills into a new nerve. I awake to the/ pitiless gloom of the first person to blankly/ gaze at a spate of pellicles evoking the "I"/ to stir the canon roused by a dare. (55)

A seriously elliptical mouthful from an author who states that he "major[s] in opacity" (56)! An online search for "spiritus" not only pulls up the Latin terms for spirit or breathing but also notes it as a title for a journal of Christian spirituality as well as a high proof Polish vodka. As a modernist myself, I can't help recalling Wallace Stevens's questioning "Whose spirit is this?" as he imagines the world-making significance of the female singer on the beach who has dazzled the speaker after she "sang beyond the genius of the sea" in "The Idea of Order in Key West" (1934). I also recall W. B. Yeats's invocation of the "Spiritus Mundi" (or great archetypal mind) from which the mystic Irish bard draws out the image of the "rough" apocalyptic beast as it "Slouches towards Bethlehem to be born" in "The Second Coming" (1919). Might not such a reference connect us to the "golemic hurl" image? A Golem, after all, is, like the Yeatsian beast, a monster, albeit from folklore created by Jews as protection from enemies (Wikipedia). Through the Golem reference, Harris expresses fear about creating discourse on the web that defies authorial control. Hence the reference to "pellicles evoking the 'I'." Pellicles? Online research reveals it is, among other things, a biological term defining the thin layer supporting the cell membrane in various protozoa, but also a protective cover applied to a photomask used in semiconductor device fabrication; the pellicle protects the photomask from damage and dirt (online sources). Offering an exact paraphrase of the "pellicles" passage may be a fool's errand, given its hermeticism, but one can safely say that the "pellicles" reference benefits from hyperlinked investigation into its connections with the microscopic skin of the one-celled animal and its function as another kind of protective skin for a microscopic computer reproduction device. In each case, the "pellicle" skin protects a fundamental element of biological life and technological reproduction of images, and thus, for Harris's poetics, "pellicles" represent the conservational properties of web-based literary appearance. At the same time, one senses Harris's disenchantment with the pellicled Golem. I say this because such figures for a web-based image of his voice and vision suggest an unruly monstrous Other, a skin without a body, that seems alienated from selfhood that, paradoxically, may be regarded as a retrograde act of vanity and self-commodification: "I awake to the/pitiless gloom of the first person to blankly/gaze at a spate of pellicles evoking the 'I'".

Harris's poetics are steeped in Harold Bloom's theory—outlined in his notorious 1973 study *The Anxiety of Influence*—of agonic competition among male poets from different generations engaged in an Oedipal struggle for acknowledgment and literary power. Harris also illustrates Bloom's understanding that contemporary poets are terribly self-conscious about arriving on the literary scene late in a tradition already saturated with major accomplishments by prior masters. In an interview with the author, Harris stated:

> My "hermetic style" and my "stylistic opacity" are saturated with an interpretive variability richly informed by the limits of the western canon, hermeneutics, deconstruction, postmodernism and such exemplary print poetry at Stevens, Ashbery, Celan and Hill. At its core, the strong poem (in Bloom's sense), is invention itself, wrestling with agonic tropes that cause the myths of catastrophe creation to keep breaking forward. Invention is by definition historiographic. From the amalgam of disparate traditions demanding honor and bypass, arises the new poem. The demands are great. (Morris)

One feels the "anxiety" referenced in Harris's book title is Janus-faced. His burden as an author is Bloomian because it stems from his desire to distinguish his elliptical stylings from merely imitating past masters ranging from Rashi to Celan to Kafka to Stevens to Ashbery.[2] What makes Harris's anxiety about belatedness unique, I'd argue, is that he is also concerned with the frightfully sublime challenge of confronting a virtual format that threatens spatial and temporal moorings of traditional page poetry.

Let me explain. Harris's fascination with wordplay and the amplification and distortion of meaning, sound, and graphic significance is indebted to Kabbalistic acrostics, but may also be likened to mid-twentieth-century concrete poetics that materialized language to upset the transparency of representation and thus challenge the order of things. Although written in a hermetic style that disrupts a tight fit between sign and signification, and thus defies easy reading for "meaning" or "content"—"The Agon Poems" reflect his self-consciously Bloomian account of belatedness. What makes Harris's agon peculiar is that his temporal problem in relation to innovation, contra Bloom, involves arriving at poetic maturity *prior to*, rather than *in the aftermath of*, major developments in the field. For Harris, I am saying, belatedness, ironically, means appearing on the scene too early to fully engage creatively with a new electronic field that has, from his perspective, arrived too late for him to take full advantage of its resources.

---

2 In terms of literary forebears, Harris is clearly indebted to international modernism. One hears in Harris's peculiar admixture of conversational, philosophical, and self-consciously sonic and playful discourse the poetics of Wallace Stevens's "The Idea of Order at Key West." His poetry, again like Stevens, is Emersonian, in its essayistic quality. One has the sense of a mind working through concepts, ideas, and problems related to imagining and disseminating the poet's voice, self, and authorial imagination not only in and through the artificial form of page poetry, but in a hypertextual environment where notions of body, community, acknowledgment, authorship, and visibility, as well as issues of void, chaos, and loss of control of one's text, and a radical hermeneutic instability are major concerns, as is the issue of the transmission of culture and the preservation of the human image across time. Besides the Stevensian strains, we notice the punning and love of wordplay found in James Joyce, and the wicked self-criticism and implication in authorial hypocrisy found in Eliot and Baudelaire. The very concept of "anxiety"—foregrounded in the book title—is itself a modernist emotion, suggesting an interior disease that Auden referred to as a modern affliction in "The Age of Anxiety." One does not associate the postmodern condition with anxiety, but rather, as in Deleuze, with the ecstatic synesthetic rush of schizophrenia. Of course, "anxiety" is a keyword in Jewish gnostic Harold Bloom's theory that "strong" major poets are engaged in a private intergenerational agon, if the hermeneut is able to read the hidden code. Harris is intensely concerned with ancestral relationship, as the genealogical section of his website reveals.

Given his obsessive concern with literary forebears, Harris is not what Marjorie Perloff, in *Unoriginal Genius: Poetry by Other Means in the New Century*, would consider as an avant-gardist, or a writer interested in discovery and detachment from past aesthetic models, but rather as an arriere-gardist, one committed to recovery in new formats of disregarded predecessors (67). Writing that the arriere-garde "treats the propositions of the early twentieth-century avant garde with a respect bordering on veneration (56)," Perloff, referring to Brazilian concrete poets, explains,

> The *arriere-garde*, then, is neither a throwback to traditional forms—in this case, the first-person lyric or lyric sequence—nor what we used to call *postmodernism*. Rather, it is a revival of the avant-garde model—but with a difference. When, for example, Oyvind Fahlstrom makes his case for the equivalence of form and content, his argument amalgamates Khlebnikov's zaum poetics of the Russian avant-garde with principles developed by the French *lettristes* who were his contemporaries. (58)

Arriere-gardist in Perloff's sense of the term, Harris's book bears affinities with the *Zohar* (Radiance/Splendor), the legendary Kabbalistic text of esoteric Torah commentary authored by Moses de Leon, the thirteenth-century Spanish Jew who claimed his writings were based on Aramaic midrash from the Second Temple period. The *Zohar* was later redacted between the fourteenth and eighteenth centuries in Italy, Germany, and Poland by Jewish and non-Jewish scholars, mystics, and theologians.[3]

The key long poem "The Ballad of Don Notarikon" illustrates Harris's fascination with wordplay. His approach bears affinities with how linguistic creativity occurs through acrostics in the *Zohar*, but also with the writings of modernists such as Wallace Stevens and James Joyce, and with hyperlink poets such as those associated with the Flarf movement who turn to the Web itself as a postmodern resource for a peculiar kind of self-expression that manipulates prior texts:[4]

---

3 "For more information on the Zohar, see the Wikipedia entry on "Zohar" as well as Moshe Miller's "The Zohar's Mysterious Origins" on the Kabbalah Online website. https://www.chabad.org/kabbalah/article_cdo/aid/380410/jewish/The-Zohars-Mysterious-Origins.htm".
4 "While traditional notions of writing are primarily focused on 'originality' and 'creativity,' the digital environment fosters new skill sets that include 'manipulation' and 'management' of the heaps of already existent and ever-increasing language," writes Kenneth Goldsmith in *Uncreative Writing: Managing Language in the Digital Age* (15).

> This earnest/
> quip to know thyself is paravisual, emblem/ of italics that hints at bereshit—the proper/
> name of Don Notarikon is a tetragrammaton:/ the T-B-D-N syllabary styled on rabbinic/ acronymics. "The," courtly article, bringer/ of names and potency. "Ballad," its prosodic/
> reach in twenty stanzas of twelve line tropes. /"Don," head dominus, Don Juan, don a Don/ Quixote chivalric self to anoint your reader/
> S Panza, or Horatio or a Don Paterfamilias,/ Don Immanuel the courtier of Zeona, Spain,// who survives being burnt at the stake in 1492/to wear the eyes of Don Notarikon. (50)

In such a passage, one glimpses how Harris connects a mystical Iberian strain of Jewish hermeneutics with digital poetics and the realm of hyperlink. In *Uncreative Writing: Managing Language in the Digital Age,* Kenneth Goldsmith argues,

> The Internet and the digital environment present writers with new challenges and opportunities to reconceive creativity, authorship, and their relationship to language. Confronted with an unprecedented amount of texts and language, writers have the opportunity to move beyond the creation of new texts and manage, parse, appropriate, and reconstruct those that already exist. (http://cup. columbia.edu/book/978-0-231-14990-7/uncreative-writing)

Goldsmith's emphasis on "reconceive[ing] creativity" as a process of appropriation and reconstruction of prior texts recalls the alchemical method Kabbalists employed to derive spiritual meanings from Bible text through rearranging words and sentences. In both computer generated poetry as described by Goldsmith and the dissemination of text in Harris poems such as "The Ballad of Don Notarikon" the emphasis is on textuality and plurivocality. "The Ballad of Don Notarikon" also reflects on Harris's mixed relationship to web era poetics and Jewish hermeneutics through his invocation of the Greek term for a Kabbalistic method of rearranging words and sentences in the Bible to derive the esoteric substratus and deeper spiritual meaning of the words (Wikipedia).[5] In the ballad (a venerable narrative

---

5 Besides signifying the Kabbalistic idea that Torah words are formed from the first letter abbreviations of other Hebrew words, the word "Notarikon" is also itself an online

folk genre that precedes print culture as well as disrupts the association of lyric subjectivity with a single author), Harris writes, "The circuitry/for this hardware is offline. Tech support says 'Dead Don Walking' spins codes of hyperlink/as the original alias remains camouflaged on/the edge of mad stanzas built like Babel to/First crisis."

The passage quoted above is itself a coded pastiche. It tropes on a 1995 film by Tim Robbins starring Sean Penn and Susan Sarandon about a condemned man befriended by a nun as he is about to perish on Death Row in Louisiana, and then likens the unruly dissemination of many languages characteristic of a web environment to the "Tower of Babel" story from Genesis 11:1–9. The Babel story is an etiological explanation of the origins of multiple languages as God's response to concerns about human freedom and power that, God decided, needed to be divided to create misunderstandings and miscommunications through the confusion of tongues (Wikipedia). The Babel story speaks to Harris's fascination with roots, origins, and genealogy. In an essay that appears on his website—"Strangers and Friends—Cultural Identity and Community"—Harris urges readers to unearth "the forgotten histories within ancestral memories and places" so "we might have a starting point for healing a change." Interested in the "fertilizing and benevolent presence of strangers in traditional societies," Harris notes that the "Golden Age of Spain" in which Jewish mysticism and learning thrived for 200 years on the "anxious edges of the Inquisition" because of "relatively little resistance from clerical and royal powers."

The Babel story also raises questions of authorship, as well as the issue of linguistic control of texts one disseminates via digitalized media in which everyone is potentially an author and conceptions of the audience are bewilderingly estranged from traditional ideas of the intimate union between solitary writer and solitary reader. This is so even as, in the passage quoted above from the "The Ballad," Harris, in Derridean fashion, self-consciously mocks his anxiety about the relationship of author, voice, text, and originality through description of the source of Don Notarikon's language and perspective. "The circuitry [...] [for the] mad stanzas"—stems from an "original" source "offline" that is associated with a still living, but doomed "Dead Don," but one that is itself fictive—an "alias" that is itself a subterfuge—"camouflaged."

---

software application that allows users to search and find Bible codes such as acronyms and numerical values. (Wikipedia)

Don's poetry, he comments, is, like the biblical city and tower, meant to confront what he calls a "First crisis." Harris is a liminal figure situating his poetry at a "crisis" point—an in-between space or turning point that, while itself a time of uncertainty and confusion, will pivot the course of future events markedly in one direction or another. The "online" world is thus not a comfortable home for the Don—he prefers the "offline" realm of "hardware" as opposed to "software."

In a long, tour de force passage from late in "The Ballad of Don Notarikon," Harris, recalling the persona (or mask) poems of Eliot in "Prufrock" (1915) and Pound in "Mauberley" (1920) reflects with his characteristic deep ambivalence on an alchemical process and diasporic journey of transfiguration from flesh and blood human existence to avatar in the "wide empty" of an intelligent machine.

> I, lifted alias, potency and low politique to/ mediate between demiurge and apeiron, my/ body chrysolite with mineral silicates of iron,/ part topaz, olive, clay—man of light—light/ man of green—morphed as Notarikon across/ the wide empty filled with steps. I am born/ or pre-born, stillborn not still, nor implied/ coupling as no couple has yet to rub sweet/ swells of comfort on cicatrix or schism that/ I am. I am Don Notarikon. I, in sound mind/ and amygdale, am the ars poetica of a winged/ devarim who scaled heights of darkling tiers//to decrescendo in faults of a man made out/ of words. Here's one: anthropos, arms curved/ to the knuckle of a prehensile hand marking/ basalt with spurs. Here's one: pantomorphos,/ shape-master, "All-Shaped" whose covering/ cherubs and ministering angels bask in rays/ of cabalic privacies. I am now their dread a,/matriculant in the School of Contraction, with/ an emerging student body of tympanic shapes./ I major in Opacity, minor in Limited Down./ First things first. I have taken a step. My body/ is oblongi [...] (56)

The speaker is "morphed," symbolically devolved, and reinscribed into another, non-human form. I take the image of the anthropos (first man) and the apelike figure with the prehensile hand to represent the Devo experience. Devo is then reconceived as an Odysseus, metamorphic figure—the pantomorph—who then is electronically reborn from the primitive cellular forms of the mind (the computer mind as new biological/evolutional incubator of creative breath, the Yeatsian "spiritus mundi," the Kabbalist's notion of the Hebrew letters of the Bible as acrostically generative of new words and new worlds). I say "electronically reborn" because "amygdale" refers to the almond-shaped structures associated with groups of nuclei located deep within the medial temporal lobes of the brain, and linked with memory and emotional reaction. The speaker brags in bravura tones over his appearance as a Kabbalistic version of a Stevensian "man made out of words"—"[I] am the ars poetica of a winged devarim who scaled heights of darkling tiers"— devarim is the Hebrew term for "words," and also the Torah portion from *Deuteronomy* in which Moses begins his repetition of the Torah to the assembled Children of Israel [Chabad.Org]. At the same time, the "demiurge" (or subordinate deity who fashions the sensible world in the light of eternal ideas; Merriam Webster Online) who mediates an unlimited, infinite space—the "apeiron"—is DOA. The Great Don, like the Stevensian Emperor of Ice Cream who, in a famous poem from 1922, rules with his phallus (the big cigar) a frothy insubstantial realm of "concupiscent curds," is merely a spectral figure. He is "stillborn." Further, the poem references the language of a last will and testament ("I, in sound mind [...]"), and there is a suggestion that while the image of the Don may be infinitely reproducible via the web, he is impotent. He exists in an asexual, disembodied environment in which his trace is likened to a scar:

no couple has yet to rub sweet/
swells of comfort on cicatrix or schism that/ I am

Given that "cicatrix" refers to the scar left by the formation of new connective tissue over a healing scar or wound (Free online dictionary), one can infer that Harris regards the Don's web-based representational appearance as absence-based (non)existence. (Harris picks up on the theme of electronic appearance as a smoke ring-like trace, an aftermath of embodied life, in "Noone": "without words/soars the severed skull free/of human shape" and "Noone was here/is/ smile the leg/the road//without body" [11]).

Like T.S. Eliot, Harris addresses the relation of tradition and the individual talent, as well as the place of embodied existence altogether. According to Harris, "People are obsessively concerned with identity. There is an insufferable desire to be understood but honor what has come before. The danger is that we could be living in a vacuum of platitudes where everything is cliché" (Schneider). As DePauw Religion and Literature professor Beth Hawkins Benedix notes in a full-length introductory essay to the volume, lines from Harris's poetry such as "Does anyone ask about identity?," "Do we live here?," "Too many/writers and not enough readers," and the author's parodistic comment that his task may be to "self-publish the urbanism of lonely obfuscations" speak to what Benedix calls the "wish for connection, for a listening Other, [which] sits side by side an equally compelling need to expose the naiveté of this wish" in the dizzyingly intangible virtual space of New Media. An utterly contemporary and postmodern condition for poetry, as witnessed by recent studies of poetry in the digital age by Adelaide Morris, N. Katherine Hayles, Marjorie Perloff, Kenneth Goldsmith, Kevin Stein, and C. T. Funkhouser, Harris suggests current practice is resonant with ancient Jewish mystical traditions (associated with, for example, Moses de Leon) of esoteric creativity through the decidedly Jewish and diasporic Derridean processes of dissemination, textuality, and plurivocality that characterize web-based communications.

It is important to distinguish Harris's mixed response to poetry in a New Media era from that of leading theoretical proponents of e-poetry such as Goldsmith, Hayles, Perloff, and Funkhouser. Closer in spirit—if not stylistics—to Kevin Stein, who offers a judicious commentary on e-poetry from the perspective of a page poet in *Poetry's Afterlife*—Harris is a fascinating cusp figure with a deeply modernist sensibility. His tonal touchstones (Stevens, primarily), focus on interiority, anxiety, wordplay, allusiveness, verbal opacity, and an assemblage/collage aesthetic all put him in modernist camp even as the modernist is confronting a consuming postmodern realm of electronic reproduction. Like Eliot, Pound and Walter Benjamin in the *Arcades Project*, for Harris originality and innovation are, paradoxically, contingent upon extraordinary scholarly efforts to compile and collate esoteric wisdom texts, political tracts, and sacred and secular literature.

Flarf writers and e-poets such as Funkhouser and Jim Andrews and installation artist-poets such as Mary Flanagan generate decentered texts by, for example, linking URLs, thus creating hypertexts as "readers" may proceed through webpages by linking on to whichever webpage the "readers" decide to click upon—thus creating a thematically dizzying number of possible versions of the "original" version of text the Flarfist originally "programmed" into being. Harris, by contrast, publishes page poetry on online 'zines such as *Zeek* and via his website, but is at bottom a twenty-first-century modernist in that his forums are primarily obscure print little magazines and small presses—*Hyperlinks of Anxiety* appears with Cervena Barva Press of Somerville, MA.

Works Cited

Harold Bloom. *The Anxiety of Influence: A Theory of Poetry*. New York: Oxford University Press, 1973.

Kenneth Goldsmith. *Uncreative Writing: Managing Language in the Digital Age.* New York: Columbia University Press, 2011.
Daniel Y. Harris. *Hyperlinks of Anxiety.* Somerville, MA: Cervena Press, 2013.
———. Lecture on "Post-Digital American Jewish Poetry" at the University of California, Irvine, Winter 2013.
Daniel Morris. "Interview with Daniel Y. Harris." Conducted via email. March 2014.
Marjorie Perloff. *Unoriginal Genius: Poetry by Other Means in the New Century.* Chicago: University of Chicago Press, 2010.
Kevin Stein. *Poetry's Afterlife: Verse in the Digital Age.* Ann Arbor: University of Michigan Press, 2010.

CHAPTER 10

INTERVIEW WITH ADEENA KARASICK ON *CHECKING IN*

Note: Born of Russian Jewish heritage in Winnipeg, Manitoba in 1965, educated in Canada, and currently teaching at the Pratt Institute in New York City, Adeena Karasick's

> Kabbalistically inflected, urban, Jewish feminist mashups have been described as "electricity in language" (Nicole Brossard), "proto-ecstatic jet-propulsive word torsion" (George Quasha), noted for their "cross-fertilization of punning and knowing, theatre and theory" (Charles Bernstein) "a twined virtuosity of mind and ear which leaves the reader deliciously lost in Karasick's signature 'syllabic labyrinth'" (Craig Dworkin); "demonstrating how desire flows through language, an unstoppable flood of allusion (both literary and pop-cultural), word-play, and extravagant and outrageous sound-work." (Mark Scroggins).[1]

In this interview, Daniel Morris discusses Karasick's *Checking In*, published by Talonbooks in 2018.

> **DM**: Adeena, the title poem of your new book covers around the first half of the volume and weighs in at over thirty pages of text. "*Checking In*" is a playful phrase of many meanings. So many meanings that I find myself wanting, in admittedly ludic fashion, to take a shot at deciphering your title. Hopefully, amidst my musings you can find a question or two that will spur a response!
> I think of the term's use in 12-step recovery programs. You allude to the connection between Checking In and recovery programs in the line:

---

1 https://www.pratt.edu/people/adeena-karasick/

"Schoenberg is starting a 12-Step Program." (p. 18). The reference to 12-Step programs and Schoenberg alludes to his development of a revolutionary music composition technique. Anthony Tommasini describes "twelve tone" music in the *New York Times* (2007): "Schoenberg's use of systematized sets of all 12 pitches of the chromatic scale—all the keys on the piano from, say, A to G sharp—was a radical departure from tonality, the familiar musical language of major and minor keys."

So, the slippery texture of the title, *Checking In*, has taken me to Schoenberg. I now want to ask you about the relation between Schoenberg's "departure from tonality, the familiar musical language of major and minor keys" and your poetics in *Checking In*. With your whimsical, punning, and allusive method, you most certainly do depart from a literary language that distinguishes between "major" and "minor" referents. By that I mean Where's Waldo, Abba, the musical *Annie*, Dr. Doolittle, and Carly Rae Jepsen's "Call Me Maybe" take pride of place alongside "Highbrow" literary, theoretical, musical, and avant-garde references to heavy hitters from Bakhtin, Baudrillard, Benjamin, and Brecht to Mrs. Dalloway, Maria Damon, and Moby Dick.

But, to return to my inquiry about the title *Checking In*. So many other resonances besides Schoenbergian 12-stepping. To check in is to announce one's arrival, to die, to communicate about one's status (as in, I'm checking in on the status of that manuscript your press has been sitting on for three years), simply talking, recording something, returning something (such as checking in a book back to the library), and, of course, signing oneself in for treatment (I'm checking myself in to rehab).

But the question I want to ask you is about the meaning of *Checking In* in terms of checking in to read one's email or social media. The graphic design for the long poem "Checking In" resembles a digital-social mediation: Twitter or Facebook. On the bottom of each page one finds icons— "like," "comment," and "share"—representing how users' responding to Facebook/Twitter communications. And yet your book is decidedly NOT a digitalized experiment in new media poetics where users can directly respond to your missives. "Checking In" is not a hypertextual electropoetic digital audio project I associate with folks like Chris Funkhouser— whom you acknowledge in your book. Your book is most definitely a book. It is intertextual, polyreferential, semiotica in flavor for sure, but it reads like a book. (I think of Campbell's hearty soup ads of yore in which the manly canned stew "eats like a meal," but we should use a spoon so as not to miss a drop.) It is a beautiful thing, your book. A lovingly crafted small indie press poetry object. I am interested in such in-between poetic projects. I've written, for instance, on Noah Eli Gordon's *inbox*, an independent press poetry book composed of actual emails that appeared in Gordon's inbox concerning the alt-poetry community.

Adeena, Both of us born in the 1960s, we preceded the digital revolution. (I started my dissertation in the late 1980s on a typewriter, and switched to a first-generation boxy Apple around Chapter 2 of my project on WC Williams). And so, I am interested in between-er projects such as *Checking In* in terms of its relationships to the tradition of alternative press small run poetry books AND to the Born Digital electropoetics to which your text alludes and imitates in its semiotic layers and comfort with plays on major/minor disruptions: HD meets Dr. Doolittle and the like.

Please, then, reflect on the status of *Checking In* as a book? Issues of audience reception come to mind. I was very comfortable with your range of references because I am in your circle in terms of years on the planet and attractions to Jewishness, music, avant-gardism, and theory. I am proud to have published a story in my undergraduate literary magazine that referenced Pere Ubu (the band and the play). And so, I am a target audience. I like. But, as for the question, do you think much about distribution, audience, communities of interpretation? Would you think about those questions differently if "Checking In" was not published as a book? What if "Checking In" existed exclusively online, in a format where folks could actually respond with "like," "share," "comment"?

AK: Ah Daniel, you offer so many interesting "probes" here and I have to say it's so refreshing and heartwarming to have such a close and thoughtful reader to respond to. So yes, *Checking In* navigates between a mediatic territory of both book (sculptural text object) yet is firmly entrenched in the world of digital media as the title poem's very premise is grounded in Facebook updates. As both author of now 10 books and creator of media art / videopoems / pechakuchae, I inhabit both of these worlds—and though I love, with the advent of new media and digipoeisis the new possibilities available for language, my heart is (as has always been) firmly rooted in the notion of the book—physical, material and viscerally accessible. Dedicated to that, I recently designed the newly established "Book Minor" at Pratt, where students can literally study all things book—historically, aesthetically, philosophically, exegetically.

So yes, *Checking In* for me as art object, is both a repository and a meaning generator marked by production, consumption and (non)utility. Each page a sculptural space of ever-signifying variables; aromatic, tactilic, and sensorially alive. And to this end, I am *so* grateful to my indie press, Talonbooks (who has stood by me for 25 years and giving in to my "spark joy" maximalist aesthetic; generously allowing me the freedom of design, of covers, of interiors with full-color, genre-blurring collage essays, "excessive" typographical, concrete / vispoetic play—none of which are available as e-books--inviting the reader to play this book as music, turning its pages, caressing its text, *hearing* it.

And so, I adore how you mention the Schoenberg line—because in fact there are so many zones of intersection with his thinking. Most notably perhaps, in the way that *Checking In* moves between major and minor referents in the jouissey mash-up of pop culture and Kabbalistic hermeneutics, media theory and midrash, contemporary poetry, philosophy, semiotics, movies and pop songs; all commenting on each other asking us to re-hear or see them from different vantage points. And this ironic / paradoxical juxtapositional play of otherness *is* kinda Schoenbergian—the way his dodecaphony ensures all twelve notes of the chromatic scale are sounded as often as one another—while not fetishizing any one note. Similarly, all multigeneric and "all–access" with *Checking In* there's a kind of de-hierarchizing of information, a levelling out (where say "King Ubu is dining at Nobu, Gargantua and Pantagruel are listening to They Might Be Giants, Immanuel Kant liking No Doubt, and Uber Allis is driving for Lyft"). Taking the reader on a satiric tour through the shards and fragments of literary and post-consumerist culture, to put it in Schoenbergian terms, it too, avoids being in a specific key. Not just the title poem, but in fact the whole book moves through a wide variety of tones, microtones, feels, foci—whether that be homophonic translations, (Pound, Olson, Wittgenstein, Cicero); the infusions of vispo, a re-setting of bpNichol's "blues", "Score for Diacritics", (a satirical mashup of the markers of pronunciation); the repurposing of *Lorum Ipsum* (Cicero's, 45 BC treatise on the theory of ethics re-translated as a passionate love poem). Full of transpositions, and inversions, it's continually "checking in" with itself—*itself* which is always something other.

And in the spirit of "otherness," I love how for you, the title reminds you of checking in to a clinic. In that sense, the book would offer a zone of recovery ha! I was thinking more in term of dis-covery, i.e. how "Checking In" not only refers to the act of reporting, enrolling, registering or recording one's arrival or status, but also hidden in its homonymy, "checking in" as "shakin'", ripping one from their normative reading habits. *Chacque'n in,* intralinguistically highlighting how the "same" is always different, how (in the words of Derrida), "every other is every bit other." Or "checking" as in "checked" as a multicolored, harlequinesque cubist motif, patterns of repeating elements; or "checkered" in the sense of a past of varied fortune, credible and incredible incidents ever re-presenting themselves. Or "checking" as in an account, an accounting; an economy of exchange. So all checking and re-checking, *shickered* up, "shooketh" 'n shirkin responsibility, or in a Beyoncé-esque sense of "Check It Out", "Checking In", also references the sense of checking as examining something, scanning, surveying, scrutinizing it in order to determine its condition, detect the presence of something; asks the reader to stop or slow down, as one peruses, probes, analyses, inquires.

So yes, "Checking In" does become so much more than just the beckoning of the Facebook platform. For me, there is one other reference that I am continually haunted by, and kinda underscores everything—If according to Kabbalistic hermeneutics the world was created through letters, their very expansion and contraction (mirroring the very act of meaning production), then in some ways the world can be seen as some giant 3-D pop-up artist book that we live in and recreate with every "reading". And in a kind of Jabèsian way, we enter its warm flesh; enter it sometimes through the skin of its meaning, its form. Enter it with vigilance through its thresholds, agonies and garrulousness, through its illegibilities and dissimulation, disguises, dreams, affirmations and displacement between the writing and the written and the yet to be written where all is shattered fragmented; wandering and rebellious between borders, orders, laws, flaws, codes, idioms, territories, terrortories, deserts and promises, questions, probes, anxieties, abandonments absences abscesses, obsessions and flourishes. And literally BOOK ONESELF IN, enter it as a dwelling place to inhabit—a giant AirBnB to which we are forever "Checking In."

*

As per your question about audience, you raise a good point—as you, Daniel, (with a similar aesthetic / philosophic / literary and cultural background) are an ideal reader, but it's clear to me not everyone will get all the references. It was my great hope, though that there're so many trajects, and enough "accessible" moments, that it would be able to speak to a range of audiences. The book took four years to write, and in that time, I tested it with a radical array of receivers readers / listeners—not only poetry crowds but those focused on Media Ecology, General Semantics, Jewish audiences, international audiences (through India, Italy, France, Czechoslovakia, Austria, Canada, United Kingdom and the United States), learning how to highlight, underscore certain flavors for different occasions—i.e. "Fancy Bread is in thy heart and in thy head […] and also at Balthazar" would be edited for whatever international bakery was most famous in that place. When reading abroad, a lot of the culturally specific references went over their head but they laughed at the Literary references. The Media Ecologists didn't get the Poetry but loved the McLuhan, Postman, Korzybski, and all that relates to television, movies, and songs. The Jews love the Jewy stuff: "Salomé is listening to the Talking Heads," "Moses is Smashing His Tablet," "Samson is Reading the Rape of the Lock." It's been a kinda great learning experience.

Also, interesting you ask about having the book versus working within an arena of digital media—as in collaboration with digital media vispo guru, Jim Andrews, we created a pretty trippy digital version of the title poem. I provided him with about 500 images that relate to the text and using dbCinema, a graphic synthesizer he developed, "brushes" sample from these images, essentially using them as "paint." The images are fragmented, palimpsested, bifurcated, and in some ways highlights the construction of memory, meaning production, the materiality of language and the ever-recombinatory swirling nature of communication; how language is always-already intertextatically layered and proprioceptively received. Its seductive swathes of color texture, image typographies are synechdic of how meaning unveils itself as an ever-spiraling space where "Origin" is unlocatable; where everything is a re-articulation of a re-articulation, translation of a translation, where the past is palimpsestically re-passed, surpassed in an irrepresentable present non present or resonant present that continually escapes itself—

A still from this collab became the cover image for the book:

—and also the six-page full-color "Similily" in the center of the book was created from this method as well (though in this case using 613 images of Monet's Water Lillies).

So YES, love the digital media and these hypertextual electropoetic digitized excursions into new media—but like the age-old conundrum between orality and textuality, each medium a distinct yet confluential experience and I think (or hope) one can find pleasure through all its myriad manifestations.

Here's the link to the full vispoetic *Checking In* text :)
https://www.youtube.com/watch?v=p-syLYJ4Ma8

DM: "Checking In" is funny. You use puns and other playful language styles to draw surprising and humorous connections between and among culture makers one would not often draw together, but, which, do belong together: T. S. Eliot and the Who (teenage wasteland), Cindy Sherman and Whitman (song of selfie), Lady Macbeth and Annie (tomorrow). Can you discuss humor in your poetry? Koch, O'Hara, Ginsberg, and Irving Feldman come to mind, but there isn't a ton of funny serious poetry. Is there something subversive about bringing humor (even silly humor) into avant-garde poetics? Along these lines, irony and puns do create a relation of closeness between the joke teller (speaker) and the listener (the audience). *Checking In* has in its title the theme of connecting speaker to reader/listener/audience. Does your use of humor contribute to your wish to make connections with readers who must "get" the joke?

AK: I think the role of humor in poetry is such an interesting question and something that I love pushing the boundaries of—though over time it's gotten me into a whack of trouble—You may remember, "I got a Crush on Osama" (2000) which was a parody of the Obama Girl video, collected in *The House That Hijack Built*, was featured on Fox News. In the aftermath of 9/11, everyone was literally obsessed with finding Osama bin Laden, so for me, it was a satiric intervention, "imitation with a critical difference," (as Linda Hutcheon might say), an ironic investigation and commentary on how we are so shaped by the media apparatus, our national obsession with celebrity, how we deal with fear. At the time the video was made, the entire nation was consumed with terror, anxiety, fixated on where he was hiding. So, the piece is audacious, subversive, provocative, and (in the true definition of "irony") explodes ontologically and cuts into the fabric of things; the smooth functioning of the quiet comfortability, or the "homeyness" of our world. But in so many ways, that is the role or art. And though I wasn't thinking of it at the time, it kinda operates on the same kinda Warholian pun of "Most Wanted Men."

This sense of disruptive comedy bleeds through much of *Checking In*. Perhaps, in part, one could see it as an "assimilationist" brand of Jewish humor; not of bombastic neurosis, but one that threatens to unleash chaos, creates unsocialized anarchy, embodies unpredictability Impassioned, engaged, shticky, outrageous and earnest all at the same time—in a post-Woody Allen (Jon Stewart / Sarah Silverman / Sandra Bernhard / Joan Rivers / Chelsea Handler) kinda way.

So much about stand up / about joke telling, really at bottom is the juxtaposition of otherness—and how that enables us to say the unsayable, elevate the mundane, mixing, combing, spinning, twisting reference, syntax, idioms—providing different avenues of connection. And, though they often get a bad rap, in some ways, for me, punning is the highest art form, inhabiting what Freud might call a "psychic economy," opening up the possibilities for infinite signification ;) This sense of parodic commentary / satire has always been my preferred mode. Even as a young girl growing up in Canada, when everyone else was trading hockey cards, I collected Wacky Packages.

DM: Let me quote some things about "genre" and the rise of the construction of the canon and the idea of national literature from *Doing English: A Guide for Literature Students* by Robert Eaglestone (Routledge):

"Also important for the construction of the idea of canon is the concept of *genre*. The poets and writers of the Renaissance (roughly 1450–1650) also produced lists, ranking the most important types, or *genres*, of writing ('genre' basically means 'kind' or 'type' of literary text). The British poet Sir Philip Sidney (1554–1586) produced a list that classed poetry by type: epic, lyric, comic, satiric, elegiac, amatory, pastoral sonnet, epigram. Epic poetry—about the origins of nations and peoples—was the greatest, most enduring, and most significant form, while short poems about love were the most transient and insubstantial [...] By the eighteenth century, it was common to find debates not only over the worth of particular genres of poetry but over the worth of particular poets [...] The ideas of authority, authenticity, genre value and nationalism began to come together even more closely in the nineteenth century. Perhaps most influential in the formation of the canon were the many anthologies of poetry popular in the nineteenth century." (60–61)

I thought of these passages on genre, national identity, canon, and literary value as I experienced *Checking In*. *Checking In* is a genre-busting text. The poem "Checking In," for example, conceptualizes a Facebook or Twitter page as a found text. "Score for Diacritics" is a concrete poem version of a musical composition score. It includes an international array of diacritical marks (umlaut; circumflex) as signs for musical notes, accompanied on the same page by a lot of white space and a line or two of doggerel verse that combines cultural theory with twisted versions of pop tunes: "let's get pataphysical" (49), a Madonna-esque punning take on Jarry's sly take on whimsical science/metaphysics. You devote four pages to a colorful art/word assemblage you co-created with Jim Andrews ("a still from the seven-minute Vispo video" [85]). In the art/text assemblage, the word "Similily"—a portmanteau that blends simile and lily and silly and simulacrum—appears in layers of chunky but transparent fonts of various sizes filled with bits of Claude Monet's "Nympheas" water lily paintings. Your book also includes concrete poetry—"Eros"—poems designed by Olsonian spatial field ("In Cold Hollers"), and even a list poem made up of lines of titles for poems yet to be written. In a sense, your book is a contemporary anthology of texts that resist easy categorization. You self-consciously challenge traditional genre categorizations of what belongs (and what doesn't) in a book of "serious" poetry.

Please reflect on *Checking In* in terms of genre. Can you pay special attention to the connection between genre, national identification, authorial status, and the canon? You are Canadian, but you teach in New York at Pratt and travel and perform widely, so your situation challenges identification of authorial identity by nation. You are a multimedia artist/performer who does sound recordings, video poems, and whose work has appeared in many media contexts including television.

AK: For all those reasons, the notion of genre and compartmentalization has plagued me always, and as you probably know, my second book was titled "Genrecide" (1994) and features a genre-busting collage essay blurring critical theory, poetry and visual elements overtly addressing the relationship between Genre and Nationalism as a kind of totalitarianistic, somewhat fascistic means of discrimination that is saturated with outmoded ideas of Truth, Authenticity, and Closure, marked by inherent hierarchies that close down dialogue—

Perhaps it's interesting to think about genre in some ways as Marshall McLuhan speaks of Acoustic Space, an "inner landscape, fields of relation, elation, erration; a space which is dynamic and in flux, creating its own dimensions *out of itself.*" *This* is the landscape of *Checking In*—not just merely mashing up "high and low" discourses but an ongoing negotiation of power, definition, resistance; inscribing a language of textual hybridity and jouissance where genre explodes into an intra-subjective matrix of differential locations, allocations, r'elations displacing all sites of discrimination and domination—

And especially now whereby our "reality" is increasingly constructed (and navigated) from within our webbed networks, and our locus, a colloquy of illocatable locution recollated through screens, mirrors, phones, walls, all twittering and blogoscopic, how can we even see nation (like genre) as a thing-in-itself? Maybe better to see it as an *iter[]ation;* an emaNation, a dissemiNation forging (or 5G'ing itself), through 280 characters patterns; structures, codes, logics, idioms; a merger'Nation, of multiple aesthetics, styles, embodying a range of difference, errance, an invagiNation of communication strategies and procedures, of creases caverns, infolded crevices, or an *enjambiNation* of riffs, drifts, grifts, a calculus of constructs, foundations; an immersioNation of links, subversions excursions perversions, generating a contiguous infolding of meaning—

So yeah through all the work and especially in *Checking In*—there is a sense of displacement, in both form and content, highlighting how all webbed up and *sticky*, intratextual and hyperlinked, we can continue to re-negotiate language, meaning, being, from new perspectives—

*

As you point out, my very identity *en process* (between Canada and America, between a variety of ethnic, political and religious identities, aesthetic communities, between genres—as poet, performer, essayist, lecturer, media artist), there is inevitably a sense of exile, ex-staticism that bleeds through all the work; a sense of vagrancy nomadicism, that gets played out / or splayed through hyperspatial interplays. *Checking In* travels (*travailles*) through a complex of codes, texts, borders; logic systems saturated with a palimpsestic his/herstoricities, unpredictability, promiscuity, possibility, and location becomes not a specific site but an abseit cite, parasite-ations of the proper, improper, inappropriate (impropriotous, riotous), which is depropriated, exappropriated and repels, re-appelles or propels itself *into* place or displaced between readability and resistance; a sapirous reciprocity of paracitation, quotation, restoryation, appendices which binds a range of differences and discriminations that inform the discursive and political practices of racial and cultural hierarchization.

Heidegger says, "a boundary is not that at which something stops, but is that from which something begins its presencing," and in a way this is the domain of *Checking In*, "a collection of points," an excess of borders (or *deborder*, excess)—re-locating location not as a fixed, contained and stable place, but as a collusion of locution; illicit loquations, colloquations, correlations of illocatable collation, a hybrid space between ethnicities, cultures, codes; between structures of power, authority, domination; between genres, languages, dialects and ways of speaking.

And maybe, full of echoes, murmerings, it can remind us how borders themselves are always already a series of traces, echoes, cinders inscribed in a spectral economy of exile, rupture, gaps, caesuras, silences and uncertainty, and the old strongholds of genrefication have to be renegotiated.

DM: Adeena, I must ask you about your poem "Contour XLV: With Asura." It is, as Austin Powers would say, "very groovy."

I am not a Poundian, but I am familiar with Canto XLV and its anti-Semitic subtext. Myself a Jew, Pound's screed against usury rings in my ears as I play recordings of him reading it in my classes at Purdue. So, when I read your poem, I weirdly hear Pound's voice as well as your voice in duet. Instead of an anti-Semitic rant on monetary policy, however, the focus is on Asura. You offer a gloss of the obscure term: *"asura:*Yiddish for 'forbidden'; particularly noteworthy in Rabbi Kook's 'The Whispers of Existence'" (84).

Asura has connections with Jewish mysticism, but also Buddhist and Hindu associations with the spirit world. We can connect the term with the main character of a video game: Asura's Wrath. How do you imagine the relations between usury and Asura? Both associated with something forbidden? If we connect Asura with forbidden spirits, do you regard Pound as the daemonic ghost? Pound railed against credit, interest, borrowing money, Jews as moneylenders. He was into the idea of hard currency. But, as with usury, you borrow from Pound and pay him back, with interest.

It is clever, witty, and provocative to turn Usury, the anti-Semitic trope, into Asura, a term connected with Jewish and Eastern religious mysticism, and with the "forbidden." In your version, you link the "forbidden" with the perspective, experience, and language usage of "woman."

So, the forceful, playful, and mellifluous voicings in your poem take power from a "forbidden" source—one of Pound's most notorious anti-Semitic expressions—that is also, in terms of poetics, a resource for contemporary avant-gardists. The avant-garde is a term of war. You use Pound, the avant-gardist extraordinaire, against himself in a battle for your own juicily excessive *Écriture féminine*.

Is the Pound poem part of what is the "forbidden" you translate into a version of your voice? Is the "forbidden" quality of Asura related to something else we have discussed: your willingness to animate your "serious" poetry with jokes, silliness, pop referents, and punning imitations that some might view as the opposite of Highfalutin' Poundian epic modernism: the woman as "hoarder of giddy tomes" who wonders if her "cred [is] ever more than stalwart gags." And also I ask you about the focus in your Asura poem on the woman—the Jewish woman, the erotic/ "kinky" woman of "amorous terrain," the linguistically gifted and literary-historically empowered female poet whose "COUNTER RANT" brings "pulsing to breed" while "battling the languerous grid and the bridled gloom."

AK: Daniel, Daniel, I love how through your beautifully close reading you unpack so much of what I'm doing and extend it in ways I didn't even intend. For me, "With Asura," is a juiced-up Jewy femme-powered "Counter Rant" highlighting both *Asura* as forbidden and the Sanskrit *Asu*—whereby the "daemonic" ghost of Pound literally, figuratively, and acoustically haunts the text. *But,* I was not aware that Buddhist texts from ancient India define "asura" as "titan," "demigod" or "antigod! How fabulously synchronic especially in that these "asuras [...] are addicted to [ ] wrath, pride, envy, insincerity, falseness, boasting, and bellicosity" and how "the state of an asura reflects the mental state of a human being obsessed with ego, force and violence"!

I too have obsessively listened to Pound's textured reading of the original Canto, and was interested in creating a homophonic response whereby reading the two simultaneously provides a kind of trippy echography, ("with mounting treats, strong flavours / with asura the lines grow thick/ with asura [] curled re-creations [...]") explodes aspects of forbiddeness. As we both know, in Hebrew, the word *asura* signifies that which is forbidden (referring not just to the exclusion of women, but say, the consuming of pigs or the unlawful mixing, i.e.. milk and meat, cotton, and linen), I was always also intrigued with how in Swedish, forbidden is förbJUDEN—hiding *in its very name*, prohibitions against Jews. Also interesting is that etymologically, from OE *forbidden* (from *for* "against" + *beodan* "to command," from PIE root *bheudh,* is to "be aware, make aware." So through the forbidding, foreboding, this sense of asura carries within it a sense of uncovering and "making aware." *(((((((t'root will set us free)))))))* And also, of course—the shift from *usar* to *asur* highlighting the non-utilitarian / consumerist aspect of art.

All to say, I was less interested in re-inscribing it with disjunctive infusions as "pure play," but more about having it speak to that antisemetic / woman hating "bellicosity"—borrowing from the Pound text and supplanting it with all that is forbidden / policed (culturally, politically, and aesthetically), underscoring the dirty practice of lending, while explosively vibrating within it, (more than) a pound of flesh ;)

Through an economy of exchange, I wanted to pay it back, pay it forward, not just *with interest* but also thinking about currency as in contemporary idioms, or a *coeur*rency all kinky and amorous yet (dis)heartened, opening a space for the ugly, the crooked, the passionate, for a fleshy um pounding. To this end, I love that you brought to my attention, one other reference for Asura, that I didn't know, but how in Fandom, the Asura is the main protagonist of the 3D action beat 'em up game, *Asura's Wrath* a powerful combatant, hot-tempered, good-hearted warrior who shows an absence of fear. *In for pound.*

DM: Adeena, I found myself thinking about the theme of "leakage." You enact "leakage" throughout your book and focus upon it in the poem "Your Leaky Day." Please reflect on the leaky meanings/relations between image and text in your reframing of a Victorian era postcard-type sentimental style color drawing of an old fashioned image of Little Bo Peep that appears in your book with the label "Ceci n'est pas une peep."

As you can imagine, there is a lot of "deviant" art related to Little Bo Peep imagery. A good deal of it reimagines the Victorian version of Little Bo Peep in ways that subvert the stereotypical version in your book. You offer the traditional image of Little Bo Peep a la Mother Goose rhyme. She is a virginal prepubescent. She is blond-curled, blue-eyed pastoral European white girl set in nature. Gazing away from the viewer, her body is concealed in an abundant array of pink skirts and petticoats and long sleeves, red vest, sun hat fastened by elaborate pink bow around neck and sturdy work boots. Her delicate right hand clutches the legendary shepherd's crook. The crook is adorned with a blue bow and a songbird perch atop the object.

May I ask why you selected the unthreatening image of Little Bo Peep rather than one of the contemporary versions that unleash the powers, libidinal impulses, and embodied diversities suppressed in the archetypal Little Bo Peep image in your book?

Can you talk about this image as it relates to your poetics? Overall, your book plays in the space between revelation and concealment, between showing and not showing, between showing and not telling?

My question pertains to your ambivalent relation to the modernist avant-garde, a question that came up in my inquiry on Pound's "usury" Canto as a "forbidden" aspect of your repertoire. Here, in the Little Po Peep image, you are contextualizing Mother Goose with a complex play on Magritte's "The Treachery of Images—This is Not a Pipe."

Your image text of Little Bo Peep/"Ceci n'est pas une peep" literally and figuratively faces in a dual-page format your poem called "Lov3r's Squall." This poem is a mockup, according to your helpful notes, of Khalil Gibran's "A Lover's Call XXVII." (I should say that your book is quite a network of textuality; I've done a lot of googling to try to keep up with your referentiality!). By placing the NOT Little Bo Peep in dual face with your revision of Gibran's "A Lover's Call," you literally make NOT Little Bo Peep appear to be uttering your version of "A Lover's Call." Your NOT Little Bo Peep, in other words, is not in search of wandering sheep, but rather, in search of "my beloved" (Gibran). And yet, in your version of "A Lover's Call," the desire for the beloved is cast in terms of the desire to find one's own voice in song: "Where are you, my bevelled aria? (57). Your image of Not Little Bo Peep motivated me to read the Mother Goose poem "Little Bo Peep." The version of the poem that appears on the Poetry magazine website is quite stunning in its surreal weirdness and Freudian potentialities. The Mother

Goose poem alludes to dream, desire, loss, mourning, and even castration and death when Bo Peep awakens to find: "their tails, side by side, / All hung on a tree to dry." Your work certainly encourages a form of active reading/reception of intertexts, both within and among your texts, and in relation to your sources texts: Mother Goose, Magritte, Gibran, and the "deviant" versions of Bo Peep that I found via Google images.

AK: OMG Daniel your exegesis, your attention is startlingly astute, observant—again all the ways I consciously intended and so many others that I wasn't even aware of in the writing. With "Ceci n'est pas une peep" I was motivated predominantly by the pun of it—and opted for the most, albeit clichéd image to pair it with, because like a cliché itself, I love the idea of taking some old worn out phrase, revitalizing, recycling it; hijacking it and dyssemically thrusting it into new socio-linguistic zones. And I was totally attracted to the simple ridiculousness of juxtaposing the "stereotypical" Mother Goose image with the Magritte, sifting it through a kinda 'pataphysical historicity and having each cultural referent "leak" into the other—which for me felt "deviant" all on its own.

It is so exciting though to be made aware of these other transgressive bo peep images—which I had no knowledge of. Particularly thrilling was this one:

While I was writing *Checking In*, I was firmly enmeshed in the *Salomé: Woman of Valor* project—(my spoken word opera, with composer, Frank London), revisioning the apocryphal figure through a Jewish Feminist lens and liberating her from the anti-semitic, somewhat misogynist Oscar Wilde text and back into her rightful place in history as a powerful, Jewish matriarch. So, this image you found of bo peep literally beheading the sheep is so beautifully synchronous with the beheading of John the Baptist—

And in both images, the decapitated head needn't be seen as a trophy *per se*, but a site of multiplicity, dialogy. Separated, the head foregrounds the thinking body, a site of the absent present, of lost referents, of apostrophic spectrality. Or thought through a Kabbalistic lens, the separation of the head from the body pays homage to the separation of the primordial letters. *Heady!!*

In any case, when constructing "Ceci n'est pas une peep," (maybe because of my working on Salomé and consumed with how she was scapegoated throughout history), I was thinking about sheep in relation to goats and how, as you know according to Jewish tradition in Temple times, the Priest would put all the sins of the people onto the goat and send it into the forest or sacrifice it. So, was thinking about poor bo peep and wondering how in fact DID she lose her sheep??? How they were maybe "on the lam." In the words of Christopher Smart, I was totally "Rejoicing in the Lamb, the Lamb from bedlam, or as Blake says in Little Lamb, "giving clothing of delight [...] making all the v[eil]s rejoice!" *she, sheepishly, says*—

Also, it's interesting that you highlight the fact that the bo peep image I use in *Checking In* is one of the "the virginal prepubescent"—because that is exactly what Salomé has been historically represented as. And in both cases, I am recontextualizing these virginal girls, imbuing them with something "other" a kind of weightier history.

And in *Checking In*, yes, she is yes, my bo is indeed peeping with her gaze not toward her wandering sheep, but toward the homophonic tran'elated Gibran—because for me she is calling out and into *all that is wandering* as in *diferrance*, all that cannot be contained, all that is inscribed with difference, desire, highlighting how all of language and meaning production is a process of veiling and unveiling, of avails, values, volés; of clarity and obfuscation, how nothing is what it is, (ceci n'est pas une [ ]), as I lay "their ta[le]s, side by side, / hung [as treats] to [t]ry."

SECTION 3
To Teach is to Learn Twice: Poetry, Poetics, and Pedagogy

CHAPTER 11

CONVERGENCE CULTURES: MODERN AND CONTEMPORARY POETRY AND THE GRAPHIC NOVEL

Author's Note

It is not easy to change course—literally and figuratively—as a late-career university professor. Prior to 2018, when I began teaching in a general education program at Purdue designed for first-year students who were majoring in STEM fields, I saw myself as a senior scholar in the niche area of avant-garde twentieth-century poetics. I am proud of my accomplishments in my research area: scholarly monographs, edited collections, books of my own original poetry, presidency of two learned societies, a decade of co-editorship of a scholarly journal, NEH, Fulbright, and College of Liberal Arts Excellence in Discovery awards. Nonetheless, as I enter my thirtieth year at Purdue, I am adjusting my perspective on my career. With the assistance of staff and fellow faculty, I have succeeded, late in my career, to transform myself from a field specialist in modern and contemporary poetics to an innovative instructor in what some—often disparagingly—refer to as a "service" course. As this book indicates, I still publish scholarship, but I now see my main professorial task as developing fresh ways to initiate young students into poetry studies. As this chapter demonstrates, I've learned a lot about the relationship between poetry and graphic novels, a genre familiar to many first-year students. Combining poetry with comics, a popular culture form, I have not compromised my commitment to a humanistic education characterized by active reading as a form of critical engagement. I continue to offer a pluralistic approach to textual analysis that includes formal, ethical, and historical contexts.

My signature assignment in my first-year humanities course asks students to "transform" a poem into a "comics" format, and then to present to class a "how to" speech about their process and their product. Based on lessons we learn through class discussions concerning Scott McCloud's self-reflexive graphic novel, *Understanding Comics: The Invisible Art* (1994), my public-speaking assignment encourages students to enact, and then to explain, the relationships between "form" and "idea," between reception and creation of meaning through a verbal/visual performance of poetry in the comics format.

Traditionally, as in the art criticism of the eighteenth-century German philosopher Gotthold Ephraim Lessing, aesthetic theorists prior to post-modernism distinguished painting and poetry from each other. The visual form, it was argued, excels at representing a single object or person in space, whereas a poem was favored to represent a series of actions in time. Because comics are a sequential art, the form demonstrates how genres matter in the construction of meaning, but also how media can be combined to display ideas, moods, and kinds of beauty ranging from the photographic to the abstract to the cartoonish. By crafting a comics version of a poem, students must think about formal issues. They must consider how to sequence panels, how to use the "gutter" as a negative space to create viewer involvement, and how to combine image and word to convey ideas and emotions. Students must also articulate why they made their formal choices. Formal choices, we learn, are always meaningful choices. Form and idea, I teach, cannot be separated in poetry or in any other creative art. In Deweyan terms, students learn this lesson by doing it. The following chapter, originally written for a volume intended to help teachers and students approach the graphic novel as a significant literary form, stems from my ongoing interest in finding new ways to help students engage with poetry in the contemporary classroom through association with popular visual cultures.

***.

In some ways, a lack of critical attention to the correlation between poetry and graphic novels makes perfect sense even as W. J. T. Mitchell has noted that in our era of "the pictorial turn" it has become challenging to "keep visuality and visual images out of the study of language and literature" (1995, 542). Graphic novels are, as Will Eisner famously argued, a "sequential" form. Most lyric poetry, by contrast, displays tonal dynamism but is limited in temporal scope: a spot of time recollected in tranquility, to combine Wordsworthian formulations, or time halted through a "momentary stay against confusion," to quote Frost's observation on the value of formal poetry in modern times in "The Figure a Poem Makes" (553). Setting aside narrative or epic modes—neither, with notable exceptions, predominant since the Romantic era—it is difficult to imagine a sustained graphic novel based, say, on an imagistic poem by H.

D., a philosophical meditation by Wallace Stevens, or a deconstructed autobiography in prose poem form by West Coast Language-oriented poet Lyn Hejinian. As Dave Morice, who since the late 1970s has been among the most influential advocates for poetry comics, acknowledges, "[s]ome poems, such as Lewis Carroll's nonsense masterpiece, 'Jabberwocky,' can't be rendered literally, because there is no literal interpretation possible. What's a *tove*, a *borogove*, a *rath*, and a *Jabberwock*?" (2008b, 31). At the same time, Morice states, he has "drawn eleven different versions of that [Lewis Carroll] poem." His admission indicates that translating poetry into a comics format should be understood as a creative collaboration between poet and illustrator. The interaction that, implicitly, occurs between poet and comics artist emphasizes the latter's imagination, formalist concerns, and interpretative actions. Reflecting on the process of drafting cartoons based on poems "by Whitman, Dickinson, Shakespeare, Blake and others" for *Poetry Comics*, a magazine he started in 1977 at the University of Iowa, Morice recalls his relationships to poetry shifted from passive consumer to active co-creator: "Previously I was a spectator, but now I was a teammate of the superpoets of history" (2008a, 28). Four decades after Morice's ground-breaking experiments, however, bringing poetry into conversation with the graphic novel remains an eccentric, but potentially beneficial, endeavor. Combining poetry with comics may elevate the significance of both genres. At the same time, combining genres may challenge German Enlightenment philosopher and aesthetician G. E. Lessing's view in *Laocoön: An Essay on the Limits of Poetry and Painting* (1766) that poetry and the visual arts must remain divided from each other because the former is a temporal (narrative) form while the latter is spatial and still. Contra Lessing—influential to modernist proponents of formal purity such as Clement Greenberg and critiqued by contemporary interarts theoreticians such as W. J. T. Mitchell—John R. Parket observes, "the visual rhythms of comics are just as pronounced as the verbal cadences of poetry; many modern poems place importance not just on the words, but the actual location of words on the page and movement of the human eye" (Parket 2011). This essay does not, however, focus on the relationship between poetry and abstract comics (see Molotiu 2009), on the one hand, and the emergence of what Tamryn Bennett (2014) calls the "graphic poem," on the other hand. My focus is on interarts translation. What happens, I ask, when a comics artist transforms a poem, first published as words on a white page, into a new graphic form? Paradoxically, it turns out, the disjunctive, spatial, allusive, collaborative, and sequential features of T. S. Eliot's seminal modernist epic, *The Waste Land* (1922) and Allen Ginsberg's mid-twentieth-century Beat classic, *Howl* (1956), have provided the source texts for Martin

Rowson and Eric Drooker to craft the two most celebrated, if controversial, graphic novels based on long twentieth-century poems. As Stephen Tabachnick has argued, Eliot's poem challenges the reader to "leap from line to line, and section to section, trying to find order, but is almost never sure about how to connect the new line or section with the one preceding it" (Tabachnick 2000, 84). Ironically, given the common misperception that experiencing comics is merely a leisure activity for juveniles that requires little creative effort on the reader's part, Eliot's notoriously inscrutable pastiche may in fact be the type of poem best suited to the comics medium, which Tabachnick and Brian McHale, following Scott McCloud, note, "moves in terms of readerly leaps from panel to panel across the empty 'gutters' between them" (2010, 84).

Composing a sequential series of intermedial images, the comics artist uses standard elements of the format—gutters, panels, thought bubbles, speech balloons, story boxes—to produce what theorist Hannah Miodrag calls, "the radical heterogeneity of visual signification, which subsumes an array of different codes such as size, color, texture, and location, very different to language's finite pool of like units" (2013, 10). As Miodrag's commentary indicates, scholarship on graphic novels tends toward establishing a language peculiar to the form, but such analyses, I will argue, resonate with topics addressed by poetry scholars. In their introduction to a special issue of *Critical Inquiry* devoted to the topic, editors Patrick Jagoda and Hillary Chute, for example, ask questions about the "art and design," "rhetorical patterning," "typography," and the "graphics" of comics that resonate with how critics respond to poetry in a new media environment. Jagoda and Chute also imagine comics as a hybrid form. Noting a "transmedia turn in popular culture" (Chute and Jagoda 2014, 2), they place the genre in "transmedia ecologies" (7) in a period media theorist Henry Jenkins has defined as characterized by a "convergence culture." Following their lead, I see my essay on poetry and the graphic novel as an intervention in transmedia studies. Basing the graphic novel on canonical twentieth-century poems such as *The Waste Land* and *Howl*, the artist, I contend, produces a genuinely innovative transmedia text. Words (often handdrawn) and the more overtly visual dimension of the work function separately (as semiotician Miodrag points out, written language is arbitrary but visual language is motivated), but interactively, with the preeminence of writing challenged. Discussing comics from the perspective of reception, Chute and Jagoda argue that the form is oriented toward an open-ended, active, or participatory response. It is for them "a form that gestures at robust readerly involvement; it actively solicits—through its constitutive grammar the participant's role in generating meaning. Further, comic pages do not function directively as some other forms of media; the correct direction of reading is often unclear; and deliberately so. The relationship between word and image is often disjunctive, even within the space of one frame" (4). Modern and contemporary poetry often shares with comics the qualities of disjunction, readerly orientation, open-endedness, and what Rachel Du Plessis calls "segmentivity." At the same time, I interrogate what happens to that open-endedness when a poem such as *Howl* or *The Waste Land* is, quite literally, imagined in a graphic novel context. Does the comics' frame add to or detract from the "robust readerly involvement" that Chute and Jagoda claim the genre "actively solicits"? In assessing the convergence of poetry and graphic novel animation, we must address questions of canonicity, audience reception, and the issue of how contextual frames influence the significance of cultural artifacts. My essay questions the degree the animation of difficult modernist poetry such as Eliot's may contribute to the reception of the poetry in a pedagogical space that increasingly favors visual display. On the opposite side of the coin, I ask to what degree does the affiliation of poetry with comics disrupt the "street cred" associated, for example, with R. Crumb and Alison Bechdel at a point when the genre's status undergoes revision?

There are only a few bona fide graphic novels devoted to twentieth-century poems in the English and American literary tradition.[1] By invoking the phrase "bona fide graphic novels," I exclude the quite common instances of short lyrics printed with an accompanying illustration that interacts with the words in a one-dimensional way. Lance Tooks's 2011 illustration of Paul Laurence Dunbar's "Sympathy" (1899), however stylish it may be, is a case in point (Pomplun and Tooks, 74). Dunbar's poem, written on the cusp of modernism but displaying traditional features, consists of three elegantly written stanzas, each containing seven, four-beat lines, each rhymed (ABCCBAA, ABAABAA, ABCCBAA), and with each stanza beginning and ending with a variation on the famous exclamation, picked up by Maya Angelou for her 1969 memoir, "I know why the caged bird sings!" (Angelou, 1969). Co-editor of a collection of

---

1 Besides the efforts by Rowson and Drooker that I will discuss below, Bianca Stone's *Poetry Comics from the Book of Hours* (2016), which features what the Louisiana State University publisher's page for the volume describes as "a mixture of dreamy expression and absurdist wit that is entirely her own. Her watercolor panels are filled with anthropomorphic horses and baffled ballerinas that guide the reader through the poet's graphic dreamscape," is a prominent recent example. http://lsupress.org/books/detail/poetry-comics-from-the-book-of-hours/ (last accessed 19 Sept. 2017).

illustrated African American classics and a former assistant editor at Marvel Comics, Tooks sets Dunbar's poem beside his colorful portrait of the bust of an attractive young African American female, cast in a sidewise profile, absorbed in dreamlike reverie.[2] Tooks emphasizes her large closed eyes, thick lashes and brows, aquiline nose, bluish shadows over her cheeks and neck, and streaks of black hair tightly kept in a bun surrounded by lipstick red flourishes that suggest the spontaneous quality of the artist's sketchy compositional method. Above the maroon ink marks and the top of the woman's head, Tooks imposes an image of a cylindrical bird cage containing an abstracted (presumably male) peacock-like bird with long purplish wing feathers, curvilinear neck, beak, and small head from which stems four plumes, and an arrow-shaped orange breast (pointing downward toward the young women). The bird's thin beak, languid neckline, and the downcast turn of its head all mirror the woman's image beneath it suggesting, as does Dunbar's poem, an emotional connection between the caged bird and the poem's speaker. The caged bird, however, is, unlike Dunbar's caged bird, neither singing nor beating its wings until "its blood is red on the cruel bars" (Pomplun and Tooks, 74). Further, Tooks does not depict notable features of the poem such as the relationship the text draws between the caged bird and the prayer-like song it intones to register detachment from a romanticized setting of flowing rivers, budding, perfumed flowers, and sun-lit slopes. Tooks's illustration moves "Sympathy" in the direction of female suffering in silence (mouth closed) and without seeing (eye closed), whereas most readers of Dunbar's poem connect the lyric "I" to Dunbar, the male African American author who was born in Dayton, Ohio in 1872. In fact, one could argue that Tooks revises the theme of Dunbar's poem away from a political one focused on African American suffering in the face of Jim Crow-era segregation and toward a visual narrative that connotes

---

2 As the *Graphicnovel Reporter* website states:

> African-American Classics presents great stories and poems from America's earliest Black writers, illustrated by contemporary African-American artists. Featured are "Two Americans" by Florence Lewis Bentley, "The Goophered Grapevine" by Charles W. Chesnutt, "Becky" by Jean Toomer, two short plays by Zora Neale Hurston, and six more tales of humor and tragedy. Also featured are eleven poems, including Langston Hughes's "Danse Africaine" and "The Negro," plus Paul Laurence Dunbar's "Sympathy" ("I know why the caged bird sings [...]").

http://www.graphicnovelreporter.com/reviews/african-american-classics-graphic-classics-volume-(last accessed 19 Sept. 2017).

unrequited female desire. I say this because the image of the caged male bird appears to be a thought bubble depicting what the woman is imagining while her eyes are closed. Nancy Barnhart argues: "In a poetry comic, each comic frame blends image with text to help anchor meaning, much like illustrations in picture books. The pictures help students visualize hard to grasp lines by making the abstract concrete" (2009, 23). As my reading of Tooks's illustration indicates, however, a comics image may do more than "help anchor meaning" in relation to a poem, but rather may impose an entirely new meaning upon it. At the same time, because Tooks's illustration is separated on the page from Dunbar's writing, one could say that even as his painting of the young woman fantasizing about the caged male bird redirects our reading of the lyric toward an expression of female desire and away from the theme of African American protest against racial discrimination, Tooks maintains the integrity of the poem's formal features in ways that, I will now show, many other comics artists who take on poetry do not achieve.

In the more robust poetry/comics hybrids I discuss below, poetry is, quite literally, re-visioned, often radically so, well beyond the assistance in "anchor[ing] meaning" described by Barnhart. An ekphrastic process, but reversed, in which a written text is interpreted in a medium that is oriented toward visuality, Morice's comics version of portions of Walt Whitman's proto-modernist "Song of Myself" (1855) in "The Adventures of Whitman" (1982) illustrates why we may consider the comics versions of poems as much acts of reading and interpretation by the artist as they are acts of rewriting and visualization of the original poem in order to anchor its meaning. Using bold blacks and solid whites (no grays) for a cartoon that spans 42 panels of various sizes and shapes, Morice, in the first four panels, imagines Whitman as a shaggy haired, bearded, bespectacled figure (think Clark Kent combined with Jerry Garcia) wearing a wide-brimmed farmer hat comparable to the one Whitman donned for his engraving of the poet as everyman in laborer's clothes that appeared on the frontispiece for the 1855 First Edition of *Leaves of Grass*. Morice figures Whitman as a contemporary American couch potato. He swills generic beer from a lounge chair with his feet propped up on a round ottoman while staring at a news announcer on the tube. In subsequent panels, presumably animated to action upon listening to disturbing information from the newsman depicted on the screen, Whitman tears off his street clothes to reveal a Superman-type outfit, but with a "W" instead of an "S" stamped on his chest and cape. Indicating the intertextual quality of poetry comics, Whitman as superhero resembles William Blake's depiction of God as an Architect in an illustration from *The Ancient of Days*. "Paumanok Starting," he proceeds to "FLY LIKE A BIRD" over a Gotham-style cityscape and into outer space where the Whitman/Superman goes "SPEEDING WITH TAIL'D METEORS" to punch his way through cosmic debris to confront aliens who inhabit a spaceship (223). Morice does not display—does not *try* to display—anything like a standard academic version of why Whitman is regarded as a major figure in American literature and a precursor to modernist poetry. He does not focus, for example, on Whitman's Civil War era poetry ("The Wound Dresser," "Calvary Crossing a Ford," "A Vigil Strange I kept One Night," and his elegies to Abraham Lincoln are examples), or on Whitman's ground-breaking poetics, which anticipated modernism by refusing accentual syllabic verse patterns and end rhymes in favor of what the poet viewed as the more democratic (because not difference based) strategy of cataloging very long lines with anaphora and by replacing rhyme with parallel structures that align end-stopped lines. In "The Adventures of Whitman," the figure of the poet is, in McCloud's terms, an icon, through which the author can enter into Whitman's persona in an idiosyncratic manner that projects Morice's fascinations with mid-twentieth-century popular culture—he transforms the *Superman* television program's "It's a bird, it's a plane [...] it's superman [...]" into "IT's A BARD [...] IT'S A POET [...] IT'S WHITMAN" (223)—and his commitment to political liberty through his surrealist visions of the good gray bard as a cosmic fighter against Cold War conformity. Ignoring the poet's long line, arguably his most important contribution to, in Pound's terms, "breaking the back of the pentameter," Morice splices bits from at least five different Whitman poems into thought bubbles, speech bubbles, and story boxes that, in Morice's terms provide, "[i]nformation that is necessary to the narration—such as, stage directions, moods, time changes" (Appendix: *Poetry Comics: An Animated Anthology*). Since Morice describes Whitman as a figure on the side of good as well as evil—"I AM NOT THE POET OF GOODNESS ONLY,// I DO NOT DECLINE TO BE//THE POET OF WICKEDNESS ALSO"—it is difficult to fit his Whitman hero into the unambiguous Cold War-style binary that animated the depiction of mid-twentieth-century American heroes such as Superman (223). That said, Morice's Whitmanic hero reflects a sensibility especially critical of extraterrestrial figures who appear to be identical automatons. The rows of floating mannequins with black-and-white mask-like heads and faces lack human traits such as an awareness of mortality and embodied desires. It is this challenge to basic signs of human feeling, individuality, and awareness that compels the superhero-poets to battle the aliens even as in the final panels Whitman identifies with the "THE DUPLICATES OF MYSELF" as the source of his own guilty relationship to conformism. Implying his complicity with a monotonous environment, the final panel includes Whitman's interrogation of an alien figure, apparently the leader of the "LITTLE PLENTIFUL MANNIKINS," about his guilty secrets. In "How to Make Poetry Comics," Morice has himself rightfully noted that in "moving from poem to cartoon, you take a given group of words and create a visual environment around them. The change automatically affects the tone of the poem. The results can be illustrational, satirical, critical, or surreal" (2002, 116). In the case of "The Adventures of Whitman," Morice most certainly achieves something well beyond an "illustrational" result.

In *The Beats: A Graphic History* (2009) and *Hip Hop Family Tree* (2013), writers such as Harvey Pekar and graphics artists such as Ed Piskor have combined their talents by narrating the history of outsider poets such as Allen Ginsberg and Diane DiPrima and rap and hip-hop wordsmiths such as LL Cool J and Kool Moe Dee. These two informative graphic novels contribute to the canonization of ground-breaking movements in twentieth-century transgressive poetics, but how does the casting of a canonical modernist poem in comic book format itself challenge the initial work's meaning(s), and especially the association of poetry with reader access to the cultural capital associated with the prestige of an elite form such as modernist poetry? Here Martin Rowson's ambivalently loving, book-length parody version of *The Waste Land* (1990) is an especially paradoxical example of how the graphic novel may simultaneously inspire a new generation to appreciate Eliot's achievement without reproducing any of the language the quintessential modern poet put forward in his most celebrated poem. Rowson interprets Eliot's poem with a combination of irreverence and a genuine feeling for what Tabachnick regards as the text's "imitation of the distorted characters and sinister atmosphere of the Gothic and from the gaps in meaning that constitute much of the Modern element in the original" ("Gothic," 87). Reflecting the atmosphere of urban decay and spiritual uncertainty evident in Eliot's poetry from the 1920s, Rowson imagines *The Waste Land* as

> a Dashell Hammett-Raymond Chandler hard-boiled detective novel, using people and events drawn from John Huston's film version of Hammett's novel *The Maltese Falcon* (as well as from Chandler's novel *The Big Sleep*) to fill in some of the many gaps in the plot and characterization of *The Waste Land*. (So, for instance, in Rowson's graphic novel, Mr. Eugenides looks like Sidney Greenstreet, who played the "Fat Man" in the film version of *The Maltese Falcon*). (Tabachnick 2000, 84)

Rowson's selection of the detective story as narrative template, Brian McHale has argued, is especially appropriate for a graphic novel treatment of a poem that encourages a vigorous type of reading that may be likened to an "epistemological quest" (2010, 252). Rowson addresses readers as "detectives who piece together more or less plausible scenarios from fragmentary choices" (1990, 252).

The most discussed example of a graphics novel based on a twentieth-century poem, Rowson's work is controversial because his book challenged, however unsuccessfully, the status of Eliot's poem as a copyrighted text. First published with ample quotations from Eliot's poem in the United States in 1990, Eliot's executors denied Rowson the right to quote from the poem in a subsequent UK edition.[3] A celebrated London cartoonist born in 1959 whose work regularly appears in the *Guardian*, Rowson, forced to revise his graphic novel for its English edition without access to direct quotations from the poem, relied upon his wit and ingenuity to convey Eliot's themes, tones, movements, and cultural environment by finding verbal substitutions.[4] Frederick Williams and Edward Brunner note, for example, that Rowson takes a dig at the poet's own appropriative tendencies by substituting the children's rhyme "Tom Tom the Piper's son stole a pig and away he run" for the "London bridge is falling down" rhyme that appears in Eliot (Williams and Brunner 2015, 190). As the website *HipComic* reports, Eliot also suggests cultural context by representing Marlowe trolling a

> nightmare world where Robert Frost, Norman Mailer and Edmund Wilson drink in the gloom of a London pub; where Auden is glimpsed entering the men's room; where Henry James, Aldous Huxley and Richard Wagner share an ice cream aboard a Thames pleasure steamer; and where, out of

---

3 Following the lead of *Modernism and Copyright* (Saint-Amour 2010), my brief analysis of Rowson's *The Waste Land* thus considers the question, raised by Paul K. Saint-Amour, "how is the study of modernism today being affected by expanding copyright regimes?"
4 As Kevin Jackson has observed:

> In Britain, a lengthy period of horse-trading between Penguin and the lawyers resulted in a version which was more or less intact pictorially but in which many of the wittiest verbal gags (this is a strip in which the Sanskrit word DA is transformed into the local DA) were at best muffled, at worst ruined. Phlebas the Phoenician had to become Mike the Minoan, Stetson became Idaho Ez and the nightingale from "The Fire Sermon" now says "Quack". (Jackson 1994, online unpaginated)

luck and out of clues, Marlowe finally tracks down T. S. Eliot and Ezra Pound. (HipComic unpaginated)

Rowson also transforms Eliot's notoriously disjunctive poem into a comparatively lucid hardboiled noir murder mystery. Replacing Eliot's clairvoyant figure, Tiresias, who is depicted by Rowson as "a cross-dressing sex worker whose age has reduced him to abject propositions" (Williams and Brunner 2015, 186), as the narrative voice, Rowson's visual format, often associated by critics with textual defamiliarization, reduces the disorienting effect of a verbal collage that Eliot scholar Nancy K. Gish regards as "a set of moods, often without concrete bases in situation or event, along with dramatic scenes and stream-of-consciousness meditations on desire, sexuality, loss, life and death, and the possibility of change, hope, and restoration of value" (1988, 30). A master of what we would today think of as sampling, Eliot mashed together bits of text ranging from religious works such as the *Bible* and *Upanishads* to classics of English poetry and drama by Spenser, Shakespeare, and Thomas Kyd to touchstones of modernism ranging from Baudelaire to Joseph Conrad's *The Heart of Darkness* to riffs on ragtime jazz music and on to what Gish refers to as "the Perilous Chapel of the Grail legends as interpreted by Jessie Weston" (1988, 26). Rowson's version, too, is something of an intermedial pastiche. It features a Humphrey Bogart-style detective named Chris Marlowe who, holding office in the Bay Area at the beginning of the graphic novel, travels to London to investigate the murder (which in the end turns out to have been faked) of his partner Miles Fisher, as well as search for a stolen chalice, but, as Williams and Brunner point out, "the chalice that all had been greedily fighting over ends up in Marlowe's possession, and having no use for it, he hands it over to the corpulent expatriate Marie" who "converts [the] chalice into drinking goblet" (2015, 190). By referencing the grail legend that served as one of Eliot's archetypal templates, but treating the goblet as only useful for a drunken woman to imbibe toward the end of the graphic novel, Rowson pulls the legendarily High Cult classic down to earth.[5] Similarly, what Williams and Brunner refer to as

---

5 As is the case with Eliot's poem, which imposes several layers of archetypal motif involving a grail quest and a legend concerning a wounded Fisher King that shares "with the ancient rituals the restoration of a waste land to life and fertility" (Gish 1988, 43) upon the fragmented modern scene characterized by what Gish calls "a prevailing mood of fear, loss, and unease" (31), Rowson plays with the grail myth and the death of his partner, appropriately named Fisher, to impose a narrative dimension upon what would otherwise appear to be a cacophony of Eliotic archetypes, allusions (including references to other

Rowson's use of "ever-shifting and freewheeling arrangement[s] that recalls the sensational layouts that the production designers for *Classics Illustrated* favored to compete for the attention of adolescents in the American comic-book market in the 1940s and 1950s," combined with imagery drawn from the pop cult realms of pulp fiction, detective genre fiction, and Hollywood film, contribute to the reframing of a modernist touchstone as an ironic, if tender, postmodern pastiche (Williams and Brunner 2015, 183).

Rowson combines classics of modernist poetry and detective fiction within a graphic novel format that itself tips a hat to tropes associated with modernist classics of film and painting. Alluding to a scene from Michael Curtiz's 1942 film starring Humphrey Bogart and Ingrid Bergman, one panel, for example, depicts a propeller airplane flying over a map that features a broken line indicating the path Marlowe travels from Los Angeles to London with Casablanca listed on the map alongside the names of some of the other "unreal cities" that Eliot lists in his poem. In terms of modernist painting, another panel combines imagery from Georges Seurat's "A Sunday Afternoon on the Island of La Grande Jatte" (1884) and George Bellows's "Forty-Two Kids" (1907) as a group of downtrodden working-class men loiter on the bank of the Thames while also in the foreground one man bathes in the dirty water with the Tower Bridge, its suspension bridge lifted to allow a steamship with the name La Paloma (the Dove) to cross it, apparent in the background. The intermedial references to noir detective fiction, film, and modern painting create a peculiar, even paradoxical, effect in Rowson's satire of Eliot's high cult poem. Rowson is at once parodying and mirroring Eliot's strategy of managing cultural references, both high and low, in a context that at first glance appears to cohere into an archetypal narrative, but, as Rowson himself claims, is, like Eliot's poem, in fact a bricolage of red herrings:

> The way [*The Waste Land* is] taught, certainly at A-level, is as a detective story where you rummage through the quotations and allusions and try to find what all of them mean [...] it's presented as a kind of mystery which you have to delve into, and at the end there's no real conclusion. Moreover, it matches brilliantly with the Chandleresque detective story where there

---

Eliot poems such as "The Love Song of J. Alfred Prufrock" and the Sweeney poems), imagery, characters, and allusions to Chandler novels such as *The Big Sleep* and *The Long Goodbye*.

are red herrings and McGuffins all over the place and you're never quite sure what's going on. (qtd. in Jackson 1994, unpaginated)[6]

Like Eliot in *The Waste Land*, whose speaker says he wants to "shore these fragments against my ruins," we also can interpret Chandler's Marlowe as a perplexed modernist hero, attempting to bring ethics, courage, order, and justice to a sordid world that defies cut-and-dried interpretation. Unlike Eliot's *The Waste Land*, however, in which traditional notions of lyric voice are decentered through the poet's sampling of texts ranging from Dante and the *Upanishads* to ragtime jazz, Marlowe's role as hero and especially as narrator controls our reception of the visual text through his wisecracking tone of voice. Counterintuitively, Rowson's visual idiom (often associated by comics theorists with defamiliarization) limits the unruly quality of Eliot's verbal bricolage as it, in Brian McHale's term, *"narrativizes The Waste Land"* (McHale, 34).

In contrast to Eliot's disruptive literary executors, Allen Ginsberg encouraged New York artist Eric Drooker's visualizations of his poetry to the point we could describe *Howl: A Graphic Novel* (2010), which features artwork Drooker had originally designed as an animation for the Rob Epstein/Jeffrey Friedman biopic *HOWL* (2011) as well as his prior effort, *Illuminated Poems* (1996), a sampling of 34 poems Ginsberg published between 1948 and 1992 accompanied by Drooker paintings and drawings that had originally appeared in the *New Yorker*, as genuinely collaborative endeavors. From the late 1980s, when Ginsberg collected Drooker's politically radical posters—the Leftist Jewish poet would notice the public art and then clandestinely tear it off brick walls and lampposts on his wanderings around the Lower East Side of Manhattan—and until his death in 1997, Ginsberg admired Drooker's art and sought his services as early as 1993 when the author tapped Drooker to create a poster for his poem

---

6 Rowson continues:

> And then an image came into my head, which was of Phlebas the Phoenician (from Book IV, "Death by Water"), but which was also the scene from *The Big Sleep* where they dredge the Packard out of the bay. After that, these curious coincidences started arising. I discovered that Chandler and Eliot were both celebrating their centenaries in the year I started doing it, and then, re-reading *The Long Goodbye* in order to gen up on the genre, I discovered these wonderful quotations, such as: "She is very languid and very shadowy and you can't lay a finger on her because in the first place you don't want to and in the second place she is reading *The Waste Land* or Dante in the original [...]" (Rowson quoted in Jackson, 1994 unpaginated)

"The Lion for Real" for a St. Mark's Poetry Project New Year's Day Benefit. For Ginsberg, the artist's "scratchboard print" style was reminiscent of how progressive artists depicted "Weimar American 1930s Depressions" (Ginsberg and Drooker 2006, xii). Drooker's posters, in Ginsberg's terms, were appealing because the art conveyed in "such vivid detail that the authoritarian reality horror of our contemporary dog-eat-dog Malthusian technoeconomic classwar became immediately visible" (Ginsberg and Drooker 2006, xii). Drooker's art in *Howl: A Graphic Novel*, however, as Michael J. Prince rightly remarks, offers "virtually no direct correspondence in content from text to image. Rather than showing us what the text is telling us, the pictures themselves beg their own 'poetic' interpretation."[7] In a comment featured on the inner sleeve of *Howl: A Graphic Novel*, Ginsberg, undisturbed by the lack of interdependence between text and image, explains that he perceived Drooker's project as an innovative method to introduce key themes and images from his most famous poem concerning, and here I again quote Prince, "poverty, solidarity, sex, drugs, and a symbolic fall and redemption," to a new, visually oriented, audience of media consumers: "I thought that with today's lowered attention span TV consciousness, this would be a kind of updating of the presentation of my work" (Prince, 2012) One may regard Ginsberg's appreciation of the graphic novel format as in line with his own interest in reaching new audiences for poetry by performing his poem in jazzy settings such as at the Six Gallery in San Francisco in 1955 and then publishing *Howl and Other Poems* in 1956 with the Pocket Poets Series from City Lights. Ginsberg was especially impressed with how the artist depicted the "megalopolis" and "gigantic skyscraper vision" from the "Moloch" Section 3 of "Howl." As Drooker points out: "I made Moloch, the God of War, look more or less like a Greek minotaur, [...] It has the head of a bull and the body of Schwarzenegger. It's a terrifying character. We send our

---

7 Prince observes:

> The reader / viewer of this volume would encounter many more "parallel combinations" where word and image function distinctly, such as line 66, "Who threw potato salad at CCNY lecturers [...]" on pages 118–119, which is printed over a red and green close up of a screaming face. Even more disjointed is the parallel combination of the near identical flying translucent skeletal figures on pages 182–183 and 208–209, which accompany the radically different texts as line 109—I'm with you in Rockland where there are twenty-five thousand mad comrades all together singing the final stanzas of the Internationale—and line 123—"Holy New York Holy San Francisco [...]." (Prince 2012)

firstborn to war, in ancient times as well as in modern times" (Messer 2010). Along with his appreciation of Drooker's rendering of the cityscape, Ginsberg has also commended Drooker's sensitive rendering of how his poem's thematizing of poverty, madness, addiction, and despair may also lead individuals to connect with other sufferers as well as encourage visionary insights. Drooker's painting over a two-page spread of two urban hoboes warming themselves beside a barrel that emits a flame shaped like "Mohammedan angels staggering on tenements roofs illuminated," illuminates how Ginsberg addresses the redemptive potential in human suffering (24–25). Overall, Ginsberg viewed Drooker's *Howl* as a way for an artist from a "later generation" to make his poetry from the mid-1950s "still relevant, even inspiring" for the twenty-first century.

In their analysis of the Rob Epstein/Jeffrey Friedman biopic version of *Howl* (2010), starring James Franco as Ginsberg, and which focuses on the composition, performance, and obscenity trial that followed San Francisco publisher Lawrence Ferlinghetti's release in 1956 of *Howl and Other Poems*, Bruhn and Gjelsvik report on how the poem is mediated in the film. Epstein and Friedman represent "Howl" the poem "through a poetry reading, but it is also read out loud as evidence in court; furthermore, we see the poem as written text, but also visually transformed into the animation work of artist Eric Drooker" (Bruhn and Gjelsvik 2014, 350). As in the movie version, Drooker's art in the graphic novel interacts with Ginsberg's poetry in a manner that is simultaneously transformational, media-specific, and integrative. Drooker represents "Howl" the poem in a visual format that often strays from the poem's mimetic content, but the illustrator foregrounds a retro-looking typeface (it is probably "My Underwood," "Special Elite," "Love Letter," or "Gabrielle," all of which are font designs that indicate reference to mid-twentieth-century technology—the manual typewriter) when transcribing Ginsberg's language in a way that directs the reader back to a seminal graphic feature of the original manuscript. As Prince notes, one may accuse Drooker of "mangling" an essential aspect of Ginsberg's poetics by, for example, "artificially extend[ing] over three pages" the first line that was designed to "reflect the human breath." Four images that Drooker juxtaposes on pages six and seven of *Howl: A Graphic Novel*, however, point the reader back toward the poet's authority over his composition by depicting the 29-year-old poet as he types the original "Howl" manuscript in his Bay Area apartment in 1955. One of these images is a contemporaneous black-and-white photograph, taken by Ginsberg's lover, Peter Orlovsky, one is a color still of James Franco as Ginsberg in the filmic version of *Howl* (2010), and two are Drooker paintings, one of Ginsberg, abstracted in an iconic fashion against a light hazy blue background as he smokes a cigarette and types in his white undershirt, the other a close-up, which, as Prince (not paginated) writes, is viewed from the poet's perspective, and also cast in blue tones, of his fingers as they are about to press keys on the manual typewriter. These images foreground Ginsberg's authority and the graphic appearance of his typewritten language as the source for Drooker's subsequent animation. Simultaneously, by transforming the poet into an icon, which, in McCloud's definition of the term, universalizes, amplifies, and abstracts a realistic version of the image in a way that McCloud argues makes the image seem more personal, the viewer is encouraged to project himself or herself into the image and thus to identify with Ginsberg's authority. I stress the iconic quality of Drooker's image of the poet as I conclude my remarks because I believe it captures the reception orientation of his version of "Howl," an emphasis on the reader as co-producer also evident in Rowson's *The Waste Land*.

In this chapter I have built on various scholars such as Brian McHale and Jan Baetens, who, in Tamryn Bennett's terms, address "the need to move beyond narrative analysis" by noting "the impact of other features of comics like fragmentation, spatial arrangement, line, and rhythm" (Bennett 2014, 107–108). I have focused on the challenges the comics artist faces when retaining the distinct graphic features of the poem by maintaining fidelity to what John R. Parket calls, "the actual location of words on the page and movement of the human eye" (Parket 2011)—that is, the poem's lineation, line breaks, use of white space to indicate silence, narrative trajectory, and spatial form—while transferring the poem's themes, moods, tropes, and tones into what Parket refers to as the "visual rhythms" of the comics version.

Works Cited

Primary Texts

W. Craghead III. *How to Be Everywhere*. Bethesda: Gallery Neptune, 2007.
P. L. Dunbar. "Sympathy." In *African-American Classics: Graphic Classics Volume 22*, edited by Lance Tooks and Tom Pomplun. Mount Horeb, WI: Eureka Productions, 2011, p. 74.
R. Epstein, and J. Friedman, dir. *HOWL*. Perf. James Franco, Jon Hamm, Mary-Louise Parker. *Werc Werk Works*. 2010 (Star Media Entertainment 2011 DVD).
R. Fawkes. *One Soul*. Portland: Oni Press, 2011.
A. Ginsberg, poet, and E. Drooker, animation. *Illuminated Poems*. New York: Thunder's Mouth Press, 2006 [1996].
———. *Howl: A Graphic Novel*. New York: Harper, 2010.

R. Kick, Editor. *The Graphic Canon: Volume 2. From "Kubla Khan" to The Bronte Sisters to The Picture of Dorian Gray*. New York: Seven Stories Press, 2012.

D. Morice. "The Adventures of Whitman." In *The Graphic Canon: Volume 2. From "Kubla Khan" to The Bronte Sisters to The Picture of Dorian Gray*, edited by R. Kick. New York: Seven Stories Press, 2012, pp. 222–226.

———, Editor. *Poetry Comics: A Cartoonverse of Poems*. New York: Simon and Schuster, 1982.

———, Editor. *Poetry Comics: An Animated Anthology*. New York: T&w Books, 2002.

H. Pekar, and P. Buhle. *The Beats: A Graphic History*. New York: Hill and Wang, 2010.

E. Piskor. *Hip Hop Family Tree. Volume One*. Seattle: Fantagraphics, 2013.

T. Pomplun, and L. Tooks, Editors. *African–American Classics: Graphic Classics, Volume Twenty Two*. Mount Horeb: Eureka Productions, 2011.

M. Rowson, animator, and T. S. Eliot, poet. *The Waste Land*. Hammondsworth: Penguin, 1990.

S. Stone. *Poetry Comics from the Book of Hours*. Baton Rouge: Louisiana State University Press, 2016.

Secondary Texts

M. Angelou. *I Know Why The Caged Bird Sings*. New York: Random House, 1969.

N. Barnhart. "Words and Images: Using Poetry Comics with Young Students." *Teachers & Writers* 41, no. 2 (2009): 23–26.

T. Bennett. "Comics Poetry. Beyond 'Sequential Art.'" *Image (&) Narrative* 15, no. 2 (2014): 106–123.

J. Bruhn, and A. Gjelsvik. "Ginsberg's Animating Typewriter: Mixing Senses and Media in *Howl*." *Word & Image* 30, no. 4 (2014): 348–361.

H. Chute, and M. DeKoven. "Introduction: Graphic Narrative." *Modern Fiction Studies* 52, no. 4 (2006): 767–782.

H. Chute, and P. Jagoda, Editors. "Comics." *Critical Inquiry* 40, no. 3 (2014): 1–10.

N. Cohn. *The Visual Language of Comics: Introduction to the Structure and Cognition of Sequential Images*. New York: Bloomsbury, 2014.

R. B. DuPlessis. *Blue Studios: Poetry and its Cultural Work*. Tuscaloosa: University of Alabama Press, 2006.

W. Eisner. *Comics and Sequential Art*. Tamarac: Poorhouse Press, 1985.

R. Frost. The "Figure a Poem Makes". *Collected Poems of Robert Frost*. New York: Holt, Rinehart, and Winston, 1939. Reprinted in *The Bedford Anthology of American Literature*. Volume 2: 1865 to the Present. Second Edition. Susan Belasco and Linck Johnson, editors. Boston: Bedford, 2014.

J. Gardner. *Projections: Comics and The History of Twenty-First Century Storytelling*. Palo Alto: Stanford University Press, 2012.

N. K. Gish. *The Waste Land: A Poem of Memory and Desire*. New York: Twayne, 1988.

HipComic. *The Waste Land* SC VF martin rowson parody - t.s. eliot - ezra pound – detective. n.d. https://www.hipcomic.com/listing/the-waste-land-sc-vf-martin-rowson-parody-ts-eliot-ezra pound-detective/1834946 (last accessed September 19, 2017).

K. Jackson. "T S Eliot: The Sequel: First that Film, Now this Waste Land Opera based on a Comic. No Wonder Lawyers Acting for the Eliot Estate are So Busy." *Independent*. May 3, 1994. http://www.independent.co.uk/arts-entertainment/t-s-eliot-the-sequel-first-that-film-now-this-waste-land-opera-based-on-a-com (last accessed: September 20, 2017).

H. Jenkins. *Convergence Culture: Where Old and New Media Collide*. New York: New York University Press, 2008 [2006].

G. E. Lessing. *Laocoön: An Essay on the Limits of Poetry and Painting*, translated by E. A. McCormick. Baltimore: Johns Hopkins University Press, 1984 [1766].

S. McCloud. *Understanding Comics: The Invisible Art*. Northampton: Kitchen Sink Press, 1993.

B. McHale. "Narrativity and Segmentivity, or Poetry in the Gutter." In *Intermediality and Storytelling*, edited by M. Grishakova and M.-L. Ryan. Berlin: De Gruyter, 2010, pp. 27–48.

A. Messer. "Eric Drooker: Graphic Novel of Ginsberg's '*Howl*'." *SFGATE.com*. September 30, 2010. http://articles.sfgate.com/2010-09-30/entertainment/24103909_1_graphic-novel-pixar-moloch (last accessed September 19, 2017).

M. Miodrag. *Comics and Language: Reimagining Critical Discourse on the Form*. Jackson: University of Mississippi Press, 2013.

W. J. T. Mitchell. *Blake's Composite Art: A Study of the Illuminated Poetry*. Princeton: Princeton University Press, 1978.

———. "Interdisciplinarity and Visual Culture." *Art Bulletin* 67, no. 4 (1995): 540–542.

———. *Picture Theory: Essays on Verbal and Visual Representation*. Chicago: University of Chicago Press, 1994.

A. Molotiu, Editor. *Abstract Comics: The Anthology*. Seattle: Fantagraphics, 2009.

D. Morice. "How to Make Poetry Comics." Appendix to *Poetry Comics: An Animated Anthology*. New York: Teachers & Writers Books, 2002.

———. "Poetry Comics: Taking Poems Out of Church." *Teachers & Writers Magazine* 39, no. 4 (2008a): 27–30.

———. . "Three Poetry Comics Exercises." *Teachers & Writers Magazine* 39, no. 4 (2008b): 31–33.

J. R. Parket. "Comics and Poetry: The Rhyme and Rhythm of Sequential Art." *Comics Alliance*. May 2011. http://comicsalliance.com/comic-books-poetry/ (last accessed September 19, 2017).

C. Pizzino. "The Doctor versus the Dagger: Comics Reading and Cultural Memory." *PMLA* 130, no. 3 (2015): 631–647.

B. Postema. *Narrative Structure in Comics: Making Sense of Fragments*. Rochester: RIT Press, 2013.

M. J. Prince. "*HOWL: A Novel Graphic*: Authenticity and Irony in Eric Drooker's Adaptations of Allen Ginsberg's '*Howl*'." *Scan: Journal of Media Arts Culture* 9, no. 1 (2012). http://www.scan.net.au/scan/journal/display.php?journal_id=164 (last accessed September 19, 2017).

P. K. Saint-Amour, Editor. *Modernism and Copyright*. New York: Oxford University Press, 2010.

S. E. Tabachnick. "The Gothic Modernism of T.S. Eliot's *Waste Land* and What Martin Rowson's Graphic Novel Tells Us About It and Other Matters." *Readerly/Writerly Texts* 8, no. 1 and 8, no. 2 (2000): 79–92.

———. "Introduction." In *Teaching the Graphic Novel*, edited by S. E. Tabachnick. New York: MLA, 2009, pp. 1–15.

F. Williams, and E. Brunner. "Eliot with an Epic, Rowson with a Comic: Recycling Foundational Narratives." In *Son of Classics and Comics*, edited by G. Kovacs and C. W. Marshall. New York: Oxford University Press, 2015, pp. 179–200.

CHAPTER 12

RESISTING BILLY COLLINS: ON TEACHING "INTRODUCTION TO POETRY" IN INTRODUCTION TO POETRY

It is especially challenging to teach critical reading skills on the site of Billy Collins's poetry. His poetry has been lauded by well-known poet-critics and in the popular media as especially seductive. John Updike ("lovely poems"), Edward Hirsch ("an ironist with a funny bone"), and Richard Howard ("funny, moving, brainy") have all testified to the emotional pleasures of reading Collins's best-selling verse (Merrin 202). *The Minneapolis Star-Tribune* considers the poet to be "absolutely charming and irresistible" (Fink 100), and the *New York Review of Books* declares that "It is difficult not to be charmed by Collins" (Fink 101). The 2001 U.S. Poet Laureate's own critical essays point us in the direction of reading poetry for pleasure not for critical thinking. In "How Do Poems Travel?," Collins states, "More interesting to me than what a poem means is how it travels. In the classroom, I like to substitute for the question, 'What is the meaning of the poem?' other questions: 'How does this poem go?' or 'How does this poem travel through itself in search of its own ending?'" (396).

Collins's essay, "Poetry, Pleasure, and the Hedonist Reader," speaks to his fascination with the seductive elements of poetry. In a section of this essay on the "music of the poem," Collins notes that rhythm, pacing, and phrasing "cast a modest spell over us" (4). At its most seductive, Collins argues, poetry causes readers to become irrational. Merging with the object of desire—the poem—and projecting themselves onto it as if they were its creator, not its recipient, readers are encouraged to relinquish their critical faculties. They are to surrender to the "pleasure of the page": "a poem pulls us in through the power of the speaker's consciousness, which temporarily replaces our own reader-consciousness" (15). Like Alice entering the hallucinatory space of Wonderland's rabbit hole, readers are "carried off suddenly into a new conceptual zone, to be slipped through a secret passageway and into the extraordinary rooms of the imagination" (20). Describing poetry reading as a form of travel, the exotic destination not a tropical island, but a vacation in the pleasure dome created by the gifted wordsmith, Collins writes, "we gain access to the other consciousness by submitting to the speech-world of the poem" (14). Reading poetry, for Collins, is a deliberate attempt to relinquish control of our critical faculties. Apollonian in orientation, we fail to resist the hedonistic temptation of the poet's language games. Is it too far-fetched to describe the dynamic at play in Collins's theory in terms of sexual conquest? Is not the poet imagined as a Don Juan who, metaphorically, drops Alice the pill that will inaugurate her yielding to the lyric's synesthetic play?

Collins argues that there is a significant cultural motivation for him to emphasize textual delights over critical interpretation. From his point of view, America has simply become too brainy. To counteract our obsession with thoughtful analysis, the poet must write in a way that encourages us to suppress our cerebral bent. Collins derides the "interpretive fallacy" that underwrites the tendency of teachers to "put the greatest emphasis on finding out what the poem means." He states that this pedagogy of meaning is merely a symptom of a wider crisis that "reveals the supremacy of reason in our culture, its dominance over the somatic and the sensory" (Collins 29). Given Collins's pop sensibility, I must admit his comments suggest he does not watch TV, and that he does not pay attention to our political discourse, which most observers would agree promotes emotional response to candidates instead of reasoned judgment.

In "Poetry, Pleasure, and the Hedonist Reader," Collins states that he wants to put "meaning into the kind of hedonist perspective [that] might help to remove the shadow of the poetry teacher from the page and allow the reader to indulge more fully in the cluster of poetry's imaginative and physical pleasures" (29). By contrast, when I teach a course entitled Introduction to Poetry each year at Purdue, I take as my charge the task of sharpening students' abilities to evaluate poetry beyond saying, in an impressionistic fashion, whether they "like" a poem on a gut level. I also want them to move beyond saying, as they often do at the start of the semester, that "poetry means something different for each of us."

I open my first session of Introduction to Poetry at Purdue by offering students a cluster of works that call for different types of reading strategies and foster different kinds of emotional and ethical response. "Introduction to Poetry" (1996), a lyric by longtime Lehman College (CUNY) English teacher Collins, which self-consciously reflects on the project of teaching poetry to undergraduates, is one of them. I don't tell students this upfront, but in truth "Introduction to Poetry" is not my cup of tea. My trouble with Collins is that in spite of his possession of what one critic has called the "generous dollop of regular-guy jokiness" that has made his works into best-sellers (Merrin 205), his "Introduction to Poetry" harks back to the "art for art's sake" movement that informed the archetypal statement of High Modernist poetics in Archibald MacLeish's "Ars Poetica" (1926): "A poem should not mean / but be." In the end, I hope my class will join me in resisting the seductive discourse that lays out Collins's aestheticism, but I want class discussion to center on what is at stake when an author treats the poem as a surreal, thingy object designed for diversionary pleasure, not critical reflection. For that is what Collins's poem is all about.

Discussing "Introduction to Poetry" on day one will also foreground things to come in subsequent classes because it concerns an issue that I will also explore when we turn to the objectivist poetry of William Carlos Williams and its relation to the found art of Marcel Duchamp. In my presentations on Collins, and then on Williams's "This is Just to Say" and Duchamp's "Fountain," I will be thinking about poetry as "framed" within institutions of meaning that affect our reception and even our understanding of what counts as poetry worth teaching and what doesn't. In Collins's typical tongue-in-cheek fashion, "Introduction to Poetry" addresses the fact that poetry reading today occurs primarily in the classroom. Institutionalizing poetry in the academic context troubles Collins because he follows in the footsteps of avant-garde movements such as Dadaism that challenged the association of poetry with rational discourse. Collins regards poetry as an inappropriate site to perform meaning-oriented readings that consider social and biographical contexts. In an interview with Michael Meyer, Collins stated:

> One thing to keep in mind is that readers of poetry, students especially, are much more preoccupied with "meaning" than poets are. While I am writing, I am not thinking about the poem's meaning. I am only trying to write a good poem, which involves securing the form of the poem and getting the poem to hold together so as to stay true to itself. (Meyer 409)

Collins's criticism of how poetry is taught to young people in the interview with Meyer and in his poem "Introduction to Poetry," I would argue, is an example of bad faith, or at least an ambivalent one, given his own relationship to academia. Does not symbolic and economic value accrue in Collins's poetry through its repeated exposure in anthologies and on course syllabi?

Would "Introduction to Poetry" make any sense at all if teachers refrained from presenting poems in college classrooms? A poet and pedagogue, Collins is decidedly ambivalent about placing the poem in the classroom. In his essay, "The Companionship of a Poem," Collins reflects on the value of teaching poetry to undergraduates:

> I came to realize that to study poetry was to replicate the way we learn and think. When we read a poem, we enter the consciousness of another. It requires that we loosen some of our fixed notions in order to accommodate another point of view—which is a model of the kind of intellectual openness and conceptual sympathy that a liberal education seeks to encourage.

Setting up an adversarial "I versus Them" dynamic in his poem entitled "Introduction to Poetry," Collins contradicts his stated intent to accommodate another's point of view by fostering "intellectual openness and conceptual sympathy." In his poem, Collins imagines himself as an increasingly frustrated instructor whose students resist his aesthetic. In the last two stanzas of the seven-stanza poem, he rages against his students for their desire to read for meaning, as teachers have trained them to do in high school, and as they will need to do to say something coherent in a paper or final exam. In the first stanzas of the poem, the teacher "asks them" politely to experience the poem's zany, synesthetic pleasures. The teacher instructs the students to hold a poem up to the light like a color slide and to press an ear to it, as if it were a buzzing hive. Despite his efforts, he laments in increasingly condescending tones his failure to prevent students from reading for meaning:

> But all they want to do
> is tie the poem to a chair with rope
> and torture a confession out of it.
> They begin beating it with a hose
> to find out what it really means. (lines 12–6)

Collins critiques didacticism, but we notice how the poet has chosen images to stack the deck in a polemical argument that discourages deep reading and promotes surface appreciation. Is connecting a poem to an author's life, which Collins discourages through his image of the reader as water-skiing "on the surface" of the poem while waving to the author "on the other shore," comparable to torturing a suspect during an interrogation?

Collins casts students as little terrorists because they want to dig beneath the surface of a poem. Ironically, in another of his anthologized poems, "Taking Off Emily Dickinson's Clothes" (2002), Collins gets his kicks by unveiling the surface appearance of the Belle of Amherst. Critic Tom Fink has described the process of undressing in the poem as, "a male poet's fantasy implying violation of the reclusive Dickinson's privacy and her poem's complex interior life" (102). On the one hand, Collins's critique of reading poetry to torture a confession out of it can be read as his assertion of a distinctive place in literary tradition by distancing himself from the 1950s and 1960s "confessional movement" led by Lowell, Berryman, Plath, and Sexton. On the other hand, I wonder if Collins's distaste for probing the relation between the author and text is a defense mechanism that enables the poet to engage in fantasies of abuse—of students in "Introduction to Poetry" and of Dickinson in "Taking Off Emily Dickinson's Clothes"—without taking responsibility.

I agree with Collins that asking students to write papers about poetry in a graded environment may not foster appreciation of the poem's "isness." But it does not follow that Collins should verbally beat up students by parodying their efforts at finding meaning. Shouldn't a teacher respond with empathetic understanding to students who are merely reacting to opaque texts with the interpretive tools prior teachers have given to them? Recalling their own experiences of excessive symbol hunting in high school—the word *buoy* in Hemingway's *The Old Man and The Sea* (1952) read by one teacher as *boy*; the color of the sky as blue in another poem representing a state of mind—many students find relief in Collins's privileging of tactile experience over intellectual rumination. Demonstrating his roots in modernism, I pair Collins's poem with Archibald MacLeish's "Ars Poetica," but I also encourage students to resist Collins's seductive and yet ironically polemical claims by placing his poem beside work by other lyricists for whom "meaning" is something essential to their intent.

Selecting a poem to contrast with Collins's that is set in an environment likely to be familiar to Purdue students, I pair "Introduction to Poetry" with Jared Carter's "The Purpose of Poetry" (1993). Born in Elwood, Indiana in 1939, Carter sets his metapoem—a poem about poetry—at a crucial moment of cultural transformation in a rural part of the Hoosier State near the Mississinewa River. Unlike Collins, who urges his students to separate aesthetic experience from mimesis, Carter, avoiding the didacticism one finds in Collins, connects poetry to life. In calm, uninflected tones, Carter offers the tragic story of an old man, a cattle farmer, who shoots his beloved dogs and then commits suicide after an official from the courthouse arrives at his farm to inform him "how the new reservoir / was going to flood all his property."

As my mentor Allen Grossman reminded students in lectures at Brandeis, poetry is a radical act because it is a breaking of the cosmic silence. Why does Carter, I ask my students, decide to break silence to enter the space of the poem? For Carter in "The Purpose of Poetry," the answer is not, as in Collins, to imagine the poem as a space of escape from the pressures of reality or as a diversionary form of entertainment. Instead, we note, a change has come to pass in the world familiar to the poet that sets up a sharp contrast between then and now. The sense of "always," as Carter describes the quotidian rhythms of the old man's predictable life before the visit from the courthouse official, has been upended. Threatening the Jeffersonian image of the yeoman farmer, the courthouse official brings news of a new chapter in the relationship between people, place, and state, one associated with economic growth through the harnessing of the river's powers for the sake of community progress. Because the old man suffers a social death at the hands of an agent of the state, it follows that the man decides to take action himself. He becomes the agent of his own death and of his beloved dogs.

I ask students to consider whether or not the final line of the poem to be ironic. How can the purpose of a poem about death be to "tell us about life"? One answer is that Carter is demonstrating how conflict, change, and the rights of the individual versus the needs of the community may come into play when more than one party lays claim to something as scarce and valuable as land. We must acknowledge that this old farmer is not the first one to be pushed off the land in the name of progress. Isn't the state of Indiana named as such because it was once the "Land of the Indians"? Following the bitter logic of poetry, we notice in the name of the local river, the Mississinewa, the appearance in language of the vanished presence of the native peoples. The poem becomes a reservoir for the layers of persons who have occupied the same piece of land, if we recall that the word has roots in the Old French term that means "reserve." "The Purpose of Poetry" records the old man's death, but the poem is an archive that preserves (like a reservoir) the story of the old man. Poetry cannot change what happens in life, but it can "tell us about life."

To offer a bold contrast to Collins's New Critical aesthetic, I also play a recording of "Talkin' Union" (1941) by iconic Left-Wing folkie Pete Seeger. The overtly political lyric demonstrates that even in the realm of "low"—folk or popular—culture, many songwriters would adamantly disagree with Collins's focus on poetry as mere respite from worldly concerns. Student responses to Seeger's lyric vary. One student accused Seeger of writing "propaganda" not "poetry." This comment leads us to examine what we mean by "propaganda" and whether we could, or should, draw such a distinction between "poetry" and "propaganda." Could we not argue that Collins's poem is, ironically, propaganda via its willful dismissal of the social value of art? One student argues that propaganda occurs when an author wants to motivate his audience to "do" something in the world outside the text. Authors write propaganda and protestors paint picket signs when they feel strongly about something: religion, unionization, World War II, the environment. Focusing on communal values and public controversy, rather than individual meanings and introspection, "Talkin' Union" is not, the student continued, as in traditional lyric poetry, concerned with generating strong feelings in the listener. But another student disagreed. Wasn't Seeger's lyric meant to arouse vehement emotions in members of his intended audience of non-unionized factory workers? Didn't he want his words to help workers find the courage to dismiss charges of being Un-American—Red—and choose to unionize?

Seeger's folk lyric resists the ideology of unbridled capitalism, but here again I bring in the concept of "resistant reading" to critique Seeger's seductive poetics. I encouraged students to read Collins's "art for art's sake" aesthetic with both an empathetic understanding and a critical perspective that examines the manipulative nature of Collins's ironically polemical poem. I also wanted students to think critically about how Seeger portrays the "boss" and the unions. I wanted students to notice how Seeger uses images, humor, voice, repetitions, and concrete details to portray the Boss as a heartless and cruel wife-beater and the union as the royal road to the good life for workers and their families. Does Seeger accurately portray unions? Does he deal with the critique of unions as corrupt and overly involved in political campaigns to the point where social critics on the right often accuse unions of being another special interest group? One thinks of a classic movie such as Elia Kazan's *On the Waterfront* (1954) in this regard. Did the unionization of the Ford motor plant, celebrated in Seeger's poem, ironically contribute to how Ford and other American automakers have struggled to compete in a global context in which non-Union workers build Hondas and Subarus in "right to work" states such as Indiana? Is Seeger's overtly political poem merely a period piece that lacks the enduring significance of great poetry? My main point in playing Seeger off Collins is to demonstrate that Collins's aestheticism did not account for lyrics such as Seeger's. Both works were indeed about meaning and values and neither could be separated from the political realms and institutional frames in which they exist. The lesson is that we as readers, critics, and students cannot adopt a one-size-fits-all approach.

In week one, I also bring to class a poem called "in loving memory," published on the seventh anniversary of the death of a young woman named Trisha Gochenour (11/19/1978 to 01/09/2003) in the Lafayette, Indiana *Journal and Courier*. A poem one would never find in an anthology such as Norton or Heath—unless it were framed as a negative example—"in loving memory" was written by the unskilled hands of her parents and friends—it is signed, "Love, Mom, Dad, Sequoya, Julie, Troy, Seth, Zach, Jacob, Michael, Tony & Matt." It was published as a paid advertisement and accompanied by a color mug shot of Trisha in the obituary section of our town's local paper on January 9, 2010.

Like Collins's, Carter's, and Seeger's, "in loving memory" caused us to ask questions about aesthetic criticism, evaluative criticism, and the purposes of poetry. Written in a traditional iambic measure and with rhyme, the poem lacks the funky imagism, contemporaneity, and creative surprises of Collins's poem. But it is clear the authors went to considerable time and expense to self-publish their commemorative words in a recognizably poetic form. Somehow, they believed that poetry was the proper medium to communicate their grief to readers, many of whom may have known Trisha. The authors are not skilled wordsmiths, and they are certainly not up on modernist movements such as Surrealism or Objectivism, but they paid to see their lyric in print because it expressed in public their continuing memory of a lost loved one. The poem is also a statement of religious faith that the family would come together again in the next world through the will of God when, they wrote, the "chain" that had been "broken" with Trisha's death would be refastened in God's hands. I mentioned in class how this poem's expression of religious faith stands in contrast to the iconic critique of Christianity's emphasis on the next world's pleasures in "Sunday Morning" (1915) by Wallace Stevens.

Many students felt the poem was corny, sentimental, and generic in its statements. It was too much like a Hallmark Card to qualify as serious poetry worthy of class discussion. One student said you could place a picture of any other deceased person, or even of a beloved pet, beside Trisha's elegy, and the poem's sentiments would apply to those other persons or animal. In creative-writing workshop parlance, the poem *told* us how the authors felt about the deceased person. It didn't *show* or enact, through imagery and anecdote, who Trisha was or why readers should feel for her or those who knew and loved her. Some students, however, didn't mind the discursive, even generic, quality of the poem. Lyric poetry, they argued, was supposed to be universal. Even as Keats wrote "When I have fears that I shall cease to be" in 1818 to come to terms with his own fading health, the impending death of his brother Tom, and his affection for Fanny Brawne, each reader should be able to step into his shoes and empathetically identify with his knowledge of death. I take up the issue of the privilege of the universal "I" unselfconsciously adopted by Keats when we discuss Langston Hughes's "Theme for English B" (1951), but the student has a point. Some students felt the lack of specific information about Trisha was actually a good thing. Readers, especially those who knew Trisha prior to reading the poem in the local paper, could apply their memorable images and anecdotes to the poem's general sentiment that Trisha was a kind and loving person who remains deeply missed. I added that it was possible to critique the poem's lack of concrete details about the subject's life because it was as if the poem was not registering the life of the subject but instead rehearsing how readers are supposed to feel about her. The poem, I argued, offers readers the after-effect of having read a powerful poem, rather than the poem itself being an experience about which we should have strong feelings. (I was offering students a definition of kitsch.) I wondered why the poem doesn't offer a more complex analysis of the subject's life. Was the subject really all sweetness and light? Wouldn't representing her quirks have made the subject that much more memorable? Maybe not. At least according to some students, we want to remember the deceased in the best light. We don't need to go over the darker, upsetting, ambivalent feelings.

But then I played for them a song by Lucinda Williams—daughter of acclaimed Arkansas poet Miller Williams—called "Little Angel, Little Brother" (1992). The song didn't paper over the problems in Little Brother's life. It discussed how the singer, the subject's sister, would find him passed out in the back seat of his car in the parking lot of a bar with an empty bottle on the floor. Williams doesn't shy away from representing his alcoholism, but she also describes him as a quirky, creative spirit who loves Shakespeare, chess, Ray Charles, and wisecracks. Was Lucinda Williams's lyric in bad taste? Would her brother be upset when he heard the song? Would it be a wake-up call for him to get clean and sober? Should that even matter? Could we as readers accuse Lucinda of muddying the reputation of a loved one? Or do we appreciate what some students called "the realism" of Williams's song? Do we honor Williams's courage to be honest about the brother, who exists in a gray zone that contrasts with the black-and-white world painted by Seeger in "Talkin' Union" or the authors of the elegy for Trisha? Was poetry not at its best when it expressed ambivalence, another word for seeing the gray, rather than the black and the white?

Placing Collins beside Jared Carter, Lucinda Williams, Seeger, and the authors of Trisha's elegy only complicated our class discussion, thus allowing us to improvise as new melodies entered the composition of class discussion. By "new melodies" I mean that we were then able to ask different questions about how we value poetry, and especially how we distinguish quality via the criteria of originality and complexity. Comparing and contrasting "Little Angel, Little Brother" with "in loving memory" brought us into the area of aesthetic judgment. Why were some of us so uncomfortable with the unvarnished "sentimental" statements of love, loss, faith, family, and care that were put forward so directly in the poem published in the *Journal and Courier*? Why did we think originality was such an important value to uphold in poetry? Was it always that way? I mentioned how lyric poetry came out of the ancient idea of the traveling bard, who strummed a harp-like lyre while reciting folk memories around the fire as he sang for his supper. The ability to remember set pieces of narrative, myth, and folk history and then to combine these well-known elements in compelling ways was much more important to the success of the ancient singing bard than originality in topic or perspective. Was the focus on newness and innovation a sign that we live in a commodity culture in which the economy depends on convincing buyers that they need to purchase the new model of the same old automobile to remain in fashion?

My decision to move in week one between a poem by Collins grappling with its place in official poetry culture, Carter's poem about change in Indiana, a union song, an amateur elegy in the local paper, and a well-crafted piece of contemporary country music speaks to how I bring a "jazz aesthetic" into my choice of texts. By "jazz aesthetic," I am saying that I put forward the basic melody or "riff" that I wanted to achieve in the first week of class by playing Collins and MacLeish off Carter, Guthrie, Lucinda Williams, and the semi-anonymous elegy that appeared in the local paper. But I had no way to predict how the other soloists, the students in the class, would react to this basic melody. And I didn't know for sure how their reactions would set off my own memories, cultural contexts, thoughts, beliefs, and reflections. All of this happened together in the real time of the classroom. It was a one-off experience, and I am sure it will be different when I teach the course next year.

Works Cited

Jared Carter. "The Purpose of Poetry." *Darkened Rooms of Summer: New and Selected Poems.* University of Nebraska Press, 2014
Billy Collins. "How Do Poems Travel?" In *Poetry: An Introduction*, edited by Michael Meyer. Boston: Bedford Books, 2013.
———. "Introduction to Poetry." In *The Apple That Astonished Paris*. Fayetteville: University of Arkansas Press, 1996.

———. "Poetry, Pleasure, and the Hedonist Reader." In *The Eye of the Poet: Six Views of the Art and Craft of Poetry,* edited by David Citino. New York, NY: Oxford UP, 2000, pp. 1–33.

———. "Taking off Emily Dickinson's Clothes." In *Sailing Alone Around the Room: New and Selected Poems.* New York: Random House, 2002.

———. "The Companionship of a Poem." *Chronicle of Higher Education* 48, no. 13 (2001): B5.

Thomas Fink. "Poetry, Charm, and More: Billy Collins and Mei-Mei Berssenbrugge." *Talisman: A Journal of Contemporary Poetry and Poetics* 27 (Winter 2003): 100–107.

Archibald MacLeish. "Ars Poetica." In *Anthology of Modern American Poetry,* edited by Cary Nelson. New York: Oxford UP, 2000, p. 331.

Jeredith Merrin. "Art over Easy." *Southern Review* 38, no. 1 (2002): 202–214.

Michael Meyer. "On 'Building with Its Face Blown Off': Michael Meyer Interviews Billy Collins." In *Poetry: An Introduction.* Boston: Bedford, 2013.

Dad Mom, et al. "In Loving Memory." *Lafayette Journal and Courier.* January 9, 2010.

Joan Murray. "Taking Off Billy Collins's Clothes." In *Poetry: An Introduction*, edited by Michael Meyer. Boston: Bedford, 2013.

Pete Seeger. "Talkin' Union." *Pete Seeger's Greatest Hits.* Columbia Records, 2002.

Lucinda Williams. "Little Angel, Little Brother." *Sweet Old World.* Chameleon, 1992.

CHAPTER 13

AMIRI BARAKA'S AESTHETIC RADICALISM: *DUTCHMAN*'S MODERNIST ROOTS

I teach *Dutchman* in a survey of American literature since 1865. I place it in the final third of a reading list that stretches back a century before Amiri Baraka (1934–2014), then known as LeRoi Jones, wrote the Obie Award-winning drama (honoring off-Broadway productions) that premiered in New York City's Greenwich Village in 1964. My training in modernism, with special emphasis on poetics, informs my approach. My students read Baraka as a playwright, but he is best known as a poet who merged avant-garde aesthetics with Black nationalist ideology. Baraka was featured in *The New American Poetry: 1945–1960* (Allen; 1960), an anthology containing works in the tradition of experimental modernists such as Ezra Pound, William Carlos Williams, and Louis Zukofsky. The collection included politically radical and formally innovative writers identified with beat, Black Mountain, San Francisco Renaissance, and New York school poetics. It is also worth recalling that the young Baraka edited work by the Black Mountain poet Charles Olson, whose "projective verse" was characterized using form as an extension of content and by spontaneity and improvisation (Sollors 33).

Certainly, we should locate *Dutchman* within the context of civil rights and Black liberation politics to understand Baraka's ambivalent treatment of Clay Williams. A young urban Black man, Clay masks anger at a racist society through an assimilationist posture. He suggests that art—even the traditional African American artistic expression in the blues and jazz—sublimates a desire for vengeance. Baraka invokes and critiques disparate models of Black male identity in the 1960s. Clay's initial persona is a bourgeois with bohemian flair—Lula notes that he is "trying to grow a beard" and that he reads "Chinese poetry" (8). At the end of scene 2, Clay becomes a militant who can no longer contain his rage: "And I sit here, in this buttoned-up suit, to keep myself from cutting all your throats" (34). Through Clay, Baraka mocks conformist tendencies among middle-class Black people, and Clay embodies Baraka's belief that the arts, including drama, should serve social protest. As Houston Baker remarks, Baraka's conception of "Black as a country—a separate and progressive nation with values antithetical to those of white America—stands in marked contrast to the ideas set forth by Baldwin, Wright, Ellison, and others of the fifties" (*Journey* 106). Ellison, for instance, believed that African Americans are profoundly American and are crucial to defining American identity. Baraka, by contrast, moved toward a Black separatist ideology. In a slightly later work, a manifesto entitled "The Revolutionary Theatre" (1965), he said drama "should force change": "[white] Americans will hate the Revolutionary Theatre because it will be out to destroy them and whatever they believe is real" ([National Humanities Center] 3). Unquestionably, Baraka intended to shock audiences and readers through Lula's murder of Clay—and through the suggestion that another Black male awaits her knife blade after the curtain closes.

Yet there are other important contexts, in addition to the civil rights and Black liberation movements, in which the play should be read. *Dutchman* was "designed to shock" through "its basic idea, its language and its murderous rage," as a *New York Times* reviewer states on the back cover of the Morrow edition (*Dutchman & The Slave, Two Plays*. New York: Morrow Press, 1964), and, in this regard, the play belongs to a continuum of twentieth-century transatlantic culture that Werner Sollors calls an "international camp of aesthetic protest and antibourgeois Bohemianism" (18). Lula's sexual advances toward Clay on a subway are themselves a manifestation of modernism's intent to scandalize. So is her Dadaist performance of screaming, dancing, throwing items out of her purse, and chanting suggestively lyrical nonsense phrases: "Red trains cough Jewish underwear for keeps! Expanding smells of silence. Gravy snot whistling like sea birds" (31). When Clay was in college, he fancied himself a "Baudelaire"—and Lula mockingly calls him a "Black Baudelaire" (19)—but, as Sollors notes, Baraka may be a "Black Breton" (127). In his "Second Manifesto of Surrealism" (1930), André Breton advocates an art "not afraid to make for itself a tenet of total revolt, complete insubordination, of sabotage according to rule" (125). Stylistically, Baraka follows Breton in crafting deliberate anti-art. *Dutchman* is an answer to the "well-made play" epitomized in Black theater of this period by such works as Lorraine Hansberry's *A Raisin in the Sun* (1959). Lula's demeaning chatter (e.g., "Screw yourself, Uncle Tom. Thomas Wooly-head" [32]), Clay's physical intimidation and verbal aggression (e.g., "I could murder you now. Such a tiny ugly throat" [33]), and, of course, Lula's murder of Clay recall Antonin Artaud's theater of cruelty, to which Baraka's "The Revolutionary Theatre" is explicitly indebted. As Matthew Rebhorn writes, "Baraka engaged in innovative theatrical techniques—techniques built on earlier twentieth-century experimental dramaturgy. [...]Artaud wrote that what modern society really needed was 'a theater that wakes us up: nerves and heart'" (799).

When my class reaches *Dutchman*, students have already discussed American modernisms, including Gertrude Stein's Dadaism, the mythic strains of T. S. Eliot's *The Waste Land* (1922), and the images of bourgeois alienation in Eliot's "The Love Song of J. Alfred Prufrock" (1915). We've discussed the racial context of modernism: Harlem Renaissance writers' lyric expression of their "individual dark skinned selves" (Hughes, "Negro Artist" [Belasco and Johnson] 561). When interpreting *Dutchman* as "radical," therefore, I want students to consider the adjective's Latin etymological meaning. We think of "radical" as meaning "root" rather than exclusively viewing radicalism as a drastic change.

Among *Dutchman*'s various roots are the radical modernist aesthetics of the early twentieth century. As is typical of modernism (e.g., *The Waste Land*), *Dutchman* is a compositional pastiche, depicting Baraka's creativity through his appropriation of other texts. The materials that Baraka appropriates are derived from early-twentieth-century experimental arts movements, albeit recast to represent issues of race, interracial desire, violence, and masculinity in urban America in the 1960s. As Sollors puts it, Baraka "appropriates modern poetry to his own uses" (37), and Baraka himself recalled his early "Eliot period," albeit as a "shell" from which he needed to emerge (qtd. in Sollors 38). "Eliot is certainly present in Baraka's works," Sollors further argues, "even if Eliot's 'objective,' 'academic' art is what Baraka struggles away from" (38). In what follows, I discuss the focus of my course unit on Baraka's *Dutchman*, the play's appropriation of not only an Eliotic mythopoesis but also Eliot's work itself. Through this appropriation, I explain to my students, Baraka represents the peril of the Black subject's seeking recognition on the other side of the color line.

In "*Ulysses*, Order, and Myth" (1923), Eliot praised James Joyce's experimental novel for its "mythical method" (178). Creating "a continuous parallel between contemporaneity and antiquity" provided Joyce with "a way of controlling, of ordering, of giving a shape and a significance to the immense panorama of futility and anarchy which is contemporary history" (177). Baraka, too, undergirded his radical art with myth. The play's setting is "the subway heaped in modern myth" (*Dutchman* 3). From the earliest scholarship on the play, critics have noted affinities between *Dutchman* and the archetypal imagination of modernists who framed their period with templates from long ago.

Tom Reck, writing in 1970, implicitly connected *Dutchman* to the modernist "mythical method":

> *Dutchman* is, in fact, worked around the most archetypal of all myths: the seduction of the male by the beautiful but deadly female, with particular inference to the myth of Adam and Eve in the Garden of Eden. The name of the Negro male, Clay, seems to suggest an Adam and Everyman; and the white temptress, Lula, is not only a direct descendent of Lilith, Circe, and Delilah, but particularly of Eve. (67)

In 1979, George Levesque took a similar approach to the play and made explicit Reck's linkage of *Dutchman* to transatlantic modernism. Baraka follows August Strindberg, for example, in building conflict by drawing male and female figures as "representative" types rather than as the particularized characters that one expects from realist drama (Levesque 34).

Baraka renders Clay and Lula as types, even as stereotypes, to suggest how their conflict illustrates general concerns. At the start of scene 1, Lula is described in stage directions as "the face," implying that, for Clay, Lula represents the oppressive gaze of white America. When Lula tells Clay, "I lie a lot. It helps me control the world" (9), we read her remarks as Baraka's assessment of America as an empire whose dominion is predicated on deceit. As Victor Leo Walker has argued, those more general cultural concerns recall a tradition of African American authors—W. E. B. Du Bois, Paul Laurence Dunbar, and Ralph Ellison—who challenged stereotypes such as Uncle Tom and Jim Crow and who asserted their identities despite a felt need to "wear the mask," to conform to white expectations for behavior and appearance. Following Alain Locke, Walker writes, "[W]hite America has historically controlled African American public images [...] using symbolic types such as 'Uncle Tom' to represent assimilationist roles that have been forced upon them" (237). Walker argues that, at the end of *Dutchman*, Baraka invokes and then destroys the Uncle Tom archetype.

The play's title is itself an expression of Baraka's archetypal imagination:

> [The] Flying Dutchman, a ghost ship in several maritime legends, was a sign of bad luck, particularly for sailors. In most versions, the ship appeared off the Cape of Good Hope, the southern tip of Africa. The legend was inspired by the story of a Dutch sea captain named Vanderdecken who

boasted that he could complete the journey around the cape during a fierce storm. He swore that he would do so or keep trying forever. As punishment for his rashness, he was condemned to sail around the cape until the end of time. ("Flying Dutchman")

The *Flying Dutchman* achieved lasting fame through Richard Wagner's opera of the same name (1843). In this variant, the captain returns to land once every seven years, and if he can find a faithful wife during one of these respites, the curse will be lifted. Baraka appropriates this legend to dramatize a racially inflected romantic conflict. Rebhorn writes that the play projects "the relationship between the doomed sailor and his lover onto Clay and his 'loving' and erotic murderess Lula" (796).[1]

In reading *Dutchman* as an expression of a modernist mythopoetic imagination, we link the play to Eliot's work, which we encountered earlier in the semester. Furthermore, we discover that Eliot's work is some of the "modern myth" in which Baraka's subway is "heaped." In remarkable ways, *Dutchman*'s tone, setting, characterization, and plot allude to "Prufrock." Here Eliot depicts a purgatory environment prior to the paradiso that he glimpses at the end of *The Waste Land*. *Dutchman*'s plot involves two strangers who cast eyes on each other, flirt, and argue as they consider the prospect of going to a party together. Scene 2 begins with Clay and Lula imagining how they will behave at the party, how others will regard them, and what will happen after they leave. The implied narrative in "Prufrock" is strikingly like this action: a neurotic, bourgeois man strives, and fails, to reach a party with another. "Let us go then, you and I," Prufrock pleads, envisioning a room in which "the women come and go / Talking of Michelangelo" (672). Baraka alludes to "Prufrock" when Lula and Clay discuss the party's aftermath. Lula's prediction—"After the dancing and games, after the long drinks and walks, the real fun begins" (24)—recalls the following lines from "Prufrock":

> And would it have been worth it, after all,
> After the cups, the marmalade, the tea,
> Among the porcelain, among some talk of you and me,
> Would it have been worth while.... (675)

---

[1] In 1991, Baraka said in an interview that the idea of representing the subway as a modern ghost ship was suggested in part by advertisements for Albert Lewin's 1951 film *Pandora and the Flying Dutchman* (*Conversations* 255), a revision of Wagner's opera (1843).

Lula, who, as George Knox writes, "'comes on' as a kind of Prufrockian 'lady' carried to an erotic extreme," is taunting Clay with her comment (245–46). Her innuendo of sex after the party is twisted later in scene 2 when Lula uses her knife as a deadly phallus. In Eliot, Prufrock's skepticism, ennui, self-consciousness, and inability to live in the present tense render him unable to meet those women talking about Michelangelo. Clay, too, is eager to know and be known by another—to project himself across the color line—though *Dutchman* ultimately suggests the hopelessness of this desire.

Baraka again references Prufrock's struggles to convert chatter into physical intimacy when Lula tells Clay, "You don't know what I mean" (28). Throughout Eliot's poem, Prufrock feels misconstrued by women even as his female interlocutors feel he misunderstands them. Any affirmation he makes is likely to be rejected with the words "That is not what I meant at all. / That is not it, at all" (675). Like Prufrock, Clay is a split self. His desires for sex and an integration of appearance and reality, character, and body, cannot be satisfied. Lula reads Clay not as a unique individual but as "a well-known type" (12)—so much so that Clay feels that she controls his image. Similarly, Prufrock avoids the party because he feels others will judge his age, body, masculinity, and overall appearance:

> (They will say: "How his hair is growing thin!")
> My morning coat, my collar mounting firmly to the chin,
> My necktie rich and modest, but asserted by a simple pin—
> (They will say: "But how his arms and legs are thin!") (673)

The unruly dialogue between Lula and Clay, set in a subterranean urban setting, resembles Prufrock's linguistic labyrinth, which Eliot figures as sinister streets that the speaker travels without reaching his destination. When Lula drifts from her conversation with Clay to muse about a life "[h]ugged against tenements, day or night" (13), readers may recall Prufrock's wanderings through "certain half-deserted streets" that "follow like a tedious argument / Of insidious intent" (672). Lula's "argument" turns out to be similarly treacherous, and Clay's struggle for recognition just as hopeless as Prufrock's. Clay waits far too long to abandon his fantasy of truly crossing the color line.

In focusing on the connections between "Prufrock" and *Dutchman*, my class looks closely at one of the play's engagements with early-twentieth-century modernist aesthetics. Other instructors may choose to place *Dutchman* and Baraka's other works in conversation with post–World War II modernisms (or even with early postmodernisms). As William J. Harris has argued, Baraka's "jazz aesthetic" draws significantly on Olson's lessons about open-form poetry. Harris writes, "From the Projectivists, and from Olson in particular, Baraka absorbed his sense of the poem as open form, his sense of line, his sense of the poem as a recorder of process, and his conception of the poem as definition and exploration" (35). In fact, as the Poetry Foundation website notes, Baraka is most often associated with experimental poetry that developed after World War II:

> The white avant-garde—primarily [Allen] Ginsberg, [Frank] O'Hara, and leader of the Black Mountain poets Charles Olson—and Baraka believed in poetry as a process of discovery rather than an exercise in fulfilling traditional expectations. Baraka, like the Projectivist poets, believed that a poem's form should follow the shape determined by the poet's own breath and intensity of feeling. ("Amiri Baraka")

Furthermore, it is certainly the case Baraka came to Dada, surrealism, and the theater of cruelty through his involvement in the new American poetry and other post–World War II avant-garde movements.

Yet Eliotic mythopoesis is one of *Dutchman*'s roots, and I have found that exploring *Dutchman*'s appropriation of this tradition opens up the play for my classes. Many students come to my survey course already interested in archetypal texts and prepared for the kinds of analysis that these texts require. Also, by the time we study the play, my students have learned about the history of modernism, and they have begun tracing literary genealogies. To be sure, there is much more to be said about *Dutchman*'s many roots, but our work with the play's mythopoetics is one worthwhile exploration along these lines.

CHAPTER 14

TWO INTERVIEWS WITH THOMAS FINK

Interview One: Wednesday, April 28, 2010

On Teaching *Clarity and Other Poems*: A Conversation between the Teacher, Daniel Morris, and the Poet, Tom Fink

About this conversation
Daniel Morris:

This conversation took place online in late April 2010, shortly after I taught Tom Fink's *Clarity and Other Poems* (Marsh Hawk Press, 2009) in the final week of my upper-division undergraduate course on modern and contemporary poetry at Purdue. In recent years, each time I teach this course, I include on the syllabus one volume of contemporary poetry published by a small independent press. I do so for several reasons. It is valuable to introduce students to poets, poems, and presses that are ignored by the available anthologies. By exposing students to very recent work by authors who publish with alternative presses, I believe I help sharpen my students' sensibilities as readers because they cannot rely on preestablished frames of evaluation. Fink's *Clarity* did not come before the students with labels such as "great" or "canonical" or "major" attached to it. Further, by assigning a book-length volume, students must find their own way into a poet's aesthetics and social views without the filtering process that goes on when a small set of poems is selected as highlights for an anthology. I encourage students to think about the composition of the book, which is especially important with a poet such as Fink who creates works in series, such as his "Yinglish Strophes" or "Nonce Sonnets."

Fink's poetry is avant-garde, experimental, and difficult to decipher. I take these unsettling elements of Fink to be a good thing for my students to confront. As unusual as are the poems in *Clarity*, by the time we read them in class, students had been exposed to strains of twentieth-century poetics (Cage, Stein, and Ashbery among them) that influenced Fink (b. 1954). Student readings in the assemblage/collage traditions, surrealist and Dadaist poetics, New York School writing, as well as the multicultural dynamics that inform the "Yinglish Strophes" all served to allow students to get their bearings. We noticed how even a poet as seemingly eccentric as Fink has roots in work that has already entered the tradition I teach. To generate class discussion, I broke students up into groups of four or five. Each group was charged with developing five questions they wished to ask of a specific poem in Fink's book. After each group generated their questions, we then spent the remaining class sessions responding to these prompts. What follows is my summary of the questions and issues that arose in those sessions, as well as Tom Fink's responses.

***

DM: My class was drawn to poems in the ironically titled *Clarity and Other Poems* where we could glean at least the residue or remnants of more conventional elements of narrative or lyric poetry. Your poems are often disjunctive, opaque, and difficult to comprehend (in terms of mimetic meaning). But after initial Steve Martinesque cries of "I'm So Confused!," we calmed down. We realized your playful but forbidding texture foregrounded our awareness of our disposition as readers. As readers in search of conventional meanings, we struggled to create, co-create, intuit, or flat out imagine, your poems as reflections on a world anterior to the text. This was the case regardless of how resistant the poems might be to our desire to imagine that there indeed IS a world outside of text.

TF: Dan, no, my intention in writing was not to posit that there is not a world outside the text.

DM: Your poems caused us to acknowledge how conservative we are as readers, conservative in the sense that we wished to conserve status quo notions of "voice," "lyric subjectivity," "literary actors or agents within the space of the poem," an implied authorial perspective that could be gleaned from the text if we only worked hard enough to decipher the words. We yearned to connect your texty text to "real" life scenarios, and biographical, historical, and autobiographical contexts.

TF: Having the text try on "real" life scenarios is probably a good idea, but forcing a fit is not. Perhaps getting one leg in a pants leg and not the other is an interesting readerly experience. One can hop around.

DM: As much as your poems self-consciously thematized a resistance to a transparent reading of the social text on political grounds, we resisted your resistance tooth and nail.

TF: Well, maybe I try to make my poems resist "transparent" reading but that still leaves a great deal for a reader to do. I'm not against close reading; I do a lot of it myself as a critic.

DM: And so we were drawn to poems such as "Pyramid Assembled" because we felt it had enough conjunctions of imagery and topic that we could go buzz like dutiful worker bees fantasizing about what Tom Fink was "trying to say." (As much as your poems resist what the New Critics called "The Heresy of Paraphrase," paraphrase we did!). We became involved with what W. J. T. Mitchell calls the "semantics [or meaning-bearing element] of form" as we analyzed the visual shape of "Pyramid Assembled." Was it a scar? A sideways pyramid? Both? Neither? Neither and both? We noted that the poem described "The scar could/be masked by ascot, but it/ seems contemptuous of anonymity." This was the discursive link between form, content, and extra-textual meaning that we were waiting to pounce upon so we could start spinning interpretations that made sense (even as, to quote David Byrne, you wanted to "Stop Making Sense"). If indeed we were correct in reading the visual shape of the poem as a scar, then were you saying that language was itself the scarring agent or the victim of some scarring agent?

TF: To me, the shapes of "Pyramid Assembled" are abstract. But any abstract shape in any artwork can be read as figurative, so why should I resist? I don't see language as the "victim of some scarring agent" in the poem, yet it well could be: language is abused all the time. Maybe I'd say that people are the victims of manipulative uses of language, and wisecracks like "It's new/ and I/ recall it/ from/// adolescence" are meant to counteract the verbal violence.

DM: Were you saying that conventional meanings, which confirm a normative social text—the very meanings of your poems that we were attempting to tease out—were the trace elements of psychic and/or physical pain in your poem, the meaningful scars that couldn't be hidden from your disjunctive poetics? We teased out themes of wage labor, gendered work, and a narrative of exploitation in "Pyramid Assembled." We were noticing a story line that involved a server who lives on tips, but must spend a tipless hour closing the café. (I learned from students that a server only earns $2.14 an hour without tips). This brought us to the association of the poem with the assemblage of the pyramid in your attractive title. Were you comparing the exploitation of wage laborers in an urban café to the enslaved Jews of the *Exodus* story? How did this association align with the sideways pyramid reading of the visual shape of the poem?

TF: $2.14 an hour is obscene! I wonder if there are differences between Indiana, California, and New York. I'm not worried about the negative impact of "conventional meanings," just verbal distortions, bullshit, etc. I do believe that you're right to perceive various thematic continuities: "psychic [...] pain" involved in "wage labor, gendered work, and a narrative of exploitation." I wasn't trying to hide these themes, but to develop them in ways that weren't obvious. And your reading of the "pyramid" trope makes fine sense, though I didn't consciously think about a "sideways pyramid reading of the visual shape."

DM: Your poems are filled with self-referential, often self-mocking moments: "We impanel the ostensibly nonaligned"; "Through vaudeville veneer I speak"; "Drained pseudo-/defiant blubber patch"; "Bet you're stumbling wanly through/another bland/ maze, vaguely blue"; "Don't stop tinkering with the borrowed"—this last a mishearing of the Fleetwood Mac song. Given this self-referential quality of your poems, we wondered about the "assembled" part of the title of your first poem. How did a poem that thematized exploited work resonate with your own self-styled position of poet as assembly worker? Was your work with the materiality of language a form of undercompensated labor?

TF: A worker who assembles the "parts" of a "collage" isn't an assembly-line worker who faces mind-numbing drudgery and job-related physical problems. I enjoy this work, and fretting about the degree of compensation would be a pointless distraction from this enjoyment.

DM: As stated, we gravitated toward poems that did not only provide us with the Barthesian pleasure of the text through your gift at punning, zany humor, and witty, often surrealistic juxtapositions of images such as "rubber scoreboard," "pediatric perm center" and "Dildo/pasta" from "Your Preppie Blizzard."

TF: Well, you know, speaking of "Your Preppie Blizzard" (35), pages 28 through 36 of *Clarity and Other Poems* pick up on sound-effects in conjunction with surreal "narratives" that I was working with in parts of my previous two books, *After Taxes* and *No Appointment Necessary*, and I'm not sure that my "experiments" with this mode continue to satisfy me as a reader. The narrative components seem too arbitrary. A few months ago—less than two years after the book came out—I tried to rewrite some of these poems, and the effort didn't work. I don't regret writing the poems in the first place, because, even when experiments aren't successful, they can be the mulch for strong later developments. The question is: Should I regret publishing them? As I finish up my next collection, I'm trying to be very careful not to include poems that I might find unsatisfactory a few years after publication. But then again, those readers who come at a poem like "Your Preppie Blizzard" from a very different perspective than either your students "in search of conventional meanings" or me (at this time) could convince me that it has virtues I haven't noticed.

DM: We were very interested in the various ways history and politics did inform your poems, and so we focused on poems in which we could decipher the multiple levels on which you engage politically. Sensing your commitment to pacifism in the context of an increasingly militarized culture during the period of the Bush Wars in the Middle East, equitable labor practices, housing and social class issues, food and diet, cancer and smoking, "Homeland Security," anti-consumerism, and sensitivity to environmental concerns, we did wonder why you didn't treat these topics in a more direct, accessible fashion. On the back cover of your book, Joanna Fuhrman notes that your "brilliant constructions should help us in this struggle" for "Aspiring Democracy." Given the difficult texture of your work, we wondered how. I told the class that I thought you wanted to activate a kind of readerly relationship to texts (both your own poems and the social text enforced by the mass media) that would foreground a vigorous reading as co-creation process while at the same time deconstructing the mind-numbing slogan, ads, billboard wisdom, and headline sound bite social text that your work often mimics in a parodic fashion. (I mentioned to the class how important humor, and especially humorous wordplay à la Groucho Marx, has been to diasporic Jews as a way of dealing with social absurdities and linguistic defamiliarization.) I told the class that I got the sense that you felt if you wrote about (rather than enacted in the strangeness of your text) your political commitments you would be merely integrating your oppositional perspective into a discursive system—the prison house of language spoken of by Wordsworth and Jameson—that has the power to absorb dissident subjectivities.

TF: Much of your explanation works very well. However, I wouldn't argue that direct articulation of political commitments always results in the dilution of "oppositional perspective," though clichéd expression almost invariably does. Carefully articulated, nuanced discursive formulations are one vital component of any significant social change, and these can occur in poetry. My poems are not intended to be proscriptive but to provide ways to read and just to explore (without definitive conclusions) culture and politics—while at the same time giving pleasurable attention to resources of language (and organization of those resources into new forms) that are not inherently "political"—and perhaps at times to hint at fruitful alternatives to typical operations, as in the eco-themed "When the Ad."

DM: I told them that I felt you understood language itself as a political instrument. But your poems, we felt, were also conventionally political in topic and theme. For example, the poem "Ralph's Mama" concerned the limitation of traditionally gendered work practices that, your poem argued, inhibit progressive relationships to work and liberatory feminist entrepreneurship. You describe how the mother has failed to "hush his ambient/macho and steer him to intricate,/intimate acquaintance with her household/cultivation moves, Alice could/have extended/her donut/powdering/career."

TF: A lot of poems in the book are "conventionally political in topic and theme," especially the "Nonce Sonnets," but others, like the two poems from the "Dented Reprise" series, could be associated with not particularly politicized love or lust, and still others like "Dangerous Intersection" with family situations. And I hope that political themes are often "invaded" by topoi that aren't obviously or primarily political. Though I've been a Nichiren Shoshu Buddhist for 36 years, I've been reluctant to develop religious themes in my work, because I didn't want to distort the teachings. Yet in a review of *After Taxes* in *Jacket*, Shivaji Sengupta noted that a Buddhist sense of transience or impermanence was important to the work, and that probably continues to be so. Evocations of transience are not reducible to the political, though the thematization of consumer culture is a very good "place" to include them. Also, for a Buddhist, notions of compassion— which, I hope, governs some of my decisions while writing or editing a poem—are not always equivalent to social action on a broad scale.

Going back to "Ralph's Mama," I took Ralph and Alice to be specific figures in popular culture, and "donut/ powdering" is a highly particular allusion. Of course, they could also signify otherwise, and I'm not one to stop that.

DM: In "Introducing Wallpaper" we felt we were overhearing a critical discussion about the Gulf War and our national dependency on oil, the flow of which is protected or facilitated by militarism.

As an assimilated, hyper-educated, middle-class Jew with grandparents who came over from Russia and Latvia via the Ellis Island experience, I was particularly drawn to your "Yinglish Strophes," which we spent a good deal of class time discussing in terms of contemporary multi-lingual-hybrid-diasporic poetics. As in the previous examples, we as a class tried to pull together a narrative, thematic elements, and characterizations of personae in these voice-driven strophes. We imagined the speaker (here I was projecting my own experience) as a living remnant of an increasingly moribund Eastern European Jewish Yiddish cultural experience. We spoke of the Shoah and Isaac B. Singer and how what is left of Yiddish, itself a hybridic mongrel language made up of German, Hebrew letters, and other elements of Jewish wanderings, is, in your Strophes, undergoing still more mongrelization/hybridization as the grandmother's diction, tone, syntax, and grammar delightfully represents a collision of American English and Yiddish. As much as the grandmother/speaker's lexicon and grammatical structures are transformed through her transplantation from Eastern Europe to New York City, we noted that your own poetics is delightfully impacted by the Yiddish grandmother's speech patterns and word choices. American English in Fink becomes itself a porous, flexible hybridic lexicon that is absorbing international influences, be it the Yinglish of your poetry ("meshuga" is the first word in the first of the series of "Yinglish" strophes) or the Spanglish dimension of other multiculturalist poeticists. At first, we thought of the grandmother and the son (hyper-educated, science-oriented, and avant-garde poet) to whom we imagined her speaking (often in a scolding, "I know better than you" grandmotherly tone!) as belonging to two utterly distinct linguistic spheres and thus epistemological universes. In "Yinglish Strophes 15," for example, we at first viewed the grandmother speaker and hyper-educated New World grandson in these binary terms: Grandma's good greasy Jewish soul food including white flour versus enlightened whole wheat Health Food diet that doesn't "agree" on a taste-test level with grandma's culinary aesthetics; "tasty [...] maternity feeds" versus nutrition and child-rearing theories of "newspaper scientists"; Grandma's cleaning habits (a broken broom, not a vacuum please!) and critique of air conditioning versus contemporary critiques of pollution; the personal testimony of the grandmother concerning her husband's smoking Camels and living to "almost 90" and the scientific data which would be surprised by his longevity, and "education science" versus the sassy intelligence "inside second smoke" that the grandmother's wisdom represents. As different as are the world views, aesthetics, and linguistic dispositions of the grandmother speaker and the grandson, I ended up feeling that you were suggesting how each participant in the polylingual discourse was literally and figuratively feeding off of each other, learning from one another, expressing affection in a dialogic relation to one another as elements of each other's discursive community seeped into the other.

TF: As I read "Yinglish 15," the grandmother figure is not a spokesperson for pre-modern views but someone in transition who is attentive to uncertainties. She understands that whole wheat is good for most people but, given the strange specificity of each individual constitution, not her. She is impatient with "newspaper scientists" because the "wisdom" is always changing, not because she wants to defend "good greasy Jewish soul food." She wants the scientists to get it right, and she's frustrated with them, as well as with the makers of vacuum cleaners, who should make their products capable of extirpating residues of air pollution, which she sees as a menace. This speaker knows that smoking is bad for you, and she is probably puzzled that science can't seem to account for her husband's longevity. So, from a Bakhtinian sense, double-voiced discourse in this particular poem exists within her, and there isn't necessarily any need—as there is in some other poems in the series, like 8—to posit the grandson or someone else of a different generation as listener, as dialogic partner.

DM: As much as the grandmother's broken syntax and suggestive but not quite right word choices ("sugar we refine on") reflect her position as a displaced person, we realized that your own poetics reflects a kind of dissociated sensibility at odds with mainstream ways of seeing and saying. Just like the grandmother, the poet uses humor, puns, mishearing, and criticism of the status quo to suggest his own uneasy relationship with mainstream discourse.

TF: Yes, and thank you.

Interview Two: December 2, 2022

Exchange with Thomas Fink on Reading Poetry with College and University Students: Overcoming Barriers and Deepening Engagement

DM: Tom, as I read your critically mature book, *Reading Poetry with College of University Students: Overcoming Barriers and Deepening Engagement* (Bloomsbury Academic, 2022), I was thinking about how you could have framed your study in different ways to appeal to different audiences. For example, since you display an impressive grasp of a wide range of approaches to poetry, you could have donned your "theorist" hat, and directed your book to readers interested in exploring the relationships between various critical theories and reading contemporary poetry. I say this because you do such a good job engaging with Stanley Fish's idea of "interpretive communities," suggesting that it is possible, and desirable, to move among and between various communities in coming to terms with ambivalent, and often contradictory, poems. Elsewhere, you make a strong case that Derridean deconstructive strategies can help readers perceive, and trouble, hierarchical relationships between characters in poems that focus on, for example, an analyst and an analysand, such as Julia Alvarez's "The Therapist." You turn to postcolonial theory and ecocritical modes in intriguing ways to discuss A. K. Ramanujan's "Death and the New Citizen," a poem that enumerates how to use corpses and how to dispose of them. Queer theories of assimilation, difference, gender, and non-binary identity inform your readings of Timothy Liu's "The Prodigal Son Writes Home" and

Trace Peterson's "Trans Figures." You work with Eve Sedgwick's notion of "reparative reading" to read Denise Duhamel's "Egg Rolls." Alternatively, you could have written a book that makes a case for how and why older, perhaps less fashionable, formalist, aesthetic, and myth critical approaches to reading poetry still matter today. Relying on formalism, but often combining that way of reading with historicism, you explore not just "what" a poem means, but also "how" a poem means through the decisions a poet makes about syntax, grammar, lineation, meter, tropes, figures, allusion, and adherence to traditional stanza patterns or modes such as the praise poem, as you show Gwendolyn Brooks doing in a tribute to Langston Hughes. A third option could have been for you to appeal to a general readership by simply collecting a book's worth of your stellar readings of individual poems, a project similar to one Stephanie Burt undertook in *The Poem Is You: 60 Contemporary American Poems and How to Read Them* (2016).

You could have positioned your study in these and other ways, but you didn't. Instead, you decided to focus on poetry and pedagogy. Your task was to help teachers do better with helping students read poetry. Given that you are yourself an accomplished poet and critic, would you reflect on your decision to write a book from the perspective of your position as a teacher whose task it is to help other teachers work with poetry in the undergraduate classroom? Why did you imagine this aspect of your identity, that of instructor, and this audience—classroom teachers—as the dialogic participants for this conversation about poetry at this point in your life?

TF: I haven't had a solid new idea for a book of poetic criticism since my last one in 2001, though I published quite a few articles and reviews before deciding to focus mostly on interviewing poets about five years ago. During the previous decade, I kept looking at my published work to see if there was a "thesis" or cluster of interacting "theses" that would bring the essays together into a book. No luck. When it came time for me to apply for a sabbatical from LaGuardia Community College of the City University of New York, where I've taught since 1981, I decided that, since I'd heard over the years from quite a number of colleagues who were obviously extremely good at teaching fiction, drama, and critical theory that they found teaching poetry difficult, I would address that issue in an article.

My sabbatical spanned from September 2020 to August 2021, and I got a head start over the summer. By October, after doing substantial research, "prewriting," and outlining, I realized that this wasn't going to be an article;

I had three interrelated articles that, topped off by an integrative conclusion, would be enough for a modestly sized book, and perhaps I could get a rough draft two of those articles (chapters) done by the time I returned to teaching. This was in the thick of the pandemic. During that time, on average I left my home once or twice a week and traveled minimally. It gave me great pleasure to do research for this project and write many hours a day; I'd never gotten quite as much joy from just writing about poetry or theory in the other ways that you so aptly describe. Perhaps I felt that pedagogical writing would be of greater practical use. In any case, because I had a sabbatical during the relative isolation of the pandemic, I finished a draft of the book by mid-summer 2021. I even enjoyed making mostly stylistic changes prior to submitting the book for Bloomsbury's consideration at the beginning of Spring 2021.

DM: In your response to my first prompt, you mention that you have taught at LaGuardia for over forty years. For this prompt, I'd like you to narrow your focus a little more than you do in your book, by discussing the specific opportunities you experience for "deepening engagement" with students at LaGuardia, as well as some of the barriers you try to overcome in teaching poetry at LaGuardia. Your college is in Queens, which you mention in your discussion of Paolo Javier's poem "Feeling Its Actual" is "one of the United States' most ethnically and racially diverse areas" (43). Reading your discussion of Javier—who, I learned, is "originally from the Philippines" and has served as "Poet Laureate of his current home borough, Queens" (43)—I found myself thinking that addressing what you call the difficulty of "syntactic deviation" poetry such as Javier's may be of special importance when working with students for whom English is a Second Language. In your discussion of unconventional English usage in Javier's "Feeling Its Actual," for example, you emphasize the immigrant speaker's "emotional authenticity" as well as "self-reproach" over linguistic "errors" (43). As you observe in your discussion of syntax in "Feeling Its Actual," "Having the makeshift adverb 'concedingly' modify the verb 'can be' suggests that the speaker chooses to behave provisionally in response to a particular context rather than to succumb permanently to pessimism" (46). Would you agree with me that your analysis of "Feeling Its Actual" may serve as a "reparative reading" for some of your LaGuardia students who, like Javier's speaker, may be made to feel ashamed of language usages that, in truth, represent "imaginative constructions of meaning" (43)?

TF: Our student population at LaGuardia is extremely heterogeneous, and I hesitate to make large generalizations. In my composition and literature classes, I'd estimate that between 20% and 70% of the students might indicate that English is not their first language. (This semester, one student characterized English as her *fourth* language.) And some others may have grown up bilingual. But within the population who have a different first language than English, there are students who received rigorous instruction in English *grammar and syntax* in their native land and thus have conventional usage and only occasional idiomatic lapses, as opposed to those who report speaking and writing very grammatically in their native tongue but find the grammatical and syntactic move from that language to English difficult. Still others suggest that they are not particularly in control of grammar and syntax in their native language, as well as American English. If memory serves, when I taught Javier's poem about seven or eight years ago, I had a large number of native English speakers. For most of them, Javier's poem did seem to enhance their respect for what non-native speakers go through *and* their ability to produce "imaginative constructions of meaning." Though I don't remember any saying so, I imagine that the analysis of "Feeling Its Actual" and poems like it does serve as a "reparative reading" for some former-ESL students, and this often has something to do with the affective process of identification, though that might occur in the first contact with the poem, prior to interpretation. On the other hand, other students may find the affirmation to be found in the poem superfluous. Why? Proud of their primary language and culture, they take its primacy in their life as a matter of course; some may even find the acquisition of standard English skills a nuisance, irrelevant to the career goals that comprise their reason for going to college. A student might even interpret the poem as evidence of that perspective, regardless of what a "majority opinion" in the class is.

When I teach Louise Bennett's dialect poetry, students of Jamaican origin frequently enjoy their position as "guide" or "native informant" to their non-Jamaican colleagues and professor. For some, reading a poem like "Colonization in Reverse" may indeed be reparative, especially if they have experienced culture clashes or discrimination in NYC. The non-Jamaican students tend to find the process of understanding the dialect elements either delightful and intriguing or burdensome.

DM: I'm writing my third prompt to you on the afternoon of November 8, 2022, midterm election day in the United States. I don't know how the results of this election cycle will turn out, but it is not breaking news to say that few observers would regard current American political discourse as featuring the qualities of nuance, ambivalence, and ambiguity that, you demonstrate, teachers encourage students to regard as admirable features of poetry.

Political advertisements and remarks by candidates in debates traffic in misleading "sound bite" versions of opponents' positions on what are inevitably complex issues. Turning political discussion into a game of "gotcha," it is considered a mortal sin if a politician has changed her mind about an issue. The context in which an opposing candidate had once cast a vote or made a claim is rarely considered when the meaning of the vote or claim is taken up in the new context of a debate or in an attack ad.

It strikes me that the model you advocate for how to read, write about, and discuss poetry in the classroom might serve as a usable model for how I, for one, wish political discourse were treated in the public square. In contrast to the cherry-picking aspect of political soundbites, for example, you discourage readers of even such a controversial poem as Amiri Baraka's "Somebody Blew Up America" from engaging in "contextual synecdoche," that is, from acting "as though a relatively small part of the text is its essence, and this allows them to draw a frame around the entire text and ignore counterevidence" (137). At another place in the conclusion to your book, you advocate for students to offer provisional, partial, and suggestive readings of poems, and to avoid the goal of attempting to offer an airtight one hundred percent correct analysis of a poem. You write, "After a thorough discussion of a text, various members of an intellectual community often will not reach consensus, yet an attitude of dialogic openness and a desire to enhance whatever understanding is possible is far preferable to the use of conversation to serve egotistical bids for dominance. When students address interpretive differences rooted in ideological disagreement, they can do so in an atmosphere devoid of ad hominem and ad feminam offensives." (138). Your book does not overemphasize the theme of poetry and politics, but would you care to comment on how your recommendations for how to approach poetry in the classroom could serve as a model for how citizens might engage with political discourse?

TF: I'm writing my reply to you the night after the midterm elections, and I interpret the results so far as an encouraging rejection, for the most part, of MAGA extremism.

Your analogy is wonderful! Why can't a flexible, open approach to poetry interpretation provide a sense of how *political* interpretation can be lifted out of the mud—or better yet, a tar pit like LaBrea in LA? Supersubtle modulations of phrasing in some literary criticism only partly disguise polarizing rhetoric and even knee-jerk emotionalism that is so egregiously on the surface in U.S. political life. An organization called *Common Ground* stages dialogues and makes them accessible as podcasts to explore how those with divergent ideologies can find ways to transcend gridlock, the kind that's plagued Congress for decades, to solve pressing problems. As these conversations indicate, a precondition for the realization of areas of agreement between those with irreconcilable positions would be engagement in the process of *reading* an "other's" tenets, reasoning, tropes, and examples, with more than the sole picture of total victory in a debate. Openness to *whatever* might be found, including an area of compromise, however provisional, is required.

In the case of Baraka's "Somebody Blew Up America," it may be tough for some readers with subject positions to settle down to the kind of open reading that we're talking about, because of the poem's emotionally charged, declamatory style and a few assertions of wrongdoing that may not be verifiable. However, this is precisely what I think they should do. And if they do, there's a chance they'll see that Baraka is not being anti-Jewish but trying, among other things, to challenge the equation of Jews and Israel. In fact, anti-Zionist Orthodox Jews would agree with him on this one point.

DM: Tom, I'd like to ask you to reflect on student resistance to difficult poetry. I ask because, as you mention in your book, innovative poet-critic Hank Lazer has noted that "today's 'multitasking' millennial and post-millennial student are already acclimated" to "an open encounter with collage-poetry," and yet students may struggle with poems that "lack a single, immediately discernible frame" (25). Given that students, as you point out, "enjoy collage effects in other media than poetry," can you home in on why students tend to resist poems that lack a conventional narrative structure and autobiographically inflected lyric speaker (26)? I believe your response may move our conversation in the direction of reflecting on the problem of situating poetry in the classroom, and on student expectations that the poetry presented in the classroom must be comprehended in a conventional sense of that term, but I'd like to hear your views on the matter.

TF: Some members of my literature classes have understood and appreciated the connection between collage-poetry and collage-effects in other media and are ready to do the kind of close reading that accounts for big thematic shifts. Ashbery's short poems sometimes elicit this kind of response. On the other hand, many students enjoy collage effects in other media because they can relax, skate lightly on surfaces, and engage in what Tan Lin calls "ambient reading;" they don't feel the pressure of paying acute attention to each part or ponder the relation of parts to the whole. But when they're in a college course and know that they have to write an essay on a poem, these readers don't perceive the poem as something to enjoy or a source of relaxation. They often presume that this essay must have a thesis, and all the body paragraphs of poetic interpretation have to support this thesis or build up to it. If the poetic text is disjunctive and hence seems to present a severe barrier to thesis-building and, hence, essay completion, then the students can get annoyed and frustrated. How does my explanation of these two different tendencies jibe with your experience of teaching disjunctive poetry at Purdue?

DM: I currently use a textbook by Susan Holbrook that includes a first chapter entitled, "What Makes Poetry Poetry and Why Are We So Afraid of It?" The chapter features Holbrook's experience of teaching "Blues" (1966) by Canadian experimentalist bpNichol.

As you can see (and I mean see, because this poem is as much a visual/graphic experience as it is a text to read), "Blues" is a literary riff on Robert Indiana's legendary series of "Love" sculptures and paintings that originated in 1964. Never mentioning the musical form of the blues, or the color, or the melancholic state, the poem consists of four lowercase letters splayed across a white space eight times, forwards and backwards. As we start our unit on poetry with this text in a general education course, I regularly teach to first-year STEM students at Purdue, my goal is to help students realize they are not alone if they feel uncomfortable speaking in public about difficult texts. To facilitate class discussion, I ask students to address questions such as the following prompts based on comments Holbrook makes about the poem in her opening chapter:

Chapter one: Introduction: What Makes Poetry Poetry and Why Are We So Afraid of It?

1. Why do you think a student in Holbrook's class called bpNichol's poem "Blues" an example of "Avant-Garde Toilet Paper"?
2. According to Holbrook, "How does poetic language differ from the language of prose?"
3. In what way is language in poetry like a "stained glass window"?
4. Thinking about the example of "Blues," what is Holbrook getting at when she says "meaning [in poetry] is shaped in multiple ways by its medium"?
5. In relation to "Blues," why do you think Holbrook brings up the fact that the word "poet" has roots in ancient words that meant "to make" or "to build"?
6. Poets often like to put forward words that convey multiple meanings and associations. Name three associations or meanings for the word fragment, "evol."
7. With "Blues" in mind, why do you think Holbrook urges poetry readers not to "feel pressure to reduce the poem to a simple summarizing sentence"?
8. Why do you think Holbrook says "Blues" is a "meditation on love, but also on language itself"?
9. Why do you think Holbrook considers you, the reader of the poem, to be "the most important piece" of the puzzle in determining what a poem means? Do you agree with Holbrook?

When dealing with "difficult" poems, students appreciate having specific, but open-ended, prompts that enable them to develop their own responses to specific aspects of the "difficult" poem. I would add here that one of the things I enjoy doing in class when addressing "Blues" is to use the poem as an opportunity to introduce related art forms and cultural movements. Relying on resources available on YouTube, I show clips about blues music, Duchampian readymades, the meaning of "avant-garde," and on Robert Indiana's Love sculptures.

Tom, my comments above about teaching "Blues" in a general education program for STEM majors at Purdue lead me to my next prompts: Given the neoliberal world of contemporary academia today, how do we make a case that helping students find pleasure in poetry matters? You address this issue in chapter two, "Emotional Enticements and Aversions," but I wonder if you could reflect here on how you try to encourage students to embrace the multiple pleasures of reading, talking about, and writing about poetry, while at the same time making the case to other stakeholders such as administrators, trustees, and tuition-paying parents and guardians that what we do in the poetry classroom has vocational significance in developing "soft skills" and "critical thinking"?

TF: Dan, your questions for the STEM students provide a useful set of contexts for entering a meaningful analysis of Nichol's poem and for discouraging an (old—by now, ancient!) New Critical approach. As for Holbrook calling the poem "a meditation on love" and "language," I think that really stretches the term "meditation." If she said that "Blues" occasions the reader's meditation, I could accept that.

You are undoubtedly highly aware of this already, but I'll talk about a recent trend for the benefit of members of our audience who don't teach in literature departments. On their websites, English departments throughout the United States are currently making a solid case to both students and "administrators, trustees, and tuition paying parents and guardians" that English majors, contrary to superficial journalistic soundbites, consistently get good jobs in a variety of fields (other than teaching). The departmental statements tend to attribute this to how employers recognize the very "soft skills" and "critical thinking" that you mention in job seekers who are English graduates. The caveat is that English majors also need to take courses outside the field—such as in the domain of computer technology—that will show prospective employers that they can combine "hard" and "soft" skills to provide "value" for a company. In addition, because of what they learn in our courses that sharpens their communication skills and ability to understand and solve complex problems, our majors tend to have staying power and the opportunity to advance in ways that allow them to make increasingly decent salaries, even if STEM majors frequently have higher starting salaries.

College and university websites promoting the benefits of the English major are referring to the study of literature in general rather than the study of poetry. That's appropriate. I would remind those faculty who tend to valorize concentration on the other genres and tacitly marginalize poetry that lyric poetry's relative economy of scale—and even long (epic or anti-epic) poems tend to be shorter than novels—provides significant pedagogical benefits. Critical thinking involves a continual vacillation between scrutiny of details and consideration of larger cognitive structures. When this is practiced on a short text, the interpreter can focus on a greater quantity of details in relation to the text as a whole and does not have to engage in as much synecdoche: closely citing and reading some parts of the text and ignoring other, equally potentially salient parts. In that sense, critical thinking relies less on arbitrary selection that, in some way, diminishes criticality.

In the last four pages of my Conclusion, I concentrate fully on how the reading and analysis of poetry develops interpretive abilities and flexible patterns of thought and action that reflect many of the attributes that English department websites foreground to show students that the major can lead to a rewarding career. Rather than repeating those points here, I'll just circle back to your question about the relevance of openness toward multiple interpretations to the U.S. political arena and my affirmation of the connection that you see. If this kind of ability to entertain multiple perspectives fully, to avoid rushing into rigid postures, and to articulate complexities is germane to our national political life, it's also valuable in guiding thought and behavior in commerce, the law, medicine, and arts and entertainment in general.

DM: Tom, my previous questions have focused on students and student learning, but I'd like to focus now on what it takes for you to prepare for and to conduct a successful course involving poetry analysis. Your book demonstrates your dedication to teaching. For example, here is a passage that describes the steps you take to help students who may get "carried away with external historical, political, or sociological evidence" when writing about a poem (68):

"I attempt to set clear, precise guidelines for the first draft of an essay so that these kinds of things do not happen. And if the guidelines do not sink in, specific comments on the first graded draft about areas in which the student needs to demonstrate *how* the poem communicates (rather than just *what* it communicates) can help the writer compose an effective revision. These comments can be reinforced in a conference." (68)

As I read that passage, I was struck by how time-consuming your process must be as you interact from your response to a first draft, to conference, to revision of first draft, to your response to their final draft. I don't know what your course enrollments are or how many sections you teach each semester, but you must be spending a lot of your work days responding to student writing about poems. Your preparation for class discussion also suggests immense diligence:

"In group work and class discussion that take place in a literature course, I find that, aside from eliciting students' interpretive conjectures, it is often beneficial to expose them to various components of others' interpretations and rationales for them—including implicit and explicit interpretive frames. (If no one has published criticism on the poem, I devise alternative readings.)" (71).

Your analysis of critical perspectives on W.B. Yeats's "A Prayer for My Daughter" ranging from hard-line critique of patriarchy to one that reads a stanza as a "temporary endorsement of female spiritual empowerments" (81) to a reading that emphasizes Yeats's interest in Hindu symbolism illustrates how you present critical views so that students can see the poem as a "busy 'thoroughfare' that reflects the daunting complexity of Yeats's influences, pressures, ideas, and modes of persuasion that get in each other's way" (84).

You have been teaching for over four decades, and your book makes clear that your work with students remains a central task for you. How do you stay inspired? Can you discuss how you integrate your preparation for teaching poetry with other aspects of your life as a critic, poet, artist, and your other obligations as a professor?

TF: The process can be demanding but isn't as insanely time-consuming as it may seem from the passages you cite. There is a cap of twenty-eight students in Writing through Literature and the same in Introduction to Poetry. (For various reasons, a few students never show up or withdraw from a course by mid-semester.) I teach 24 hours of courses per year spread over two twelve-week terms and one six-week term; depending on how many hours each week a class is, that could be seven or eight classes. There are three high-stakes assignments in the Writing through Literature course.

It doesn't take a lot of time to read and provide feedback on the brief low-stakes assignments (that involve some aspect of high-stakes ones). The first draft does receive a lot of commentary, but conferencing can occur either in class during group work or designated office hours, and students have the option not to revise the first draft if it is passing. Many don't, so the first draft is the final one.

As for preparation for class discussions in Writing through Literature and Introduction to Poetry, I don't do exhaustive and exhausting research on more than one poem in the former course and a handful in the latter. Sometimes, preparation consists of re-reading a poem twice or thrice and making a few scribbles, and often, that suffices, because one is drawing on years of thinking about poetry and poets. And I tend to do the fullest kind of research for teaching at times when I'm not teaching—well before the actual course in which the poem will be covered takes place. During the summer months, I often prepare syllabi and course schedules for most classes I'll be teaching in the following year, and the rest gets done during other downtime.

I've just emphasized these points about how preparation doesn't have to be excessively burdensome, because one way to stay inspired is not to overwork. For example, insisting that every student revises every paper is not good for the faculty member, and it's not pedagogically sound for students whose first draft is strong and those who may have a good deal to improve but are juggling a lot of other responsibilities and are just going to make "cosmetic" revisions. Further, I try to be very organized in accomplishing my "other obligations as a professor" so that I don't take more time on them than they require. Another way of staying inspired is to find the middle ground between two extremes: each semester, I try to make sure I teach a substantial amount of literature that I've never taught before *and* some work that I taught a few years earlier or even a long time ago. The first approach keeps everything fresh, while the second enables me to find dimensions of the work (and, for research papers, criticism on the text) that I hadn't noticed in the previous classroom interpretation and wouldn't have noticed if I'd taught it the previous term. The excitement of the poetry itself, the temporal unfolding of consensus, dissensus, and oscillation in the process of dialogue about a poem, and individual students' manifestation of eureka moments continue to motivate me.

The most obvious way to stay inspired is to notice and strengthen connections between different realms of activity. When I put a lot of effort and thought into something like the orchestration of competing critical claims about Yeats's "A Prayer for My Daughter," I know it will eventually have (at least) an indirect impact on some facet of a problem that I pursue in criticism and even find its way into a poem—either through the play of language or some thematic fragment. When I teach poets who are new to me, their work may show the way to trying something in my own poetry that I had never considered. And my poetic or artistic practice sometimes leads me to questions that poems promise to answer, and so I decide to teach those poems.

SECTION 4

In My End Is My Beginning: Reviewing Peter Dale Scott and Philip Guston

CHAPTER 15

REVIEWING PETER DALE SCOTT/ REVIEWING MYSELF

Author's Note

I consider reviewing books of poetry and scholarship in my field to be a vital part of my "thirty-year creative reading workshop." I have published at least 35 reviews since my first effort, which, according to my CV (I just checked), is "Redefining the Canon of Modern American Poetry." *Retrospection* (University of New Hampshire Graduate Journal of History). In the last few months, I reviewed two books on subjects related to my earlier book projects. Deborah Dash Moore's *Walkers in the City: Jewish Street Photographers of Midcentury New York* resonated with my *After Weegee: Essays on Contemporary Jewish American Photographers*, published in 2011. Dara Barnat's *Walt Whitman and the Making of Jewish American Poetry* dovetails with my interest in a Jewish way of reading and writing poetry unrelated to the religious affiliation of the author or reader, as indicated in Norman Finkelstein's casting of Wallace Stevens as a "Dark Rabbi." Book reviewing has served different purposes for me at different points in my academic journey. Reviewing poetry for the *Harvard Review* when I was a lecturer at Harvard from 1992 to 1994 let me see my name in print and enabled me to feel like my opinions mattered outside my circle of friends and associates. Later, establishing myself as a scholar at Purdue, reviewing helped me stay abreast of developments in my field, and, sometimes, to promote the work of colleagues whose writings deserved a wider audience. Now, nearer to the end of my career than to the beginning, it is gratifying to be asked to review in areas where I have established my reputation through publications. Book reviewing remains a critical aspect of professional service.

The two reviews that follow this "Author's Note" shed light on the meaning of this book project. The first, on Peter Dale Scott's *Listening to the Candle: A Poem on Impulse* (1992), spurred me to learn about Scott's research into "U.S. covert operations, their impact on democracy at home and abroad, and their relations to the John F. Kennedy assassination and the global drug traffic" (Peter Dale Scott's website). Scott's poetry, published by James Laughlin's New Directions Press, the house of my dissertation subject, William Carlos Williams, showed me that a contemporary long poem could be lyrical and relevant as social commentary. Unlike the conservative social formations propounded in long poems by modernists such as T. S. Eliot and Ezra Pound, here was an accomplished literary practitioner whose mission was to critique American imperialism. The poet-critic Robert Hass has written (*Agni*, 31/32, p. 335) that Scott's "*Coming to Jakarta* is the most important political poem to appear in the English language in a very long time." My review of Scott's *Listening to the Candle* in 1992 suggests my yearning to find examples of political poetry, a topic I would learn more about in subsequent decades, culminating in my editing of the *Cambridge Companion to American Poetry and Politics since 1900*, published in 2023. The second review, on Scott's *Poetry and Terror: Politics and Poetics in Coming to Jakarta* (2018), which I reviewed for *Notre Dame Review* in 2022, revealed how a writer and activist I admire has, late in life, engaged in his own act of "learning twice" by revisiting the circumstances and personal inflections of his trilogy of poems about American involvement in the massacre of more than a half million Indonesians in 1965.

***

Listening to the Candle: A Poem on Impulse by Peter Dale Scott. New Directions Press, 1992

(Review first published in *Harvard Review* Volume V. Number One. '92. 57-63.)

The central problem of how to acknowledge the significance of "the mystery of dailiness" and the sanctity of "inner" life in light of the facts—the political horror—that a worldly figure such as Peter Dale Scott (b. 1929) cannot avoid witnessing and speaking out against leads the poet in his second book-length poem into a search for a perspective from which to make sense out of, or at least to embrace the nonsense of, his life and times:

> the choice of being
> diminished by what one sees
> to the point of anonymity
> or enlarged by solitude
> to visions of madness
> flickering to the north
>
> of the restricted regions
> where we deal in words

While Scott resists the Eliotic attempt to extinguish personality in order to tell the story of the culture as a whole, he also chooses to write a poetry which is distinct from the work of Frank O'Hara or the very late notebook poetry of Robert Lowell, which, in Scott's terms, would be to "express the personal" as in the phrase "I have forgotten my umbrella." Rather, like the poets once associated with the Black Mountain School (Olson, Creeley) to whom his "field of action" poetry bears a formal allegiance, Scott attempts to "communicate/ what can be received." The experience of the pain of separation from a loved one, from this perspective which waits to judge, can be understood as an opening toward some new possibility, some new peace. Like Rilke, who believed that the intensity of our love increases in the absence of the beloved, Scott can find consolation even in the separation from his wife of 30 years, Maylie, whom we learn during the poem has left domesticity to become a priest:

> as we move out beyond
>   the fulfillment of marriage
> gives us each the space
>
> to sit as I do now
>   in this plane coming down
> over the fields of Mexico
>
> to rejoin its shadow
>   this vacancy distance
> of separation
>
> we can only call a *gift*

The wisdom that Scott achieves in this poem, and that he embodies in the flexible, inclusive structure, is that we must search for a way between what he calls the "brutality" of civilization and the mindless anarchy that he says will soon lead to brutality; the way is achieved by a pleasure in the act of making, as Scott advocates "the instruction of play [...] instead of custom dance."

The son of a Canadian diplomat and civil rights champion whose death is among the personal losses suffered by the poet that enable this meditation, Peter Dale Scott has been since the 1950s in a unique position to attempt to write a non-egotistical form of a personal/political poetry. His involvement in informed protest against covert government operations has made the experience of this "outsider" seem paradigmatic of those persons in the United States who have been outraged at the excesses of the imperial presidency. From 1957 to 1961 he was the Canadian member of the UN General Assembly before coming to the United States as a professor at UC Berkeley, where he published books about the Vietnam War and the assassination of John F. Kennedy. His most recent political nonfiction concerns the Iran-Contra connection and "Cocaine Politics." The commitment to exposing and unraveling covert American involvement in international affairs is absorbed into *Coming to Jakarta* (New Directions, 1989), Scott's first book-length poem, which was triggered by the bloody Indonesian invasion in 1965.

In *Listening to the Candle*, the second long poem in a planned trilogy, Scott moves away from a focus on politics without ignoring the scars he has incurred by witnessing events that have precipitated his move to "more inward/solitary landscapes." The Gulf War, international terrorism, ethnic violence, South African apartheid, as well as the suppression of Scott's own books in the UC main library, and possible involvement by the CIA in drugging members of the radical left at Berkeley in the 1960s, are among the subjects that inform the fear, outrage, and perhaps, conciliatory escape in *Listening to the Candle*. The kind of protest that Scott now envisions is of the beautiful and non-tragic sort that for a brief time took place in Tiananmen Square, where, Scott writes, protest occurred and the world heard it "without unlocking the terror/in the hearts of colonels/that has always led to bloodbaths."

Scott's focus, however, is on personal matters, on the death of his father, on the separation from his wife, on the personal question of whether the "normalcy" he associates with academic life has been for him a good decision, on his less-than-successful attempts to mediate between his literary and political ambitions and his desire to be a good father, and on a growing sense that his academic "normalcy" masks a "fear of losing control." For this reason, it will be disappointing to readers who have come to expect from Scott, as perhaps we have come to expect from Carolyn Forché, poetry that witnesses and explains the uses and abuses of power by a government with imperialistic designs. Like much of the so-called L=A=N=G=U=A=G=E poetry, which also originates from Berkeley, California, Scott's poetry is concerned with "those limits of memory/beyond learning to speak," with the difficulty, in other words, of returning to the personal past or to political truths through language, and with a sense of the worlds' movement toward illegibility and what Scott calls "endarkenment." The book's message about the social efficacy of art is not optimistic. This is not at all to say that *Listening to the Candle* is a gloomy book, but it is to say that the poet has come to a place where the truth and simplicity of the Zen practice of sitting quietly and with a straight back has become, as in a different context as it was for Eliot in the *Four Quartets*, the source of strength and consolation for a writer once deeply engaged in trying to change the world:

> ... the joy
>   always available to us
> of this spine-hung breathing
>
> that hold the earth
>   close up against the strained
> cross of legs beneath

"This spine-hung breathing" is an appropriate metaphor for the speech rhythms of Scott's poem. The imaginative act of making poems, as it was for Stevens and for Blake, becomes itself a sufficient and highest good, as well as a temporary stay against the feeling of helplessness to inaugurate social change. Zen practice, after all, with its distrust of a goal, or even of a clear course, while at the same time stressing mindfulness and openness to all experience without judgment upon it, is the poetry of what Scott calls "the enduring practice." The poet's attempt to "comprehend" rather than to "impose" order—his openness to patterns that happen to exist—is a feature of the poem's effortless style. Scott presents to readers a way toward the making of a less aggressive (which is to say, contemporary) form of modern poetry.

Internal Turmoil and State Violence in Poetry and Terror
Peter Dale Scott and Freeman Ng
Lexington Books 2018
286 pages
(Review first published in the *Notre Dame Review* in 2022)

From 1966's *The Politics of Escalation in Vietnam* to 2014's *The American Deep State: Big Money, Big Oil, and the Attack on U.S. Democracy,* Peter Dale Scott published fourteen nonfiction prose books. In these books, many co-authored, Scott's research into government documents unravels CIA mischief involving cocaine, assassinations, and misinformation campaigns in Indonesia, Afghanistan, and Central America. Given *Poetry and Terror* (2018) is collaborative historiography, this time with his former UC Berkeley student Freeman Ng, published in a series called "Asia World," and dedicated to Daniel Ellsberg, the RAND corporation whistleblower who released the Pentagon Papers in 1971, you may assume Scott, now 90, has published his fifteenth political documentary. *Poetry and Terror* is about the relations between covert operations and American imperialism, but its main contribution will be to poetics, as well as to reception, genre, and trauma studies. Focusing on *Coming to Jakarta: A Poem About Terror* (1989), the first volume in his trilogy *Seculum*, *Poetry and Terror* demonstrates how a contemporary long-form poem can simultaneously explore the terror of internal turmoil as well as document an under-acknowledged exhibition of state terror.

Like *Cocaine Politics* (1991) and *The Iran-Contra Connection* (1987), *Poetry and Terror* critiques American power by exposing actions committed by agents of what Scott, writing from the Left and well before Trumpists adopted the term, calls the "deep state." (For Scott, "deep state" refers to the "interrelated topics of organized non-official violence, crime, drugs, and oil" that constitute "the zone of the unspeakable and undefinable that poets, and indeed all of us, need to be aware of" [199]). Unlike his prior collaborative projects, however, *Poetry and Terror* offers a self-reflexive interrogation into a "politics under the surface, of all these other forces accumulating and asserting themselves and not part of the world as we think about it rationally" (77). The author addresses his own minor, but long suppressed, collaborative relationship to U.S.-sponsored terror abroad. He acknowledges his complicity with his university's involvement in training Indonesians who took part in the 1965 massacre:

> The Berkeley campus had trained people who went back and helped prepare to take over the country.//I remember that the first time I wrote about this massacre, I tried to excuse the University of California. I wrote an article in a book published in England that took issue with the critic who has said that the "Berkeley Mafia" (a term used in Jakarta about Suharto's economic team) were at the heart of it.//So what in me had tried to say, "Oh, no! not the *Berkeley* Mafia"? It *was* the Berkeley Mafia! [...] And in III .ii I acknowledge that I am part of the enemy. And in an odd way, that's a reassurance. [65–66]

In 1980, Scott's acknowledgment of second-hand complicity with General Suharto brought him psychic pain, but also initiated a burst of creative activity. As Scott writes in his "Introduction" to *Poetry and Terror*, the first draft of *Coming to Jakarta* "was written after a night of panic, and which came slowly to focus on the US-backed massacre of Indonesian leftists in 1965" (xiv).[1]

---

1 As *Inside Indonesia's* Robert Cribb and Michele Ford report in "The Killings of 1965-66": "In the course of little more than five months from late 1965 to early 1966, anti-communist Indonesians killed about half a million of their fellow citizens. Nearly all the

Scott has struggled for more than 50 years to overcome psychological inhibition and the mainstream media's veil of secrecy to convey what happened in Jakarta in the early 1960s. He treats censorship in broad terms. Censorship includes his denial of "the Berkeley Mafia," but also how Simon and Schuster held off publishing his study of the JFK assassination in 1980. The *New York Times*, Scott also notes, refused to publish his editorial challenging a misleading story in November 1965, which stated North Vietnam "insisted that the Americans *must pull out before* a peace conference could be considered" (114). Scott admits that we all "repress memories that do not fit our everyday reality" to stay sane (170). He observes that for years he blocked a memory "of meeting a witness to opium on CIA planes in Southeast Asia" who "wouldn't talk to us, because somebody had burned a hole in his car door" (172). The overall trajectory of *Poetry and Terror*, however, trends toward the uses of poetry and commentary to work through repressed personal memories as well as to expose the "colossal repression of the truth" of U.S. complicity in massacres in Jakarta and East Timor in the 1960s and 1970s (173). Scott destabilizes Manichean thinking about who is accountable for terror.

Poetry and Terror contributes to trauma theory and reception studies, as well as to the study of poetics. Scott reimagines *Coming to Jakarta* as less of a stable work, and more of a fluid text. Scott discusses, reconsiders, and reclaims his long poem in a 40-year process of knowledge transmission through poetic commentary. *Poetry and Terror* also asks us to think more flexibly about genre. The book combines poetry and prose, contemporary lyric "confessionalism" and modern impersonalist poetry with history, epic and elegy. Scott questions the Romanticist notion that only the bohemian outsider may challenge state power. Like T. S. Eliot, Robert Lowell, and James Merrill, Scott hails from a family of elites, in his case Canadian politicians and academicians. A former diplomat who served in the Canadian consulate in Poland for two years, Scott, a paradoxical insider activist, criticizes the toxic masculinist need to dominate events and the subsequent corrupting influence of power on Allen Dulles and Henry Cabot Lodge, privileged American foreign policymakers during the Cold War.

Scott wrote *Coming to Jakarta* and *Poetry and Terror* in the service of psychic health. In this sense, Scott's compositions resemble Ezra Pound's assemblage of the *Pisan Cantos* in 1945. Scott believes Pound's writing was "part of a healing

---

victims were associated with Indonesia's Left, especially with the Communist Party (PKI) that had risen to unprecedented national prominence under President Sukarno's Guided Democracy." https://www.insideindonesia.org/the-killings-of-1965-66

process in which he says a lot of things which contradict the ideology of his earlier cantos" (20). *Poetry and Terror* is, however, an unsettling text that resists the healing balm of psychic closure. The author as reader, Scott becomes a belated receiver of his own poem. He regards history, both personal and political, as an unfolding procedure that requires, in Scott's case, almost four decades of composition to make sense out of the initial crisis. However, Scott wonders, can we locate the initial crisis? Because he links poetic inspiration to cognitive studies by "letting the neurons do their own far-out choosing rather than having the frontal lobes do the sensible choosing," it is folly to limit Scott's psychic troubles to his role in concealing Cal Berkeley's responsibility for the Indonesian massacre (6). *Poetry and Terror* reveals that the psychic reclamation that animates *Coming to Jakarta* includes recovering childhood memories involving violent behavior, fear of mortality, and a mystic bent. The poet was eight when he "saw a ghost coming towards me" during "a frightening all-night snowstorm" (6-7). There was a near-death drowning experience when he was a child, and a reckoning with his "own violence" when young Scott threw a rock at other boys in a "rough part of Montreal" in the Depression era to prevent them from stealing his ski sled (62–63). One cannot so easily unfold and sort out the strands of a life that combines politics and personal reflection, violent impulses, and peaceful gestures.[2] Scott delimits the significance of *Coming to Jakarta* in *Poetry and Terror* by expanding the idea of coming to terms with Jakarta well beyond confronting the Indonesian massacre of 1965.

Scott is a tenacious researcher into the seedy doings of what *Nation* correspondent Larry Bensky calls, "an old-boy network of far rightists, gonzo adventurers, profiteers, drug-and gunrunners, religious fanatics, and intelligence freelancers who intersect regularly with the various government agencies they once served." (https://www.poetryfoundation.org/poets/peter-dale-scott). He is also a McGill- and Oxford-trained multicultural classicist. His poetics makes a case for how a robust background in world literature can amplify a critique of covert state power. In a chapter of *Poetry and Terror* titled

---

2 We can, however, make out a chronology of crucial events, reaching back over a half century, that inform the composition of *Poetry and Terror*: the 1965 Indonesian massacre, Scott's published denial in 1975 of Berkeley's "responsibility for the 1965 massacre" (47), the 1980 panic attack and psychological breakdown in Watertown, Massachusetts, after the Reagan election that precipitated Scott's drafting of the first part of *Coming to Jakarta*, the publication of the three volumes of *Seculum* 1988–2000, the interviews with Freeman Ng conducted in 2012, and the actual publication of *Poetry and Terror* in 2018.

"Truth and nonviolence," for example, Scott discusses how, in one thread of *Coming to Jakarta*, Gandhi interpreted the *Bhagavata Gita* from "a war epic, the *Mahabharata*," in an allegoric manner to promote non-violence.

> The explanation is that Gandhi allegorized the Gita. He understood it as not to be taken on the literal level of a battle between the Pendawa and their cousins. It's an allegory about the soul.//Arjuna represents the soul becoming detached from the passions of the battlefield. So, Gandhi turned it into an argument for *ahimsa* as he practiced it, which is *not-fighting, nonviolence*. This is the literal meaning of the word, which gets inverted in the Gita and then gets re-inverted to its original meaning by Gandhi. (166)

Like Pound's *Cantos*, *Coming to Jakarta* includes history and world literature: Virgil, Homer, Aeschylus, the Bible, the Bhagavad Gita, as well as Wordsworth, Eliot, and Milosz; all make appearances in *Poetry and Terror*. Homeric epics amplify Scott's figurative journey through an interior space: "Achilles in the *Iliad* and later Odysseus in the *Odyssey*, escape ruin by a process of confronting the irrational in themselves, and establishing a more integrated relationship to it" (168). Such archetypal features of ancient literature as the heroic journey into the underworld are important to Scott. Framing *Coming to Jakarta* in relation to *Antigone*, he asks whether individuals are culpable agents of history or merely pawns in larger epochs in which fate trumps the individual will. Jakarta is not only a specific geopolitical space but also an Everyman's Underworld.

In the end, we think of the long poem he published with New Directions in 1988 as, really, just one of Scott's ongoing attempts at coming to (terms with) Jakarta. Scott upends the idea that Jakarta has already happened. As in Faulkner's comment from *Requiem for a Nun*, "The past is never dead. It's not even past," Scott writes, "In editing *Poetry and Terror*, I have come to see my poem as also an elegy, not just for the dead in Indonesia, but for the decay of my first marriage, and for the passing of the Sixties era, when so many of us imagined that Movement might achieve major changes for a better America" (181). Scott is still "coming" to Jakarta in a multi-mediated unfolding that leads him to reconceive his epic as elegy.

CHAPTER 16

IN MY END IS MY BEGINNING: SEEING DOUBLE AT *PHILIP GUSTON NOW* IN THE SUMMER OF 2023

Philip Guston, the influential North American painter who died in 1980, has been on my mind lately. This chapter is about why. It is also a belated thank-you note to him. I say this because, half a lifetime ago, my awareness of this hero/bad boy of twentieth-century art saved my hide. Or, more realistically, to take my grandiose appreciation of his efforts down a few notches, a job talk I gave at Purdue about Guston in 1994 clinched my unlikely shot at a permanent academic career in the humanities. (I am ashamed to admit that when I was thirty, landing safely on the tenure track felt like a life-or-death matter.) Can I recover what Guston's art meant to me back then on a gut level? I can certainly remember the outlines of my precarious situation back then, and why Guston's late trauma-filled work would have appealed to me on a deep personal level.

In Boston in the early 1990s (Somerville, actually), I was a dime-a-dozen unemployed humanities PhD. In debt, I paid bills as a secretarial temp. My only marketable skill was the fact that I could touch-type. My living-as-married girlfriend had just broken up with me. I couldn't pay attention to her needs because I was too stuck on my fear I would never catch on as an academician after spending my twenties in training to do so. My father, himself a failed teacher, had died when I was 11. (By coincidence, Guston's father, an émigré from Odessa by way of Montreal, hung himself in Los Angeles when Philip was 10.) I mention my father's passing since I felt shadowed by his untimely demise at age 45. Not getting a teaching gig meant I was my father. He died weak, heavy, and in debt. His marriage was failing, and he was *worried about losing his job* for losing control of his sixth-grade class at Hicksville Elementary School in Nassau County, Long Island, New York. I didn't acknowledge back then that he had untreated diabetes. The disease, not incompetence, is what lulled him to sleep at his desk in front of his unruly students. It was the disease that compelled him to gulp Tropicana orange juice directly from the triangular spout of the half-gallon carton. He drank the juice at night in front of the fridge in his underwear and black work socks after another humiliating day in which his pupils asked him how to spell "fuck" and "shit" until the principal stepped into his classroom to halt the mayhem.

Did I see my father in Guston's overweight frame when the Boston poet Bill Corbett introduced his work to me in 1990? Or Guston in my father? Both were heavyset Jewish men whose families had emigrated from the Pale of Settlement; Guston was born in Montreal in 1913, my father was born in Brooklyn in 1929. Guston changed his name from Goldstein; my father's grandfather changed the family name to Morris from Kleshefsky when he landed in Scotland en route to New York after abandoning the Pale. I think of my father when I gaze at Guston's signature late painting, *Painting, Smoking, Eating* (1973). I stare at that plate of wood plank-like French fries resting on the blanketed chest of the artist's unshaven Cyclops late imago. The fries appear like a wicked treasure. Cyclops knows if he lifts his arms out of his blanket and grabs a handful of those fries, they will trigger another coronary. The thought is tempting. The fries signify a ticket to take him out of his misery—signified by an index finger pointing to a backdrop of shadowy icons associated with traumatic memories including the horseshoe boot heels, all painted in a bloody cadmium red. Oh, how my father lived and died for a paper boat serving of Nathan's thick crinkle-cut fries! For Guston, all three—painting, smoking, eating—were killer addictions. For my father, mostly it was the eating, although he did enjoy a cigar after grilling a T-bone steak in the backyard.

Thirty years ago, I wasn't consciously thinking, as I am now, about how Guston's late work indirectly reflected my own traumatic history. When I gave my job talk at Purdue about his work, I was laser-focused on scoring academic points. I argued that Guston (and the Belgrade-born American poet Charles Simic, who died this year at age 84) represented a rejection of postmodern simulacra. Both engaged in figuration, objectivism, and social history without falling into confessionalism's trap of mistaking representation for voice or personal image for the painter's real presence. In my job talk, I contrasted Morris on Simic's poem "My Shoes" ("secret face of my inner life") and Guston's representations of boot heels as synecdochic registrations of human suffering with Fredric Jameson's dance with Warhol's Halston-influenced "Diamond Dust Shoes" (1980) and (Guston's close friend) Meyer Schapiro's earlier detection of the Heideggerian life force bottoming up from Van Gogh's 1886 still life painting *A Pair of Shoes*. Simic/Guston footwear synthesized Warhol and Van Gogh;

something old married to something new to create a *post*-postmodern aesthetic. Like Warhol, Simic and Guston acknowledged the stagey dimension of personhood associated with straight-up postmodernism of a Baudrillardian variety. Both were serious, but also playful. Both embraced popular culture, and the self-referentiality one typically associates with a postmodern aesthetic. I can rehearse the argument, but, at 30, I had not lived long enough to appreciate, as I do now, how Guston's late work reflected the expressions of a trauma artist. Unable to separate past wounds from current predicaments, Guston, a damaged survivor, represented the entanglement of Then on Now. One did what one could, in Freud's terms, to "work through" early trauma. Guston's late art, however, suggests early wounds remain open and that healing was never complete. Like the excessive eating and smoking, the painting was a compulsive repetition of the hurt that remained, a residue of the "acting out."

Guston's late style (roughly from 1968 until his death in 1980) is so interesting to me now from a psychological point of view because his late-phase visual vocabulary—the white hoods, the boots, the light bulbs, the ropes, the bricks, the rubbery mangled limbs, the chunks of wood posts, the rusty nails, the trash cans and trash car covers, the irons—refer back to objects he represented to imagine historical disasters in his social realist and even quasi abstract phases from the 1930s through the 1950s. "My old interests came surging back," the artist said in *Philip Guston: A Life Lived* (1981), a documentary film directed by Michael Blackwood, on view in a screening room as part of the *Philip Guston Now* exhibit currently showing at the East Wing of the National Gallery of Art in Washington, DC. As Chadd Scott reports, iconic features of his late style resonate with personal trauma:

> Three days after his 10th birthday and just over a year after moving to Los Angeles, Guston's father hanged himself, despondent over not being able to carve out a better life for himself in America. In Canada, he worked as a boilermaker for the railroad, in California he had to settle for being a rag picker.
>
> Maybe Guston found the body; maybe his mother did. Here, again, memory and reality prove difficult to parse. In any case, ropes and porches figured prominently in Guston's work through the 1940s.
>
> Another tragedy involved Guston's brother who died in 1932 after his legs were crushed when he walked behind his car and it rolled over him. The shoes and piles of dismembered legs reoccurring in Guston's work could be owed to this trauma. Or perhaps they take inspiration from an exhibition

of large-scale photographs of liberated German concentration camps Guston saw in 1945 when teaching at Washington University in St. Louis.[1]

Guston himself stated that one spur that initiated his iconic hood pictures from the late 1960s and 1970s was the memory of how in 1933 the Los Angeles police "Red Squad" had destroyed a mural he had painted depicting Klan violence.[2] "In 1967–68, I became very disturbed by the war and the demonstrations," Guston said. "They became my subject matter and I was flooded by a memory [of the police destroying his anti-Klan mural]." We may regard Guston as a diver into the wreck of his subconscious impulses in a period when the dominant paradigm called for tricky surfaces, not manifestations of depth psychology. As Guston scholar Kosme de Barañano has remarked about the artist's later oeuvre:

> Guston's images are immersed in a sinister place of faltering breath, subjected to the cold of the simple grayish, pinkish or white primer. They contain no impasto or terrain that allows for context. The results are symbols like geographies shattered by a feeling halfway between desolation and claustrophobia. They resemble an acidic X-ray scan of a time of defeat, an existential psychodrama just as in Francisco de Goya's Black Paintings.[3]

Theorists of the relationships between trauma, memory, testimony, and representation who have written about Holocaust testimony— Dominick LaCapra, Cathy Caruth, and Dori Laub—seem more relevant to the work of Guston than do theorists of the postmodern aesthetic.

---

[1] Chadd Scott. "America's Most Controversial Art Exhibition, 'Philip Guston Now,' Debuts At MFA, Boston." *Forbes*. May 1, 2022, https://www.forbes.com/sites/chaddscott/2022/05/01/americas-most-controversial-art-exhibition-philip-guston-now-debuts-at-mfa-boston

[2] "In 1932, Guston painted a mural of a Black man being whipped by a Ku Klux Klansman as part of a larger series on racism in America, which he was making with friends in the John Reed Club, a local outpost of a network of Communist clubs. Several months later, the Los Angeles Police Department's Red Squad, a unit that went after Communists, destroyed the murals. Some Los Angeles police officers were known to be members of the Ku Klux Klan." https://www.nga.gov/stories/philip-guston-10-things-to-know.html

"Artist Spotlight: Philip Guston: 10 Things to Know" (National Gallery of Art Website).

[3] https://www.phillips.com/article/49861501/in-the-small-hours-philip-gustons-late-figurative-painting

Uncannily, I now find myself at the age—60—Guston was when he painted the trauma work that made him a rule-breaking "stumblebum" of bad taste, as the art critic Hilton Kramer declared him to be. By trauma work, I am referring to the caricature-type "hood" series of paintings that first appeared in the notorious Marlborough show of 1970. Curators deemed the "hood" series so controversial in 2020 that the comprehensive *Philip Guston Now* exhibition, currently on display this summer in DC, was postponed from its original opening date of June of that year. A half-century ago, Guston was controversial for different reasons. How could one of midcentury modernism's leading abstractions break the taboo against figuration? And not only that, but how could he choose to do so in such a crude style? Art world gatekeepers such as Kramer felt Guston's 1970 style was more appropriate for subway graffiti, trippy Robert Crumb images of big booted hipsters chanting "Keep on Truckin'" from *Zap* comix, and George Herrimann's pop anarchist *Krazy Kat* imagery from the old Sunday Funnies—Guston described the hue he selected for the "hood" series as "a nice pink Sunday comics color"—than it was for museum art by a painter who rubbed shoulders with New York School heroes such as de Kooning and Rothko.

On a stylistic level, the Klan-like "hood" paintings departed from Guston's abstract work from the 1940s and 1950s. Whereas in the "hood" pictures the paint is thinly applied, saturated into the canvas, and reminiscent of a comic strip aesthetic, the abstract paintings revel in the wedding cake frosting quality of the sensuously painted surface. In retrospect, we now see that even Guston's abstract work foreshadows motifs found in his influential (and yet reviled) return to figuration in the late 1960s. "Red Paintings" from 1947 to 1950 and abstract paintings from the late 1950s already suggest a return to pictorialism in titles such as *The Return* and *Passage*. In *The Tormentor* (1947–1948), for example, we notice elements of figurative drawing that prefigure motifs repeated in the late phase work. Outlines of familiar objects, such as the thinly inscribed horseshoe-like boot heels in black ink are apparent even as they seem to be "slowly dissolved into an acid sea of cadmium red paint," as a wall note beside the work at the exhibit describes it. That cadmium red, a Guston favorite, would reappear as splotches of paint on the artists' hoods as they smoke cigars and ponder their creations in paintings such as *The Studio* (1969).

In 2020, curators fretted about showing Guston for reasons other than his decision as a stylist to go low rather than high. There was COVID to worry about, but the primary concern was that Guston's depiction of racist terrorism and anti-Semitic violence might be too upsetting for viewers to witness in the wake of the murder of George Floyd in Minneapolis in May 2020, the violence and chanting against Jews and African Americans by white supremacists that took place as part of the "Unite the Right" protests in Charlottesville in August 2017, as well as the Tree of Life shootings in Pittsburgh in October 2018. We were not ready in 2020, the curators concluded, to deal with Guston's uncomfortable message about his, our, and the art world's complicity with violence and terror. As Dana Carvey's imitation voice of George H. W. Bush might have said, had he remained a cast memory on *Saturday Night Live*: "Complicity. Not going to do it." Guston's "hood" paintings were, however, all about complicity. He pointed the finger at himself, and at what Musa Meyer, his daughter, and head of the Guston Foundation, describes as "white culpability":

> They plan, they plot, they ride around in cars smoking cigars. We never see their acts of hatred. We never know what is in their minds. But it is clear that they are us. Our denial, our concealment. My father dared to unveil white culpability, our shared role in allowing the racist terror that he had witnessed since boyhood when the Klan marched openly by the thousands in the streets of Los Angeles.[4]

Philip Guston Now has opened this summer in DC, but with the following warning placard set on the wall beside the narrow entrance to the room that features "hood" paintings from the Marlborough Show:[5]

> Please be advised that this exhibition contains anti-Black racism and anti-Semitism, including images of lynching, the Ku Klux Klan, and victims of Nazism. If you prefer to bypass the large paintings with hooded figures, please walk through the hallway to your left, where the exhibition continues.

I believe Guston may well have chuckled, shrugged his shoulders, shook his head from side to side, taken another puff from his cigarette, and quoted from his beloved poet T. S. Eliot's "Prufrock": "that is not what I meant at all." For

---

4 Quoted in "America's Most Controversial Art Exhibition, 'Philip Guston Now,' Debuts At MFA, Boston."
Chadd Scott. *Forbes*. May 1, 2022
5 A National Gallery Press Release Announcing the Show reports, "As Guston contemplated his complicity in the injustices of his time, he made 'self-portraits' of artists in Klan hoods in works such as *The Studio* (1969). *Philip Guston Now* includes the largest reunion of paintings from his pivotal Marlborough Gallery show—in total 12 of the original 33 paintings shown. At the National Gallery, these include the imposing *Courtroom* (1970)."

Guston, the "hood" paintings did not require trigger warnings, or at least not for the reasons stated on the sign. They were not designed as mimetic objects to reflect in social documentarian fashion on events outside the painter's studio in Woodstock, New York, where he famously painted late into the night, as if his goal were to conjure the imagery and associative logic that occur to us unconsciously, when we usually are sleeping and dreaming. Turning inward, as in Freud, rather than outward, as in Marx, the "hood" paintings mark a rethinking of his contributions to the social realist tradition such as is found in his impressive 1934 anti-fascist fresco mural, *The Struggle Against Terrorism*, painted with Ruben Kadish after visiting Mexico to study with Leftist Mexican social realists David Alfaro Siqueiros and Diego Rivera. Guston is challenging his conception of the artist as producer of "dangerous" content for viewers to consume in an art world context. The painter no longer perceives the museum as a relevant space for political action. He finds morally suspect his inevitable process of aestheticizing the suffering and violence of others that is already evident in the 1930s in *The Struggle Against Terrorism* and in his first important easel painting, *Bombardment*.

Bombardment (1937) is a major example from the early period of neoclassical social realism that Guston rejected in the "hood" paintings from three decades later. A "vortex of mayhem," is how the panel beside the painting interprets the work in the current DC exhibition. Here is how the website for the Philadelphia Museum of Art, the work's permanent home, describes *Bombardment*:

> Philip Guston painted *Bombardment* after reading newspaper reports of atrocities carried out during the Spanish Civil War, which began on July 17, 1936, when General Francisco Franco led a military coup against the democratically elected Republican government. The emotionally charged scene, which reflects the artist's recent exposure to the activist art of the Mexican mural movement, depicts the aerial bombardment of a civilian population by Franco's warplanes. However, the traditional tondo (circle) format, typically identified with Italian Renaissance painting, suggests that Guston intended to create a universal icon decrying human hatred and destruction rather than a specific commentary on the war in Spain.[6]

Bombardment is shown in a wide-open room at the front end of the exhibit space. It bears no special warning signs that the imagery might offend viewers. In fact, on one of my visits this summer, a friendly and knowledgeable guard

---

6 https://philamuseum.org/collection/object/305249

encouraged me and my friends, Ethan and Marianne, to take a closer look at *Bombardment*, to compare the classical draperies on the mother in the front left part of the picture to how her drapery was cast in a preliminary drawing that appeared on the wall next to the painting. It is only the "hood" work from around 1970 that merits the warning note. And yet, one could argue, *Bombardment* depicts a much more historically resonant scene of political terror than does a "hood" painting such as *Courtroom* (1970). I say this because *Bombardment* represents an active scene of destructive terrorism and indiscriminate murdering of a civilian population. Guston portrays a naked boy who is about to be thrown from his mother's arms, blown to bits. In the center point of the tondo (circle) format, streaky shards of white-and-black smoke and yellow and red rays of fire signify the blast. The bomb bursts like a volcanic eruption out of the deep core of the painting's surface. It explodes into the foreground of the picture plane, splattering a naked man, a character wearing a gas mask and red cape (an aid worker), and the boy's mother, who clings to the wailing child as he comes loose from her arms. In the background toward the top middle of the painting, we see a squadron of dark fighter planes—the Luftwaffe Hitler gifted to Franco as a kind of trial run for Germany's 1939's blitzkrieg invasion of Poland—receding into the painting's border. *Bombardment* is documentary art. To a degree I believe Guston would lament in his later phase, it could be argued that what *Bombardment* really showcases is the artist's skill at dealing with the technical problems of composing a jumble of material into a unified, properly proportioned whole within the peculiar tondo format—with its resonances to his beloved Italian Renaissance painting as well as to Picasso's neoclassical phase work.

Besides the problem of aestheticizing violence, apparent in *The Struggle Against Terrorism* and *Bombardment*, Guston had concluded by the late 1960s that another problem of social realist work is that artist and audience immediately understand exactly where to point the accusatory fingers at the culprits. The finger points outward, at the easy targets. In Guston's early work that means the following basket of deplorables: Franco, Hitler, Mussolini, Spanish inquisitors, the Ku Klux Klan. There was no conversation, no self-reflection, no blurring of the lines between them and us in Guston's political art from the 1930s.

Guston, of course, was not interested in defending criminals, bigots, anti-Semites, murderers in his "hood" series. In *City Lights* (1969), however, the hoods seem more like us than like them. Tooling around in a silly little roadster, possibly a Model T Ford, it is as if the homegrown terrorists are also middle-class working stiffs, carpooling to or from a day at the office in the city. Are they heading back to the suburbs for a TV dinner, a beer, or a bourbon, while catching Walter Cronkite on the CBS Evening News before trudging upstairs to bed to watch Raquel Welch and Jonathan Winters entertain Johnny Carson? Guston was interested in exploring the uncanny, the banal, the complacent, and the quotidian aspects of terrorism. He investigated human behaviors, including art making, in their contradictory, unsettling, and often tragic dimensions. This is not to say there are not in Guston iconic tokens representing the victims as separate figures from the victimizers. There are the white hooded figures, and then there is the pile of rubbery, elongated pipe cleaner legs attached to oversized boot heels, discarded in a trash can, or lined up like a decapitated chorus line in *Rug* (1976). The images suggest the "victims of the gas chambers," according to Aruna D'Souza in a *New York Times* review of the exhibition.[7] In *Rug*, one might assume that Guston is suggesting a clear-cut distinction between the iconic perpetrators of mass violence—the hoods—and the iconic image of victims of mass killing—the chorus line of legs. But here's the thing: we never see the bottom half of the hooded figures, nor the top half of the legs. Guston's point is that the hooded heads and skinny legs stem from the same imagination: his own. Revealing an intense identification with victimizer and victim, Guston resembles one of his key influences, the Odessa-born Jewish storyteller Isaac Babel (1894–1940). In the *Red Cavalry* stories (1926), Babel chronicled his experience during the Polish-Soviet War when in 1920 he accompanied the Red Cavalry Army, who had murdered fellow Jews in the Pale of settlement.[8] In *Odessa Tales* (1931), Babel narrated the doings of a Jewish gangster, Benya Krik. Contributing to a political discourse that might

---

[7] "Where's the Controversy in 'Philip Guston Now'?" https://www.nytimes.com/2023/07/19/arts/design/philip-guston-national-gallery-washington.html
[8] Gregory Freidin writes:

> In the spring of 1920, under a Russian-sounding pen name, Kiril Lyutov, Babel joined Semyon Budenny's First Cavalry Army as a reporter for YugROSTA (the southern branch of the Russian Telegraph Agency) and was soon thereafter assigned to the 6th Division of the army for the duration of the Russo-Polish War. While there he also performed staff duties at the division headquarters, contributed to the army broadsheet *Red Cavalryman*, and on occasion accompanied his detachment into action. Much of the fighting done by Budenny's Cavalry Army took place in the ethnically diverse borderlands between eastern Poland and western Ukraine, a region long settled by traditional, largely Hasidic, Jewish communities.

https://www.britannica.com/biography/Isaac-Babel

transcend our current situation of divisive finger-pointing, Guston refused to separate his own destructive urges from the compulsions enacted by the crude killers he depicted. It was as if the "hoods," like the legs in *Rug*, were the other within the self. In *Painter's Forms No. 2* (1978), Guston draws the outlines of a jaw, a cheek, and a more forcefully rendered wide-opened mouth painted with thick red lips and a set of teeth that remind me of a white picket fence. Spewing into or out of the opened mouth, we not only see white cylinders resembling cigarette filters, but also piles of limbs, boots, and boot heels, some painted in such an abstract manner that they resemble geometric shapes. The painter of *Paintings, Smoking, Eating* is suggesting in *Painter's Forms No 2* that Guston's voracious appetites included the need to ingest, digest, and regurgitate iconographic remnants of catastrophes such as the Holocaust and white terrorist Klan activity. It is as if these historical disasters had become translated into "painter's forms," the visual vocabulary through which he could explore his psyche in his night studio during the last decade of his life.

In Guston, aesthetic styles—neo-Italian Renaissance, surrealist, social realist, Ash Can school, abstract expressionist, underground comix—come and go. As he matured, however, the associative logic and connotative effect of the familiar elements of his restricted visual vocabulary became increasingly internalized, dissociated from sociopolitical reference. Autobiographical, philosophical, and art world meanings take over as political tropes become digested and regurgitated in the late phases. A social realist style drawing from 1930 for the painting called *Conspirator*, which was undertaken in support of the Scottsboro Boys, for example, includes a grouping of hooded Klan figures, brick walls, ropes, and a crucifixion scene in the background. These elements of Guston's visual vocabulary reemerge in cartoonish form, virtually dissociated from their historical context, almost four decades later. One could argue that the "hoods" in the late work may also be interpreted as ghosts, spectral imaginings of Guston's traumatic memories. *Martial Memory* (1941), regarded as his "first mature easel painting," similarly portrays images and objects that Guston would recycle 30 years later. As in Foucault's theory of history as genealogical, subjective, and a concept which "opposes itself to search for 'origins'," *Martial Memory* is itself Guston's collation of a cluster of personal memories and aesthetic references stemming from the long history of Western art.[9] Janus-faced, *Martial Memory* points in the direction of the art that was

---

9 In the 1971 essay "Nietzsche, Genealogy, History," Foucault spells out his adaptation of the genealogical method in his historical studies. First and foremost, he says, genealogy

to emerge in his later phases. The painting is itself a revision of Pierro Della Francesa's *The Torture of the Jew* (1447–1466). As the exhibition text that accompanies the painting explains, Guston here is "turning a scene of torture into one of mock combat among street kids." What is most important to me about *Martial Memory* is that this early painting that represents a childhood memory of "mock combat" features so many elements of the visual vocabulary that would become the iconic language Guston reconfigured in the "hood" paintings from the late 1960s and 1970s: bricks, rope, pieces of wood, trash can lids, the tea kettle, triangular headgear that serve as precursors to the Klan hoods. The figurative dimension of *Martial Memory*, if not the stylistics, recurs throughout his career in ways that increasingly associate destructive impulses with the internal drives of the creator, rather than with the more traditional, and, in my view, less provocative, earlier work in which Guston points the accusatory finger at others besides himself.

On the level of pictorial "content," *Bombardment* is a more disturbing display of politically inspired terrorism against an innocent civilian population than is a "hood" painting such as *Courtroom*. By contrast to *Bombardment*, the controversial "hood" paintings lack scenes of immediate terror. It is all about the before and the after, not the during. It is about the artist, in his studio, doing a double take on a creative process that defies ethical considerations. In *Courtroom* (1970), icons that symbolize victimization now appear as mediated elements of the visual vocabulary that stimulated his ferocious imagination and narratological impulses. In *Courtroom*, Guston casts a pair of skinny legs in concentration camp-type striped pants that is stuffed face down in a trash can as a trope in a completed canvas. Set behind the hooded artist, the cloak splattered with red cadmium paint, the skinny legs and trash can are tucked in the background nearby other tools the artist will need to put together his next work of art. Behind the image of the legs in the trash can, we notice pieces of an easel, a stool or chair, and blank or only partially completed smaller canvases of scenes that remind me of Guston's late landscapes, seascapes, or shorelines.

Why is *Courtroom* the troublemaker, but not *Bombardment*? We may find an answer if we consider what Guston selected to appear at the center of the picture plane in *Courtroom*. We recall the smoke and flames of an exploded air bomb on an innocent civilian population as the central imagery in *Bombardment*. In

---

"opposes itself to the search for 'origins' (Foucault 1977, 141). That is, genealogy studies the accidents and contingencies that converge at crucial moments, giving rise to new epochs, concepts, and institutions." https://plato.stanford.edu/entries/postmodernism/#3

Courtroom, it is the lit cigar, clipped, Groucho Marx style, between two red fingers (gloved) of the "hood" who dominates the foreground of the composition. This is the image of the artist as brooding revisionist, ruminating over technical aesthetic problems. The painting is not primarily about political violence, although it bears resonances to historical catastrophe, but about Guston's transformation of real horror into a dark imaginative playscape. *Courtroom*'s referential elements are less political critique than features of a visual vocabulary that Guston would, as a statement attached to the exhibit explains, "combine in endless variations to create larger, more complex canvases." Guston is condemning the character of the artist in love with paint. "I'll just take white and I'll take cadmium red medium, which is my favorite color, and mix it up and make a pink. That mess of pink make me want to paint," Guston stated.

The composition also includes another symbol that points to another culprit: the viewer of the painting. I say this because Guston manipulates objects in the foreground of the composition to lead the viewer's gaze back to himself or herself. On the right side of the large canvas, an oversized cartoon version of a thick red hand sticks out of a black robe. This large red hand features a large red index finger that is pointing to the black slits (the eyes) behind the Klan like, red-splattered hood of the main figure who dominates the center of the painting. This red finger is Guston's Kafkaesque figure for the Superego, a projection of displaced self-blaming. In terms of the composition, however, the large red finger also leads the viewer's eyes to the cigar, which protrudes out of the hood's twinned fingers and directly outward, as if beyond the picture plane, and toward the viewer. Guston is now pointing the finger at patrons of the art world. As Guston himself stated, "The canvas is a court where the artist is prosecutor, defendant, jury, and judge." The unchecked, monomaniacal power of the artist to judge the world he imagines becomes one of Guston's great themes in the late work. As with eating and smoking, Guston was addicted to an art process that involves taking something from outside the self, ingesting it, and transforming it into something else: smoke, waste, another canvas that regurgitates historical atrocity as a piece of art:

> The [Vietnam] War, what was happening to America, the brutality of the world, what kind of man am I, sitting at home, reading magazines, going into frustrated fury about everything—and then going to my studio to adjust a red to a blue?

As in Guston's oeuvre, the Now of the exhibit was deferred because of the impact of historical traumas upon the meaning of art that was already saturated in personal disturbance and political catastrophe. *Philip Guston Now*—entangled as it is with the controversial history of the show itself—thus must reemerge in a different historical moment, a different Now, and with additional concerns attached to the grisly imagery. Guston's art is all about the deferred impact of Then on Now. Isn't that what trauma is all about? It is only now, at 60, when I have walked most of the hallway through what Yeats, in "Among School Children," called *The Long Schoolroom*, I realize why Guston's favorite line from his favorite poem from his favorite book of poetry was, "In my end is my beginning," from "East Coker," from T. S. Eliot's *Four Quartets* (1943). And I know now why Guston, after hospitalization for a heart attack, decided in 1979—he died in 1980—to paint a displaced self-portrait called *East Coker – tse*. Scarred with streaks of blood around the cheeks, chin, and neck, the grotesque head in profile resembles Eliot's. This is a different type of unmasking (and remasking) of the artist's previously hooded self than was the Cyclops in other late works such as *Painting, Smoking, Eating* (1973). I also realize why in the late "self-portrait" of the artist as Eliot on his deathbed, Guston painted the poet's ear so prominently with the elongated lobe one associates with representations of the Buddha. In an interview, Guston noted that Eliot had become attracted to Buddhism later in his life. I invoke "In my end is my beginning" *here* as well as the association of Eliot with Buddhism in the context of my remarks about how Now and Then persistently become encircled within each other throughout Guston's work. For Guston, art-making is not a linear journey in which creative discovery requires abandoning prior versions of the self to imagine new ones. Rather, art-making consists of a continual turning and returning upon prior fixations. Now and Then become coterminous. Guston remarked, "The only thing one can really learn, the only technique to learn, is the capacity to change." He also spoke of the "continuity of time." More precisely, the exhibition highlights a transformational imagination. As we stroll through the retrospective, we notice Guston returning to compose strange new things within the self-imposed restraint of manipulating a small set of iconic objects—book, clock, rope, hood, trash can lid, horseshoe-shaped boot heel, pointing finger, brick wall, plank of wood, paintbrush that doubles as bullwhip. Closer to my end than to my beginning, I face (and not through reproductions) a half-century of his metamorphic work at the *Philip Guston Now* exhibit on display at the East Wing of the National Gallery in Washington, DC.

CONCLUSION: GOODBYE, HEAVILON HALL

I conclude my 30-year creative reading workshop on a downbeat note and in an elegiac mood. It is May 2024. In recent times, I have lost too many friends in poetry and related arts to be cheerful as I end this book. Beloved poet, critic, and teacher Tyrone Williams, subject of Chapter 7, passed away at age 70 of cancer. David Shapiro, a member of the Marsh Hawk Press advisory board, succumbed to Parkinson's disease at age 77. Not a poet, but a legendary culture maker, Steve Albini, the producer of such iconic bands as Nirvana, leader of the metal punk group Big Black, member of my 1984 graduating class from Northwestern, and an acquaintance from my college years, has died at age 61 of a heart attack. Louise Glück, whom I first heard perform her work in a spellbinding, trance-like presentation style in the children's room of the Watertown (Massachusetts) Public Library in 1984, died in Cambridge at age 80, now a Nobel Laureate, in October 2023. As I mention in Chapter 4, I knew of the distinguished reputation of Boston-area poet Thomas Lux when I was a graduate student, but I did not study his work until I found "Refrigerator, 1957" in an anthology I use at Purdue. Teaching his poetry led to an email exchange, and, eventually, to the chapter I include in this book. Lux died in Atlanta, age 70, in 2017. My chapter on my mentor, Allen Grossman, was written for a commemorative collection after he passed away in 2014 at age 82. The Belgrade-born, New Hampshire-based poet Charles Simic, who died in 2023 at age 84, was, as I discuss in Chapter 16, the author of writings on shoes as symbolic carriers of trauma that I compared with Philip Guston's memory-laden paintings of boot soles in my "job talk" at Purdue in 1994. Lyn Hejinian, who helped usher in the Language movement with Barrett Watten in the Bay Area in the 1970s, as I discuss in Chapter 6, died at age 82 in February 2024. The two most prominent critics in my field, Helen Vendler and Marjorie Perloff, have died in recent months. I hope my project may serve as a memorial to all of these inspiring creative souls.

Closer to home, and relevant to my remarks on Guston, Heavilon Hall, home to Purdue's English department since the 1950s, and the site where I gave my job talk in the third-floor lounge about the Jewish painter of cartoonish "hoods," will be torn down later this summer. By the time classes start this fall, there will be no physical trace of the environment in which I taught courses in the first-floor classrooms, held office hours on the first and third floor, participated in 40 or 50 graduate prelim exams and thesis defenses in seminar rooms with long tables instead of rows of desks, and even served in the administration office. The space in which my "Thirty-Year Creative Reading Workshop" took place, in other words, will only exist in the memories of those who worked and studied in Heavilon for generations.

The reason behind the Purdue administration's decision to demolish "Heave," as students have referred to the building where they became initiated into college writing, reading, and critical thinking, remains obscure to me. One legitimate reason for taking down the building is in the interests of public health. English faculty, graduate students, and staff have for years complained that the building may be uninhabitable because it is infused with asbestos and mold. The administration has countered that the university hired experts to evaluate the building for toxicity, and reported that the inspectors have deemed Heavilon as safe for occupation. Public health concerns, therefore, cannot be the main reason the building is going down. In contrast to state-of-the-art halls that house more privileged units such as business (named after former governor and Purdue President Mitch Daniels), computer science, and aerospace engineering (named after Purdue graduate Neil Armstrong.) "Heave" may be habitable, but it is not the easiest building to love. A generic 1950s style academic building with long dark narrow hallways, no open common areas, smallish boxy classrooms, little natural light, windows that are bolted shut in many offices, and certainly no performance spaces or quarters for the Starbucks or Au Bon Pain outlets that one finds in the contemporary buildings on campus, "Heave" remains, for better or worse, as the academic space where I grew up as a teacher, mentor, scholar, colleague, and person. My feelings about Heavilon Hall are thus similar to those Neil Young expressed about his childhood home in north Ontario in the song "Helpless": "All my changes were there." A decade ago, colleagues with an architectural bent gathered in committee to draw up plans for a replacement building that would serve the English department as an attractive, upbeat space for students, faculty, and staff to gather, collaborate, teach, learn, perform, and chat informally at the café over a coffee and croissant. Other units of the liberal arts such as sociology and anthropology have expanded in recent years, but a smart new building for the English department is not part of the college's plans for development.

When I arrived 30 years ago, Purdue English was, not figuratively, on the move. We were a thriving unit featuring 60 tenure and tenure track faculty with equal distribution among the three main ranks of assistant, associate, and full professor. A big tent or, better, crazy quilt, of a department, our faculty in my early years helped train 200 graduate students working in fields ranging from rhetoric and composition, a discipline more or less invented by Purdue faculty in the 1980s, linguistics, English as a Second Language (ESL), creative writing, American studies, gender studies, ethnic and race studies, cultural theory, English education, technical writing, philosophy and literature, writing program administration, professional writing, and literary studies from Beowulf to Toni Morrison to Sherman Alexie and beyond. The department's Writing Center and Online Writing Lab (OWL) were state of the art. The presence of journals, including *Modern Fiction Studies* and *Sycamore Review*, symposia, a "town and gown" lecture series called Books and Coffee, and Literary Awards, a venerable event dating back to the 1920s, which each year featured a distinguished guest speaker (the likes of William Carlos Williams, Robert Frost, and Carl Sandburg in the early decades) and a banquet to honor student writers from Indiana high schools, all contributed to a vital cultural community. We were simultaneously honoring traditions and bringing current ideas and creative offerings to Northwest Indiana.

The year I was hired as an assistant professor, the department also brought in three other junior colleagues. A student of the leading Marxist literary theoretician Fredric Jameson, one had just published a book with Duke University Press in the emerging field of television studies. One was a Queer theorist from the University of Virginia who would publish a groundbreaking book, also with Duke, on the intersection of race studies and Queer studies. A third, with a graduate degree from Michigan Tech, was a postmodern rhetorician with a specialty in electronic media. The three other members of my cohort left Purdue for other positions years ago; one has since passed away. In retrospect, I now see my incoming class of assistant professors as part of the heyday of English as a major research department at Purdue.

The only one of the junior hires from 1994 that remains on faculty, I feel like a remnant of something fine that my colleagues had built over decades, but which now exists in a diminished state. To put the windfall hiring year class of 1994 into perspective, it has been 15 years since Purdue English has hired anyone on the tenure track in any field of literary or cultural studies. A department that now numbers around 40 members, even as the overall undergraduate population has risen from 35,000 students when I arrived to 50,000 today, Purdue English currently has no tenure-track assistant professors on the roster. The average age of the faculty is now 57. With a number of faculty nearing retirement, I expect our department will in the near future consist of thirty members, or half the number compared to when I started out in 1994. Our nationally recognized graduate programs, which produced generations of teachers and scholars who work all over the globe, have dwindled to the point that most units no longer admit any graduate students each year. For the incoming English department class of 2024–2025, for example, only a handful of graduate students will matriculate, most in the rhetoric and composition wing of the department. A handful of new students is hardly enough to run the seminars necessary to administer a graduate program even in one area of what once was really a small college that consisted of seven or eight distinct areas. The demolition of Heavilon Hall this summer thus feels like a literalization of the figurative dismantling of advanced literary and cultural studies at many universities in the United States.

It has been an emotional experience this May to unlock the door to my office (123 B) in Heavilon with the task of sorting through 30 years of books, letters, papers, poster displays, photographs, and other memorabilia in my corner of a soon-to-be demolished building. Since I currently teach online due to health concerns, I have not been offered one of the limited number of English faculty cubicles currently being constructed in another old building, Stanley Coulter, which is already crowded because it houses faculty in language studies other than English. I need to box up and take home what stuff I want to keep by June 1. I must also choose between bins marked "recycle" and "landfill" for everything I don't want to keep, except for books, which are now being stacked by faculty and graduate students in the lounge where I gave my talk on Guston 30 years ago. After rolling another cartful of books from my office into the elevator and on to the lounge where I will deposit them on the floor, on chairs, on couches, or on remaining spots on a seminar table in an adjoining room, I take one last look at anthologies that I've underlined and marked up for class discussion, but which I have no room for at home, and so must abandon. In truth, I've forgotten the plot of most of what I've taught in these old anthologies. I'll need to make fresh marks and underlines on the pages of whatever stories and poems I choose from the new edition I order for future course preparations.

Conclusion: Goodbye, Heavilon Hall 259

The lounge, now filled with thousands of "free books," mine joining the textual detritus of other teachers, feels like another symbol of the current state of university literary studies and of academic publishing, not only at Purdue, but in general. These books have no monetary value anymore and the Purdue library is uninterested in adding them to its collection. I worry that when my generation of publishing literary scholars retires, there will not be a next generation to replace them. Who will be on faculty to recover the significance of classic authors by developing innovative approaches that will appeal to the sensibility of tomorrow's students? I think of how much I learned from my mentors—Allen Grossman, Paul Breslin, Mary Kinzie, Leslie Epstein, Daniel R. Schwarz, and Frank Bidart—, but also how in my teaching and writing I have tried to take my field in new directions. I feel like I'm part of a broken link at the end of a long chain of cultural transmission, especially when I stare at all of the discarded critical studies left behind on the lounge floor.

Unloading books from my cart before finding increasingly scarce places for them in the lounge, I notice a young woman who is staring intently at a volume someone else has already deposited near where the lectern at which I did my job talk on Guston still stands. "Are you a literature student?" I asked her. "Well, I'm a lecturer here." "What do you teach?" "Mostly basic writing and comp. Whatever they can offer me. It changes from semester to semester." We chatted a little bit more. It turns out she has already earned a PhD in Early Modern and Shakespeare studies from a prestigious graduate program in English Literature. As I return to my cart to unload more books, conflicting thoughts cross my mind. If this accomplished young woman had started her academic journey in the 1990s, as was the case with me, it is likely she would have been up at the lectern giving her job talk in the lounge at Purdue or another major university seeking a "cutting edge new hire" in Early Modern Studies. Instead, like countless other newly minted PhDs in literary studies of her generation, she must leave the profession or accept temporary appointments that lack the job security, appropriate salary, research leaves, retirement benefits, and professorial visibility that I have had the privilege to enjoy over my lengthy career. I feel embarrassment, even shame, at my good fortune. And yet I feel bitter that my department will not replicate itself, and that the building where I enacted my 30-year creative reading workshop will only exist in memory. I feel angry at the ridiculously lousy job market in literary studies and angry at universities for taking advantage of this lousy market by hiring exquisitely prepared young scholars to do piecemeal work at the introductory levels while affording them little time or financial resources to develop their scholarship or to share their new findings with advanced students. I feel angry at my university for all but completely closing down our graduate programs in English, but then I must acknowledge that continuing to train smart young people for careers that do not exist is not an answer either. I empathize with the raw deal that the young woman lecturer with the high-powered doctorate has been handed, but I regard my situation as a remnant of a quite different English department at Purdue as being a blessing, but also a curse. I have been blessed with the professional security to teach and write about my expanding conception of my field, as the chapters and interviews in this book indicate. But I am cursed to know that professorships, such as the one I am privileged to hold, are increasingly rare to find at most colleges and universities today. As I gaze at the scholarly studies stacked all over the lounge, a fearful chill rises up in me that my scholarly efforts belong in those piles, rarely again to be consulted by anyone who doesn't know me well.

Returning to my office, my mood lightens up a little bit. I come across cards and notes from students thanking me for writing their letters of recommendation, or serving on their dissertation committee, or attending their poetry reading, or teaching a class they liked, or lending them a book that they had shown interest in during office hours. On one shelf, there are dozens of graduate thesis projects wrapped in thick black leather covers. On the first page of each thesis is the official endorsement from the graduate student's committee, and there is my name and signature along with the other committee members, many of whom have since retired. I note the variety and depth of projects these bright students have undertaken. Some have succeeded as academicians, some have left the profession, and some are no longer alive. My general impression of my academic career has been I've been too selfish with my work time. Taking the phrase "Publish or Perish" too literally, I've focused too much attention on my scholarship and editorial responsibilities, but not enough on teaching and mentoring students. But I can see from the course syllabi that I come across as I sift through my papers, and from observing the number and variety of graduate theses on the shelf, that my assessment of my career is misguided. I have been too hard on myself. It is clear that throughout my career I have dedicated myself to improving my knowledge base to help me teach undergraduates more effectively and to keep up with the innovative approaches being developed by graduate students. I feel a terrible sense of loss as I force myself to toss all of the black-covered theses into the recycle bin, shut my office, and leave Heavilon Hall behind me.

Concluding my 30-year creative reading workshop at Heavilon Hall, as well as the chapters and interviews in this book that reflect my development, does not mean that I plan to close up shop. I remain committed as a teacher to finding new ways to introduce students to poetry via the online, synchronic (real time) classroom. Currently, I am preparing a version of my "Introduction to Poetry" class for Fall 2024 in which I will introduce students to book-length narratives in verse: Vikram Seth's *The Golden Gate*, Elizabeth Acevedo's *The Poet X*, Archibald MacLeish's verse drama *J.B.*, and *Loving vs. Virginia*, Patricia Hruby Powell's documentary novel in verse about the landmark Supreme Court case. I will continue my affiliation with the Marsh Hawk Press collective, including publishing my fifth book of poems in 2025. I also plan to further the legacy of Peter Dale Scott and Tyrone Williams, two poets I discuss in these pages, by editing collections of critical essays on their ground-breaking work. In one of the final conversations I had with Tyrone Williams before his passing, I was lamenting the headwinds poetry faces in an era of book bans, AI-generated poetry and criticism, the closing of Small Press Distribution, which until recently had been the distributor of books put out by independent presses such as Marsh Hawk, and the diminishing role of advanced literary studies at universities such as my own. Tyrone did not seem worried by these developments: "Poetry marches on," he said. "In spite of it all, poetry marches on." Amen. —May 24, 2024, West Lafayette, Indiana.

INDEX

Note: Page numbers followed by "n" refer to notes.

A (Zukofsky) xvii
"A Lover's Call XXVII" (Gibran) 161
abstract expressionism xii
Acevedo, E.: *Poet X, The* 261
Achembou, R. 90n13
"Additional Notes" (Williams) 103, 113
"Adoration of the Magi, The" (Durer) 104
Adorno's Noise (Harryman) 89
"Adventures of Whitman, The" (Whitman) 173–75
Aeneid (Virgil) 33
Aeropagitica (Milton) 83
aesthetic apartheid 109
aesthetic attitude 60
aesthetic radicalism 199–205
After Taxes (Fink) 211, 213
"After Walker Evans" 112
After Weegee: Essays on Contemporary Jewish American Photographers (Morris) 231
"Agon Poems, The" (Harris) 135, 138
Albini, S. 255
Alexander, E. 117–18
Alexander, L.: "Dark Brother, The" 102
Alfred, W. 7
"All Along the Watchtower" (Dylan) 39
Allen, D.: *New American Poetry, The* 90
Allen, W. 155; *Zelig* 37–38
Alphabet, The (Silliman) 86–87

Alter, A. 36–37
Althusser, L. 114–15
Alvarez, J.: "Therapist, The" 215
American Deep State: Big Money, Big Oil, and the Attack on U.S. Democracy, The (Scott) 235
American Family, An (Goldsmith) 53
American Prayer, An (Morrison) x–xi
Ancient of Days, The (Blake) 173
Andrews, J. 144, 152, 156
Angelou, M. 171
anti-establishmentarianism 44
Antin, D. 17, 127
Anxiety of Influence, The (Bloom) 137–38
Apollinaire 51
Ararat (Glück) 34
Arcades Project (Benjamin) 52, 144
Arlen, H. 119
Armory Show of 1913 xvi
Armstrong, L. 119
"Ars Poetica" (MacLeish) 189, 191
Ashbery, J. x, 13–14, 17
"Asia World" (Ng) 235
Aspen: The Multimedia Magazine in a Box (Graham) 51–52
"Asphodel, that Greeny Flower" (Williams) xvi
"Attack of the Difficult Poem, The" (Bernstein) 95n5, 118
"Authenticity of Difference, The" (Williams) 117
avant-garde journalism 132
avant-gardism xx–xxi, 49–54, 109, 149

Babel, I.: *Odessa Tales* 249; *Red Cavalry* 249
Bacharach, B. 119
Bad History (Watten) 84
Baetens, J. 182
Ball, H.: "Karawane" 51
"Ballad of Don Notarikon, The" (Harris) 136, 140–43
Baraka, A. xx, 79, 83, 88–89, 99, 106, 125; aesthetic radicalism 199–205; *Dead Lecturer, The* 77; *Dutchman* xxi, 199–205; *New American Poetry: 1945–1960, The* 199; "Revolutionary Theatre, The" 200–201; "Somebody Blew Up America" 219–20
Barnhart, N. 173
Barnum, P. T. 52
Barok, D. 53
Beats: A Graphic History, The (Pekar and Buhle) 175
Bechdel, A. 171
Being and Time (Heidegger) 66n3
Bell, A. 102
Bellamy, D. 128
Bellow, S. 31, 36
Bellows, G.: "Forty-Two Kids" 178
Benedix, B. H. 143
Benjamin, W. 144; Janus-faced Angel of History 75; "Work of Art in the Age of Mechanical Reproduction, The" 112
Bennett, T. 169, 182
Bensky, L. 238
Bergman, I. 178
Berkeley in the Sixties (film, 1991) 80–82
Bernhard, S. 155
Bernstein, C. xx–xxi, 95, 124–25, 147; "Attack of the Difficult Poem, The" 95n5, 118; *Line in Postmodern Poetry, The* 131–32
Bernstein, L. 119
Bernstein, M. A.: "Reticence and Rhetorics: The Poetry of George Oppen" 76
"Between Walls" (Williams) 49–50, 54
Bidart, F. 3, 6–14; *Book of the Body, The* 12; "Ellen West" 12, 15–16; *In The Western Night: Collected Poems 1965–90* 16

"Bird's Blake" (Robertson) 102
Bishop, E. x, 3, 9–10, 16, 18; "In the Waiting Room" 13; "Poem" 6
bitter logic 23, 25, 192
Black Arts movement x, 77, 97, 100, 102, 106
Black Chant: Languages of African-American Postmodernism (Nielsen) 94–95n4
Black History Month 99
Black Lives Matter movement 36, 116
Blackwood, C. 8
Blackwood, M. 243
Blake, W. 83, 102; *Ancient of Days, The* 173
blasphemy 70
Bloom, H. 56–57, 135; *Anxiety of Influence, The* 137–38
Bloomfield, M. 32
"Blowin' in the Wind" (Dylan) 33, 39
"Blues" (Holbrook) 221–22
Bob Dylan Behind The Shades: A Biography (Heylin) 37n3
Bob Dylan: Prophet, Mystic, Poet (Rogovoy) 32
Body in Pain, The (Scarry) 103
"Body of Michael Brown, The" (Goldsmith) 53–54
Bogart, H. 178
Bombardment (Guston) 247–48, 251
Book of the Body, The (Bidart) 12
Brakhage, S. 52
Brawne, F. 195
Braxton, A. 119
Brazil, D. 129
Breslin, P. xvii; *Psycho-Political Muse: American Poetry Since the Fifties, The* x
Breton, A. 130, 200; "Second Manifesto of Surrealism" 200
Broadway: *Miss Saigon* 74, 74–75n8
Brodsky, J. 36
Bromwich, D.: *How Words Make Things Happen* 96n6
Brooks, G. x, 97, 216
Brooks, M. 24
Brossard, N. 147
Brown, J.: "Say It Loud ~ I'm Black & I'm Proud" 97
Brown, L. A.: "Fashion Show Poetry Event" 128

"Brown v. Board of Education" 98
Browne, H. 99
Brownian Motion 105, 106n15
Browning, R. 35
Brunner, E. 176–77
Bryce Passage (Morris) 16
Buhle, P.: *Beats: A Graphic History, The* 175
Burroughs, W. 51
Burt, S. 11; *Poem Is You: 60 Contemporary American Poems and How to Read Them, The* 216

Cage, J. 85
"Call Me Maybe" (Jepsen) 148
Callas, M. 12
Campbell, M. 11
"Can't Get Enough of Your Love, Babe" (White) 25
Capital (Goldsmith) 87
Capital: New York, Capital of the 20th Century (Goldsmith) 87
"Carded" (Williams) 113, 117
Carmichael, H. 119
Carroll, L.: 'Jabberwocky' 169
Carter, J. xxiii; "Purpose of Poetry, The" 191–92
Caruth, C. 244; *Unclaimed Experience* 88
Carvey, D. 246
categorical imperative xiv
Catullus 14
Cervena Barva Press 144
Chandler, D. H.-R. 175, 179
Chaucer, G.: "Wife of Bath" 14
Checking In (Karasick) 147–64
Chute, H. 170–71
City Lights (Guston) 248–49
Civil Rights Movement 98
Clarity and Other Poems (Fink) 207–27
Cloud, D. 38n5
Cocaine Politics (Scott) 234, 236
Cohen, H. xx
Coleman, O. 119
Collected Poems (Lowell) 10, 12, 14
collective diversity 35
Collins, B.: "Companionship of a Poem, The" 190; "How Do Poems Travel?" 187; "Introduction to Poetry" ix, xi, xxi, xxiii, 187–96;

"Poetry, Pleasure, and the Hedonist Reader" 187–88; "Taking Off Emily Dickinson's Clothes" 191
Coltrane, J. 119
"Comedian as the Letter C" (Stevens) 107
Coming to Jakarta: A Poem about Terror (Scott) xxii, 232, 236–39
Common Ground 220
"Companionship of a Poem, The" (Collins) 190
compulsory heterosexuality 13
conceptual poetry 85–86
conceptualism 17, 79, 110, 112
confessional poetry 45
confessionalism x, xxiv, 11, 14, 27, 134, 237, 242
"Confessions of a Blogger" (Harris) 133–35
Conrad, J.: *Heart of Darkness, The* 177
Conspirator (Guston) 250
Constructivist Moment, The (Watten) 88
Contemporary Women's Writing (Durgin) 126
"Convergence Cultures" (Jenkins) xvi, xxi, 170
Corbett, B. 7, 242
Corbett, W. xii
Cory, R. xii
Courtroom (Guston) 246n5, 248, 251–52
Crane, H. xiv, 4
Crane, S.: "Open Boat, The" 97
Crania Americana; A Comparative Views of the Skulls of Various Aboriginal Nations of North and South America (Morton) 104n14
Creeley, R. 90, 124
critical thinking 223–24
Cronkite, W. 249
cross-cultural exchange 35
Crowther, G.: "On the Friendship and Rivalry of Sylvia Plath and Anne Sexton" xin1
Crumb, R. 171, 245
Cruse, H. 98
cultural capital 10, 175
Cummings, A. 95, 97
Cunningham, J. V. 11
curation 49–54

Curley, J. 17
Curtiz, M. 178

Dadaism 201
Dalton, D. 33
Damon, M. 127
"Dangerous Intersection" (Fink) 212
Daniels, D. 51
Danto, A. 60
"Dark Brother, The" (Alexander) 102
Dasein 66n3, 74
David, H. 119
Davis, G. 36
"Day Lady Died, The" (O'Hara) 14–15
de Barañano, K. 244
Dead Lecturer, The (Baraka) 77
"Death and the New Citizen" (Ramanujan) 215
Deep Image x
Demuth, C.: *I Saw the Figure 5 in Gold* xvi
"Dented Reprise" (Fink) 212
Dershowitz, A. 46–47
Dickinson, E. 21, 24, 45n15, 89, 107–8, 191
DiPiero, W. S. x
Disability Studies 125–26
Disability Studies in the Humanities Listserve (DSHUM) 127
Dixon, D.: 'No More Auction Block' 33
Doing English: A Guide for Literature Students (Eaglestone) 155
Donahue, J. 68
double consciousness 96
double-voicedness 101n11
Drooker, E. 170, 179–82
Drucker, P. 10
DSHUM: *see* Disability Studies in the Humanities Listserve
D'Souza, A. 249
Du Bois, W. E. B. 98, 202; *Souls of Black Folks, The* 96, 103, 118
Du Plessis, R. 171
Duchamp, M. xvi, 110; "Fountain" 55, 189; *L.H.O.O.Q* 50; "Nude Descending a Staircase" xv

Duchamp is My Lawyer (Goldsmith) xxii; curation 49–54; late avant-gardism 49–54; populism 49–54
Duhamel, D.: "Egg Rolls" 216
Dulles, A. 237
Dunbar, P. L. 102–3, 109, 172–73, 202; "Ships That Pass in the Night" 108; "Sympathy" 171–72
Duncan, R. 87–89, 103
Durer, A. 103; "Adoration of the Magi, The" 104
Durgin, P. xx, 123–32; *Contemporary Women's Writing* 126; *Hannah Weiner's Open House* 123, 125, 127; *Route, The* 123
Dutchman (Baraka) xxi, 199–205
Dworkin, C. 107, 147
Dylan, B. 31–47, 72; "All Along the Watchtower" 39; "Blowin' in the Wind" 33, 39; "Hard Rain's a-Gonna Fall, A" 39; "Highway 61" 32; "Highway 61 Revisited" 32–34, 46–47; "It's Alright, Ma (I'm Only Bleeding)" 44; *Love and Theft* 33; "Masters of War" 44; "Only a Pawn in their Game" 44; "Times They Are A Changin,' The" 44; "Who Killed Davey Moore" 34

Eaglestone, R.: *Doing English: A Guide for Literature Students* 155
"Egg Rolls" (Duhamel) 216
Eisner, W. 168
Eliasson, O. 128
Eliot, T. S. xiv, xxi, 11–12, 23, 25, 97, 154, 170, 176–77, 237; *Four Quartets* 235, 253; "Love Song of J. Alfred Prufrock, The" 201; "Prufrock" 142, 203–4, 246; "*Ulysses*, Order, and Myth" 201; "Waste Land, The" 114, 169–71, 175, 178–79, 182, 201, 203
Eliotic impersonaliam 134
elitism 51
"Ellen West" (Bidart) 12, 15–16
Ellison, R. 98, 202
Ellsberg, D. 235
"Emoticon" (Harris) 133

"En Face" (Hejinian) 100
enjambment xv, 12–13, 55
Epstein, L. 26
Epstein, R. 179, 181
experimentalism: American 125
"Face *Qua* Flash Card" (Williams) 117

Fahlstrom, O. 139
"Fallacy of Paraphrase" x
fame 28
"Fashion Show Poetry Event" (Brown) 128
Faulkner, W.: *Requiem for a Nun* 84, 239
"Feeling Its Actual" (Javier) 217–18
Fidget 52–53
Fields, J. 94n4
"Figure a Poem Makes, The" (Frost) 168
Figure Five, The (Indiana) xvi
Fink, T. 17, 191; *After Taxes* 211, 213; *Clarity and Other Poems* 207–27; "Dangerous Intersection" 212; "Dented Reprise" 212; "Introducing Wallpaper" 213; *No Appointment Necessary* 211; "Nonce Sonnets" 207, 212; "Pyramid Assembled" 209–10; "Ralph's Mama" 212–13; *Reading Poetry with College or University Students: Overcoming Barriers and Deepening Engagement* 215–27; "Yinglish Strophes" 207–8, 213–15
Finkelstein, N. xx–xxi, 231; *On Mount Vision: Forms of the Sacred in Contemporary American Poetry* 65, 69–70; "Oppen at Altamont" 65–76; *Ratio of Reason to Magic: New & Selected Poems, The* 65
"First Person" (Robertson) 102
Fishbane, M. 46
Fisher, M. 177
Fitzgerald, E. 119
Five Biggest Lies Bush Told Us about Iraq, The (Sheer) 79–80
Flanagan, M. 144
Flanzbaum, H. xx
Flood, A. 37n2
Fluxus, A. K. 52

"Flying Inland" (Spivack) 18
"For the Union Dead" (Lowell) 4
"Forty-Two Kids" (Bellows) 178
Foster, E. 68
Foucault, M. 250
"Fountain" (Duchamp) 55, 189
Four Quartets (Eliot) 235, 253
Francesa, P. D.: *Torture of the Jew, The* 251
Franco, J. 181
Fredman, S.: *Menorah for Athena, A* xvii–xviii
Free Speech movement 85; at Berkeley 77, 81; at Cal 81–82
Freidin, G. 249n8
Freud, S. 155, 247
Friedman, J. 179, 181
From the Other Side of the Century: A New American Poetry 1960–1990 (Messerli) 124
Frost, R. xii, xiv; "Figure a Poem Makes, The" 168; "Mending Wall" 25
Fuhrman, J. 211
Fuller, J. 36
Funkhouser, C. T. 144

Garcia, J. 173
Gates, H. L. 110–11, 115; *Poems on Various Subjects, Religious and Moral* 111; *Signifying Monkey, The* 101n11; *Stony the Road: Reconstruction, White Supremacy, and the Rise of Jim Crow* 104n14; "Talking Book" 101
genre 155
"Genrecide" (Karasick) 156
George, U. 6
Gewanter, D. 14
Gibran, K.: "A Lover's Call XXVII" 161
Gimme Shelter (film, 1970) 67, 69, 74–75
Ginsberg, A. x, xvi, 3, 17, 68, 71, 73, 81, 90, 182; *Howl: A Graphic Novel* 169–71, 179–81; *Howl and Other Poems* 180–81; *Illuminated Poems* 179; "Lion for Real, The" 180; "Sunflower Sutra" 13
Girard, R. 68; theory of violence 70

Gish, N. K. 177
Glass, P. 127
Glück, L. 18, 31–49, 255; *Ararat* 34; *Meadowlands* 34; *Triumph of Achilles, The* 34–35, 39, 45–47; *Vita Nova* 34
Goffman, E. 42
Golden Gate, The (Seth) 261
Golding, A. xx, 67
Goldman, J. 100, 112, 127
Goldsmith, K. xvi, 49, 86–87, 144; *American Family, An* 53; "Body of Michael Brown, The" 53–54; *Capital* 87; *Capital: New York, Capital of the 20th Century* 87; *Duchamp is My Lawyer* xxii, 49–54; *Uncreative Writing: Managing Language in the Digital Age* 53, 140–41
Gordon, N. E. 149
Gould, H. 68
Graham, D.: *Aspen: The Multimedia Magazine in a Box* 51–52
Grand Piano, The (Watten) xxi, 78–79, 83–85
graphic novels 167–82
"Great Figure, The" (Williams) xvi
Grossman, A. xi–xiv, xvi–xvii, 7–9, 16, 129–30, 192, 255; on bitter logic 23, 25; as hermetic elitist 23; *Long Schoolroom: Lessons on the Bitter Logic of the Poetic Principle, The* xiii, 253; on personhood 22–23; radical simplicity 21–29; *Sighted Singer: Two Works on Poetry for Readers and Writers, The* xiii; "Woman on the Bridge Over the Chicago River, The" 26–27
Guesdon, J.-M. 32–33
Guest, B. 17
Guston, P. ix, xii, xxiii, 241–53, 255–56; *Bombardment* 247–48, 251–52; *City Lights* 248–49; *Conspirator* 250; *Courtroom* 246n5, 248, 251; *Martial Memory* 250–51; *Painter's Forms No. 2* 250; *Painting, Smoking, Eating* 242, 253; *Rug* 249–50; *Struggle Against Terrorism, The* 247; *Studio, The* 245, 246n5; *Tormentor, The* 245
Guston Foundation 246
Guthrie, W. 37

Hall, R. 52
Halliday, M. xiii–xiv, 11, 27
Halpern, R. 100
Handler, C. 155
"Hannah Weiner at Her Job" (Weiner) 128
Hannah Weiner's Open House 123, 125, 127
Hansberry, L.: *Raisin in the Sun, A* 200
"Happy Fault" (Williams) 113–14
"Hard Rain's a-Gonna Fall, A" (Dylan) 39
Hardwick, E. 14
Hardy, T.: "Convergence of the Twain" xii
Harmonium (Stevens) 107
Harris, D. Y. 133–45; "Agon Poems, The" 135, 138; "Ballad of Don Notarikon, The" 136, 140–43; "Confessions of a Blogger" 133–35; "Emoticon" 133; *Hyperlinks of Anxiety* xviii, 133, 144; "Post-Digital American Jewish Poetry" 133
Harris, W. J. 204–5
Harryman, C.: *Adorno's Noise* 89
Hartman, G. 36, 44
Hasidism, L. 38–39
Hass, R. 232
Hatlen, B. 73
Hawk, M. 16–17
Hayden, R. 99
Hayles, N. K. 144
Haynes, T. 38
"He Doesn't Move" (Spivack) 18
Heaney, S. 7
Heart of Darkness, The (Conrad) 177
Heidegger, M. 76, 157–58; *Being and Time* 66n3
Hejinian, L. 83, 101, 169, 255; "En Face" 100
Hell, R. 128
Heller, E. 11–12
Hemingway, E.: *Old Man and The Sea, The* 191
hermeneutics: Jewish 133, 135–37, 140–41; Kabbalistic 150–51
hermeticism 137
Herriman, G. 245
Hesiod: *Works and Days* 21

Heylin, C.: *Bob Dylan Behind The Shades: A Biography* 37n3
"Highway 61" (Dylan) 32
"Highway 61 Revisited" (Dylan) 32–34, 46–47
Hindus, M. xvii
Hip Hop Family Tree (Piskor) 175
Hofer, J.: *Route, The* 123
Holbrook, S.: "Blues" 221–22
"Home After Three Months Away" (Lowell) 14
Homer 28, 36
Hong, C. P. 94–95, 99
House That Hijack Built, The 154
"How Do Poems Travel?" (Collins) 187
"How to Make Poetry Comics" (Morice) 175
How Words Make Things Happen (Bromwich) 96n6
Howard, R. 187
Howe, S. 101–2; "Thorow" 69–70
Howl: A Graphic Novel (Ginsberg) 169–71, 179–81
Howl and Other Poems (Ginsberg) 180–81
Hughes, L. 216; "Theme for English B" 195
Hunt, E. 97, 100, 103
Hurston, Z. N. 100–101, 115: "Some Characteristics of Negro Expression" 100
Hutcheon, L. 154
Hyperlinks of Anxiety (Harris) xviii, 133, 144
"I Am Not Proud To Be Black" (Williams) 96–99

I Saw the Figure 5 in Gold (Demuth) xvi
"Idea of Order at Key West, The" (Stevens) 24, 136, 138n2
Ignatow, D. 17
Illuminated Poems (Ginsberg) 179
I'm Not There (film, 2007) 38
imperialism 51
impersonality xiv, 7, 11, 29, 35
in-between 103
"in loving memory" 194
"In the Waiting Room" (Bishop) 13
In The Western Night: Collected Poems 1965–90 (Bidart) 16

Indiana, R. 221, 223; *Figure Five, The* xvi
intentional fallacy 4
interpretive communities 215
intersectional 103
"Introducing Wallpaper" (Fink) 213
"Introduction to Poetry" (Collins) ix, xi, xxi, xxiii, 187–96
Iran-Contra Connection, The (Scott) 236
"It's Alright, Ma (I'm Only Bleeding)" (Dylan) 44

J
'Jabberwocky' (Caroll) 169
Jackson, K. 176n4
Jagger, M. 68–69, 71, 75
Jagoda, P. 170–71
jamcloset 55
"Jane Poems" (Spivack) 18
"Jane Witnesses the Destruction of the World" (Spivack) 17
Javier, P.: "Feeling Its Actual" 217–18
jazz aesthetic 196
J.B. (MacLeish) 261
Jefferson, T. 113
Jenkins, H.: "Convergence Cultures" xvi, xxi, 170
Jepsen, C. R.: "Call Me Maybe" 148
Jewishness x, xxiii, 18, 31–32, 35, 37–39, 43, 127, 149
Jin, H. xx, 11
Johnson, G. D. 111
Johnson, R. 32
Jones, L. 105
Joubert, J.: *To Teach is to Learn Twice* ix
Joyce, J. 52, 138n2, 139, 201; *Ulysses* 35, 53
Juan, D. 188

Kant, I. xiv
Karasick, A.: *Checking In* 147–64; "Genrecide" 156; *Salomé: Woman of Valor* project 163; "Your Leaky Day" 160
"Karawane" (Bell) 51
Kazan, E.: *On the Waterfront* 193
Keats, J. 23, 109, 194; "When I have Fears" 22
Keller, L. 43

Kent, C. 87, 173
Kerouac, J. 4, 33
Kerr, C. 82
Killian, K. 100, 129
Kimmelman, B. 17
Kinzie, M. x
Kirk, R. 119
Klappert, P. 17–18
Knox, G. 204
Koch, K. 17
Kramer, H. 245
Krupskaya 99, 115
Kunitz, S. 3, 10

Labors of Othello Simpson, The 99
LaCapra, D. 244; *Writing History, Writing Trauma* 88
L=A=N=G=U=A=G=E movement xx
language poetry: history and/as 77–91; resistance to hegemony 77; torqued 93–119
Laocoön: An Essay on the Limits of Poetry and Painting (Lessing) 169
late avant-gardism 49–54
late capitalism 110
Laub, D. 244
Laughlin, J. xvi, 232
Lawrence, D. H. 52
Lazarus, E. 43
Lazer, H. 220
Leader, M. 11
Lease, J. xii
Leaves of Grass 173
Lee, L.-Y. xix
Lennon, J. 23, 128
Leon, M. de 135, 144
Lessing, G. E. 168; *Laocoön: An Essay on the Limits of Poetry and Painting* 169
Levertov, D. 90
Levesque, G. 202
Levine, S. 110, 112
L.H.O.O.Q (Duchamp) 50
Lieu, J. xix
Life Studies (Lowell) 4, 14
Line in Postmodern Poetry, The (Bernstein) 131–32
"Lion for Real, The" (Ginsberg) 180
Lipkis, J. 26

Listening to the Candle: A Poem on Impulse (Scott) xxii, 231–32, 234–35
Little Red Book (Mao) 82
Liu, T.: "Prodigal Son Writes Home, The" 215
Lodge, H. C. 237
London, F. 163
"London Bridge is Falling Down My Fair Lady" xii, 25–26
Long Schoolroom: Lessons on the Bitter Logic of the Poetic Principle, The (Grossman) xiii, 253
Lord Weary's Castle (Lowell) 4
Love and Theft (Dylan) 33
"Love Song of J. Alfred Prufrock, The" (Eliot) 202
Loving vs. Virginia (Powell) 261
Lowell, R. x–xi, 3–5, 7–11, 16, 45, 135, 237; *Collected Poems* 10, 12, 14; "For the Union Dead" 4; "Home After Three Months Away" 14; *Life Studies* 4, 14; *Lord Weary's Castle* 4; "Man and Wife" 14; "Memories of West Street and Lepke" 4; mental illness 5; "Quaker Graveyard at Nantucket, The" 7; "Skunk Hour" 4, 14; "To Speak of Woe that Is in Marriage" 14; "Waking in the Blue" 4, 14
Lux, T.: "Refrigerator, 1957" 50, 54–61, 255

Mac Low, J. 85, 124, 130, 132
Mackay, N. 103, 128
MacLeish, A.: "Ars Poetica" 189, 191; *J.B.* 261
Malamud, B. 31
Malone, C. 45
"Man and Wife" (Lowell) 14
Mao: *Little Red Book* 82
Marcus, G. 128
marginal 103
Margotin, P. 32–33
Marlowe, C. 177, 179
Marsh, A. 16
Martial Memory (Guston) 250–51
Martinesque, S. 208
Marx, G. 212
masculinism 51

"Masters of War" (Dylan) 44
"Mauberley" (Pound) 142
Mayer, B. 127
Maysles, D. 67
McCloud, S. 170, 182; *Understanding Comics: The Invisible Art* 168
McDowell, F. 32; "61 Highway Blues" 33
McGarrigle, K. 119
McHale, B. 170, 176, 179, 182
McKay, C. 103
McLean, D. 125
McLuhan, M. 156
McRae, C. 119
McTell, B. W. 32
Meadowlands (Glück) 34
Meir, G. xvii
Melson, B. 6–7
Melson, G. 6
"Memories of West Street and Lepke" (Lowell) 4
"Mending Wall" (Frost) 25
Menorah for Athena, A (Fredman) xvii–xviii
Mercer Arts Center 128
Merrill, J. 13, 129, 237
Messerli, D.: *From the Other Side of the Century: A New American Poetry 1960–1990* 124
Metamorphosis (Ovid) 114
Metcalfe, S. 41
Metres, P. 84
Meyer, M. xx, 189, 246
Midwest Jewish Studies Society xvii
militarism 51
Miller, S. P. 17
Milton, J.: *Aeropagitica* 83; *Paradise Lost* 83–84
Minnie, M. 36
Miodrag, H. 170
Miss Saigon 74, 74–75n8
Mitchell, W. J. T. 168–69, 209
Modernism 36
Monet, C.: "Nympheas" 156
monomania 52–53
Moore, D. D.: *Walkers in the City: Jewish Street Photographers of Midcentury New York* 231
Moore, J. P. 77–79, 83, 87

Moore, T. 128
Moriarity, L. 100
Morice, D. 169, 173–74; "How to Make Poetry Comics" 175
Morris, A. 123–32, 144
Morrison, J.: *American Prayer, An* x–xi
Morton, S. G.: *Crania Americana; A Comparative Views of the Skulls of Various Aboriginal Nations of North and South America* 104n14
mourning 70
Mullen, H. 96–97, 100, 109
"My Shoes" (Simic) 242
Myers, N. xix
Myles, E. 128
mythical method 201–2
"Mythmaking" (Spivack) 18
negation, definition of 78n2
Neo-Liberal fetishization 78
New American Poetry: 1945–1960, The (Baraka) 199
New American Poetry, The (Allen) 90
New Criticism ix–x, xiv, xxiii, 12, 90–91, 192, 209, 223
New England transcendentalism 4
New Gnosticism 68, 88
Ng, F.: "Asia World" 235; *Revisiting Jakarta: Internal Turmoil and State Violence in Poetry and Terror* xxii
Nielsen, A. 94; *Black Chant: Languages of African-American Postmodernism* 94–95n4
Nijinsky, V. 11
No Appointment Necessary (Fink) 211
'No More Auction Block' (Dixon) 33
"Nonce Sonnets" (Fink) 207, 212
North, A. 41
Not Born Digital 123
"Nothing Compares 2U" xii
Nowak, M. 129
"Nude Descending a Staircase" (Duchamp) xv
"Nympheas" (Monet) 156

Objectivism xvii
Objectivist movement xvii
O'Connor, S. 23
Odessa Tales (Babel) 249

Of Being Numerous (Oppen) 66–67, 72–73, 76
O'Hara, F. 13, 17, 233; "Day Lady Died, The" 14–15; "Step Away From Them, A" 15
Old Man and The Sea, The (Hemingway) 191
O'Leary, P. 68
Oliver, M.; 18
Olmstead, F. L. 5
Olson, C. 12, 199, 205
"On Being Brought from Africa to America" (Wheatley) 111
On Mount Vision: Forms of the Sacred in Contemporary American Poetry (Finkelstein): "Making The Ghost Walk About Again and Again: History as Séance in the Work of Susan Howe" 65
"On the Friendship and Rivalry of Sylvia Plath and Anne Sexton" (Crowther) xin1
On the Waterfront (Kazan) 193
"Only a Pawn in their Game" (Dylan) 44
"Open Boat, The" (Crane) 97
Oppen, G. x, xvii, xxi, 17, 65–76; *Of Being Numerous* 66–67, 72–73, 76
"Oppen at Altamont" (Finkelstein) 65–76
O'Reilly Factor, The (TV show) 79–81
Orlovsky, P. 181
Osherow, J. 35
Osmond, M. 51
Ostriker, A. 35
"Outboard Engine" (Spivack) 18–19
outsideness xiii–xiv, 50
Ovid: *Metamorphosis* 114

Painter's Forms No. 2 (Guston) 250
Painting, Smoking, Eating (Guston) 242, 253
Pair of Shoes, A (Van Gogh) 242
Paley, G. 31
Palmer, M. 8
Paradise Lost (Milton) 83–84
paranoid narcissism 130
Parker, C. 102
Parket, J. R. 169, 182

Parks, R. 99
Paterson xvi
patriarchy 18, 44, 46–47, 225
Pease, D. 87
Pekar, H.: *Beats: A Graphic History, The* 175
Peltier, L. 130
Pere Ubu 149
Perelman, B. 79
"Periodizing the Present" (Watten) 84–85
Perloff, M. 91, 144, 255; *Unoriginal Genius: Poetry by Other Means in the New Century* 139
Perrault, J. 127
personhood 22–23, 28, 104, 135, 243
Peterson, T.: "Trans Figures" 216
Philip Guston: A Life Lived (film, 1981) 243
Philip Guston Now exhibition (2020) 243, 245, 246n5, 253
Philpot, C. 50
Picasso 51
Pictures of Brueghel (Williams) xvi
Pinsky, R. xx, 7
Pisan Cantos (Pound) 134, 237, 239
Piskor, E.: *Hip Hop Family Tree* 175
Plath, S. x–xi, 4, 6, 7, 10, 45
pluralistic approach to textual analysis 167
"Poem (As the cat [...])" (Williams) 49, 55
"Poem" (Bishop) 6
Poem Is You: 60 Contemporary American Poems and How to Read Them, The (Burt) 216
Poems on Various Subjects, Religious and Moral (Gates) 111
Poet X, The (Acevedo) 261
Poetics Program, UB 124
"Poetry: A *Basic* Course" 24
"Poetry, Pleasure, and the Hedonist Reader" (Collins) 187–88
Poetry and Terror: Politics and Poetics in Coming to Jakarta (Scott) 232, 235–39
"Poetry and the Politics of the Subject" (Silliman) 109
Poetry Comics from the Book of Hours (Stone) 171n1
Poetry Foundation 205

Politics of Escalation in Vietnam, The (Scott) 235
Pollock, J. xvi
Pope, A. 110
populism 44, 49–54
Porter, C. 119
postmodernism 139
Pound, E. x, xiv, xviii, 11, 158–59, 174; "Mauberley" 142; *Pisan Cantos* 134, 237, 239
Powell, P. H.: *Loving vs. Virginia* 261
"Prayer for My Daughter, A" (Yeats) 225, 227
Prince, M. J. 180, 182
Prince, R. 128
"Princess and the Pea" xv
"Private Pain in Time of Trouble" (Spivack) 18
proceduralism 86, 107; arbitrary 87
"Prodigal Son Writes Home, The" (Liu) 215
"Proletarian Portrait" (Williams) xiv–xvi, 49
"Prufrock" (Eliot) 142, 203–4, 246
psychic economy 155
Psycho-Political Muse: American Poetry Since the Fifties, The (Breslin) x
"psycho-social" disability 126
"Purpose of Poetry, The" (Carter) 191–92
"Pyramid Assembled" (Fink) 209–10
"Quaker Graveyard at Nantucket, The" (Lowell) 7

Quasha, G. 147
Queer studies 257
Questions of Poetics: Language Writing and Consequences (Watten) xx–xxi, 77–91; "On the Advantages of Negativity" 79

Ra, S. 119
racial insensitivity 99
racial science 104
radical mimesis 110–13
radical mimicry 111–12n21
"Radio" (Watten) 88
Raisin in the Sun, A (Hansberry) 200
"Ralph's Mama" (Fink) 212–13

Ramanujan, A. K.: "Death and the New Citizen," 215
Ransom, J. C. 5
Raphael: *School of Athens, The* 12
Ratio of Reason to Magic: New & Selected Poems, The (Finkelstein) 65
Rawls, J. xiv
Ray, M. xvi
Reading Poetry with College or University Students: Overcoming Barriers and Deepening Engagement (Fink) 215–27
Rebhorn, M. 201
Reck, T. 202
Red Cavalry (Babel) 249
Reed, I. 99
"Refrigerator, 1957" (Lux) 50, 54–61, 255
religious Calvinism 4
reparative reading 216
"Republic of New Africa" 97–98
Requiem for a Nun (Faulkner) 84, 239
resistant reading 187–96
"Reticence and Rhetorics: The Poetry of George Oppen" (Bernstein) 76
Revisiting Jakarta: Internal Turmoil and State Violence in Poetry and Terror (Scott and Ng) xxii
"Revolutionary Theatre, The" (Barack) 200–201
Reznikoff, C. xvii–xviii
Rich, A. x, 5, 11, 17; on compulsory heterosexuality 13
Richter, G. 128
Ricoeur, P. 135
Rimbaud, A. 33
Ringstrom, A. 40n7
Rivera, D. 247
Rivers, J. 155
Robbins, T. 141
Robertson, E.: "Bird's Blake" 102; "First Person" 102
Robinson, E. A. xii
Roche, M. 119
Roethke, T. 10
Rogovoy, S. 33, 37–38; *Bob Dylan: Prophet, Mystic, Poet* 32
Romanticism 36, 102
Ros, S. 128
Rosenthal, M. L. 5, 14

Rossman, M. 82
Roth, P. 31
Rothenberg, J. 65, 103, 127
Route, The (Durgin and Hofer) 123
Rowson, M. 169–70, 175–78, 179n6, 182
Rug (Guston) 249–50
Rukeyser, M. 17
Russell, J. 4, 55
Ryder, M. 107

Salomé: Woman of Valor project 163
Savio, M. 82
"Say It Loud ~ I'm Black & I'm Proud" (Brown) 97
Scalapino, L. 130
Scarry, E.: *Body in Pain, The* 103
Schapiro, M. 242
Scheiber, A. H. 128
Schmidt, M. 37n2
Schnabel, J. 51
Schneemann, C. 127
Scholem, G. 135
School of Athens, The (Raphael) 12
Schopenhauer, A.: "World as Will and Idea, The" 14
Schreier, B. 31, 36
Schwartz, L. 6–7
Schwarz, D. R. 26
"Score for Diacritics" 155–56
Scott, C. 243–44
Scott, P. D. xi, xxii–xxiii, 231–39, 261; *American Deep State: Big Money, Big Oil, and the Attack on U.S. Democracy, The* 235; *Cocaine Politics* 234, 236; *Coming to Jakarta: A Poem about Terror* xxii, 232, 236–39; *Iran-Contra Connection, The* 236; *Listening to the Candle: A Poem on Impulse* xxii, 231–32, 234–35; *Poetry and Terror: Politics and Poetics in Coming to Jakarta* 232, 235–39; *Politics of Escalation in Vietnam, The* 235; *Revisiting Jakarta: Internal Turmoil and State Violence in Poetry and Terror* xxii; *Seculum, Poetry and Terror* 236
Scroggins, M. 147
"Second Manifesto of Surrealism" (Breton) 200

Second Wave Feminist x
Seculum, Poetry and Terror (Scott) 236
Sedaka, N. 24
Sedgwick, E. 83, 216
Seeger, P. xxiii, 192–93
segmentivity 171
Seldess, J. 128
Sensational Fix 128
September 11, 2001 109
Serra, R. 51
Seth, V.: *Golden Gate, The* 261
Seurat, G.: "Sunday Afternoon on the Island of La Grande Jatte, A" 178
Sexton, A. xi, 3–7, 10, 16
Shadows in the Night (album, 2015) 37
Shakespeare, W. 24
Shapiro, A. x, 11
Shapiro, D. 17
Sheeler, C. xvi
Sheer, R.: *Five Biggest Lies Bush Told Us about Iraq, The* 79–80
Shepard, T. S. 15
Sherman, C. 154
"Ships That Pass in the Night" (Dunbar) 108
Shreiber, M. Y. 35
Sidney, Sir P. 155
Sighted Singer: Two Works on Poetry for Readers and Writers, The (Grossman) xiii
Signifying Monkey, The (Gates) 101n11
Silko, L. M. xiii
Silliman, R. 83; *Alphabet, The* 86–87; "Poetry and the Politics of the Subject" 109
Silverman, S. 155
Simic, C. 243; "My Shoes" 242
Simpson, O. J. 99
Singer, I. 36
Siqueiros, D. A. 247
"61 Highway Blues" (McDowell) 33
"Skunk Hour" (Lowell) 4, 14
Smith, P. 128
Sollors, W. 200–201
"Some Characteristics of Negro Expression" (Hurston) 100
"Somebody Blew Up America" (Baraka) 219–20
"Song of Myself" (Whitman) 173

Sonic Youth: Goodbye 20th Century 129
Souls of Black Folks, The (Du Bois) 96, 103, 118
Spahr, J. 87, 127
Spencer, A. 99
Spivack, K. xi, 3–19; "Flying Inland" 18; "He Doesn't Move" 18; "Jane Poems" 18; "Jane Witnesses the Destruction of the World" 17; "Mythmaking" 18; "Outboard Engine" 18–19; "Private Pain in Time of Trouble" 18; *With Robert Lowell and His Circle* 3; "Young Woman Who Went Deaf, The" 19
Spivack, M. 6
Spivak, G. 82
Spring and All (Williams) 90
Spring Showers (Stieglitz) xvi
St. Augustine 134
Stalling, J. 130
Starbuck, G. xi
Steele, T. 11
Stefanile, F. xix
Stein, G. xvi, 54, 201
Stein, K. 144
Steinberg, S.: "View of the World from 9th Avenue" xix
"Step Away From Them, A" (O'Hara) 15
Stern, G. xx
Stevens, W. 27, 74, 109, 136, 140, 169, 231; "Comedian as the Letter C" 107; *Harmonium* 107; "Idea of Order at Key West, The" 24, 136, 138n2; "Sunday Morning" 22, 193; "This Solitude of Cataracts" 75; "World Without Peculiarities" xiii
Stewart, J. 155
Stieglitz, A.: *Spring Showers* xvi
Stone, B.: *Poetry Comics from the Book of Hours* 171n1
Stone, S. xv
Stony the Road: Reconstruction, White Supremacy, and the Rise of Jim Crow (Gates) 104n14
Strand, M. 9
"Street Works" (Weiner) 128

Strindberg, A. 202
Struggle Against Terrorism, The (Guston) 247
Studio, The (Guston) 245, 246n5
"Study of a Negro Head" (Williams) 100, 103–5, 114
sublime despair 98
suffering 28
Summer, D. 25
"Sunday Afternoon on the Island of La Grande Jatte, A" (Seurat) 178
"Sunday Morning" (Stevens) 22, 194
"Sunflower Sutra" (Ginsberg) 13
"Sympathy" (Dunbar) 171–72
Syrkin, M. xvii
Szilar, I. 53–54

Tabachnick, S. 170
"Taking Off Emily Dickinson's Clothes" (Collins) 191
"Talkin' Union" 192–93
"Talking Book" (Gates) 101
Talking Heads 128
Tankle, B. 116
Tarn, N. 101–3
Tate, A. 5
Tennyson, A. L. 35
The (Zukofsky) xvii
"Therapist, The" (Alvarez) 215
"This Is Just to Say" (Williams) 49–50, 54, 56, 58–60, 189
"This Solitude of Cataracts" (Stevens) 75
Thomas, L. 95, 100
Thomas, R. F. 34; *Why Dylan Matters* 33
"Thorow" (Howe) 69–70
Time Capsules (Warhol) 50
"Times They Are A Changin,' The" (Dylan) 44
"To a Poor Old Woman" (Williams) 49
"To Speak of Woe that Is in Marriage" (Lowell) 14
To Teach is to Learn Twice (Joubert) ix
Today 85
Tormentor, The (Guston) 245
Torture of the Jew, The (Francesa) 251
Towery, M. 22–23
"Trans Figures" (Peterson) 216

Transatlantic Slave Trade 103–4
transgression 70
Triumph of Achilles, The (Glück) 34–35, 39, 45–47
Trott, D. 40n7
Trump, D. 44
Trumpian isolationism 44
Twentieth Century Literature and Culture conference, University of Louisville xx

UbuWeb xxii
Ulysses (Joyce) 35, 53
"*Ulysses*, Order, and Myth" (Eliot) 201
Unclaimed Experience (Caruth) 88
Uncreative Writing: Managing Language in the Digital Age (Goldsmith) 53, 140–41
Understanding Comics: The Invisible Art (McCloud) 168
Universal Music Publishing Group 42
Unoriginal Genius: Poetry by Other Means in the New Century (Perloff) 139
Updike, J. 187

Valpato, G. 12
Van Gogh: *Pair of Shoes, A* 242
Vaughan, S. 119
veil of ignorance xiv
Vendler, H. 7, 35, 255
Verlaine, T. 128
Virgil 36; *Aeneid* 33
Vita Nova (Glück) 34

Wachtel, C. xix
Wagner, R. 203
"Waking in the Blue" (Lowell) 4, 14
Walcott, D. x
Walkers in the City: Jewish Street Photographers of Midcentury New York (Moore) 231
Wang, D. 106n16
Warhol, A. 54, 127, 243; *Time Capsules 50*
"Waste Land, The" (Eliot) 114, 169–71, 175, 178–79, 182, 201, 203
Watten, B.: *Bad History* 84; *Constructivist Moment, The* 88; *Grand Piano, The*
xxi, 78–79, 83–85; "Periodizing the Present" 84–85; *Questions of Poetics: Language Writing and Consequences* xx–xxi, 77–91; "Radio" 88
Watts, C. 75
Weeks (Weiner) 123
Weinberg, J. 82
Weiner, H. xx, 123–32; "Hannah Weiner at Her Job" 128; *Hannah Weiner's Open House* 123; "Street Works" 128; *Weeks* 123
Welch, R. 249
West, E. 11
West Coast Language movement xxi
Weston, J. 177
Wheatley, P. 110–11, 113; "On Being Brought from Africa to America" 111
"When I have Fears" (Keats) 22
White, B. 36; "Can't Get Enough of Your Love, Babe" 25
White, D. 66n1
White, H. 11
white Buddhism 130
white culpability 246
white supremacy 104
Whitman, W. xii, 13, 54; "Adventures of Whitman, The" 173–75; "Song of Myself" 173
"Who Is It" (Williams) 96
"Who Killed Davey Moore" (Dylan) 34
"Why Can't We Be Friends?" 53
Why Dylan Matters (Thomas) 33
"Wife of Bath" (Chaucer) 14
Wilbur, R. 41
Wilde, O. 163
Wilkinson, J. M. 96, 99–100n8
Williams, F. 176–77
Williams, L. 195
Williams, M. 103
Williams, T. xx–xxi, xxiii, 93–119, 255, 261; "Additional Notes" 103, 113; "Authenticity of Difference, The" 117; "Carded" 113, 117; "El Negro" 103; "Face *Qua* Flash Card" 117; "Happy Fault" 113–14; *Heretofore* 119; "I Am Not Proud

To Be Black" 96–99; "Open and Closed forms in 20th Century American Poetics" 99; "Study of a Negro Head" 100, 103–5, 114; "Who Is It" 96
Williams, W. C. xix, xxii, 54, 123; "Asphodel, that Greeny Flower" xvi; "Between Walls" 49–50, 54; "Great Figure, The" xvi; *Pictures of Brueghel* xvi; "Poem (As the cat [...])" 49, 55; "Proletarian Portrait" xiv–xvi, 49; *Spring and All* 90; "This Is Just to Say" 49–50, 54, 56, 58–60, 189; "To a Poor Old Woman" 49; "Young Sycamore" xvi
Wimsatt, W. K. 90
Winters, J. 249
With Robert Lowell and His Circle (Spivack) 3
Wolff, T. 102–3
"Woman on the Bridge Over the Chicago River, The" (Grossman) 26–27
Wordsworth, W. 103
Wordsworthian self-expressionism 134
"Work of Art in the Age of Mechanical Reproduction, The" (Benjamin) 112
Works and Days (Hesiod) 21

"World as Will and Idea, The" (Schopenhauer) 14
"World Without Peculiarities" (Stevens) xiii
Wright, J. x
Wright, R. 98
Writing History, Writing Trauma (LaCapra) 88

Yau, J. 96n6
Yeats, W. B. 18, 22, 25, 129, 136; "Prayer for My Daughter, A" 225, 227
"Yinglish Strophes" (Fink) 207–8, 213–15
Young, N. 256
"Young Sycamore" (Williams) xvi
"Young Woman Who Went Deaf, The" (Spivack) 19
"Your Leaky Day" (Karasick) 160

Zelig (Allen) 37–38
Zimmer, R.: "Chicago Statement" 80–81
Zohar (Radiance/Splendor) 139
zone of uncertainty 103
Zukofsky, L. 66, 90; *A* xvii; *The* xvii
Zwerin, C. 67

www.ingramcontent.com/pod-product-compliance
Lightning Source LLC
Chambersburg PA
CBHW020639230426
43665CB00008B/243